Islamist Politics in the Middle East

For over three decades, Islamist politics, or political Islam, has been one of the most dynamic and contentious political forces in the Middle East. Although there is broad consensus on the importance of political Islam, there is far less agreement on its character, the reasons for Islamist's success, the role of Islamist movements in domestic and international affairs, or what these movements portend for the future.

This volume addresses a number of central questions in the study of Islamist politics in the Middle East through detailed case studies of some of the region's most important Islamist movements. Chapters by leading scholars in the field examine the Egyptian Muslim Brotherhood, Hamas, Hizbullah, Morocco's Justice and Benevolence, the Jordanian Muslim Brotherhood, the Sunni Insurgency in Iraq and Islamist politics in Turkey and Iran. The topics addressed within this volume include social networks and social welfare provision, Islamist groups as opposition actors, Islamist electoral participation, the intersection of Islam and national liberation struggles, the role of religion in Islamist politics, and Islam and state politics in Iran, among other topics.

All of the contributing authors are specialists with deep knowledge of the subject matter who are committed to empirically based research. These scholars take Islamists seriously as modern, sophisticated, and strategic political players. Together, their work captures much of the diversity of Islamist politics in the region and will contribute to the scholarship on a topic that continues to be important for the Middle East and the world.

Samer S. Shehata is an Assistant Professor of Arab Politics at the Center for Contemporary Arab Studies at Georgetown University. He is the author of *Shop Floor Culture and Politics in Egypt.*

Islamist Politics in the Middle East

Movements and change

Edited by
Samer S. Shehata

Routledge
Taylor & Francis Group
LONDON AND NEW YORK

First published 2012
by Routledge
2 Park Square, Milton Park, Abingdon, Oxon OX14 4RN

Simultaneously published in the USA and Canada
by Routledge
711 Third Avenue, New York, NY 10017

Routledge is an imprint of the Taylor & Francis Group, an informa business

British Library Cataloguing in Publication Data
A catalogue record for this book is available from the British Library

Library of Congress Cataloging-in-Publication Data
Islamist politics in the Middle East: movements and change / edited by Samer S. Shehata.
p. cm.
Includes bibliographical references and index.
1. Middle East--Politics and government--1979- 2. Islam and politics--Middle East. I. Shehata, Samer S. (Samer Said), 1967-
DS63.1.I747 2011
320.5'570956--dc23
2011038102

ISBN 978-0-415-78361-3 (hbk)
ISBN 978-0-415-78362-0 (pbk)
ISBN 978-0-203-12631-8 (ebk)

Typeset in Bembo
by Taylor & Francis Books

MIX
Paper from responsible sources
FSC® C004839

Printed and bound in Great Britain by the MPG Books Group

For Riem

Contents

Acknowledgments

The dramatic political events that took place in the Arab world in 2011 led some observers to mistakenly conclude that Islamist politics in the Middle East was in decline. After all, Islamist movements were not behind the mass uprising that brought down Zein Al-Abidine Ben Ali in Tunisia, after 23 years in power. Similarly, the organizers of the January 25, 2011 protests that led to Hosni Mubarak's ouster in Egypt were largely liberal, Internet savvy, youth activists, not the Muslim Brotherhood. The same can also be said of the uprisings that shook Libya, Yemen, Syria and other parts of the Arab world.

One year after the beginning of the Arab uprisings, however, there can be no doubt about the importance of Islamist politics in the region. Across the Middle East and North Africa, Islamists are on the march. In October 2011, the Islamist Annahda party won nearly forty percent of the vote in elections for Tunisia's constituent assembly, the first elections since Ben Ali's departure. One month later, Morocco's Islamist Justice and Development Party secured a plurality of the vote in the country's first elections after the Moroccan king instituted constitutional reforms. In Egypt's first legislative elections in the post-Mubarak era, Islamist parties – the Muslim Brotherhood's newly formed Freedom and Justice Party and the *Salafi* Islamic Alliance – won more than seventy percent of parliamentary seats. And earlier, in June 2011, Recip Tayyib Erdogan's Justice and Development Party became the first Turkish party in history to win three consecutive parliamentary elections with an increasing percentage of the vote in each election.

This volume is about Islamist politics in the Middle East. It is the outcome of a two-day symposium held at Georgetown University's Center for Contemporary Arab Studies (CCAS). Leading scholars from Europe, the United States, and the Middle East were invited to present research about political Islam and some of the region's most important Islamist movements. The work of many of those who participated is included in these pages.

Such projects require an enormous amount of planning and effort and this one was no exception. Many people and institutions deserve thanks for making the conference and the resulting volume possible. Of course, the authors deserve praise for their scholarship and patience in seeing a collaborative project through fruition. I would also like to thank everyone who participated in the symposium, including those whose contributions are not included here.[1] The Center for Contemporary Arab Studies and its staff deserve tremendous thanks for sponsoring the conference and supporting this volume. CCAS faculty, staff, and the symposium steering committee provided invaluable assistance at every stage of the endeavor. Two previous CCAS directors, Barbara Stowasser, director at the time of the conference, and Michael Hudson, have remained particularly supportive of the project. Two other CCAS colleagues, Mimi Kirk, formerly Publications Editor, and Nancy Farley also generously provided expert editorial advice on many of the volume's chapters.

I owe a more personal debt of gratitude to a number of individuals and institutions for supporting my own research, some of which is included here. Georgetown University's Edmund A. Walsh School of Foreign Service has provided an encouraging environment in which to pursue scholarship that is engaged with real world politics. Fellowships from the Woodrow Wilson International Center for Scholars and the Carnegie Corporation of New York have enabled me to carry out research and writing about the Egyptian Muslim Brotherhood's electoral participation, some of which is included in chapter seven. A CCAS Oman Faculty grant also partially funded two short research trips to Egypt during elections.

A number of former students were also kind enough to read and comment on the introduction, chapter seven, and other sections of the manuscript. I thank Adam Farrar and Benjamin Stevenson for sound suggestions and editorial advice. Mostafa Hefny and Nada Ramadan provided outstanding research assistance. Ayoung Shin and Nicholas Garcia-Mason read the introduction and chapter seven very closely, improving both considerably. Niels Lee cheerfully completed much of the meticulous work involved in standardizing references and creating bibliographies. And Joe Whiting, Suzanne Richardson, Lisa Williams, Emma Hart and their colleagues at Routledge have been a pleasure to work with as I prepared the manuscript for publication.

I am also extremely grateful to Nezar AlSayyad for graciously hosting me as a Visiting Scholar at the University of California at Berkeley's Center for Middle Eastern Studies (CMES) during the 2009–2010 academic year. CMES provided an ideal, distraction-free environment in which to put the finishing touches on my chapters and complete some of the editorial work involved in a project such as this. I also thank Emily Gottreich and CMES's extremely helpful staff, Mejgan Massoumi and Priscilla Minaise, for making my year there both productive and enjoyable.

As always, my greatest debt goes to my family, Riem, Omar, and Mariam. Nothing I write here can express my love for them or my appreciation for their endless support.

Samer S. Shehata (ed.)
Islamist Politics in the Middle East: Movements and Change

Note

1 It is worth noting that Mohamed Saad El Katatny participated in the conference on which this volume is based. At the time, Katatny was the head of the Egyptian Muslim Brotherhood's Parliamentary Bloc during the 2005–2010 parliament. He became the Secretary General of the Muslim Brotherhood's Freedom and Justice Party when it was established and was recently elected as speaker of the Egyptian parliament.

Notes on contributors

Saïd Amir Arjomand is Distinguished Service Professor of Sociology and Director of the Institute for Global Studies at the State University of New York at Stony Brook. He is the Founder and President of the Association for the Study of Persianate Societies, and served as its President from 1999 to 2007. He is editor of the *Journal of Persianate Studies*, and his books include *The Shadow of God and the Hidden Imam* (University of Chicago Press, 1984), *The Turban for the Crown: The Islamic Revolution in Iran* (Oxford University Press, 1988), *Constitutionalism and Political Reconstruction* (Leiden: Koninklijke Brill NV, 2007), and, most recently, *After Khomeini: Iran under His Successors* (Oxford University Press, 2009).

Raymond William Baker is an internationally recognized authority on the Arab and Islamic world. He is the author of a series of critically acclaimed studies of Egypt, published by Harvard Press. His most recent book is the co-edited *Cultural Cleansing in Iraq: Why Museums Were Looted, Libraries Burned and Academics Murdered* (Pluto Press, 2010). Baker is College Professor of International Politics at Trinity College, Hartford, CT, and Director, International Council of Middle East Studies, Washington, DC. He is currently completing a book for Oxford University Press, *One Islam, Many Empires*, on which he draws for this chapter.

François Burgat is the Director of the Institut Français du Proche-Orient in Damascus, Syria, and was previously Senior Research Fellow and Director of Research at the National Center for Scientific Research (CNRS), Institut de Recherches et d'Etudes sur le Monde Arabe et Musulman (IREMAM) in Aix-en-Provence, France, and the Director of the French Center for Archeology and Social Sciences in Sanaa, Yemen. He is the author of multiple books on Islamist politics, including *The Islamic Movement in North Africa* (University of Texas at Austin, 1993), *Face to Face with Political Islam* (I. B. Tauris & Co. Ltd, 2003), and *Islamism in the Shadow of Al-Qaeda* (University of Texas Press, 2008), in addition to numerous book chapters and academic articles.

Janine Astrid Clark is Associate Professor in the Department of Political Science at the University of Guelph (Canada). She is the author of *Islam, Charity, and Activism: Middle-Class Networks and Social Welfare in Egypt, Jordan and Yemen* (Indiana University Press, 2004) and co-editor of *Economic Liberalization, Democratization and Civil Society in the Developing World* (Palgrave Macmillan, 2000). She has contributed to several edited volumes and has also published numerous academic articles in journals such as *Comparative Politics, Comparative Political Studies, International Journal of Middle East Studies*, and *Middle East Report.*

Rola el-Husseini is an Assistant Professor of Middle Eastern Politics at the George H. W. Bush School of Government and Public Service at Texas A& M University. Prior to joining the Bush School faculty, she was a postdoctoral associate at the Center for International and Area Studies at Yale University. Her publications have appeared in *Comparative Studies of South Asia, Africa and the Middle East, Middle East Journal*, and *Third World Quarterly*. Her first book, with the working title *Pax Syriana: Elite Politics in Postwar Lebanon*, is forthcoming with Syracuse University Press.

Amr Elshobaki is Senior Expert at the Al Ahram Center for Political and Strategic Studies in Cairo, Egypt. He is one of the leading experts on the Egyptian Muslim Brotherhood and has written both scholarly and popular work, in French and Arabic, about the group's history and current place in Egyptian politics. He is the author of *Les Frères musulmans des origines à nos jour* (Paris: Karthala, 2009) and is a frequent contributor to the Egyptian daily *Al Masry Al Youm*. He holds a PhD in political science from the University of Paris (Sorbonne).

Ahmed S. Hashim is Researcher Manager and Academic Coordinator, ICPVTR, and Associate Professor, RSIS, Nanyang Technological University, Singapore. He is the author of *Insurgency and Counter-Insurgency in Iraq* (Cornell University Press, 2006), *Iraq's Sunni Insurgency* (Routledge, 2009), *A Bright Shining COIN: Sri Lanka's Defeat of the Tamil Tigers* (University of Pennsylvania Press, 2012), and *Small Wars: 'Civilizing the Savages'* (London: Hurst; New York: Columbia University Press, 2012).

Henri Lauzière is Assistant Professor of Modern Middle Eastern History at Northwestern University. His main area of research focuses on the history of Salafism, with a particular interest in the ways in which scholars process and produce knowledge about it. He has published articles on twentieth century Islamic thought and is currently writing a monograph on the formation and transformation of Salafism through the life and thought of Taqi al-Din al-Hilali (d. 1987).

Jean-François Legrain is a Research Fellow at the National Center for Scientific Research (CNRS) at the Maison de l'Orient et de la Méditerranée in Lyon, France. He has been a researcher at the French Institute of Arab Studies in Damascus (IFEAD), the Center for Economic Studies and Documentation, Legal and Social (CEDEJ) in Cairo, and the Centre for Study and Research on the Contemporary

Middle East (CERMOC) in Amman and Jerusalem. Among his publications are *Transformations sociales et revendications nationales au Proche Orient, 1877–1945* (Centre National d'Enseignement par Correspondance, 1985), *Les Palestines du quotidian: Les Elections de l'autonomie* (Centre d'Études et de Recherches sur le Moyen-Orient Contemporain, 1996), *Internet et histoire: les Brigades des martyrs d'Al-Aqsa* (Maison de l'Orient et de la Méditerranée, 2004), and *La Ville dans la tête: Bethleem 1996–2006* (Maison de l'Orient et de la Méditerranée, 2006) in addition to many academic and policy articles. In English his writings have appeared in the *Encyclopedia of Islam*, the *Oxford Encyclopedia of the Modern Islamic World*, the *Journal of Palestine Studies*, and as numerous book chapters.

Samer S. Shehata is Assistant Professor of Arab Politics at Georgetown University's Center for Contemporary Arab Studies. He is the author of *Shop Floor Culture and Politics in Egypt* (SUNY Press, 2009; American University in Cairo Press, 2010) in addition to numerous academic and policy articles in journals such as the *International Journal of Middle East Studies*, *Current History*, and *Middle East Report*. He has received fellowships from the National Endowment for the Humanities, the American Research Center in Egypt, and the Woodrow Wilson International Center for Scholars. In 2009, he was named a Carnegie Scholar of Islam by the Carnegie Corporation of New York. He has researched and written extensively about the Muslim Brotherhood and Egyptian politics.

Jenny B. White is Associate Professor in the Anthropology Department at Boston University. She is author of *Islamist Mobilization in Turkey: A Study in Vernacular Politics* (University of Washington Press, 2002) and *Money Makes Us Relatives: Women's Labor in Urban Turkey* (second edition, Routledge, 2004), in addition to numerous academic articles. Dr. White is the former president of the Turkish Studies Association and of the American Anthropological Association Middle East Section, and sits on the board of the Institute of Turkish Studies. She also has written three historical novels set in nineteenth century Istanbul, *The Sultan's Seal* (W. W. Norton & Company, Inc., 2006), *The Abyssinian Proof* (W. W. Norton & Company, Inc., 2008), and *The Winter Thief* (W. W. Norton & Company, Inc., 2010). *The Sultan's Seal*, translated into fifteen languages, was named one of the top ten first novels of 2006 by *Booklist* and was shortlisted for the 2006 Ellis Peters Historical Crime Award.

INTRODUCTION

Samer S. Shehata[1]

Islamist politics, or political Islam, has been one of the most dynamic political forces in the Middle East for over three decades. Whether in the form of electoral politics in the region or in the form of cataclysmic events such as the 1979 Iranian revolution and the September 11, 2001 attacks, political Islam has directly shaped both local and global politics in far-reaching ways. Consequently, it has had a tremendous impact on regional as well as international affairs.

Yet, if there is broad consensus on the importance of political Islam, there is far less agreement on its character, the role of Islamist movements in domestic and international affairs, the reasons for Islamist success, or what these movements portend for the future. These subjects are highly contentious and often politicized. Moreover, because of the media and policy focus on violent groups such as Al-Qaeda and its offshoots, the most popular, dynamic, and influential Islamist movements frequently receive less attention. But it is these groups – Egypt's Muslim Brotherhood, Jordan's Islamic Action Front, and Morocco's Justice and Benevolence, for example – that have had the most profound impact on the Middle East. And it is these groups that will likely have the greatest impact on the region's future.

This volume presents original research on a number of Islamist movements and politics in Morocco, Egypt, Jordan, Palestine, Lebanon, Iraq, Turkey, and Iran, in addition to theoretical treatments of the subject. The chapters reflect the diversity of Islamist politics and address a number of themes. However, the volume does not aspire to provide a comprehensive account of Islamist politics in the Middle East. Indeed, the broad scope and heterogeneity of the phenomenon makes such an endeavor impossible. The volume's goals are considerably more limited. First, the introduction presents a brief and necessarily incomplete glimpse of how Islamist politics has commonly been viewed in the West since 1979, when it first emerged as a major subject of media, policy, and scholarly interest.[2] It then briefly addresses some of the conceptual challenges and difficulties involved in defining Islamist politics before previewing the various chapters collected in this volume.[3]

After this brief introduction, Part I of this volume includes two conceptual chapters about Islamist politics, while Part II presents a number of detailed case studies, based on original research and analysis, of different Islamist movements and groups in the Middle East. The topics addressed include social networks and social welfare provision, Islamist groups as opposition actors, the intersection of Islam and national liberation struggles, the role of religion in Islamist politics, and Islam and state politics in Iran, among others. These issues are examined through case studies of some of the most important Islamist movements in the region, including the Muslim Brotherhood, Hamas, Hizbullah, the Jordanian Islamic Action Front, and Morocco's Justice and Benevolence. The contributors come from a range of disciplines, employ a variety of research techniques, and are not bound by a single theoretic perspective. However, all of the contributors are specialists with deep knowledge of the subject matter. All are committed to empirically based research and all take Islamist movements seriously, rejecting the view that Islamist politics is necessarily anti-modern, anti-rational, or inherently anti-democratic. The result is new scholarship about some of the most important Islamist movements in the Middle East by leading specialists in the field.

"Islamic fundamentalism"

There is no single or widely accepted definition of Islamist politics or political Islam (I use these terms interchangeably here). Different scholars have proposed quite varied definitions. The subject first gained widespread notoriety in the West following the 1979 Iranian revolution.[4] At the time it was commonly referred to as "Islamic fundamentalism."[5] The dramatic overthrow of the U.S.-backed Pahlavi regime and the subsequent hostage crisis, in which over 50 U.S. Embassy personnel were held captive by Iranian revolutionary students for 444 days, squarely focused America's attention on Iran and the ideology behind the political upheaval.

The "Islamic" revolution stunned Americans.[6] It entailed the fall of a major U.S. regional ally and the emergence of a new, powerful, seemingly alien, and threatening political force vehemently opposed to the United States and the West.

Several other important historical events also contributed to the increased attention political Islam began to receive at the time. The 1979 Soviet invasion of Afghanistan and the popular resistance to the invasion generated by the *mujahidin* (Afghan and foreign Muslim fighters) and, in the same year, the violent takeover of Islam's holiest site, the Grand Mosque in Mecca, Saudi Arabia, by a small group of heavily armed messianic Islamist extremists, also produced increased interest in the relationship between Islam and politics.

Less than two years later, Egyptian President Anwar Al Sadat was assassinated by members of a militant Islamist group, the Egyptian Islamic Jihad.[7] In the span of two short years, "Islamic fundamentalism" was making regular headlines as a violent and anti-Western political ideology. By the middle of the 1980s, there was growing concern about an impending "Islamic threat," which some claimed would replace communism as the major challenge to the West.[8]

Some scholars described the phenomenon as an Islamic "revival" or "resurgence."[9] Others wrote of "Islamic revolution," while several influential commentators warned of "Muslim rage," "radical Islam," and the "revolt of Islam."[10] For example, only a few months after Ayatollah Khomeini returned to Iran, a Massachusetts Institute of Technology political scientist described "Islamic fundamentalism" as a "revolt against Western-style modernization."[11] This was not atypical. Less scholarly articulations characterized the phenomenon as "militant and violent," "authoritarian," and "anti-democratic."[12] Comparisons with communism, fascism, and Nazism were not uncommon.

There remains a widely held view that "Islamic fundamentalism" is a backward-looking and anti-modern religiously based political ideology. "Islamic fundamentalists" are assumed to want to turn the clock back on history and return to the seventh century (i.e. the origins of Islam). As an ideology it is often believed to be inherently violent. Many consider it a dangerous threat to Western values and civilization.

There are a number of problems with such facile characterizations, not least of which is the term "fundamentalism" itself. More than 30 years after "Islamic fundamentalism" first came into widespread circulation, the term has unmistakably come to convey something inherently negative. It connotes an extremist, violent, anti-democratic, and anti-Western political ideology.[13] "Islamic fundamentalism" has also come to be associated with hijackings, suicide bombings, and other forms of political violence. In popular discourse, it is frequently equated with terrorism. "Islamic fundamentalism" is now not so much an analytical category as it is a pejorative label. Yet many in the media, as well as some scholars, continue to use the term.[14]

"Fundamentalism," however, first came into usage to describe not politically active Muslims in the Middle East but late nineteenth and early twentieth century American evangelical Protestants. Fundamentalism was primarily an anti-modernist religious movement and the term was originally coined to describe conservative Protestants who were resisting attempts by co-religionists to modernize their faith. These original "fundamentalists" opposed liberal theology, German higher Biblical criticism, and evolutionary theory (e.g., Darwinism), which was entering popular consciousness and debates about the curriculum at the time, and insisted on scriptural inerrancy and a literal interpretation of the Bible.[15]

It makes little sense, therefore, to speak about "fundamentalism" in an Islamic context because, generally, all Muslims believe in the Quran's inerrancy and accept it as the literal word of God revealed to the Prophet Mohamed through the Angel Gabriel. Most Islamists are not occupied with defending the nature of the Quran. Rather, the vast majority of Islamists – whether Iranian revolutionaries inventing the institutions of a modern "Islamic Republic," Muslim Brothers designing electoral strategies, or militant Islamists detonating improvised explosive devices – hold consciously *innovative* understandings of Islam, employ modern technologies, and are actively engaged in efforts to transform the contemporary world.[16] Some Islamists, although not all, advocate increased political freedoms and social justice. Others have more radical, and sometimes violent, political agendas.

This points to yet another major difference between Protestant fundamentalism and political Islam: the vast majority of Islamist movements are primarily focused on politics, not theology (as François Burgat makes clear in Chapter 1). Islamist movements are principally concerned with changing the governments under which they live, implementing new laws, and transforming their societies. Political Islam, as the name suggests, is largely a political phenomenon. This subject is addressed at greater length below and in subsequent chapters.

In short, the differences between Protestant fundamentalism and Islamist politics are overwhelming. In this sense, it is profoundly inaccurate to use the term "fundamentalism" to describe individuals and movements that understand Islam as a political ideology.[17]

There are other problems with the both the term "fundamentalism" and the way Islamist politics is frequently represented. "Islamic fundamentalism" implies a homogeneity that is quite far from the reality of Islamist politics. As the chapters in this volume demonstrate, political Islam manifests itself in a wide variety of forms. Islamist movements differ in terms of ideology, mobilization strategies, views about formal political participation, the use of violence, the acceptance of the nation-state as the basis for political community, as well as on many other dimensions. Islamist movements are hardly monolithic. Yet "fundamentalism" fails to capture this complexity; it implies a homogenous phenomenon.[18]

Islamist politics

If one were to write a comprehensive history of trends in the literature on political Islam since 1979, two developments would also need to be highlighted. First, beginning in the 1980s a great deal of attention was devoted to examining the relationship between Islam and democracy, often posed as the question of Islam's compatibility with democracy. Historians, political scientists, anthropologists, and religious scholars argued both sides of this debate, sometimes drawing on textual sources (i.e. the Quran and hadith) to make their arguments.[19] However, much of the discussion was abstract and ahistorical, positing a singular "Islam" that somehow existed outside of time and space and which determined not only Muslims' behavior, but also their destinies.

Asef Bayat has astutely characterized the question of Islam's compatibility with democracy as "irrelevant" (one could also add, nonsensical).[20] Rather than trying to determine Islam's "essence," scholars have increasingly turned to examining the behavior and ideologies of Islamist groups and political parties. Again, much of the discussion has taken place within a democratization framework that explicitly focuses on Islamists' commitment to democracy. The following questions are often asked: Do Islamists genuinely accept democratic values and principles? Or are they simply utilizing democratic institutions such as elections instrumentally, as some have argued, for non-democratic purposes?[21]

Within this literature, and particularly within the political science discourse about Islamist politics, a great deal of attention has been devoted to the issue of "moderation" (sometimes referred to as the "inclusion–moderation" hypothesis), to the extent that this seems to have become the dominant focus in the disciplinary scholarship on the subject. "Moderation" is believed to be positively correlated with democracy in that "moderate" groups, unlike "radicals," are thought to be good for democratic transitions. In the expanding political science literature on Islamist groups, the question is often framed as whether the inclusion of Islamist groups in formal politics leads to their behavioral and/or ideological "moderation," and, hence, their acceptance of democratic values.[22]

There have been a number of outstanding studies to emerge from this approach, including Jillian Schwedler and Carrie Rosefsky Wickham's work.[23] However, much of the literature remains enmeshed within a democratization paradigm that views Islamist groups with deep suspicion: as the primary threat to democracy in the region, often forgetting that these groups (whether democratic or not) operate in decidedly non-democratic contexts. Thus, at times debates about the merits and/or risks of including Islamists in the political process obscure the primary dilemma facing these polities: entrenched authoritarian regimes, often avowedly secular, unwilling to give up power or reform. Moreover, it is also quite likely that the authoritarian political contexts in which Islamists find themselves also impact their behavior and ideology.

There are other conceptual difficulties with the moderation paradigm. Central to the approach is a distinction between "moderates" and "radicals" (sometimes referred to as "extremists"). Although such a binary can be useful for some purposes, often – especially in the policy and media discussions of Islamist groups – "moderate" and "radical" seem to correspond to little more than a group's position vis-à-vis the United States and Israel rather than to any objective criteria about "moderation." Groups that are stridently hostile to U.S. and Israeli policy are frequently viewed as "radical" or "extremist," while those less critical are said to be "moderate." When one places such classificatory schema alongside a policy discourse that contrasts so-called "moderate Arab states" (such as Tunisia under Ben Ali, Egypt under Mubarak, and Saudi Arabia) with "radical" states and groups such as Syria, Iran, Hizbullah, and Hamas, there are legitimate reasons for skepticism. After all, these "moderate" Arab states, despite being U.S. allies, have hardly been moderate when it comes to civil liberties, human rights, tolerance, or political freedoms.[24]

Finally, the concern about Islamists and the "dangers" they pose to democracy (echoed in the oft-repeated phrase "one man, one vote, one time")[25] sometimes leads to attempts to divine whether such groups have genuinely moderated (and hence are "really democratic") or whether they simply use democratic institutions instrumentally to gain power. Not only are such attempts to see into the hearts of Islamists (or anyone, for that matter) extremely difficult, if not simply impossible, such an approach seems to assume that democracy is primarily the result of, and sustained through, individual values and commitments, rather than institutional constraints on power (e.g. structures).

Despite such shortcomings, both the democratization and moderation paradigms demonstrate how scholars have increasingly adopted "Islamist politics" or "political Islam," often interchangeably (as I do here), to describe politics and political movements that claim to be based on Islam. These terms are a significant improvement on "fundamentalism" because they are not inherently biased and because they can accommodate the broad spectrum of Islamist politics. However, there remains little consensus on how these terms should be defined or how the phenomenon they describe should be understood.

A number of quite varied definitions have been put forward – so many in fact that at times it seems there are as many definitions of political Islam as there are authors writing about the subject. My purpose in this brief introduction is not to put forward yet another definition.[26] However, examining a few of the ways political Islam has been understood will highlight the extent to which definitions vary, the broad contours of the phenomenon, and the implications of adopting one definition over another.

At the most basic level, many scholars understand Islamist politics as the belief among some Muslims, although not all, that Islam should inform politics in some manner. This has been expressed in a number of ways. For example, in an early treatment, Nazih Ayubi defined political Islam as "the doctrine and/or movement which contends that Islam possesses a theory of politics and the State."[27] Others have construed this as the call to incorporate Islamic principles, concepts, and traditions into politics. Graham Fuller, for example, has written that an Islamist "is one who believes that Islam as a body of faith has something important to say about how politics and society should be ordered in the contemporary Muslim world and who seeks to implement this idea in some fashion."[28]

These ideas are sometimes expressed as the "politicization of Islam."[29] For example, Mohammed Ayoob writes that political Islam is "Islam as political ideology rather than religion or theology."[30] Ayubi, Fuller, and Ayoob also hold that political Islam is a thoroughly modern phenomenon, not simply a return to a "traditional" or "original" understanding of politics in Islam. Ayubi expresses this most emphatically, stating that "political Islam is a new invention" and "does not represent a 'going back' to any situation that existed in the past or to any theory that was formulated in the past."[31] Understood in this manner, political Islam is neither a natural condition of Muslims nor the "essence" of Islam.

Other scholars have made valuable contributions to our understanding of Islamist politics by recognizing that politics is not only about capturing the state or controlling material resources but also entails competition and conflict over meaning and symbols. For Dale Eickelman and James Piscatori, this has led to a focus on the power of, and struggles over, Islamic symbols, language, discourse, images, and vocabulary.[32] For Salwa Ismail, the attention to culture is reflected in her definition of Islamist politics as "the activities of organizations and movements that mobilize and agitate in the political sphere while deploying *signs and symbols from Islamic traditions*" (my emphasis).[33]

Briefly contrasting these definitions with another common, but, in my view, overly narrow understanding of political Islam will prove worthwhile. Political Islam is often defined as the desire to implement the *shari'a* (Islamic law) and/or create an Islamic state. Sometimes these goals are differentiated, while at other times they are considered to be two sides of the same coin, with an Islamic state being defined as one in which all law is based on the shari'a.[34] Many authors, including Bassam Tibi, for example, have argued that this is *the* central goal of all Islamists, the single objective they share, and thus the defining feature of Islamist politics.[35] According to this view, the primary difference between Islamist groups is that some attempt to achieve these goals peacefully while others do so through violence.

There are several problems with definitions of political Islam that focus exclusively on the application of the shari'a and/or the creation of an Islamic state, although these are often the ideal objectives of many Islamist groups. Such definitions can quickly lose sight of the vast majority of activities undertaken by Islamists that are not directly related to either of these goals: charitable activities, education, medical services, religious programs, propagation (*da'wa*), and even "day-to-day politics." More importantly, a definition narrowly focused on the shari'a and the Islamic state misses other dimensions of Islamist politics – for example the ways in which ostensibly non-Islamist actors (e.g. political leaders and regimes) often draw upon Islamic symbols and referents for their own purposes (discussed in the following section, p. 8).[36] This too is a form of Islamist politics. Moreover, calls for the establishment of an Islamic state often function more at the symbolic level than as realizable short-term objectives. For many, the call to implement the shari'a has simply become shorthand for the entire Islamist project, rather than the desire to implement specific laws or a concrete political program.

Any understanding of Islamist politics must be able to capture at least four dimensions of the phenomenon. First, it must be able to capture its sheer diversity. Islamist politics includes groups, movements, and states as wide-ranging as Morocco's Justice and Benevolence, the Taliban, the Algerian Islamic Salvation Front, the Egyptian *Wassat* Party, Al Qaeda, the Palestinian Islamic Resistance Movement (Hamas), the Iranian and Saudi regimes, and Turkey's ruling Justice and Development Party. These groups, parties, and governments are tremendously diverse. Some are inspired by Sufi theology, while others are committed to Wahhabi principles. Some accept the sanctity of the nation-state, while others seek to overturn the entire international system. Some are committed to reform, while others champion revolution. Some are mass-based popular movements, while others are small, clandestine groupings. Political Islam finds itself in power in places, but more often it functions as an oppositional ideology. Some Islamists are aligned with the West, while many more are opposed to American and Western hegemony. Some Islamists espouse violence, while others are committed to peaceful political participation. Any understanding of political Islam must be broad enough to capture this heterogeneity.

Second, more often than not when we think of political Islam we think of *opposition politics*; that is, Islamist groups challenging the status quo and opposing secular regimes. In fact, this has been the dominant form of Islamist politics in the Middle East. It is also worth noting that the majority of Islamist groups are primarily focused on national-level politics, with some notable exceptions, including transnational terrorist groups such as Al Qaeda. This is somewhat counterintuitive for those who might assume that Islamist groups would focus primarily on the Muslim *umma*, the worldwide community of believers and co-religionists. In fact, most Islamists are principally concerned with domestic politics: local issues within the nation-states in which they operate, and whose boundaries they largely accept.[37]

However, in addition to opposition groups and politics, political Islam also includes states that claim an Islamic basis of legitimacy. Iran, Saudi Arabia, Sudan, Pakistan, and Afghanistan (both under the Taliban as well as the current regime, whose official name is the "Islamic Republic of Afghanistan"), for example, all claim to be Islamic states.[38] Thus, political Islam finds itself both in and outside of power – an opposition ideology in some places and an ideology of state in others.

It should also be apparent that these states vary widely in terms of regime type (e.g. monarchies and republics), institutions (e.g. elected parliaments and appointed consultative councils), economic systems, levels of development, regional and international alignments, women's rights (e.g. from full legal political rights to no political rights), and personal and political freedoms. In other words, ostensibly Islamic states vary tremendously. Thus, any understanding of Islamist politics must also be able to accommodate such diversity.

Third, in addition to being an opposition ideology and an ideology of state, political Islam has also been used by regimes and leaders, including ostensibly secular ones, as a source of legitimacy. Presidents such as Anwar Al Sadat have employed Islamic symbols and images to increase their popularity and bolster the legitimacy of their regimes. Sadat, for example, famously cultivated an image of himself as the "believer president." He frequently appeared on television attending Friday prayers, holding prayer beads, and appearing observant. Sadat also often began his speeches with *Bism Allah Al Rahman Al Rahim*, the opening verses of the Quran.[39]

Saddam Hussein also employed Islam for his own purposes, as Ahmed Hashim describes in Chapter 8 in this volume. For example, Hussein's "Return to Faith" policy following the 1991 Gulf War entailed promoting religious lessons in schools, building mosques, broadcasting Quranic lessons on the radio, and banning alcohol in restaurants. It was at this time that Saddam Hussein also emblazoned the words *Allah Akbur (God is Great)* on the Iraqi flag, supposedly in his own handwriting. These leaders undertook such measures to bolster their Islamic credentials as well as those of their regimes.[40] They drew on Islamic symbols and images to appear pious, thereby enhancing their religious legitimacy. This too is a dimension of Islamist politics.

Finally, any conception of Islamist politics should be neutral: neither proclaiming the "threat" posed by political Islam nor denying that some Islamist movements are extremist. This is the necessary conclusion of recognizing the wide diversity and broad spectrum of political Islam.

Taken together, the understanding of Islamist politics presented here has implications for how we should think about this category. If Islamist politics encompasses all of the varied dimensions presented above, then it is an extremely broad domain, comprising a wide range of activity by both state and non-state actors who engage in politics with reference to Islam. As such, Islamist politics must be understood not as an explanatory framework or a predictive model. This implies that simply classifying a group as "Islamist," for example, tells us little about its specific character or orientation. It does not necessarily reveal anything about the group's positions on particular issues, strategy, tactics, or future trajectory. Islamist politics must be understood as a broad domain rather than an explanatory framework.

The following chapters

The chapters in this volume reflect the diversity and broad scope of Islamist politics. They are divided into two parts. Part I, entitled "Islamist politics: theory and critique," includes chapters by François Burgat and Raymond Baker. In Chapter 1, François Burgat argues that Islamist politics is a product of the conditions in which Arabs find themselves at the national, regional, and international levels: repressive politics, injustice, and marginalization. The most distinctive feature of contemporary Arab politics, Burgat claims, is political leaders who remain in power *despite* elections and without regard to popular will. Arabs also face repression, injustice, and marginalization at the regional (e.g. Arab–Israeli conflict and Palestine) and international levels. Burgat argues that although Islamists employ an "Islamic lexicon" or vocabulary to make claims about social justice, politics, identity, rights, and corruption, "the use of an Islamic vocabulary ... represents more an affirmation of identity than the promotion of a theocratic vision of the world" (p. 25). Islamism, according to Burgat, is a kind of resistance against the West, similar to earlier forms of resistance such as nationalism during decolonization.

If Burgat's analysis is primarily about how we should understand Islamist politics, Raymond Baker's chapter critiques how Islamist politics has been (mis)understood and (mis)represented, particularly during the George W. Bush administration (2001–09). In Chapter 2, Baker presents a powerful critique of the policy literature about Islam and democracy produced during Bush's presidency. The subject of Islam gained tremendous significance in U.S. government and policy circles following September 11, 2001. Baker argues that Islam was seen as a "colossal threat" and a "failed faith and civilization" by dominant neoconservatives at the time. Liberals adopted a "somewhat softer view" focusing on the "cultural deficiencies ... of the Islamic threat." Both groups believed "Muslims everywhere lack the liberal gene." Baker demonstrates how these discourses simply ignored history and the writings of some of the most prominent Islamist thinkers of the twentieth century to produce a distorted account of Islam that functioned to justify an imperial U.S. foreign policy. He dissects the inner workings of this discourse – how it (mis)represented Islam and Middle Eastern/ Islamic history – in order to rationalize an imperial American project. Islam became the constructed enemy of choice – a problem that had to be dealt with (by the right) or overcome (by the left). The Bush administration's democracy discourse became a tool of empire.

In the course of his analysis, Baker examines the leading proponents of "Centrist" (*Wassatteya*) Islam, whose ideas were ignored in Bush-administration-era discussions of Islam and democracy. These "New Islamists" (e.g. Muhammad al Ghazzaly, Kamal Abul Magd, Yusuf al Qaradawy, and Fahmy Huwaidy) are arguably the most influential Islamic thinkers in the past half-century, and together they put forward a vision of Islam that champions rationality, science, education, tolerance, and social justice. Much of their attention focuses on questions of rule of law, political participation, democracy, and limiting arbitrary power. Baker argues that Western scholars and policy analysts need to take these thinkers seriously – and the Islamist political organizations that have assimilated their ideas – rather than searching desperately for "Islamist liberals who can duplicate the Western path to democracy."

Part II of this volume consists of eight chapters that examine specific Islamist movements and one chapter that takes up politics in the Islamic Republic of Iran. Chapters 3 and 4 analyze the role of networks and social welfare provision in the strategy, success, and internal politics of Islamist movements. From Morocco to Malaysia, Islamists are frequently associated with the provision of social services (e.g. orphanages, schools, medical clinics, and hospitals). But what is the relationship between social welfare provision and Islamist politics? Do social services account for the popularity and electoral success of these groups, as many assume? And what are the internal politics associated with social welfare provision for Islamist groups? Jenny White and Janine Clark explore these questions through case studies of Turkey and Jordan in Chapters 3 and 4.

In Chapter 3, White argues that Turkish Islamist women activists played a major role in the electoral success of Turkey's Justice and Development Party (AKP). She describes how Islamist women activists methodically employed face-to-face networks in their neighborhoods to increase the party's standing. White argues that the success of Islamist parties in Turkey has less to do with religious conviction (i.e. Islam) or ideology than with the type of social mobilization and networks these groups employed to connect with local communities. "A major reason for the success of the WP [Welfare Party] (and after it, VP and AKP) ... was its style of mobilizing supporters," she writes. "The party perfected a face-to-face, personalized style of mobilizing 'cells' of neighbors on the basis of local solidarities" (p. 61).

White also examines the range of social and economic services local activists and Islamist groups provided residents – everything from finding an appropriate spouse and raising a dowry to economic assistance and marriage mediation. While service provision was important, it was not *the* reason Islamists did well in the polls. However, compared with other parties, Islamists were "perceived by the population to be greatly supportive" of local communities. The primary reason for Islamist electoral success in Turkey, White explains, was the combination of networks, local activists, and efficient organization.

In Chapter 4, Clark examines the politics of patronage within Islamist movements through an analysis of Jordan's Islamic Center Charity Society (ICCS). Established in 1963 and affiliated with the Muslim Brotherhood (MB), the ICCS is Jordan's largest Islamic non-governmental organization (NGO) and one of the largest NGOs in the country. Clark presents a fine-grained analysis of the politics of the ICCS based on extensive fieldwork, including interviews, site visits, and archival research.

The ICCS is a large, multifaceted institution that employs several thousand people in positions that provide prestige, authority, and patronage opportunities. By analyzing struggles over resources between different individuals and factions within the MB and ICCS, Clark demonstrates, as few have done before, how "Islamist institutions [such as the ICCS] are sites of conflict and competition" (p. 80). Unlike most of the literature about Islamist social welfare provision, Clark's analysis goes beyond examining whether this type of activity explains the popularity of Islamist groups. More interestingly (and quite originally), she analyzes the importance of patronage *within* the ICCS and explores how this impacts the institution's leadership and its role within the Jordanian Muslim Brotherhood.

Chapters 5, 6, and 7 investigate Islamist groups and parties as opposition movements through an examination of Morocco's *Al Adl wa al Ihsan* (Justice and Benevolence) and the Egyptian Muslim Brotherhood. All across the region – in republics and monarchies, in secular regimes and ostensibly religious states – Islamists have emerged as the most organized and powerful opposition forces. What are the dynamics of Islamist–regime relations in non-democratic contexts? What role does religious ideology play in countries such as Morocco where multiple opposition groups and the state claim legitimacy based on Islam? How have Islamist opposition movements fared in seemingly durable authoritarian regimes such as Mubarak's Egypt? Why have groups such as the Egyptian Muslim Brotherhood chosen to participate in elections that were routinely neither free nor fair, despite the limited benefits and tremendous costs of electoral participation?

In Chapter 5 Henri Lauzière examines the most popular Islamist movement in Morocco, *Al Adl wa al Ihsan* (Justice and Benevolence), analyzing how the religious ideology of the group's founder, Shaykh 'Abdel Salam Yasin, significantly contributed to the movement's standing in the aftermath of the May 2003 Casablanca bombings. The horrific bombings killed 45 people and shock Morocco. The attacks were perpetrated by an extremist Salafi group and many Moroccans subsequently became suspicious of all groups associated with Salafism. In this context, *Al Adl wa al Ihsan*'s Sufi-infused Islamism appeared benign and served to radically distinguish it from Salafi-inspired movements that were seen as potentially violent. Lauzière argues that because the political sphere in Morocco is made up of multiple Islamist movements (in addition to the government claiming Islamic credentials and the king serving as "Commander of the Faithful"), differences in theology, religious practice, and ideology serve to differentiate Islamist groups from each other. In this context, religious issues and theological questions are often what most clearly distinguish Islamist groups from one another. These insights are likely to have relevance far beyond Morocco.

In Chapter 6, Amr Elshobaki provides an overview of the Muslim Brotherhood's tumultuous history by charting the group's tense and often conflictual relations with successive Egyptian governments in the pre- and post-1952 periods. Elshobaki periodizes the Brotherhood's history into three distinct phases: the founding (1928) until the 1970s, the group's reemergence after years of repression, and its subsequent entrance into formal and electoral politics. Elshobaki traces the transformations within the organization – from the consequences of repression in the 1950s and 1960s, which caused the movement to retreat from formal politics and look inward, to its increasing political participation beginning in the 1980s. He argues that political alliances with opposition parties in the 1980s profoundly affected the group. These experiences "directly impacted the Brotherhood's political discourse … generating a new Brotherhood approach entirely distinct from the organization's direction under the monarchy, Nasser, and Sadat" (p. 113).

Chapter 7 further develops the analysis of the Muslim Brotherhood as an Islamist opposition movement by examining one of the most important aspects of the group's new approach to politics discussed by Elshobaki: namely, electoral participation. Samer Shehata asks why the Brotherhood chose to participate in elections that routinely lacked integrity under the Mubarak regime. In Mubarak's Egypt, like other semi-authoritarian regimes, elections were neither free nor fair. Elections did not provide an opportunity to gain power through the ballot box, nor did parliamentary membership offer a mechanism to influence government policy. Under such conditions, Shehata asks, why would a popular Islamist movement choose to participate in "limited elections"?[41]

Based on extensive fieldwork with Brotherhood candidates during elections, interviews with the organization's leadership, and analysis of the group's parliamentary activities, Shehata demonstrates that the Brotherhood's electoral participation was not primarily about "winning" votes or seats, coming to power, or influencing public policy (as much of the political science literature on parties and elections would suggest). Shehata argues that elections in semi-authoritarian regimes provide a rare opportunity to engage in politics, something that is uncommon in such polities. Semi-authoritarian regimes such as Mubarak's Egypt often allow greater political activity during election periods, and hence electoral participation itself becomes an *opportunity* to engage in politics (e.g. holding meetings, rallies, demonstrations, disseminating the organization's message, and connecting with citizens and potential voters). Shehata calls this use of elections "political *da'wa*." He uses the term to describe the Brotherhood's use of elections (and, later, the group's use of parliament) to disseminate its ideology, communicate with wider segments of the population, and gain further adherents. The goal of electoral participation, Shehata concludes, is not to win elections or influence policy, but to propagate the Brotherhood's message.

The next three chapters focus on the convergence of national liberation struggles and political Islam. In Iraq, Lebanon, and Palestine, powerful Islamist movements have emerged that are founded upon resistance to foreign occupation. How does Islam become an ideology of national liberation? How are Islamic principles and history re-imagined according to nationalist purposes? Do conflicts between Islamist and secular nationalist movements revolve around religion? Chapters 8, 9, and 10 explore such questions through detailed examinations of Hamas (Palestine), Hizbullah (Lebanon), and the Sunni insurgency in Iraq.

The role of Islam in the Sunni insurgency in Iraq is the subject of Chapter 8, by Ahmed Hashim. Islam's political role increased significantly in Iraq in the aftermath of the 2003 war as religion came to take on greater prominence in the insurgency's discourse of resistance to foreign occupation. Hashim demonstrates how the Sunni clerical establishment "began to take an activist political role to articulate Sunni grievances and … present a cohesive narrative legitimizing resistance to foreign occupation from within an Islamic framework" (p. 152). He documents the dizzying array of groups and factions involved in the Sunni insurgency, differentiating between elements he labels "nationalist-Islamist" (insurgents who referred to the struggle against occupation forces as a *muqawama*, or resistance) and the more radical "Salafi-Jihadist groups" (including Al Qaeda in Iraq) who framed the insurgency as a *jihad*, or holy struggle against both the foreign occupiers and the Shiite majority. Hashim outlines the changing alliances between insurgent groups before analyzing the important moment when the more nationalist Sunni insurgents definitively broke with Al Qaeda in Iraq. He concludes that although Islam was an important mobilizing and ideological force, it ultimately failed to function as a unifying force within the insurgency.

In Chapter 9, Rola el-Husseini analyzes Hizbullah and its role in regional politics. Reviewing the origins of the group and its ideology, el-Husseini argues that Hizbullah is "first and foremost an anti-imperialist movement" (p. 166) committed to resistance against injustice, domination, and hegemony. Seen from this perspective, Hizbullah's support for the Palestinian intifada is a natural extension of its ideology and not a product of Israel's withdrawal from southern Lebanon in 2000, as some have argued. Similarly, Hizbullah's support for the Mahdi Army in Iraq should be interpreted as an effort to support "resistance" elsewhere in the region, including resistance against imperialism and the United States. Hizbullah's ideology, el-Husseini argues, explains the Lebanese Islamist movement's support for anti-imperialist groups in Palestine and Iraq.

Like Hizbullah, Hamas is another mass-based Islamist movement that combines formal political participation with a commitment to national liberation through "resistance." In Chapter 10, Jean-François Legrain charts Hamas' transformation from a movement focused primarily on religion to one concerned largely with politics. Legrain recounts Hamas' earlier, less well-known history, including its previous and half-hearted ventures in electoral politics. Based on original empirical research and statistical analysis, he argues that a major transformation occurred in Palestinian politics during the 2006 elections. Unlike the 1996 elections, in which most Palestinian voters cast their ballots based on local allegiances of clan, kin, and geography regardless of the candidates' political affiliation, the 2006 elections, according to Legrain, were largely characterized by "party-ticket voting." He writes, "the Islamist voter in 2006 ... gave primacy to political affiliation over ethno-localism; affirming a 'party ticket vote' independent of clannish and local allegiances ... The [Fatah] electorate and candidates, on the contrary ... remained prisoners of a logic based on local allegiances" (p. 186).

Legrain extends his analysis to the critical period after the elections. By denying Hamas the governing authority it legally achieved at the ballot box, Legrain argues, Mahmoud Abbas, Fatah, Israel, and the international community are largely to blame for the subsequent deterioration of Palestinian politics. Fatah was both unwilling to and incapable of giving up power, while the United States and the international community, despite a rhetorical commitment to democracy, were loath to recognize democracy's verdict: a Palestinian Islamist movement in power.

Of course, political Islam can be both an oppositional ideology as well as an ideology of state. The final chapter addresses political Islam and state politics in Iran. In Chapter 11, Saïd Arjomand analyzes politics within the Islamic Republic of Iran and, more specifically, Mohammad Khatami's inability to realize significant political reform during his presidency (1997–2005). Arjomand traces the weakness of Khatami's presidency to institutional, economic, and political factors: Iran's constitutional structure, the resources at the disposal of the Supreme Leader and the clerical establishment, and Khatami's and a reform-minded Majles' unwillingness to challenge the Supreme Leader.

Arjomand characterizes Iran as a "theocratic republic" and a "hybrid political regime," and traces this to the country's constitution: a heterogeneous document containing divergent principles, including theocratic government, the rule of law, and participatory representative politics. Under Khatami, the office of the presidency represented both the rule of law and participatory government but faced opposition from the Supreme Leader. In addition, Arjomand argues that Khatami and the Majles were disconnected from the population and, specifically, from activist students desiring reform, which also contributed to Khatami's weakness, and ultimately to his inability to achieve meaningful political reform. Arjomand interprets Mahmoud Ahmadinejād's election in 2005 – with the backing of the Supreme Leader and the security and mobilization apparatus – as the end of the reformist movement and the culmination of extra-constitutional power in the Iranian political system.

The chapters collected in this volume present new research and analysis about a number of the leading Islamist groups and movements in the Middle East. All of the contributing authors take Islamists seriously as modern, sophisticated, and strategic political players. Together, their work captures much of the diversity of Islamist politics in the region and will contribute to the scholarship on a topic that continues to be important to the Middle East and the world.

Notes

1 I would like to thank Ayoung Shin and Nicholas Garcia-Mason for helpful suggestions on earlier versions of this chapter.

2 The literature on political Islam or Islamist politics is enormous and would be impossible to summarize in a few pages.

3 This section will be especially useful for readers who are not deeply familiar with the subject. Specialists can move immediately to the introduction's third section (pp. 9–14), which previews the following chapters.

4 Although the subject first gained widespread attention in the West beginning in the late 1970s, Richard P. Mitchell astutely pointed out that Islamist politics was an important force in the Middle East much earlier. See R. P. Mitchell, "The Islamic Movement: Its current condition and future prospects," in B. F. Stowasser (ed.) *The Islamic Impulse*, Washington, DC: Center for Contemporary Arab Studies, 1987, pp. 75–86. Islamist politics has its roots in the development of mass-based movements, including modernist, anti-colonial movements, in the Middle East and south Asia in the early twentieth century. The Egyptian Muslim Brotherhood was established in 1928 and the Jammat-i-Islami was established in colonial India in 1941. Hassan al Banna and Abul 'Ela Mawdudi, the respective founders of the groups, are considered by many to be the historical founders of Islamist politics.

5 It was also referred to as "Muslim fundamentalism," and these terms are still, unfortunately, in circulation.

6 The "Islamic" character of the Iranian revolution is contested. Many scholars claim that opposition to the Shah's regime and the protests leading to the regime's overthrow were multifaceted, with different social groups and ideologies playing a role. This perspective claims that the revolution became "Islamic" upon the return of Ayatollah Khomeini on

February 1, 1979, the dismissal of the interim government, and the emergence of the Islamic Republic.

7 The brazen assassination particularly shocked the United States and Europe, where Sadat was widely regarded as an international statesman and hero as a result of the Camp David Peace Accords with Israel. He was considerably less popular in Egypt and the Arab world, however, as a result of his increasing authoritarianism and his widely unpopular foreign policy. The group that assassinated Sadat is also known as Al Jihad and Egyptian Jihad.

8 This threat was sometimes referred to as the "green peril" or the "green menace." The first edition of John Esposito's popular book *The Islamic Threat: Myth or Reality?*, New York: Oxford University Press, was released in 1992 and addressed this question directly. Bernard Lewis' widely read and influential essay entitled "The Roots of Muslim Rage" – rage implying the irrational hostility of the adherents of an entire religion – appeared in *The Atlantic* in 1990. It was in this article that Lewis coined the phrase "clash of civilizations," later picked up by Samuel Huntington, first in an essay in *Foreign Affairs* in 1993 and then in his widely read book with the same title three years later.

9 See, for example, R. H. Dekmejian, "The Anatomy of Islamic Revival: Legitimacy Crisis, Ethnic Conflict and the Search for Islamic Alternatives," *Middle East Journal* 34, 1980, 1–12; A. E. H. Dessouki, "The Resurgence of Islamic Organisations in Egypt: An Interpretation," in A. S. Cudsi and A. E. H. Dessouki (eds.) *Islam and Power*, Baltimore: Johns Hopkins University Press, 1981, pp. 107–18; Y. Y. Haddad, "Muslim Revivalist Thought in the Arab World: An Overview," *The Muslim World* 76, 1986, 143–67.

10 See, for example, R. H. Dekmejian, *Islam in Revolution: Fundamentalism in the Arab World*, Syracuse: Syracuse University Press, 1985; B. Lewis, "The Roots of Muslim Rage," *The Atlantic Monthly*, September 1990, 47–60; E. Sivan, *Radical Islam: Medieval Theology and Modern Politics*, New Haven, Yale University Press, 1985; B. Lewis, "The Revolt of Islam," *New York Review of Books*, June 30, 1983.

11 W. E. Griffith, "The Revival of Islamic Fundamentalism: The Case of Iran," *International Security* 4, 1979, 132–38. A number of other tropes that would come to characterize much of the literature about "Islamic fundamentalism" also appeared in this early article: that Islam "knows neither the idea of progress nor any distinction between God and Caesar or church and state" (p. 133).

12 A. Perlmutter, "Wishful Thinking about Islamic Fundamentalism," *Washington Post*, January 19, 1992.

13 In fact, as early as 1985 some scholars were arguing that the term "Islamic fundamentalism" had simply become a synonym for terrorism in much popular, and even policy, usage. See Augustus Richard Norton's letter to Lee Hamilton in the Hearings before the Subcommittee on Europe and the Middle East of the House Committee on Foreign Affairs, June 24, July 15, and September 30, 1985 (pp. 414–15). The Hearings (and Norton's letter) are collected in one volume entitled *Islamic Fundamentalism and Islamic Radicalism*, Washington, DC: U.S. Government Printing Office, 1985. John Esposito and Herman Eilts also presented thoughtful analysis during these hearings.

14 Today, the term says more about those who employ it than about the phenomenon it is meant to analyze. Those who use the term are more likely to view political Islam with deep suspicion, if not hostility. They are also less likely to accept the possibility that political Islam is not inherently extremist, irrational, or anti-democratic, let alone violent. For example, Bassam Tibi has written extensively about "fundamentalism," and although at times he seems to use "political Islam," "fundamentalism," and "Islamists" interchangeably (causing even more confusion), it is clear that he has a decidedly negative view of the phenomenon. In a recent article he calls the Turkish Justice and Development Party (AKP-Party) "Sunni fundamentalists" and then states that "*Jihadism* is a branch of fundamentalism that combines the views of Islamic world order with terrorism, turning the fight into a 'holy war.' Although there are clear differences, Islamists who choose to fight an irregular war are similar to Islamists who fight through traditional institutional means, as both are committed to the idea of an Islamic Shari'a state." This

statement is problematic for several reasons. Most importantly, for Tibi and many who continue to use the term "fundamentalism," the key point is that both seemingly "moderate" Islamists such as the AKP-Party and "radical" Islamists (i.e. jihadis) are said to share basic similarities (e.g. the desire to create an Islamic shariʿa state) that are, in many ways, more important than their differences. They are believed to ultimately share the same goals even if they differ in terms of methods. Tibi's statement is also problematic for other reasons. Characterizing the ruling Turkish AKP-Party as "Sunni Fundamentalist" would seem to imply that the term "fundamentalist" means very little. After all, the AKP-Party entered government though democratic elections and advocates Turkish membership in the European Union, civilian control of the military, neoliberal economic policies, and cooperation with the United States. The AKP-Party has also not expressed a desire to create an "Islamic shariʿa state." Nor do they consider themselves Islamists, let alone "fundamentalists." Finally, their conception of such a state would undoubtedly be radically different from how "jihadists" would conceive of such a state. See B. Tibi, "Religious Extremism or Religionization of Politics? The Ideological Foundations of Political Islam," in H. Frisch and E. Inbar (eds.) *Radical Islam and International Security*, New York: Routledge, 2008, pp. 11–37. Another recent text that employs the term "fundamentalism," but consciously and more self-critically, is N. AlSayyad and M. Massoumi (eds.) *The Fundamentalist City? Religiosity and the Remaking of Urban Space*, New York: Routledge, 2011. AlSayyad is aware of the problems associated with the term. He writes that the volume's contributors "speak of fundamentalism in the plural, with an 's,'" and that their "use of the term is not an endorsement of the concept, but a pragmatic acceptance of its currency" (p. 11). Indeed, the book takes up Christian, Jewish, and Hindu "fundamentalism" and not just "Islamic fundamentalism." But AlSayyad recognizes that the term has significant negative connotations, "including bigotry, zealotry, militancy, extremism, and fanaticism" (p. 10). It is precisely in discussions of political Islam that such negative attributes have become inextricably associated with the term, making it, in my view, beyond redemption. Moreover, using the term simply because it is widespread misses the point: it is, in part, because of how widely and indiscriminately "fundamentalism" has been used that the term is no longer a useful analytical category.

15 M. O. Emerson and D. Hartman, "The Rise of Religious Fundamentalism," *Annual Review of Sociology* 32, 2006, 127–44, http://www.annualreviews.org/doi/pdf/10.1146/annurev.soc.32.061604.123141. See also G. Marsden, *Fundamentalism and American Culture*, 2nd ed., Oxford and New York: Oxford University Press, 2006.

16 Iranian Islamists famously made use of cassette tapes and fax machines in their struggle against the Shah's regime in the 1970s. In the 1990s and in the current period, Islamists (and others) have made extensive use of SMS text messaging, internet sites, digital videos, and blogs. It should also be noted that many of the movements that are described as "fundamentalist" do much more than call for a return to the "fundamentals" of Islam. In reality, many of these movements hold new and innovative understandings of Islam and desire to use the power of the *modern* state, a twentieth century apparatus, to fundamentally transform society.

17 Although Islamist politics shares little with early twentieth century Protestant fundamentalism, Ayoung Shin has correctly alerted me to some commonalities between late twentieth century Christian fundamentalism and political Islam. Christian fundamentalists in the United States became actively involved in national politics beginning in the 1970s, supporting conservative causes and candidates. Jerry Falwell's Moral Majority Movement was incorporated in 1979 and his book *The Fundamentalist Phenomenon* was published in 1981. It is quite likely that the emergence of Christian fundamentalism in the US at the time also contributed to the use of the term "fundamentalism" to describe Islamist politics. Of course, the political contexts in which both phenomena emerged (and, hence, a great deal of their focus) were radically different.

18 There are also other problems with the term "fundamentalism," including the fact that most individuals who advocate a politics based on Islamic principles do not use the term.

The Arabic equivalent of "fundamentalism" (*usulayya*) seems to have entered the discourse about political Islam in the Arab world largely as a literal translation from English.

19 See S. Huntington, "Will More Countries Be Democratic," *Political Science Quarterly* 99, 1984, 193–218; E. Kedourie, *Democracy and Arab Political Culture*, Washington, DC: Washington Institute for Near East Policy, 1992; B. Lewis, "Islam and Liberal Democracy," *The Atlantic Monthly*, February 1993, 89–98; J. Waterbury, "Democracy without Democrats? The Potential for Political Liberalization in the Middle East," in G. Salame (ed.) *Democracy without Democrats? The Renewal of Politics in the Muslim World*, London: I. B. Tauris, 1994, pp. 23–47. For a different perspective, see J. L. Esposito and J. P. Piscatori, "Democratization and Islam," *Middle East Journal* 45, 1991, 427–40; G. Kramer, "Islamist Notions of Democracy," *Middle East Report*, July–August 1993, 2–8; J. O. Voll and J. L. Esposito, "Islam's Democratic Essence," *Middle East Quarterly*, September 1994.

20 A. Bayat, "Islam and Democracy: The Perverse Charm of an Irrelevant Question" (pp. 1–15), in his excellent study *Making Islam Democratic: Social Movements and the Post-Islamist Turn*, Stanford: Stanford University Press, 2007.

21 See, for example, the articles collected in the special section entitled "Islamist Parties and Democracy" in the *Journal of Democracy*, July 19, 2008. For the direct policy relevance of this debate, see J. M. Sharp, *U.S. Democracy Promotion Policy in the Middle East: The Islamist Dilemma*, CRS Report for Congress, June 15, 2006.

22 This literature is vast and the issues are too complex to adequately address here. Although none of the chapters in this volume adopts this approach, the topic warrants a brief comment.

23 J. Schwedler, *Faith in Moderation: Islamist Parties in Jordan and Yemen*, New York: Cambridge University Press, 2006; J. Schwedler, "Can Islamists Become Moderates? Rethinking the Inclusion–Moderation Hypothesis," *World Politics* 63, 2011, 347–76. See also C. R. Wickham, "The Path to Moderation: Strategy and Learning in the Formation of Egypt's Wasat Part," *Comparative Politics* 36, 2004, 205–28.

24 A more useful distinction might be between mass-based Islamist movements that participate in formal politics and more closed organizations that reject formal political participation. Such a distinction would avoid the highly subjective terms "moderate" and "radical" while capturing important differences between distinct types of Islamist groups. For example, such a framework could distinguish between Hamas and Hizbullah, on the one hand, and Al Qaeda on the other; the former are mass-based movements that are open for membership, operate partially above ground, and participate in formal politics, including in elections and parliaments. By contrast, classification systems focused narrowly on the use of violence would group Hamas, Hizbullah, and Al Qaeda together, conflating very different types of organizations. Without justifying the use of violence, there is a qualitative difference between violence employed in the context of foreign occupation and national liberation struggles, and Al Qaeda's brand of ideological and apocalyptic mass killing.

25 The origins of this phrase date to a 1992 speech by Edward P. Djerejian, Assistant Secretary of State for Near Eastern Affairs at the U.S. State Department at the time. Djerejian stated that while the U.S. supports efforts to "broaden political participation" in the region, "we are suspect of those who would use the democratic process to come to power, only to destroy the very process in order to retain power and political dominance. While we believe in the principle of 'one person, one vote,' we do not support 'one person, one vote, one time.'" Djerejian's remarks came just six months after the Algerian military cancelled national elections that would have likely brought the Islamic Salvation Front (FIS) to power. France supported the move while the US refrained from criticizing the anti-democratic action. Also note that Djerejian's original phrase was "one person, one vote, one time." It was later widely reproduced as "one man, one vote, one time." See E. P. Djerejian, "The US and the Middle East in a Changing World," *Meridian House International*, June 2, 1992. Sixteen years later Djerejian confirmed that at the time of his speech U.S. officials were "seriously concerned at the prospect of this Islamist

radical party's [FIS] attaining power in that important country, with possible destabilizing effects on Morocco and Tunisia," and with the more general phenomenon of Islamists using elections to come to power only to undermine the democratic electoral process. See E. P. Djerejian, *Danger and Opportunity: An American Ambassador's Journey through the Middle East*, New York: Threshold Editions, 2008, p. 22.

26 Limitations of space prevent me from elaborating further on the tremendously large literature on political Islam.

27 N. Ayubi, *Political Islam: Religion and Politics in the Arab World*, London: Routledge, 1992, p. iv. This is an excellent early work on political Islam that can still be profitably read today.

28 G. E. Fuller, *The Future of Political Islam*, New York: Palgrave Macmillan, 2003, p. xi.

29 It should be noted, however, that most Islamists would reject the idea that "political Islam" is something new or different from Islam. Many Islamists would argue that what is called "political Islam" is simply (original) Islam and that religion contains within it a political dimension. For an excellent critique of the assumption that "political Islam" is an illegitimate or unnatural crossing of religion into the political domain, especially in the context of expanding state power in the last two centuries, see C. Hirschkind, "What Is Political Islam?" *Middle East Report* 205, October–December 1997.

30 M. Ayoob, *The Many Faces of Political Islam: Religion and Politics in the Muslim World*, Ann Arbor: University of Michigan Press, 2008, p. 2.

31 Ayubi 1992, op cit., p. 3. Ayubi argues forcefully against the idea that "Islam is by its very nature a 'political' religion" (p. 3). This concerns the claim made by some observers, as well as some Islamists, that Islam is inherently political and that trying to separate politics from religion in Islam is therefore impossible. Such scholars "explain" or account for political Islam in this manner, as a natural condition. Ayubi emphasizes the fact that political Islam is an innovation and not a return to an original Islam. He writes that "'Political Islam' is not an old doctrine that is being resurrected; rather it is a new doctrine that is now being invented." See N. Ayubi, "The Politics of Islam in the Middle East with Special Reference to Egypt, Iran and Saudi Arabia," in J. Haynes (ed.) *Religion, Globalization and Political Culture in the Third World*, Basingstoke: Macmillan Press, 1999, p. 91.

32 D. F. Eickelman and J. Piscatori, *Muslim Politics*, Princeton: Princeton University Press, 1996.

33 S. Ismail, *Rethinking Islamist Politics: Culture, the State and Islamism*, London: I. B. Tauris, 2003, p. 2. Ismail also writes, "In other words, it is suggested here that the deployment of religious symbols and signs and the use of frames of reference derived from religious traditions belong to a power-laden field of action and practices" (p. 17).

34 Others consider an Islamic state to be much more than simply the application of the shari'a.

35 Differentiating "fundamentalists" who use violence from those who do not, Bassam Tibi writes that "both are committed to the idea of an Islamic Shari'a state." See B. Tibi, "Religious Extremism or Religionization of Politics? The Ideological Foundations of Political Islam," in H. Frisch and E. Inbar (eds.) *Radical Islam and International Security*, New York: Routledge, 2008, p. 23.

36 These political leaders and regimes often have no interest in establishing an "Islamic state" or implementing the shari'a. These are instances of "political Islam" that fall outside Islamist opposition groups or states that claim to rule in the name of Islam.

37 For example, just as the Egyptian Muslim Brotherhood focuses primarily on domestic Egyptian concerns, Hamas focuses primarily on Palestinian national issues, while Justice and Benevolence is primarily concerned with politics and society in Morocco. Of course, these movements also care about regional and international affairs (especially relating to Palestine and other "Muslim" countries such as Iraq and Afghanistan, as well as issues relating more generally to the treatment and status of Muslims worldwide). Their primary focus, however (meaning their attention, resources, and activities), is domestic politics in the countries in which they operate and to which they belong.

38 Morocco and Jordan also claim an Islamic basis of legitimacy (although quite different from the Islamic states listed here). The Moroccan king claims lineage from the Prophet

Mohamed and holds the official title "the Commander of the Faithful," referring to his religious stewardship of the Moroccan nation. Similarly, the Jordanian royal family also claim to be descendants of the prophet.

39 Sadat also employed a number of other strategies to cultivate the image of "the believer president" and to enhance the importance of Islam in public discourse and political life. He released members of the Muslim Brotherhood from prison and allowed them significant freedom, increased religious programming on state television, and employed Al Azhar to justify a number of his policies, including Egypt's unpopular peace with Israel. He also amended the Egyptian constitution twice, in 1971 and in 1980, to include an article about the shari'a. Article two of the 1971 constitution stated that "the principles of the Islamic shari'a are a principal source of legislation." The controversial 1980 amendments modified this by making the shari'a *the* principal source of legislation. Sadat also increasingly used Mohamed as his first name, before Anwar. Many observers also point to the discoloration on Sadat's forehead, colloquially referred to in Egypt as a *zibeeba*, or raisin (a discoloration that develops as a result of regular prayer including frequent contact between the forehead and the ground) as another (intentionally) visible sign of his piety.

40 It should also be noted that questions about the sincerity of such measures are irrelevant for our discussion here. Moreover, leaders such as Saddam Hussein and others had no interest in implementing the shari'a or creating Islamic states, yet these activities constitute a form of political Islam.

41 The question is not specific to Egypt or the Muslim Brotherhood (or even other Islamist groups) but has wider relevance for understanding elections and electoral participation in other semi-authoritarian contexts.

Bibliography

AlSayyad, N. and Massoumi, M. (eds.), *The Fundamentalist City? Religiosity and the Remaking of Urban Space*, New York: Routledge, 2011.

Ayoob, M., *The Many Faces of Political Islam: Religion and Politics in the Muslim World*, Ann Arbor: University of Michigan Press, 2008.

Ayubi, N., "The Politics of Islam in the Middle East with Special Reference to Egypt, Iran and Saudi Arabia," in J. Haynes (ed.) *Religion, Globalization and Political Culture in the Third World*, Basingstoke: Macmillan Press, 1999.

Ayubi, N., *Political Islam: Religion and Politics in the Arab World*, London: Routledge, 1992.

Bassam, T., "Religious Extremism or Religionization of Politics? The Ideological Foundations of Political Islam," in H. Frisch and E. Inbar (eds.) *Radical Islam and International Security*, New York: Routledge, 2008.

Bayat, A., *Making Islam Democratic: Social Movements and the Post-Islamist Turn*, Stanford: Stanford University Press, 2007.

Dekmejian, R. H., *Islam in Revolution: Fundamentalism in the Arab World*, Syracuse: Syracuse University Press, 1985.

Dekmejian, R. H., "The Anatomy of Islamic Revival: Legitimacy Crisis, Ethnic Conflict and the Search for Islamic Alternatives," *Middle East Journal* 34, 1980, 1–12.

Dessouki, A. E. H., "The Resurgence of Islamic Organisations in Egypt: An Interpretation," in A. S. Cudsi and A. E. H. Dessouki (eds.) *Islam and Power*, Baltimore: Johns Hopkins University Press, 1981.

Djerejian, E. P., *Danger and Opportunity: An American Ambassador's Journey through the Middle East*, New York: Threshold Editions, 2008.

Djerejian, E. P., "The U.S. and the Middle East in a Changing World," *Meridian House International*, June 2, 1992.

Eickelman, D. F. and Piscatori, J. P., *Muslim Politics*, Princeton: Princeton University Press, 1996.

Emerson, M. O. and Hartman, D., "The Rise of Religious Fundamentalism," *Annual Review of Sociology* 32, 2006, 127–44, http://www.annualreviews.org/doi/pdf/10.1146/annurev.soc.32.061604.123141.

Esposito, J. L., *The Islamic Threat: Myth or Reality?*, New York: Oxford University Press, 1992.

Esposito, J. L. and Piscatori, J. P., "Democratization and Islam," *Middle East Journal* 45, 1991, 427–40.

Fuller, G. E., *The Future of Political Islam*, New York: Palgrave Macmillan, 2003.

Griffith, W. E., "The Revival of Islamic Fundamentalism: The Case of Iran," *International Security* 4, 1979, 132–38.

Haddad, Y. Y., "Muslim Revivalist Thought in the Arab World: An Overview," *The Muslim World* 76, 1986, 143–67.

Hearings before the Subcommittee on Europe and the Middle East of the House Committee on Foreign Affairs, *Islamic Fundamentalism and Islamic Radicalism*, Washington, DC: U.S. Government Printing Office, 1985.

Hirschkind, C., "What Is Political Islam?" *Middle East Report* 205, 1997.

Huntington, S., *The Clash of Civilizations and the Remaking of World Order*, New York: Simon & Schuster, 1998.

Huntington, S., "The Clash of Civilizations?" *Foreign Affairs*, Summer 1993.

Huntington, S., "Will More Countries Be Democratic?" *Political Science Quarterly* 99, 1984, 193–218.

"Islamist Parties and Democracy," *Journal of Democracy* 19, 2008.

Ismail, S., *Rethinking Islamist Politics: Culture, the State and Islamism*, London: I. B. Tauris, 2003.

Kedourie, E., *Democracy and Arab Political Culture*, Washington, DC: Washington Institute for Near East Policy, 1992.

Kramer, G., "Islamist Notions of Democracy," *Middle East Report*, July–August 1993, 2–8.

Lewis, B., "Islam and Liberal Democracy," *The Atlantic Monthly*, February 1993, 89–98.

Lewis, B., "The Roots of Muslim Rage," *The Atlantic Monthly*, September 1990, 47–60.

Lewis, B., "The Revolt of Islam," *New York Review of Books*, June 30, 1983.

Marsden, G., *Fundamentalism and American Culture*, 2nd ed., Oxford and New York: Oxford University Press, 2006.

Mitchell, R. P., "The Islamic Movement: Its Current Condition and Future Prospects," in B. F. Stowasser (ed.) *The Islamic Impulse*, Washington, DC: Center for Contemporary Arab Studies, 1987.

Perlmutter, A., "Wishful Thinking about Islamic Fundamentalism," *Washington Post*, January 19, 1992.

Schwedler, J., "Can Islamists Become Moderates? Rethinking the Inclusion–Moderation Hypothesis," *World Politics* 63, 2011, 347–76.

Schwedler, J., *Faith in Moderation: Islamist Parties in Jordan and Yemen*, New York: Cambridge University Press, 2006.

Sharp, J. M., "U.S. Democracy Promotion Policy in the Middle East: The Islamist Dilemma," *CRS Report for Congress*, June 15, 2006.

Sivan, E., *Radical Islam: Medieval Theology and Modern Politics*, New Haven: Yale University Press, 1985.

Tibi, B., "Religious Extremism or Religionization of Politics? The Ideological Foundations of Political Islam," in H. Frisch and E. Inbar (eds.) *Radical Islam and International Security*, New York: Routledge, 2008.

Voll, J. O. and Esposito, J. L., "Islam's Democratic Essence," *Middle East Quarterly*, September 1994.

Waterbury, J., "Democracy without Democrats? The Potential for Political Liberalization in the Middle East," in G. Salame (ed.) *Democracy without Democrats? The Renewal of Politics in the Muslim World*, London: I. B. Tauris, 1994.

Wickham, C. R., "The Path to Moderation: Strategy and Learning in the Formation of Egypt's Wasat Part," *Comparative Politics* 36, 2004, 205–28.

Part I
Islamist politics: theory and critique

1

ISLAM AND ISLAMIST POLITICS IN THE ARAB WORLD

Old theories and new facts?

François Burgat

> The question of Islam as a political force is an essential question for our time and will be for many years to come. The first condition for treating it with a minimum of intelligence is that one not begin with hatred.
>
> (Michel Foucault)[1]

> Who [then] will want to claim solidarity with throat-slitters, thieves and murderers, especially when we are dealing with people we identify – based on no other historical expectation – as "Islamic madmen," enveloped and masked under the dishonored name of Islamism, an atavistic symbol of all Eastern fanaticisms, fully able to endow racist hatred with an indisputable alibi of ethical and lay legitimacy?
>
> (Pierre Bourdieu)[2]

> Each time a political system is impeded from letting true political dynamics circulate freely through its veins, each time its channels narrow to the point of no longer being able to absorb everything flowing through them, it prepares a bed for secret organizations and other clandestine groups. … Whenever it gives birth to all sorts of legal entities having no relation with the political, social or cultural reality of a country, when it gives legal existence to what does not exist in reality whereas what exists in reality is not recognized by law, when a political system tolerates such a dichotomy between the legal and the real, … we get a true schizophrenia that risks affecting all of society.
>
> (Tareq Al-Bishri)[3]

In *L'Islamisme au Maghreb*, published in the mid-1980s, I proposed an explanatory matrix for Islamist mobilization movements in the Maghreb, insisting on the fact that they were grounded more in identity and politics than strictly in religion.[4] This analysis was then used to look at and explain other Arab regions, from Cairo to Sanaʿa.[5] Since then the international context has evolved profoundly,[6] and a new generation of activists has begun to emerge. But the template proposed in *L'Islamisme au Maghreb*[7] of an Islamist matrix – based first on identity and then giving way to a multiplicity of political means of expression that should be correlated with its context rather than with the religious dimension of its vocabulary – can, it would seem, be profitably brought to bear on the subject of Islamism today.

Thus, there remains a methodological necessity of dissociating two levels of study. The first has to do with the trans-social matrix of identity that in our perspective explains the mobilization achievements of the Islamic lexicon. The second is, against any culturalist temptation of the monist type, that of the return to the complexity of the political and the social. Thus, the observer of Islamism must patiently follow the multiple paths taken by an Islamist generation whose participants may use the same vocabulary, but whose means of expression are multiple and changing according to national contexts and political events. This patient examination should focus on three areas: national boundaries, the Arab–Israeli conflict (where two nationalisms confront each other), and, more widely, the international North–South arena.

Insisting on the diversity of national configurations, however, does have its limits. Just as trans-social interpretations give evidence of collective behaviors going beyond the limits of social groups, transnational interpretations are not necessarily out of place. From Morocco to Egypt, despite the diversity of national historical and political configurations, the pattern of Islamist growth as well as the radicalization of a fraction of this generation have crystallized through the effect of readily comparable factors. The elites, having used up their initial capital of nationalist or revolutionary resources, have gradually joined together in the mold of a quasi-institutional Arab norm where, with the sometimes passive and often active support of the West, repression tends to replace the effectiveness of electoral representation.

Once the interpretation of the Islamists' real strategies has been constructed and documented, an approach to the phenomenon of Islamism cannot substitute for the study of the conditions that led to the production of this knowledge. Distortions are introduced into the Islamist field fairly systematically by the dominant media, by the European and American people who produce and transmit neo-conservative discourse, and by certain Arab figures of state as well as segments of the academic establishment.

History has placed the generation of Islamists at the center of challenging questions regarding dysfunctional aspects in the political system, particularly those that lead to the denial of electoral representation of those who find themselves on the wrong side of various relationships of domination. Islamists may confront promoters of the militarization of American oil diplomacy, artisans of Israeli expansionist strategy, or leaders of authoritarian Arab regimes who support the international order that protects them.

The difficulties encountered in imposing a rational interpretation in the West of this political "Other" can be explained by the fact that knowledge about Islamists is embedded in resistance movements against the world political order. The restrictive image that continues to prevail is thus the result of a complex process in which the emergence of a rival vocabulary – Islamic – seems first of all to give the West, whose personal vocabulary had for a long time been hegemonic, the feeling of losing the monopoly on expressing the universal. Western perception in general, and French perception in particular, of the internal dynamics of the Arab and Muslim world is therefore marked by a difficulty to conceive of cultural difference – or at least when this difference goes beyond the area of folklore, food, or aesthetics (think couscous, mint tea, and "Andalusian" art) – and deal with politics and, even more so, protest.

The critical rereading of my hypotheses articulated in the mid-1980s can logically be organized around two poles: continuity and change. The continuity, even the exacerbations, of tendencies noted in the 1980s and 1990s far outweighs the volume and strength of changes that have evolved.

The continuity of an "Islamic" assertiveness that relates more to identity than religion

The core of the thesis we would like to revisit in 2012 can be presented in a few statements. The repositioning by societies on the African and Eastern colonial periphery of Europe, after being expressed through political independence movements, was extended to the economic realm through nationalizations and then to the cultural and symbolic realm via the "re-Islamization" of the political discourse that is at the heart of the Islamist drive. Coming out of a long colonial period in politics as well as social structure, the mobilizing virtues of Islamism are due less to its sacred than to its endogenous dimension.

My central hypothesis is that the identity matrix found in the vocabulary of Islam explains its inclination to spill over the boundaries of social groups. By this token, Islamists can no more be merely those "left behind by development" than explanatory variables can be merely socioeconomic. From this point of view, that the endogenous Islamic lexicon is a religious one only partially determines the political behavior of a population; the use of an Islamic vocabulary therefore represents more an affirmation of identity than the promotion of a theocratic vision of the world.

The affirmation of "Muslimhood" that has contributed to an in-depth reorganization of the Arab political domain cannot be reduced to the emergence of one monolithic and static political ideology, adopted only by the supporters of a social machismo or revolutionary and sectarian violence. Re-Islamization in fact nourishes a complex process of reconnection with local areas that produce almost all the political ideologies in the symbolic, rather than normative, universe of Muslim culture.

The Islamists, far from being reduced to revolutionary guerrilla warfare, use a spectrum of modes of action in their politics. A large segment clearly aspires only to take its place within the parliamentary sphere, to the extent this possibility exists, thereby consecrating a space within political autonomy and stepping far outside the boundaries of the political mechanisms of theocracy.

An attentive examination of the social practices of people stigmatized as Islamists reveals that the reintroduction into the political vocabulary of markers of Muslim culture does not, *a priori*, compromise either the dynamics of social reform or the process of political liberalization. In fact, the social or political answers formulated using the Muslim vocabulary turn out to be dependent, in a very banal way, on the questions being asked – and the nature of those questions is conditional on the educational, social, and political environment of the questioners.

Islamic assertiveness may therefore condone conservative, patriarchal, and sectarian positions or bellicose strategies. But it can just as well participate in discrediting them and legitimizing reformist positions, such as the modernizing tendency to move beyond attachment to basic groups, the struggle against authoritarianism, and the assertion of individual and collective freedoms, including those for women. Just as it was possible in Europe to legitimize the principles of social justice and respect for minorities or women's causes by reference to socialist, Christian, or simply humanist values, Islamist social and political leaders do so by using references borrowed from the broad spectrum of Muslim culture, including its religious references.

The "depoliticization" at the root of a radicalization that is more political than religious

The perpetration of political violence after the structural crisis of Palestine and the electoral thrust of Hamas now occurs in Iraq and other countries. Indeed, since the mid-2000s, the activities of armed transnational Al-Qaeda groups have spread to the Maghreb. After the murderous attacks in Morocco and Algeria in 2003 and the assassination of French tourists in southern Mauritania in April and December 2007, a single explanatory variable was brought to the fore: Islamic radicalization. To what extent has this interpretation been illuminating? From what point did it become, in the social sciences as well as in diplomacy, a decoy covering the exacting solutions needed to calm this region in a durable way?

In the Arab world, the political life of the last two decades has in fact been marked by a great number of parliamentary and presidential elections or referendums in which the common characteristic has not been the success or failure of opposition parties, whether Islamist or not, but rather the failure of elections to have the slightest effect on the distribution of power between the regimes and those that oppose them. Across all of North Africa, behind institutional façades ranging from the belief in monarchy by divine right in Morocco to the Libyan "state of the Masses," to the secular states of Tunisia and Algeria, the men holding power – who have been in place for over 40 years in Libya (until 2011), almost 46 in Algeria, 29 in Egypt (until 2011), and 24 in Tunisia (until 2011) – have remained sheltered from the electoral moods of their opponents. "He who has managed to seize all the responsibilities has likewise succeeded in becoming perfectly irresponsible,"[8] writes noted Egyptian intellectual Tareq Al-Bishri.

This striking formulation describes the political system of his country under the Mubarak regime and can in fact be extended to almost the entirety of the region. For the *vox populi*, the revolutionary slogans of the nationalist past ("by the people and for … the people") have taken on an absurd tone; the elections organized "by" the head of state are done "for him" and serve less to designate those who have an opportunity to govern than those for whom power demands that a merely cosmetic pluralism be acted out. With the timid exception of Mauritania for a brief period, where presidential elections took place in a less artificial atmosphere and where military power gave way temporarily, what shows is not so much the failure of the opposition but rather the flagrant limits of these political systems. Until the revolutions in Tunisia, Egypt, and Libya in 2011, only the deposing of Habib Bourguiba in 1987, the death of Hassan II in 1999, or the quarrels among those at the top of the government in Algeria have managed to create a semblance of political alternation in the midst of an impressive amount of stability.

When exceptions occurred, such as in Algeria in 1991 and in Palestine in 2006, and the polling stations might have set in motion a real balance of political forces, their results were disavowed by the incumbents with the active support of the international community.[9] Everywhere else the only impact made on electoral regulations has been of the cosmetic type, whether observers thought they were seeing an Islamist or oppositional triumph, as in Egypt in 2005, or a new defeat, as in Algeria and Morocco in 2007.

The triple rampart of authoritarianism

This persistence of authoritarian powers is the fruit of a strategy of defense that is threefold. First, in 2007 as was the case 20 years ago, the only opposition groups authorized to participate in the electoral process are those that are more or less "domesticated," and are thus for the most part irrelevant to the great battalions of real opposition groups. This is the case, without exception, in Morocco, Algeria, Libya, and Tunisia and Egypt until 2011.

The electoral process is also not protected from even more direct interferences, the volume of which tends to become absorbed, but where the principle still holds. For example, the number of ballots and their "color" still often reflect the mood of the leaders rather than that of the voters. Arab polling stations seem to have remained accessible only for the benefit of regimes.

If the impact of this second defense is decreasing, it is because the regimes, drawing lessons from the "bad election" of 1991 in Algeria, have finished building between themselves and the moods of their electorate a third, particularly decisive, level of defense. The ability to make decisions, which never existed within the confines of parliament, can be found less and less in ministerial portfolios. Indeed, in Ben Ali's Tunisia and Mubarak's Egypt, power was completely concentrated in the hands of the heads of state and their close associates. If it is shared in Algeria, it is only among shadowy military figures who fight over it. In Morocco, it has never been extended by the monarchy and its closest advisors to anyone other than a small number of irremovable ministers, as was the case with Interior Minister Driss Bassri (1979–99). A first electoral victory for the parliamentary left (l'Union Socialiste des Forces Populaires (USFP)) in 2002 thus revealed the very limited importance of such alternation.

In Morocco, as in Algeria, the parliamentary elections of 2007 did not so much mark a defeat of the opposition, whether Islamist or otherwise, as a new aggravation of a structural depoliticization with extremely pernicious effects – extremism. In Morocco, the results for the old nationalist Istiqlal party looked like anything but a resurgence of the nationalist left. Nor is the defeat proclaimed for the Islamist Party of Justice and Development (PJD) any more a defeat for the Islamists. Rather, it clearly signals the weakness of those who, by dint of making concessions of all kinds to the throne, have lost enormous amounts of their oppositional credibility.

The true message addressed to the world by the crushing majority of the Moroccan electorate who refused to vote (more than 80 percent in urban areas, where the vote is traditionally less easy to rig) contains no ambiguity: it is the rejection of their role as "extras" that this pluralist comedy demands, and that the European partners of Morocco and its neighbors have been comfortable with for such a long time. As such, all the voters who did not take the elections seriously were not surprised to learn that someone went to the polls in their place. The impossibility of mobilizing the popular vote too openly (particularly because of the growing role of the press and foreign observers) and the increasing difficulty of manipulating the rate of participation as systematically as in the past have, paradoxically, consecrated a right that is far from negligible: the right not to vote.

Citizens of the Maghreb have had to wait to have an effective voice in choosing those who will govern them, or simply to have a significant effect on political decisions. With the denial of representation in addition to the massive use of repression, depoliticization opens the road to all kinds of extremisms. More surely than an Islamist drive or radicalization, this is truly the first major key to interpreting the current politics of the Maghreb.

A mistaken culturalist response to the very secular dead-end of "depoliticization"

From Algeria to Palestine, violent episodes that are very quickly defined as Islamic can undoubtedly be understood in terms of the radicalization of certain political activists. We still need to determine with precision if this radicalization is of a religious or political nature, who its real beneficiaries are, and, in certain emblematic cases, its true authors.

In the Maghreb, confronted with terrorist acts that are quite real, the explanations made credible by the media and by the security and judiciary forces closest to the regimes[10] orchestrate in unison a principal criminal, the Salafi Group for Preaching and Combat (GSPC). This omnipresent group is thought to be the heir to the infamous Armed Islamic Group (GIA) and to have allied itself recently with Al-Qaeda.

The theory that certain Islamist activists are growing harsher in their strategies cannot be completely discarded as long as we do not forget its deep causes. It is not so much the result of transmission over the internet of an ideological pathology – the virus of radical Islamism – itself transmitted through an intellectual genealogy from Qutb to Bin Laden, as it is the institutional door-bolting and repression that produces those "bomb planters"[11] and increasing ranks of partisans for armed combat.

Since the new edition of *L'Islamisme en face* in 2002, the international community has seemed more than ever to be playing the role of a pyromaniac fireman, fanning the flames of the radicalization that it claims to be trying to extinguish by supporting an increase in the use of force in Palestine and other Arab regions. The impulse for democratization fleetingly brandished by the Bush administration in 2004 did not last longer than one spring. France, whose role in defining European policies in the

Maghreb is particularly important, played no small part in the banalization of "the despots of Europe."[12]

After deposed Tunisian President Zin al-Abidin Ben Ali, repeatedly reelected since 1987 with more than 98 percent of the vote (in the 2007 elections he more modestly received only 89 percent of the vote), and his Egyptian counterpart, former president Hosni Mubarak, were awarded the "Louise Michel Prize for the rights of man and democracy" by the French Republic, it was President Abdelaziz Bouteflika's turn to receive the award in 2005. Bouteflika, the civilian frontman since 1999 for the Algerian military junta in power since 1962, is thus in a long line of men in authoritarian power to receive such a prize.

Arab governments that support the world order have apparently succeeded in exploiting Western fears born of the September 11, 2001 attacks and in identifying even the most legalistic of their opponents as being among the heap of armed radical groups. Supported by the approving silence of the European Union and Russia, the U.S. went so far as to promote the right to torture the human targets of its "global war on terror" by putting torture into practice in Iraq and Guantanamo or, even more cynically, by outsourcing torture to its Arab or European state partners.

The members of the armed group arrested in Tunisia in December 2006 for murdering tourists and for a number of violent acts committed in Algeria are very likely the products of that connection. But explaining away such violence simply in terms of Islamic terrorism is too simple. If we retain the theory of the GSPC following in the footsteps of the GIA of the 1990s, then this connection must bear all its explanatory consequences.

Now on this difficult terrain, on both sides of the Mediterranean, the explanation for terrorism that wins out is systematically based on political or legal sources[13] that support the survival of Algeria's military power or the colossal financial stakes of bilateral relations between France and Algeria. There are precious few analysts[14] who willingly recall that terrorism was never the prerogative of "the other side,"[15] but that it can be a part of the secret strategy used by "this side" (i.e., state, regional, or world powers), to discredit those who resist them. The whole history of the Algerian civil war (and previously the Algerian war of independence) is there to remind us that to speak and act in the name of those against whom one fights in order to cut them off from their political environment is a weapon as old as war.

So was it really Al-Qaeda of the Maghreb that on December 11, 2007 "struck once again in the heart of Algiers," as the headline on page one of *Le Monde* blared, leaving no room for the slightest doubt? There are many indications – including the concurrent and recurrent declarations of the targets of those explosions (the clan of the President of the Republic, who at the time was trying to win a third term) – that urge us to treat this explanation with the greatest caution.[16]

This example demonstrates how the methods used by the dominant interfere very directly with those of the dominated who protest against them. How Islamists protest in the future will above all be determined by their treatment by local or international interlocutors. As such, the regimes and leaders of the Muslim world on the world stage or even in the heart of Western societies will in many respects, in the near future, have the opponents that they are in the process of creating and that they therefore, at least in certain respects, deserve.

It is clear through our analysis of Islamist radicalization and identity that analytic continuity wins out over change. Nonetheless, can we find signs of structural change in the Islamism of the 1990s compared with the Islamism of today?

What are the dynamics for renewal?

In interpreting how the Islamist phenomenon will be expressed in the future we must integrate two variables. The first, in part a generational type, concerns the relative assertiveness of the Salafi generation to the detriment of the Muslim Brotherhood. The second, for the moment limited to a few governments, concerns how Islamist rhetoric fares when it is used by the state. In the case of Iran, where it comes up in particular, one must examine the state of the mullahs' resources 30 years after the foundation of the Islamic Republic.

The Salafis after the Brotherhood: change within continuity?

Hassan al-Banna and his Egyptian, and later Arab, disciples initiated the first reactive cycle of Islamism in the context of colonial domination and its aftermath of independence. Though the dynamic identified with this Muslim Brotherhood generation remains far from reaching its term, what must be reckoned with is the assertiveness of the Salafi movement.[17] The Brotherhood pre-dated the Salafis, particularly in Egypt and Saudi Arabia, and it differentiated itself in many respects before succeeding, at least in part, in eclipsing them. The first generation of the Muslim Brotherhood can be credited with having successfully imposed the symbolic requirements of re-Islamization, even in the most secular regimes, to the point where those regimes anticipated or even sometimes exceeded those requirements that did not do damage to their power.

The disciples of Hassan al-Banna succeeded more or less everywhere in the political domain and hence in the public sphere. They mobilized troops whom they rendered eager not only to inscribe the movement within the parliamentary framework but also to mobilize the voting majority within that framework,[18] even finding increasingly systematic synergies with the secular left.[19]

One of the most credible ways of attesting to the specificity of the Brotherhood's identity is to take stock of the virulent criticism that some in the Salafi sphere aim at it. In denouncing their concessions to secularism or democracy, Al-Zawahiri, the Egyptian ideologue of Al-Qaeda, demonstrates better than anyone else that the Brothers have been vectors in the "modernization" of their society – a modernization that wields the symbolic codes of local, religious culture and that is therefore more functional than that of the secular elites.

To arrive at these legal gates to power, relying upon such innovations as the notions of constitutionalism and democracy that are foreign to a literal reading of classical Islamic thought, the Brothers have initiated profound doctrinal evolutions more or less everywhere in the Arab world.[20] Not surprisingly, these reforms have generated tensions and internal divisions that have left the field open to other, more literal-minded expressions of protest. At least some of these open spaces are occupied by those groups whom we propose to think of as an outgrowth or even a resurgence of the old Salafi domain, if one considers that the major features of the *salafiya* go back to Rashid Rida, the disciple of Afghani and Abduh.

Hassan al-Banna's disciples, even while slowly gaining a central position in the legal political field, thus find themselves facing a Salafi reaction which seems intent on taking away their monopoly as a force of protest. Still, does this Salafi generation contradict the analysis presented in *L'Islamisme en face* in which Islamist identity is based less on religion than on other cultural and political concerns? Though researchers have had less access to Salafis,[21] nothing leads us to conclude this.

The Salafi movement does not lend itself to being reduced to a monolithic reality any more than the Brotherhood does. However, at first glance, it appears homogeneous as a result of its resorting to common jurisprudential authorities rather than via the existence of a politically unified leadership, which it lacks. The first common denominator of this composite movement is no doubt its differentiation from the heritage of the Muslim Brotherhood, those *ikhwân muflisîn* ("failed brothers") that every good Salafi has to denounce. A Salafi, like a Brother, insists on the importance of the primary sources of the Qur'an and the Sunna. But explicitly, unlike disciples of al-Banna, he will refuse to perform a rational contextualization or any exegesis, as human changes to the divine message are considered a violation of the sacrosanct.

And yet, the reaffirmation of the importance of a return to sources purified of all human mediation does not produce any univocal doctrinal responses that are homogeneous or static. The Salafi method, like that of the Brothers, contains no guardrail against the inevitable divergences in interpretation of a given doctrinal body of thought. Nor does it guard the believer against the interferences of perfectly human temporal powers in the process of interpreting a divine text. Thus, not surprisingly, the relation of Salafis to politics is composite and dynamic.

Certainly, the Salafis' break with the tradition of the Brotherhood can be seen as a rejection of the categories of Western political thought the Brotherhood gradually accepted in order to become involved in the political arena and out of its respect for the requirements of pluralism. These categories of thought include the creation of parties or organizational structures, participation in elections, and access by women to the public, professional, and even political arena. This break, however, is not always complete. A portion of the Salafis, particularly those who support the *ulema* close to the Saudi regime, differentiates itself from the Brotherhood by a quietism that strips its religiosity of any expression of protest.

Increasingly, the intersection of the electoral and religious fields tends to produce three types of behavior in Arab lands: Sufis, who for the most part vote for the regime; Brothers, who call for voting against the regime; and Salafis, who tend – at least for the most part – to abstain, hence supporting the powers that be. But as we know, as was the case for Qutb and the Muslim Brothers, and as can happen again in another context,[22] the Salafis, whenever they are subjected to repression, can also provide a quota of Jihadist candidates. They then differentiate themselves from the

Brotherhood by denouncing not so much the Brotherhood's politicization but their own opposition to change.

Still others in the Salafist pietist branch in Saudi Arabia and Egypt exist side by side with revolutionary splinter groups that inscribe themselves in the temporal world and claim initiation first by Juhaymân al-ʿUtaybî, perpetrator of the attack on the great mosque of Mecca in 1979,[23] and, after him, by the Jihadist school theorized by Qutb and later Ayman al-Zawahiri. Compared with the Brotherhood, the Salafis are more naturally pluralistic in their stance towards politics due to their fragmentation.

Indeed, these divergent views come into play vis-à-vis visions of society, from the role of women to modern technologies. Thus we find ourselves quickly obliged to relativize the broad boundaries attempting to define "the Salafis," which are often transcended in place after place, year after year. Salafi groups clearly differentiated from the Brotherhood support changes that are generally comparable to those that the disciples of Hassan al-Banna carried out in their time. In Yemen, as in Saudi Arabia or Kuwait, Salafis notably agree to participate in elections or even to run for office.[24] And this "modernization," denounced as an evil justifying the condemnation of the Brothers, ironically appears to be an irresistible part of the current history of the Salafis as well.

In many respects we are therefore tempted to explain the Salafi movement primarily on a generational basis, in which a renewal of the reactive cycle initiated by the Brotherhood occurs at its expense but using a comparable logic. In the alchemy of the Salafi breakthrough of the 2000s, the "modernizing" Brotherhood could be thought of as playing the role of foil to the so-called "Westernized" elites against whom they had themselves fought. While the Brotherhood might today claim the right to greater inclusion within the public arena and political systems, the Salafis might point to its poor rate of success and persistent rejection by elites, of which they also feel themselves to be victims, through discourses and practices of exclusion.

Thus, only via the symbolic status the Western media grants it does the Salafi wave unfurl more in continuity than in change. The specter of Salafism resets, so to speak, the mechanism of sectarian stigmatization to the point where it was when the first Islamist irruption took place in the Western imagination, sheltered from any rational investigation, far "from the infinite diversity of behaviors, determinants, rearrangements and results that are, in their universal banality, the very mark of humanity."[25] Might the repulsive effect of the Islamists, mullahs, and such risk losing its edge?

Islamism undergoing the test of power

The future of Islamist mobilization is at least in part conditioned by the relation of its activists to the resources of authority. This relation differs depending upon whether the participants speak from jail cells or from the *minbars* granted them by regimes – that is, whether they have the privilege (but also the responsibility) of using the apparatus of government or whether they are trying to conquer it or protect themselves from it. Whenever Islamists rely on the dynamics of opposition to regimes which have been largely discredited through their authoritarianism or their compromises with the West, they amass the resources of an assertion of identity and of opposition to an illegitimate power.

When, on the contrary, they evolve while holding power, they take advantage of the resources of public activity but must also pay the price: the erosion that affects any holder of power. The speed at which this erosion takes place varies according to whether the appeal to religion is mobilized for the goal of merely national legitimation, such as in Morocco or Saudi Arabia, or, as in Iran, where Islamist assertiveness is a part of the spectrum of foreign policy. It is mainly, but not exclusively, given the experience of Sudan and more recently of Palestine and Turkey, in the case of Iran that such a theory deserves exploration.

For the political specialist familiar with the Arab world, a trip to Iran does not simply lead to crossing over the double border of "Arabness" and Sunni Islam.[26] It introduces one to a universe where, for the first time in contemporary history, a revolutionary break has occurred – both with the primacy of an Islamic vocabulary in internal and external discourse and practice, and also via the explicit opposition to the West in general, and to the United States and its allies in particular.

In Riyadh and Rabat, and in certain respects everywhere in the Muslim world, regimes are trying to capture the dividends of the dynamics of re-Islamization at the same time as they are being courted by Washington. Over the last quarter of a century, it is only in Iran that the affirmation of the primacy of the religious lexicon has kept pace with an explicit discourse of opposition to the American masters of the world order and their supporters in the Muslim world. It is only in Tehran that the endogenous nature of a reference to Islam is being exploited to its full extent as a mobilizing force to set up a distance from the West which touches not only its symbolic universe but likewise its political order. Indeed, the Tehran regime is being criminalized and fought for the political scope of its resistance rather than for the pivotal position given religion in its internal order.

Whenever Moroccan or Saudi Islamists content themselves with promoting an alternative symbolic system while at the same time accommodating or submitting themselves to the world political order, they thereby chop off a goodly portion of their ability to mobilize. It is this same oppositional deficit that limits the actions of Islamist opposition groups such as the ex-Algerian Hamas, which was launched by the regime to counter the Islamic Salvation Front. Such groups are tolerated and even encouraged by regimes that do not question their legitimacy

One of the consequences of the double revolutionary foundation in Iran is that year after year the resources of the Islamic lexicon seem inexorably deprived of their oppositional virtues. Having joined the rank of state discourse a generation ago, the political formula resting on its two pillars of Islamist affirmation ("long live God" and "down with Bush" – or his successor) no longer carries the same load of protest power as in most of the neighboring Arab countries. If by wearing the hijab in the "modern" Tunisia of Zin al-Abidin Ben Ali, or even in neighboring Morocco, a female citizen shows allegiance to an Islamist agenda, a female citizen of Iran can mark her distance from a corrupt and dictatorial regime that has imposed the practice by wearing it carelessly or looking conspicuous in it (the "bad" hijab).[27] Furthermore, the insistent and radical denunciation of the Israeli–American regional order – a subject about which Arab regimes from Jordan and Egypt to Saudi Arabia or even Yemen and Libya must moderate the zeal of their compatriots – has for its part become an intrinsic component of the "politically correct" in Iran.

If the notion of "post-Islamism" were to some day take on an effective meaning and become a widely rooted social process, would it begin in Iran? A number of Western observers are tempted to believe this. When they wander along a few avenues in the north of the capital, certain segments of the Iranian street do indeed seem to suggest this to them. And yet, how much credibility should we grant to the media that, picking up on the analyses or the hopes of certain opponents of the Islamic Republic or monarchists living in exile, periodically announce progress on the restoration of the monarchy and the immediate demise of the mullahs?

Three variables urge us to relativize such discourse. The first has to do, of course, with the considerable distance that still separates little islands in the northern residential suburbs of Tehran from the teeming masses in the sanctuaries of Mashhad that confirm the healthy numerical status of Islamist mobilization. The second, more to the heart of the matter, takes into account the fact that the political erosion of an Islamist regime, even if it were to sink into a totalitarian drift (and this does not realistically define the present situation of the Iranian regime)[28] would be far from leaving Islamism behind. Governing members who have succeeded each other since the 1979 establishment of an Islamic republic – some of them turned down for re-election at the polling booth – are far from having depleted the full gamut of tools used to keep religion in power.

However, two categories of oppositional discourse appear to be operational in contemporary Iran. One component of the intelligentsia, frequently overestimated by wishful thinking in the West, seeks to establish a legitimate space in politics outside the domination of the religious sphere. But it is not the only secularist oppositional component, and it is not necessarily the most influential. Seeking an identical result, a second reformist current[29] has been working on a way to legitimize a process whereby reference to religion would be "automatically limited" in the political arena. This Islamic reformism, seeking to adjust the influence of the religious sphere, seems for the moment to have more social support and hence more of a future than the former, which seeks more radically to expropriate it from the public domain.

A third reason to relativize the Western desire that regularly announces the ideological collapse of the Iranian regime is that to be Iranian in 2011 is also to be Muslim in an international scene that is irrationally hostile not only to the Muslim political lexicon but to almost every identity marker of being Muslim.[30] "The truth is that we continue to react, sometimes in a Pavlovian manner, to the mere mention of the post-revolutionary Iranian situation rather than think about it," notes Fariba Adelkhah.[31] To be Iranian is also to be Shiite in a Muslim world that is for the most part Sunni and prompt to give in to the sirens of sectarian division, even if it is with the assiduous help of Washington.[32]

These are reasons to think that the Islamic mobilization of the mullah regime has not yet arrived at the end of its long and complex contemporary history – and even less so for a whole political generation in the neighboring Arab world.

Notes

1 M. Foucault, *Dits et Écrits III*, Paris: Gallimard, 1996, p. 708. [Translator's note: All quotations in this paper have been translated directly from the original French paper.]
2 Pierre Bourdieu was attacking Bernard-Henri Lévy and one of his French philosopher colleagues, André Glucksman, whom he called "negative intellectuals" for having given support in the media to the orchestrated manipulations by the Algerian military authorities after the annulment of parliamentary elections in December 1991. What he found to denounce in these French "New Philosophers" was writing that was "completely oriented towards simplistic confusion, well suited to satisfy both the best and the worst of feelings, and to superficial incitement to pity and racist hatred disguised as human indignation." See P. Bourdieu, "L'Intellectuel négatif," *Liber*, January 1998.
3 Tareq Al-Bishri, an Egyptian judge close to the opposition, 1990, quoted in F. Burgat, *L'Islamisme en face*, Paris: La Découverte, 1995 (new edition: Paris: La Découverte, 2007).
4 F. Burgat, *L'Islamisme au Maghreb. La Voix du sud*, Paris: Karthala, 1988 (new edition: Paris: Petite bibliothèque Payot, 1995). (English version: F. Burgat, *The Islamic Movement in North Africa*, Austin, TX: Center for Middle Eastern Studies, 1993.)
5 See F. Burgat, *L'Islamisme à l'heure d'Al-Qaeda*, Paris: La Découverte, 2005. This work adds lessons learned from the Arabian Peninsula to the considerations in *L'Islamisme en face*. A summarized version of this problem was proposed in F. Burgat, "Les Mobilisations à référent islamique," in Elisabeth Picard (ed.) *La Politique dans le monde arabe*, Paris: Armand Colin, 2006.
6 And equally so for the volume and quality of academic thought on the phenomenon of Islamism, to which it would be extremely difficult to do justice in a few lines.
7 Burgat, 1988, op. cit.
8 T. Al-Bishri, "Sâra al mass'ul al wahîd fi addawla, ghîr al mass'ûl al wahîd fî ha," *Ad'u kum ila 'asiân*, Cairo, 2005.
9 When Yasser Arafat was perceived as being too nationalistic, the Israelis, with the support of the international community, imposed upon him a prime minister, Mahmoud Abbas, whom they considered (and rightly so) to be more malleable and, to weaken the head of the Authority, had major functions transferred to Abbas. But when parliamentary elections supported by the entire international community elected a "bad," "Islamist" prime minister, that same international community supported a second forceful maneuver, against the prime minister this time, to the advantage of the "good" president who had succeeded Arafat. With no respected local and international figures willing to continue giving it a semblance of credibility, this little game has begun to show its limits after several decades. By dint of wanting to gather their electoral roses while refusing the thorns of alternation, Arab autocrats are one by one revealing an identical political farce.
10 In his collection of chronicles, *Au Refuge des balles perdues: Chroniques des deux Algérie*, Paris: La Découverte, 2005, Sid Ahmed Semiane, an Algerian journalist in exile today, speaks ironically about the fragility of these "sources" for the Algerian press and reminds us very usefully that whenever that press brings up questions said to relate to security, it is strictly forbidden to stray from the terms contained in communiqués from the Ministry of Information. In fact, these Algerian "sources" have until today consisted of whole news columns taken from the Western press.
11 See F. Burgat, "La Recette du poseur de bombes," *Libération*, October 1995. Also available at: http://www.algeria-watch.org/farticle/Burgat2.htm.
12 According to Sihem Bensedrine and Omar Mestiri, as quoted in F. Burgat, "Les Attentes arabes vis à vis de l'Union européenne," *Note pour la Commission des affaires étrangères du Parlement européen*, 2006. English version available at: http://www.hoggar.org/index.php?option=com_content&task=view&id=370&Itemid=64&limit=1&limitstart=5. See S. Bensedrine and O. Mestiri, *L'Europe et ses despotes: Quand le Soutien au "modèle tunisien" dans le monde arabe fait le jeu du terrorisme islamiste*, Paris: La Découverte, 2004.

13 Sid Ahmed Semiane, an Algerian journalist in exile, is one of those who, with brilliant and courageous irony, dismantled the mechanisms of official information imposed in Algeria (and reproduced so imprudently by the Western press) by "sources" authorized to deal with questions relating to security. See Semaine, op. cit.

14 In *Françalgérie, crimes et mensonges d'état*, Paris: La Découverte, 2004, Jean-Baptiste Rivoire and Lounis Aggoun summarize and put in perspective the numerous testimonials that show the scope of the manipulation of Islamic violence by the Algerian secret service.

15 Including in its blindest forms the booby-trapped car; see M. Davis, *Petite histoire de la voiture piégée*, Paris: La Découverte/Zones, 2007.

16 In particular, see Lahouari Addi, François Geze, and Salimah Mellah, *Libération, rebonds*, December 20, 2007: "On December 11, two deadly attacks targeting the Constitutional Council and a United Nations building caused dozens of deaths and hundreds of wounded in Algiers. Once again attributed to Islamists, these attacks will not undergo police or legal investigation; since the perpetrators of the explosions were killed, as usual, no examination worthy of the name will be pursued." See also F. Gèze and S. Mellah, "'Al-Qaida au Maghreb,' ou la très étrange histoire du GSPC algérien," *Algeria-Watch*, September 2007. Available at: http://www.algeria-watch.org/fr/aw/gspc_etrange_histoire.htm.

17 F. Burgat and M. Sbitli, "Les Salafis au Yemen ou la modernisation malgré tout," *Chroniques Yéménites* 12, 2002. Available at: http://cy.revues.org/137?&id=137; Q. Wiktorowicz, *The Management of Islamic Activism: Salafis, the Muslim Brotherhood, and State Power in Jordan*, Albany: SUNY Press, 2001; S. Amghar, "Le Salafisme en Europe: La Mouvance polymorphe d'une radicalisation," *Politique Étrangère* 1, 2006, 67–78; S. Amghar, "Les Salafistes français: Une Nouvelle Aristocratie religieuse," *Maghreb-Machrek* 183, 2005, 13–31; B. Rougier (ed.) *Qu'est ce que le Salafisme?* Paris: Presses universitaires de France, 2008.

18 This evolution, not very central to the mainstream media, is more naturally present in academic research, particularly in the English-speaking world. "For decades the Arab regimes have used a strategy of fear to encourage the United States and Europe to support their repressive policies regarding Islamist movements, stirring up the image of anti-Western fanatics who would take over through the ballot-box," notes Amr Hamzawy. "And yet, moderate Islamists today no longer take part in that nightmare. Activists and political observers who continue insisting on the fact that there is no such thing as a 'moderate Islamic movement' omit taking into account the fact that the militant organizations in Morocco, Algeria, Egypt, Jordan, Kuwait, and Yemen have evolved after decades of failure in their opposition to repressive regimes. Instead of hanging onto mirages of theocratic states, a goodly number of Islamist movements now recognize the relevance of choosing to compete peacefully to win participation in power and to work within the framework of existing institutions to promote progressive democratic directions." For example, see Amr Hamzawy, "The Key to Arab Reform: Moderate Islamists," *Policy Brief* 40, Carnegie Endowment, July 26, 2005.

19 J. Schwedler and J. A. Clark, "Islamist–Leftist Cooperation in the Arab World," *ISIM Review* 18, 2006.

20 B. Lia, *The Society of Muslim Brothers in Egypt: The Rise of an Islamic Mass Movement, 1928–1942*, Reading: Ithaca Press, 1998; B. Utvik, *The Pious Road to Development: Islamist Economics in Egypt*, Boulder: Lynne Rienner, 2006.

21 Among the reasons why the Salafi domain seems for a while to be a dead spot for Western research is the fact that, with a few happy exceptions, Salafi activists have communicated with foreign researchers with much greater difficulty than their predecessors, the Brothers. In Egypt, at the beginning of the 1990s, the Salafi current – which had no centralized structure or, except for a few lawyers, legal showcase – was the object of an extremely violent repression; d'Abdelharîth Madani, one of our rare Salafi interlocutors in *L'Islamisme en face*, died in 1994 while being tortured in a Cairo police station.

22 Including the Sufi brotherhoods, not only during the time when they were the spearhead of resistance against colonial inroads. On the diversified forms of the Sufi return to politics, see A. Philippon, "Bridging Sufism and Islamism," *ISIM Review* 17, Spring 2006.

23 T. Heghammer and S. Lacroix, "Rejectionist Islamism in Saudi Arabia: The Story of Juhayman al-ʿUtaybi Revisited," *International Journal of Middle East Studies* 39, 2007, 103–22; P. Ménoret, "Fighting for the Holy Mosque: The 1979 Mecca Insurgency," in C. Fair and S. Ganguly (eds.) *Treading on Sacred Ground: Counterinsurgency Operations in Sacred Spaces*, New York: Oxford University Press, 2008; M. Al-Rasheed, *Contesting the Saudi State: Islamic Voices from a New Generation*, Cambridge: Cambridge University Press, 2007.

24 P. Ménoret, "Le Cheikh, l'électeur et le SMS. Mobilisation électorale et pratiques de votes en Arabie Saoudite," *Transcontinentales* 1/2e, 2005; Burgat and Sbitli, op. cit.

25 L. Bonnefoy, "Les Relations religieuses transnationales contemporaines entre le Yémen et l'Arabie Saoudite: Un Salafisme 'importé'?" Ph.D. dissertation, Science Po, 2007.

26 We rely here notably on the first comparative ventures in the Iranian field done with the aid of Bjørn Utvik (University of Oslo) in the context of a research program on Violence and Conflicts 2007–09 based at the Institut de Recherches et d'Études sur le Monde Arabe et Musulman (IREMAM) in Aix-en-Provence.

27 In the Persian language the word *bad* has the same meaning as in English.

28 F. Adelkhah (ed.) *L'Iran*, Paris: Le Cavalier Bleu, 2005.

29 Which might, for example, be represented in part, in Tehran, by liberal Islamists such as the religious figure Mohsen Kadivar, a professor of philosophy. The first current is represented notably by the association of Iranian writers (*Kanun-e Nevissandegan-e Iran*) or the members of the Popular Front (*Jebhe e meli*). The demand for secularization implies the complete separation of religion and politics or only the separation of religion and state – i.e. in the Iranian context, the abolition of the institution of the *Velayate faqih*. Such is the stance of liberal Islamists such as Nehzat Azadi, Ebrahim Yazdi, or Gholam-Abas Tavasoli. The *Jebhe-ye Mosharekat*, in which Kadivar was active, holding a parliamentary majority from 2000 to 2004, likewise militates for a so-called "pragmatic" interpretation of the constitution leading to the separation of religion and state.

30 F. Adelkhah, "Islamophobie et malaise dans l'anthropologie: Être ou ne pas être voilée en Iran," *Politix* 80, 2007, 179–96.

31 Ibid.

32 On the problematic of sectarian tensions (Sunni/Shiite) internal to the Islamist domain, cf. (for Lebanon) B. Rougier, "L'Islamisme sunnite au Liban face au Hezbollah," in F. Mermier and E. Picard (eds.) *Liban, une guerre de 33 jours*, Paris: La Découverte, 2007. For a recent Yemeni example, see S. Dorlian, "Zaydisme et modernisation: Émergence d'un nouvel universel politique," *Chroniques Yéménites* 13, 2006. Available at: http://cy.revues.org/1365.

Bibliography

Adelkhah, F. (ed.), *L'Iran*, Paris: Le Cavalier Bleu, 2005.

Adelkhah, F., "Islamophobie et malaise dans l'anthropologie. Être ou ne pas être voilée en Iran," *Politix* 80, 2007, 179–96.

Al-Bishri, T., "Sâra al mass'ul al wahîd fi addawla, ghîr al mass'ûl al wahîd fî ha," *Ad'u kum ila 'asiân*, Cairo: 2005.

Al-Rasheed, M., *Contesting the Saudi State: Islamic Voices from a New Generation*, Cambridge: Cambridge University Press, 2007.

Amghar, S., "Le Salafisme en Europe: La Mouvance polymorphe d'une radicalisation," *Politique Étrangère* 1, 2006, 67–78.

Amghar, S., "Les Salafistes français: Une Nouvelle Aristocratie religieuse," *Maghreb-Machrek* 183, 2005, 13–31.

Bensedrine, S. and Mestiri, O., *L'Europe et ses despotes: Quand le Soutien au "mode?le tunisien" dans le monde arabe fait le jeu du terrorisme islamiste*, Paris: La Découverte, 2004.

Bonnefoy, L., "Les Relations religieuses transnationales contemporaines entre le Yémen et l'Arabie Saoudite: Un Salafisme 'importé'?" Ph.D. dissertation, Science Po, 2007.

Bourdieu, P., "L'Intellectuel négatif," *Liber*, Paris, January 1998.

Burgat, F., "Les Attentes arabes vis à vis de l'Union européenne," *Note pour la Commission des affaires étrangères du Parlement européen*, 2006. English version available at: http://www.hoggar.org/index.php?option=com_content&task=view&id=370&Itemid=64&limit=1&limitstart=5 (accessed June 30, 2011).

Burgat, F., "Les Mobilisations à référent islamique," in E. Picard (ed.) *La Politique dans le monde arabe*, Paris: Armand Colin, 2006.

Burgat, F., *L'Islamisme à l'heure d'Al-Qaeda*, Paris: La Découverte, 2005.

Burgat, F., "La Recette du poseur de bombes," *Libération*, October 1995. Also available at: http://www.algeria-watch.org/farticle/Burgat2.htm (accessed June 30, 2011).

Burgat, F., *L'Islamisme en face*, Paris: La Découverte, 1995 (new edition: Paris: La Découverte, 2007).

Burgat, F., *L'Islamisme au Maghreb. La Voix du sud*, Paris: Karthala, 1988 (new edition: Paris: Petite bibliothèque Payot, 1995). (English version: Burgat, F., *The Islamic Movement in North Africa*, Austin, TX: Center for Middle Eastern Studies, 1993.)

Burgat, F. and Sbitli, M., "Les Salafis au Yemen ou la modernisation malgré tout," *Chroniques Yéménites* 12, 2002. Available at: http://cy.revues.org/137?&id=137 (accessed June 30, 2011).

Davis, M., *Petite histoire de la voiture piégée*, Paris: La Découverte/Zones, 2007.

Dorlian, S., "Zaydisme et modernisation: Émergence d'un nouvel universel politique?" *Chroniques Yéménites* 13, 2006. Available at: http://cy.revues.org/1365 (accessed June 30, 2011).

Foucault, M., *Dits et écrits III*, Paris: Gallimard, 1996.

Gèze, F. and Mellah, S., "'Al-Qaida au Maghreb,' ou la très étrange histoire du GSPC algérien," Algeria-Watch, September 2007. Available at: http://www.algeria-watch.org/fr/aw/gspc_etrange_histoire.htm (accessed June 30, 2011).

Hamzawy, A., "The Key to Arab Reform: Moderate Islamists," *Policy Brief* 40, Carnegie Endowment, July 26, 2005.

Heghammer, T. and Lacroix, S., "Rejectionist Islamism in Saudi Arabia: The Story of Juhayman al-ʿUtaybi Revisited," *International Journal of Middle East Studies* 39, 2007, 103–22.

Lia, B., *The Society of Muslim Brothers in Egypt: The Rise of an Islamic Mass Movement, 1928–1942*, Reading: Ithaca Press, 1998.

Ménoret, P., "Fighting for the Holy Mosque: The 1979 Mecca Insurgency," in C. Fair and S. Ganguly (eds.) *Treading on Sacred Ground: Counterinsurgency Operations in Sacred Spaces*, New York: Oxford University Press, 2008.

Ménoret, P., "Le Cheikh, l'électeur et le SMS. Mobilisation électorale et pratiques de votes en Arabie Saoudite," *Transcontinentales* 1/2e, 2005.

Philippon, A., "Bridging Sufism and Islamism," *ISIM Review* 17, 2006.

Rivoire, J. and Aggoun, L., *Françalgérie, crimes et mensonges d'état*, Paris: La Découverte, 2004.

Rougier, B. (ed.), *Qu'est ce que le Salafisme?* Paris: Presses universitaires de France, 2008.

Rougier, B., "L'Islamisme sunnite au Liban face au Hezbollah," in F. Mermier and E. Picard (eds.) *Liban, une guerre de 33 jours*, Paris: La Découverte, 2007.

Schwedler, J. and Clark, J. A., "Islamist–Leftist Cooperation in the Arab World," *ISIM Review* 18, 2006.

Semiane, S. A., *Au Refuge des balles perdues: Chroniques des deux Algérie*, Paris: La Découverte, 2005.

Utvik, B., *The Pious Road to Development: Islamist Economics in Egypt*, Boulder: Lynne Rienner, 2006.

Wiktorowicz, Q., *The Management of Islamic Activism: Salafis, the Muslim Brotherhood, and State Power in Jordan*, Albany: SUNY Press, 2001.

2

DEGRADING DEMOCRACY

American empire, Islam, and struggles for freedom in the Arab Islamic world

Raymond William Baker[1]

> From now on, no Eid will pass without people remembering his execution. This was the climax of a colonial farce with the court proceedings' blatant sectarian overtones welcomed by Bush and the British government as a "fair trial." The occupation also welcomed the grotesque public execution as "justice being done." Contrast this with the end of our hopes, as Iraqis in opposition, of persuading our people of the humanity of democracy and how it would, unlike Saddam's brutality, put an end to all abuses of human rights, to execution in public, and to the death penalty.
>
> (Haifa Zangana)[2]

The Bush administration's rhetoric of remaking the Middle East along democratic lines to justify American imperial assertions in Iraq and elsewhere has inevitably degraded the democratic idea. It has also stimulated a luxuriant field of commentary on the relationship of Islam and democracy. Given the context, shaped essentially by the neo-conservative imperial agenda, it will come as no surprise that most of that new literature is hostile to Islam, amounting to little more than a repackaging of tired Orientalist notions of the "exceptionalism" of Muslims when it comes to struggles for democratic freedoms and of the "self-inflicted" wounds that explain these deficiencies.

Neo-conservative thinkers with their well-documented affiliations with the Israeli right have given these formulations a particularly blunt expression, so vulgar in style that they appear more novel than they are. In fact, these Orientalist perspectives on Islam and Islamist movements are broadly shared in mainstream media and scholarship. Liberal scholars eschew overtly racist formulations, even as they endlessly bemoan the failures of the Islamic world to generate Islamist liberals who can duplicate the Western path to democracy. In its own way the left, with its attention and hopes focused elsewhere, reinforces these treatments of Islam and democracy by refusing for the most part to attribute any democratic potential to Islamist movements, ignoring historical and contemporary evidence to the contrary. These approaches raise the question: does an Islamic cultural context preclude democratic development? I aim to situate this inquiry in that grey area between policy and the particular knowledge it demands, and theory and the generalized knowledge it requires.

While this chapter opens with the compelling image of the "colonial farce" staged recently in Iraq – the public execution of Saddam Hussein – as an emblem of the ways in which American power has been used to the detriment of democratic development, it moves immediately to look at the historical roots of American empire and to other sites in the Islamic world, notably Egypt, where the theoretical issues of Islam and democracy are being worked out in a particularly compelling way among the New Islamists, a centrist intellectual school that has been active since the 1970s.

Despite these democratic inroads, almost no effort to seriously evaluate the emancipatory potential of centrist Islamist movements – including their contributions to both imperial resistance and democratic theory and practice – has been made.[3] Regardless of this lack of attention as well as the degraded democracy of occupied Iraq, democratic development in the Islamic world continues, undeterred by empire, as my treatment of Egypt's New Islamists will show.

On both the intellectual and policy levels there is less that is new in the contemporary American imperial project and its rationalizations in the alleged animus of Islam toward democracy than is sometimes supposed. In the rush to critique the neoconservative version of empire we should not forget the broader continuities of the American imperial project and the structures of attitude and settled belief that sustain it. The roots of American empire, as Chalmers Johnson and a host of others have shown, extend deep into the Cold War era.[4] Liberals and conservatives from Roosevelt to Clinton and from Reagan to Bush have sustained it.[5] The "evil empire" and "the war on terror," to cite just two examples, are refurbished ideological relics of the Reagan era that in turn had their origins in the Cold War thinking of Truman and Eisenhower.

It is also true that although the liberal legacy identified with the democrats has emphasized economic and political tools of empire, highlighted in particular by Clinton, liberals at the same time have contributed without reserve to the consensus view that the contest for global hegemony requires military exertions. Liberals also bought fully into the same Orientalist notions that support the exceptionalist thesis that democracy and Islam do not mix, in turn allowing for armed assistance from the West.

Even those on the political and cultural left who have engaged issues of Islam and democracy have not gone beyond the critique of Orientalist ideas. They have only skillfully exposed the ways in which these ideas and their institutional affiliations have misrepresented and "covered" Islam and Islamist movements. Hence the task of lifting that ideological cover that rationalizes the imperial project has yet to be fully engaged. Notions of Islam as both incapable and resistant to modernity hold sway. Thus, from the outset, the bipartisan American imperial project was identified with the task of protecting freedom at home and spreading democracy abroad, however contradictory actual policies might have been to those ideological justifications.

As a result, on both intellectual and policy levels, George W. Bush inherited an imperial project shaded in both conservative and liberal tones and complete with well-established foundations for its ideological justification, including the invocations of democratic transitions beyond the borders under benevolent American tutelage. What Bush did on the policy level was simply take existing trends of imperialist militarism and push them to the extreme; 9/11 and the skillful exploitation of that crime against humanity simply provided the rationale and necessary climate of fear for a heightened militarization of imperial policy along aggressively expansionist lines that the neo-conservatives had been planning for years. In parallel fashion, the Bush-era scholarship on Islam and democracy simply took existing conservative and liberal theoretical formulations and gave them a simplifying clarity and certitude that only extremist thought can manage.[6]

The issue of Islam and democracy remains at the heart of the debate between imperial scholarship and its critics. The inability of the Islamic world to generate democracy, by neo-conservative lights, compelled a strategy of using overwhelming military force to clear the inhospitable Islamic ground for the planting of democratic seeds from abroad. To be sure, the purifying bombardments under the banner of freedom cause some blood and tears as the empire serves as the midwife of democracy. However, only through the pain and suffering of this bloody "birthing," to borrow Condoleezza Rice's image, will Muslims at last be free, most importantly, from their major obstacle to democracy – Islam.

Indeed, in all cases the military adventurism of the United States and Israel has been justified by their much-trumpeted claims as embodiments of the democratic idea and its most effective proponents in the international and Middle East arenas. Thus, the wars against Afghanistan, Iraq, and Lebanon, with their massive human rights violations and civilian casualties, resulted, alongside the unchecked and inherently violent colonization of the remnants of historic Palestine, under the cover of the peace process.

It is now perfectly clear that the Bush policies pursued vis-à-vis the Islamic world have been monstrously destructive. However, studies of Islam and democracy produced by scholars embedded in the neo-conservative right, especially those nestled comfortably in such think tanks as the American Enterprise Institute, the Washington Institute for Near East Policy, the Jewish Institute for National Security Affairs, and the Hudson Institute, have, not surprisingly, had a largely apologetic character, quite explicitly serving the imperial project. As on a host of other issues, these scholars have dominated the national debate, and failures on the ground have not altered this reality. All this suggests that the neo-conservatives have firmly rooted their presence in American political life and will not fade away with the passing of a discredited George W. Bush.

The use of democracy for imperialist ends was apparent years ago, in the leading scholars on whom the worker bees in the think tanks rely, notably Bernard Lewis and Fouad Ajami. When the grandiose and misguided plans dissolved into death and destruction, the blame for the failures was then placed squarely on Islam's shoulders. Noble dreams of remaking the Middle East along democratic lines faltered, Ajami noted, when the damaged humans of these transformations, especially in Iraq, failed to live up to imperial expectations and assume their proper responsibilities as the "shocked and awed" country descended into devastating chaos and the "noble experiment" failed.[7]

For our purposes, Bush-era studies of Islam and democracy are of importance only for what they reveal of neo-conservative American thinking, since they have no relationship to actual struggles for democracy in the Islamic world. Nor are they intended to. They quite unabashedly transcend mere realities on the ground to serve the higher purposes of empire by riveting attention on the dangers that failed Islam poses for the West.

This flawed Western work on Islam thus does have some theoretical interest, though in unintended ways. Studies of the Islamic world – like studies of Soviet Russia during the Cold War – take as their point of departure the idea that a culture, even an evil or failed one, is a consistent unity that can be assigned a singular character that in turn is ascribed to each of its parts. By this fallacy, Islam as "failed civilization" is a coherent cultural whole that is transparently knowable through an examination of any of its parts; it is in this sense an "easy whole" to decode quite like the totalitarian Soviet system. Thus, the varieties of Islamic movements, like their communist predecessors, are quite amenable to labeling and classification, since they are merely the slightly shaded offshoots of one accessible unity. Moreover, this "available Islam" remains unchanging in its essential character, despite all the surface variation.[8]

Today this same assumed fixedness of Islam provides a boon to harassed policy makers charged with the endless tasks of managing a global empire with its most critical bases in the Islamic world. It also rescues the security and military analysts who dominate the war on terror debates from the tiresome task of learning languages and studying cultures. No need to pay much attention to the tedious details of other peoples' history or to the exotic flora and fauna of their diverse circumstances and world views because, after all, an Islamist is an Islamist with a fixed character. All the trivial details of reality and the changes it can bring fade out completely in the radiant glare of Islam as a fully apprehended, deadly abstraction.

For the dominant neo-conservatives, Islam as failed faith and civilization stands revealed as a colossal threat, precisely because of its failures and the rage and jealousy those irreparable defects stimulate. Moreover, not only is Islam evil, it is evil on a global scale that demands a military riposte. Liberals tend to adopt a somewhat softer view that focuses on cultural deficiencies rather than violent rage as the character of the Islamic threat. By these lights, Muslims everywhere lack the liberal gene and are thus, whatever their intentions or surface behavior, the carriers of irrationality, anti-enlightenment, and anti-secular values. Hence, it is the cultural deficiencies of Muslims or the jealous rage they experience facing a superior Western civilization and *not* rapacious U.S. or Israeli policies that create the dangers that threaten to engulf the civilized world in violence and flames.[9]

In fairness to Americans, the absurdities of such imperial thinking, even when stated in so unvarnished a way, do not exceed those of the British "white man's burden" or of the French "civilizing mission" of the nineteenth and early twentieth centuries. Nor are the required suspensions of rational understanding and fellow feeling for the victims of such projects any more demanding of Americans than they were of earlier British and French publics. Indeed, the legendary ignorance of the American public of anything beyond its borders has helped enormously. So too has America's history as a European settler state, as deeply entrenched stereotypes of Arabs and Islam have played a part compatible with that historic sensibility. So too has the calculated drum beat of fear of the "natives" fostered by the state and media monopolies provided essential cover for the dirty work of empire. So too, as I will argue here, have more sophisticated notions of reason and culture, our own and theirs.

Still, the American empire has too many distinctive features to speak simply of "resurrecting empire." To be sure, the parallels in distorted thinking and extraordinary violence between the American and earlier empires that the historian Rashid Khalidi and the cultural critic Edward Said, among others, have noted are compelling. What is lost by drawing the parallels too tightly, however, is a full sense of precisely why Islam functions so perfectly as the antithesis of democracy and the enemy of choice for a global age. American empire is not simply a throwback to an earlier time; it is the product of a new imperialism of a global age and no alternative enemy comes even close to Islam in its usefulness in justifying the terrible violence that a global empire entails throughout far-flung domains. The world's 1.3 billion Muslims are everywhere, like American power, and that everywhere includes the strategically important Middle East with its incomparable oil reserves.

The democratic deficiency argument would not be an easy one to make if scholars and journalists in the West had even a cursory familiarity with the writings and practice of any of the major centrist Islamist thinkers. For the most part, they do not.[10] Neo-conservative thinkers, of course, deride the very notion of an Islamic center. Mainstream liberal scholarship pays very little attention to Islamist centrists, while the left for the most part either is actively hostile or simply ignores them. As a result, the standard Orientalist arguments flow with unperturbed confidence. One can only imagine the impact of a serious engagement with the intellectual work in which centrist intellectuals have been engaged for decades, exploring the roots of Islamic conceptions of reason and culture for democratic development.

In this regard, even the most interesting work of both liberal and leftist scholars writing for Western audiences falls short of a serious engagement with the centrists as important or decisive in their own right for the future of their societies. Willful inattention is required to maintain this posture. Consider, for example, the work of the New Islamists. These Egyptian centrists have produced a full-blown body of work that addresses the most important issues facing the Islamic world, ranging from the rights of women and minorities to the modalities of resistance to Western and, particularly, American imperialism. Out of their ranks have come some of the most important figures on the Islamist moderate landscape, such as the late Muhammad al Ghazzally and Yusuf al Qaradawy.[11] Their work has provided inspiration for centrist movements throughout the Islamic world.

Typically, liberal Western scholars include such Islamist centrists in their narratives and analyses only as stand-ins for the absent, Westernized liberals for whom they endlessly search. For leftist scholars, if the centrists appear at all, they are invoked as blank slates on which their own leftist version of such Western values of justice and human rights can be inscribed.

Amr Hamzawy, previously a senior scholar at the Carnegie Endowment for International Peace, for example, makes clear his liberal orientation in assessing moderate Islamists as "the key to Arab reform."[12] With this supportive positioning and title, this article promises more than it delivers. In Hamzawy's view, the centrists play this role only by default, and the primary emphasis is not on what they bring to the table but rather on what they lack from a liberal perspective:

> It would be nice if liberal democrats among the Arab intelligentsia could be the vanguard of political reform, but they are too few and too disconnected from their bodies politic to compel resistant autocrats to open the way for representative government.

While waiting for liberals in his adopted American mold, Hamzawy is willing to settle for moderate Islamists, though he views them through a decidedly liberal lens that introduces important distortions:

> There are good reasons for the United States and Europe to support liberal parties and secular nongovernmental organizations across the region. Normatively and politically, Arab liberals have embraced the Western political value system of universal citizenship, democracy, and rule of law. Their objectives are identical with Western aspirations for tolerant, pluralist Arab societies. They speak a language that U.S. and European policy and intellectual communities understand and admire.[13]

Hamzawy does not pause to consider even the possibility that the discourse of the centrist moderates might in fact give them the capacity to say and do things that would advance the struggle for freedom in the Islamic world and perhaps even go beyond the liberal imagination in productive ways. Rather, Hamzawy cautions that these stand-in liberals have some serious shortcomings, notably in the social dimensions of their thinking as measured by traditional liberal standards, as well as the ever-present risk that they will resort to theocratic fantasies and violence to realize them.

Given this perspective, it is not surprising that Hamzawy views the democratic commitments of the Islamist moderates as totally pragmatic in the commonsense use of the term – i.e., they merely represent practical adjustments to failed policies rather than principled commitments. This dismisses decades of serious intellectual and practical work on behalf of the expansion of freedom.

Hamzawy explains that "by the end of the 1990s, Arab Islamists had failed to change political realities in their homelands despite considerable popular support." He continues: "this failure prompted various revisionist trends that gathered momentum in the aftermath of September 11, 2001. As a result, moderate movements have become increasingly receptive to democratic procedures."[14] Historically, this argument does not stand. In his treatment of Egypt's centrist Islamist al Wassat Party, for example, there is no mention of the Islamic roots of its commitments, notably elaborated in the work of the older generation of New Islamists, on whom the al Wassat activists rely explicitly.

Only when this omission is realized can one make sense of Hamzawy's claim that the emergence of the moderates is, as he puts it, a product of the post-9/11 world, when they finally abandoned their goals of religious rule by violence and opted for democracy. While this liberal story of belated awakening undoubtedly makes sense when directed to the Washington liberal alternative to the neo-cons, it remains a serious distortion of the actual history of the centrists. Readers of Hamzawy with even passing familiarity with mainstream Islamist movements will be surprised that he manages to project this "good Muslim" image with no mention at all of the consistent opposition by the Islamic mainstream to the Western imperial project and Israeli excesses. In fact, there is not a word about the centrist Islamist position on Israel. No doubt these erasures are required to facilitate Hamzawy's use of the term "moderate," which is so important for American political discourse. In that context, of course, it means little more than pro-American.

Hamzawy evinces no hint of a scholar's skepticism and simply takes for granted the rhetoric of Western democratic commitments in the Arab world, ignoring the evidence of decades of support for authoritarian regimes, often brought to power with American covert assistance, as in the case of Saddam Hussein, and systematic interventions to block and otherwise undermine democratically elected Islamists, as in the case of Hamas in the Occupied Territories. Given this willful liberal misreading of recent history, it makes sense that Hamzawy warns Western governments to proceed cautiously with any engagement with his moderates (though, given the actual history of the American role, it is quite clearly the Islamist moderates that are in need of such cautionary advice).

Leftist analysts do not accede to these liberal illusions. Stephen Zunes, in *Tinderbox: U.S. Middle East Policy and the Roots of Terrorism*, for example, provides a scathing and well-documented indictment of the real American record on democracy in the Islamic world.[15] He does so by using an effective blend of political economy arguments that underscore the interest of the American military-industrial complex in not just oil but arms sales, as well as economic and strategic dominance. His argument shows how American anti-democratic policies in the pursuit of these ends have actively contributed to the growth of Islamic extremism, while undermining centrists (though Zunes fails to make this second point). The classic case is the now well-documented American support of transnational Islamist extremists to combat the Soviets in Afghanistan.

Above all, Zunes makes it clear how extremist Islamist versions of a malevolent U.S. role are confirmed by unqualified U.S. alignment with the Israeli agenda of overt colonization of occupied Palestinian territories and the seemingly unlimited support of brutally repressive Arab regimes. The moral force of Zunes' condemnation of these unjust and unwise policies comes in the unflinching account of the ways the best of Western democratic and human rights values are trampled in practice, even as they are trumpeted rhetorically. Zunes shows how Islamist extremists capitalize on these obvious contradictions to advance their own deplorable aims. In all of these ways, Zunes makes a truly exceptional contribution.

Still, it is striking that there is virtually not a word in Zunes' overview of the Middle East "tinderbox" of the Islamic centrist resistance to Western and American imperialism, nor any consideration of the ways in which the Islamic center has actively not only resisted the West but creatively interrogated its heritage to find authentically Islamic pathways to the more just and democratic societies that Zunes would like to see emerge in the Arab world. In the end, it is disappointing that Zunes identifies no partners on the ground who might be productively engaged to advance his genuinely high-minded vision for a radically restructured U.S. foreign policy and a self-directed Arab future.

To be sure, the centrist Islamists themselves seem to barely notice this consistent neglect or misreading. Approval from the West is not their aim. They seek instead to contribute in meaningful ways to the development of democratic ideas and practices within Islamism. For the centrists, Islamic communities have a moral mission and they argue that democracy, tailored to the diverse conditions of the Islamic world, can be an important instrument.

Today, there are important centrist Islamist movements in a variety of sites in the Arab Islamic world, notably the Renaissance Party in Tunisia, the Justice and Development Party in Morocco, the Reform Party in Algeria, the Jordanian Islamic Action Front, the *Ummah* Party in Kuwait, and the Yemeni Reformist Union. Egypt acts in many ways as the most important and most inclusive node of an informal network that links such centrists today and will provide the essential wiring for more extensive and inclusive interactions in the future.

However, these groups have already accomplished a great deal. Working since the 1970s, when the current surge of Islamic awakening began, Islamists of the center have produced an extensive body of scholarship that shows how the resources of their heritage can be turned to the positive end of fostering democratic development. In these works they elaborate key questions: How should Islam be understood in its call for a community that is at once moral and political? In what concrete, practical ways does democracy respond to the needs of the nation at this historical juncture? What character will democracy take when bent to the larger purposes of Islam? And finally, how will democratic reforms in turn enhance the capacity to turn Islamic values into the lived experiences of all, including non-Muslims, who are also members of democratic, Islamic communities?

To truly understand the work of the New Islamists, one must pay attention to their sophisticated and philosophical treatment of reason and culture. The New Islamists of Egypt, in particular, have elaborated these concepts in ways that are directly relevant not only to ongoing struggles for democracy in Egypt but to parallel efforts of democrats in Islam elsewhere.

Consciously and collectively the New Islamists have sought to use a rich conception of reason to understand the new global conditions often shaped by forces in the West but impacting Islamic societies. They aim to live as much in accord with the higher purposes of Islam in this new world. Culture for them is thus not a thing to be mummified as a relic of an earlier age, but rather an active resource for dealing with the unique and daunting challenges of the current era.

To these ends, reason in the thinking and action of the New Islamists assumes three related but still distinctive forms. *Instrumental reason* that connects means and ends in practical life and cause and effect in science is very much a part of their thinking about the world and humanity's place in it. In particular, they see Muslims as quite self-consciously the heirs of a civilization that recognized the scientific achievements of the Greeks, the Indians, and the Chinese with whom they came in contact. Islamic civilization not only preserved this human treasure but contributed impressively to it in medicine, mathematics, astronomy, and, perhaps most importantly of all, in understanding the methods and aims of empirical, experimental science. In the inaugural lecture in 1996 at a center named for the great New Islamist thinker Muhammad al Ghazzaly, who had died two years earlier, Yusuf al Qaradawy chose as his theme the absolute centrality of this practical and scientific reason to Islam as interpreted by the *Wassatteyya*, the intellectuals of the Egyptian centrist Islamist mainstream. Qaradawy reminded his listeners that the very first revelation called on Muslims to use their minds:

> Read! – In the name of thy Lord and Cherisher who created man ... Read! And thy Lord is most bountiful – He who taught (the use of) the pen – Taught man that which he knew not.[16]

The New Islamists understand this verse to mean that God wanted to begin the era of rationality – of education and science – and that he was calling Muslims to play a role as leaders in its realization. Qaradawy related how Ghazzaly was deeply saddened that the Islamic community, the leading light for science and learning for a thousand years, had become backward and ignorant. But what most angered Ghazzaly was the blame placed on Islam for this backwardness. How could such an argument be sustained, he wondered, when Islam had proven itself to be the vehicle that brought science and enlightenment to the world? In Islam there was never a conflict between science and faith. "For us," pronounced Qaradawy, "science is religion and religion is science."[17]

While recognizing the centrality of the instrumental reason of social practice and scientific inquiry, the *Wassatteyya* also emphasized that Islamic civilization explored and deepened ways in which reason could not only relate means to ends and cause to effects, but also offer evaluative judgments about the hierarchy of such ends and the usefulness of such effects for the forms of collective life they sought to build. *Evaluative reason*, they argued, has played a part as important as instrumental reason in the Islamic world, as not all ends are of equal value and not all means are compatible with the achievement of certain prized community goals. Means, they quite explicitly argued, must also be compatible with the ends used for their achievement; if not, the larger goals and purposes of collective life will be distorted or undermined. No one has conveyed that insight with more force than the same Qaradawy, who pronounced unequivocally that ends do not justify means, but rather means must always be compatible with the ends they serve.[18]

Finally, reason also allowed inclusive moral frameworks by which the activities of building the world in all its dimensions – religious, political, social, and economic – could be understood, evaluated, and guided. Fahmy Huwaidy, another centrist

Islamist thinker, brought reason in this sense into very public and controversial view when he launched an attack on the excessive religiosity of what he called the *darawish*. In a candid column, Huwaidy noted that in the village of his origins people repeatedly raised monies for the *umra* (the recommended but not prescribed pilgrimage to Mecca at times other than the *hajj*) when the village was in dire need of developmental projects to improve the health and well-being of its inhabitants. Huwaidy did not question the probity of the *umra* as a supererogatory but positive act of faith. What he did was place it in the larger framework of the Qur'anic injunction to "build the world," and he concluded bluntly that those resources were better spent on social projects for collective betterment. The *darawish*, he explained, reduced their obligations as Muslims to narrow rituals and traditional religious practices in the hopes of securing God's favor. "In doing so," wrote Huwaidy, "they are striving for their own salvation as individuals and ignoring the society around them. This causes a kind of unintended selfishness in their religiousness." Huwaidy decried this distortion of the priorities that Islam establishes in the service of a larger moral whole. Reason in this third sense thus goes a step further and organizes the most valued goals and useful effects into a coherent unity.

These three understandings of reason that characterize the thinking of the *Wassatteyya* emerged out of a distinctive cultural context shaped, above all, by Islam. It will be helpful to pause briefly and make this cultural context as explicit as possible.

The idea of culture embedded in the intellectual and social products of the Egyptian *Wassatteyya* includes the notion of culture as those habits of mind and heart that are the common possession of the varied human communities of the Islamic world. Culture also has for them the additional sense of those outcomes of human effort that command attention and respect for the beauty with which they imbue the human environment as opposed to the purely natural world. Thus there is no inclination among the New Islamists to denigrate the role of the arts, of the natural and Islamic sciences, and, indeed, of all forms of creativity which are recognized as valued outcomes of the highest forms of human effort. With great courage the New Islamists have defended art and artists against what they regard as the ignorant, extremist misreadings of Islam that banish music, dance, and artistic expression.[19] They stand just as firmly against rote memorization and the divorce of learning from living.

Culture for the *Wassatteyya* is hence open and inclusive. Islam, as the mainstream interprets it, did not come into the world to homogenize it, no matter how valued its contributions to the common human project of building the world. The New Islamists insist that attention be paid to the realities on the ground as context for particular struggles and for the unique forms they inevitably take. They are quite aware, for example, that Islam in Egypt has been shaped in certain ways by its centuries-long interaction with the large number of Egyptian Christians. Other contexts boast quite different influences. No single movement or interpretation of culture could possibly be right for all times and places. The higher purposes of Islam to which humankind is called alone have such universality. The details, including particular shadings of reason's uses and culture's role, are left to be worked out by Muslims acting in their diverse circumstances.

To this end, the New Islamists present their thought as derived from Islamic principles, and they address their message in the first instance to the people of Egypt and the larger Islamic world. Yet they also strive to interpret and project their readings of Islamic heritage in ways responsive to a new time in human history, when, as Kamal Abul Magd has written, "the barriers between peoples are falling and distances are shrinking." They thus seek to make the Islamic renewal part of this new era

> when states, peoples, and cultures around the world are searching for common intellectual ground and shared interests and seeking civilizational rapprochement and cultural cooperation for the sake of values like justice, peace, freedom, and respect for human rights.[20]

In this way, the New Islamists quite consciously have cultivated a clear sense that there are parallels and compatible achievements in other cultural settings. Their historical memory of the development of Islamic civilization includes productive encounters with Greek philosophy, Iranian literature, and Chinese and Indian technologies that provide a glimpse into what might be called universal human attainments. In the current age, the New Islamists have no trouble recognizing some dimensions of American political genius that have universal importance. Such appreciation for the transcending achievements of other cultural communities does not, of course, mean that their own culture has nothing of value to contribute on the all-human scale. Nor does it imply any sense of excessive deference to external cultural attainments. For example, an appreciation for the historic contribution of American thinking and practice vis-à-vis the quest for democracy, such as the idea of executive term limits, does not preclude in any way the toughest criticism of the anti-democratic policies that the U.S. and other democratic Western powers have consistently pursued in the Islamic world and elsewhere in the Global South.

Given these impressive resources of reason and culture that can be drawn from Islam and turned to the purposes of democratic development, it should come as no surprise that the worldly Islam of the *Wassatteyya* has contributed in significant ways to the growing Islamist literature and record of concrete achievements in the quest for democracy. As Barrington Moore, Jr. has pointed out, struggles for democracy are always part of a long and inconclusive process that aims to limit arbitrary rule, replace arbitrary rules with just and fair ones, and increase the opportunity for underlying populations to participate in the making of those rules.[21] Since the 1970s, Egypt's New Islamists have actively supported movements that call for such actions. Above all, the centrists have striven to create avenues for popular participation in social and economic work that serve the common good, most often in the face of bureaucratic and political obstacles. Very little of this record is known or appreciated in the West.[22]

The American empire requires the notion that democracy cannot come to the Islamic world from internal resources of reason and culture, such as those highlighted by the New Islamists. It is not enough to ignore this evidence; diligent, if low-grade, intellectual work is required from the advocates of empire that makes the case for Islamic exceptionalism again and again. Such repetition compensates for the lack of force of the argument itself, but the slogan becomes firmly imprinted in the minds of Western publics.

Arguments for Islamic exceptionalism, it should be added, also appear persuasive to Western audiences because the ground for them has been prepared with an impressive dose of amnesia. The notion that democracy must come to the Islamic world from the outside demands the suppression of clear evidence for an indigenous constitutional and democratic tradition in a number of Islamic lands. The leadership of the movements involved cannot be described as Islamist, to be sure, though they arose out of an Islamic milieu. After all, Egypt, Iran, and Turkey all have a rich tradition of nationalist and constitutional struggles to limit arbitrary rule on both mass and elite levels.[23]

A quick survey of the literature on Islamic exceptionalism reveals two kinds of useful arguments, one historical and one theoretical. Historical arguments make the case that the Islamic world has yet to produce a single functioning democracy. This argument is reinforced by the observation that, despite the inroads made in Egypt, Iran, and Turkey, presently existing states that describe themselves as Islamic, notably Saudi Arabia, Pakistan, and the Sudan, are scandalously undemocratic. These self-evident historical truths are then explained with three kinds of theoretical arguments:

1 Muslims don't share the values that make democracy possible. They don't value individual liberty, free consensus, religious freedom, and the right to dissent against unjust authority.
2 Muslims lack the cultural resources, the traditions, and the historical experiences out of which democracy developed. Democracy's success in the Middle East would require erasure of historical memories of past attainments, full extirpation of the extant culture, and its replacement with a Western transplant.
3 Muslims overvalue tradition; Islam does not condone innovation, and hence Islamist political culture could never prize, and most likely would punish, the very sort of individual variations a democracy requires for growth.

There are negative consequences of taking these views for granted, and I aim here to mount a pragmatic challenge to their functionality as truth. For those who make the first claim about Muslims not sharing our values, what meaning does "Muslims" have and how did it come by this meaning? Can it really mean all Muslims at once and in all times and places? Clearly it cannot mean the New Islamists. Could it mean, instead, "Muslims, insofar as I understand them from American movies and television or from Western news media accounts of their doings?" There is in this sort of claim, as we have seen, a reification of culture into a monochromatic unity, a simple as opposed to a complex whole. Moreover, it is also quite unclear who "we" are. Plenty of Americans do not share democratic values; some of them hold power.

Whether any Muslims have the values necessary to rule democratically is a matter of their actions, not their origins. A value is not a permanent belief lodged in the brain's interior. It is a commitment, implicit or explicit, to a certain *life strategy*, a model for responding to like cases in like ways, where likeness is a matter of interpretation, and consistency exists across interpreters as a matter of acculturation and of social pressure. There are indeed Muslims with the values necessary for democracy, insofar as there are enough people in Muslim countries willing to take up what John Dewey called "the struggle for the democratic way of life," to combat impediments to the maximal development of each individual's potential in accordance with his/her aspirations. The New Islamists represent such Muslims.

As for the second objection about the deficiencies of Islamic tradition, what matters is, again, the practical commitment to democratic reform of society, not inheritance of this or that tradition. As Dewey writes,

> Political forms do not originate in a once and for all way. The greatest change, once it is accomplished, is simply the outcome of a vast series of adaptations and responsive adaptations, each to its own particular situation. Looking back, it is possible, to make out a trend of more or less steady change in a single direction. But it is, we repeat, mere mythology to attribute such unity of result as exists (which is always easy to exaggerate) to single force or principle. Political democracy has emerged as a kind of net consequence of a vast multitude of responsive adjustments to a vast number of situations, not two of which were alike, but which tended to converge to a common outcome.[24]

The suitability of Islam to democracy within such a pragmatic framework would clearly become an empirical question. Dewey allows a sense of democracy concrete in practical terms but loose in abstract details, thus giving an apt guide for appraising the democratic potentialities of other cultures:

> Democracy is the idea of community life itself. It is an ideal in the only intelligible sense of an ideal: namely, the tendency and movement of some thing which exists carried to its final limit, viewed as completed, perfected ... Wherever there is conjoint activity whose consequences are appreciated as good by all singular persons who take part in it, and where the realization of the good is such as to affect an energetic desire and effort to sustain it in being just because it is a good shared by all, there is in so far a community. The clear consciousness of a communal life, in all its implications, constitutes the idea of democracy.[25]

Nothing in these accounts presupposes European lineage. In fact, a great deal evokes the experience of the New Islamists of Egypt, especially the second generation that has played such a critical role in the Kefaya Movement for political reform and the collaborative and long-blocked efforts to secure legal status for the al Wassat Party.[26]

The third objection that Islam has no place for innovation appears to carry more weight because of the centrality of Muslim belief that the Qur'an is the word of God for all times and places. The *subterranean* expression of this tension is the only way I have ever been able to understand the misplaced Western worry so endlessly expressed that Muslims don't have the sense of separation between church and state that reputedly aids in developing democracy. But the simple fact is that Muslims don't have anything like a church in a Christian sense, nor can Islam easily generate theocratic rule. In mainstream Sunni Islam, for example, there is no church-like central source of authority – no infallible, Islamically sanctioned fiats free from debate and negotiation. Instead, there is *ijtihad* (an effort of interpretation of the sacred texts), as the New Islamists have so persuasively demonstrated. Thus, nightmares of inquisitions impeding the functioning of democratic power structures are our own and not theirs. However, Muslims do have nightmares of their own. Marginal, violent sects have long been a part of their history, and these extremists are capable of terrible deeds, especially when supported by external powers that bring them to rule, as in the recent case of the Taliban regime in Afghanistan. Generally, without such support similar extremists have simply faded from view. This history, while it does have its deplorable pages, is quite different from the kind of mainstream Christian theocracy against which the Western Enlightenment necessarily demarcated itself.

We also need to remind ourselves that constitutions are held constant in democracies. While the work of the founding fathers does not have the divine status of the Qur'an, guarded parallels can still be drawn without pushing the analogy too far. Though constitutions can be amended, the real source of variability necessary to adapt constitutions to the exigencies of the day comes through reinterpretation. Judges die and are replaced by new ones steeped in a changed milieu, their hearts owned by new loyalties, their dreams projected from new standpoints.

Is the centrality of the practice of *ijtihad* by the New Islamists really so different? In democracy and Islam alike, newness is articulated in more or less consistent terms by the exercise of human intellect. Few Americans want to hear about innovations to the Constitution, and likewise Muslims cannot tolerate such notions attached directly to the Qur'an. However, interpretations – even interpretations of the Qur'an – are fully human and can be accepted or challenged by new interpretations. The work of the *Wassatteyya* makes clear that the scope of activity that counts as warranted reinterpretation, and the amount of variability allowed and even encouraged at the individual level are far greater in the Islamic context than is understood in the West.

I will leave you with a telling example of the *Wassatteyya* at work in defending the democratic rights of citizenship against ruling authoritarian regimes and retrograde social forces and policies. The activists of the al Wassat Party in Egypt have been particularly noteworthy in this respect. In 2007, Muhammad Habib, formerly the second in command of the influential Muslim Brotherhood, called for an appendix to the Egyptian constitution that would assign a second class status to non-Muslims, notably the largest community of Egyptian Christians, the Copts. According to newspaper accounts, Habib explained that the new requirement would not be a return to the Ottoman-era *gizya,* although non-Muslims would pay an additional tax. In an immediate response to the newspaper reports, the co-founders of the al Wassat Party, Aboul Ela Mady and Essam Sultan, attacked such a position as totally unacceptable. Sultan said it best, announcing that the Brotherhood had failed its exam in citizenship with a straight F. Habib himself then denied the accuracy of the accounts of his statements, and debate continued for several weeks over whether or not the press had accurately reported his views on the *gizya*. What was perfectly clear from the incident was the position of the *Wassatteyya*, forcefully expressed by the Wassat Party leaders in a variety of public forums, that any such retrograde notions had no place in the contemporary understanding of citizenship.[27]

The Bush era and the scholarship that accompanied it reopened old discussions of Islam and democracy by turning the democratic ideal into a tool of empire. Those dreadful distortions did galvanize an effective critique of the worst imperial misuses of the democratic ideal by neo-conservative scholars. But successes in these efforts have been exaggerated. The neo-conservatives have very effectively institutionalized their world view, securing it in quite tangible organizational forms in a string of think tanks. Moreover, they have proven surprisingly effective in securing a strong presence on the nation's campuses through well-managed internships and employment opportunities through which the next generation of neo-conservative thinkers and activists is being trained.

Similar caution is warranted in our thinking about the willful miseducation about Islam and Islamic political movements. Islam serves imperial purposes far too well to be abandoned so easily as the constructed enemy of choice. Moreover, far too little has been accomplished in generating the kind of positive knowledge about Islam and the Islamic world that alone can eclipse the Islamist imaginary of the neo-conservatives and the Orientalist tradition on which they draw. For all the successes of the critique of Orientalism, launched with such daring by the late Edward Said, that critical trajectory has suffered from its focus on a critique of Western thinking rather than on the kind of positive, antithetical knowledge of Islam and the Islamic world for which Said called.[28]

To be sure, courageous journalists and commentators such as Robert Fisk, Tanya Reinhardt, and Dilip Hiro have provided the raw material that historians will need. And historians themselves, such as Rashid Khalidi, have begun writing in a way that brings the real history of Muslims to Western publics, perhaps not with the depth of an Albert Hourani, but quite self-consciously in more accessible ways. At the same time, scholars of Islam, such as John Voll and John Esposito, have sought to provide more secure, general foundations for our understanding of the real makers of the modern Islamic world.

What we need now are more detailed and better-grounded accounts of the thinking and acting of movements generated by the Islamic center that are waging struggles for freedom and democracy in Islamic contexts. The hard work has begun, exemplified by the pioneering study of Rashid Ghannouchi, the formerly exiled Tunisian Islamist activist and "democrat within Islamism," by Azzam Tamimi.[29] Only such detailed and fair-minded assessments of real world Islamists that engage the full complexity of their thinking and the inevitable contradictions and setbacks in their actions can give us the understanding we need of the political imperative of democracy as it expresses itself within the context of an Islamic world view and moral framework.

In addition, we have to avoid the narcissism of looking for ourselves in *their* mirror. Liberal scholars must suspend their endless desire for the emergence of Islamic liberals, saddled with the impossible demand that they speak our language and embrace our Western values as if they have emerged out of our own distinctive historical experiences. This attitude can see Islamic centrists only as second-best stand-ins, thereby ignoring the unique advantages that the Islamic heritage gives these activists and scholars in their struggles for democracy. It is precisely from these differences that we might hope to learn in the spirit of the Qur'anic verse that tells us that God created human diversity precisely so we could "know one another."[30] And what is valuable to know includes our differences alongside appreciation for our common humanity.

The left, for its part, has to let go of its narrow secular fundamentalism and realize that a good deal of what is best in Western secularism – notably a rich conception of reason and rationality – emerges naturally out of the Islamic mainstream, though expressed in a distinct vocabulary with quite different references. Given the limitations of our own democratic experience, wouldn't it be wiser to remain open to the possibility that these distinctions that come from the Islamic world might well enrich our own understanding of ways to build a more fully realized democratic way of life? Religious traditions everywhere have asserted themselves as a creative and dynamic factor that can be turned to negative purposes, as with our own neo-conservatives, as well as progressive ends, as liberation theology in theory and practice has decisively demonstrated. More than ever in our age of globalism, the left will find itself increasingly irrelevant in a world in which political orientations of all types increasingly ground themselves in cultural and religious traditions.

Islamist centrists have taken from their heritage eminently pragmatic conceptions of reason and culture that give wide scope for practical work on behalf of democratic ideas. Do the differences in vocabulary and origins really matter much when there is so much collaborative work to be done in limiting arbitrary power, generating fair and just legal systems, and encouraging meaningful mass participation? Can we in the West, especially in America, really rest on our laurels in any of these battles? Can we afford to remain oblivious to the fact that there are real struggles for freedom and democracy underway in the Islamic world, however they may differ in contextual factors from our own? We need to know more about them.

Notes

1 Carnegie Scholar 2006. The research on which this article is based was made possible (in part) by a grant from Carnegie Corporation of New York. The statements made and views expressed are solely the responsibility of the author.
2 The *Guardian*, January 5, 2007. Haifa Zangana is an Iraqi-born novelist and former prisoner of Saddam's regime.
3 See the insightful study by Mahmood Mamdani of the Cold War origins of the war on terror in *Good Muslim, Bad Muslim*, New York: Pantheon Books, 2004. Mamdani correctly draws a parallel between Islamist radicals who would "forever close the 'gates of ijtihad' and the neo-Reaganite talk of 'good' and 'evil' [that] closes the door to political reform"

(p. 259). But Mamdani's work tells us nothing about the work of those in the Islamic world who resist those calls, often heroically. One of the rare studies that does is A. S. Tamimi, *Rachid Ghannouchi: A Democrat within Islamism*, Oxford: Oxford University Press, 2001.

4 See C. Johnson, *Sorrows of Empire: Militarism, Secrecy and the End of the Republic*, New York: Henry Holt and Company, 2005.

5 Such scholars as Mahmood Mamdani have usefully documented the origins of the intellectual justifications for neo-con militarism in Reagan-era thinking.

6 To be sure, the task of making democracy the handmaiden of an imperial project requires some intellectual effort, notably a radical reduction in its meaning. To function as a justificatory slogan, democracy must be understood in terms of simple, easily manipulated symbols and behaviors. To this end, we are told that democracy is about freedom from the tyrant so that the people can engage in its quintessential act: voting. Tear down the statue of the dictator, raise the ink-stained thumbs, let the free market work its magic, and democracy is at hand! Imperial aims realized, with the new bases and the firm control of the oil industry safely tucked out of view.

7 See L. C. Brown, "The Dream Palace of the Empire: Is Iraq a 'Noble Failure'?" *Foreign Affairs*, September/October 2006.

8 See the apologetic work of Jeanne Kirkpatrick on the difference between malleable, right-wing authoritarian regimes but unchanging totalitarian, communist systems. J. Kirkpatrick, "Dictatorships and Double Standards," *Commentary*, November 1979.

9 One path to aid such a frightening Islamic world is through those cultural hybrids who have escaped it, i.e. Muslims who have found refuge in the West. The assumption is that their interactions with Western cultures will bleach out the worst of Islam's "flaws" – ostensibly its resistance to democracy but in fact its capacity for resistance. (See G. Kepel, *The War for Muslim Minds*, Cambridge: Belnap Press, 2004, especially chapter 7, pp. 241–87.) These Westernized Muslims will provide that "defanged Islam" of which RAND researchers most notoriously dream. Alternatively, and as noted on pp. 41–42, democracy may be brought to the Islamic world more directly and more forcefully on the wings of empire.

10 There are exceptions of course, like the work of G. H. Marshall Hodgson, Roy Mottahedeh, John Esposito, John Voll, and a number of others.

11 See my *Islam without Fear: Egypt and the New Islamists*, Cambridge: Harvard University Press, 2003, for a full-length study of the work of these influential Egyptian Islamist centrists.

12 A. Hamzawy, *The Key to Arab Reform: Moderate Islamists*, Carnegie Endowment Policy Brief 40, 2005. All quotations are from this text.

13 Ibid., p. 4.

14 Ibid., p. 2.

15 S. Zunes, *Tinderbox: U.S. Middle East Policy and the Roots of Terrorism*, Monroe, Maine: Common Courage Press, 2003.

16 Surah 96: 1–5.

17 Qaradawy argued that the Qur'an enjoins man to be independent in thought and to rely on reason in efforts to better the human condition. For the Muslim, "thinking for an hour is better than praying for a whole year." While noting that there were important political and economic reasons for the decline of the great Islamic civilization, Qaradawy stated that the first cause was the failure of the educational system, which did not encourage creative and independent thinking. Qaradawy's address can be found in *al Wafd*, September 13, 1996.

18 For a representative discussion, see Y. al Qaradawy, *Fiqh al Jihad*, vol. II, Cairo: Maktabet Wahba, 2009, where this thinking is elaborated.

19 See the perceptive discussion of creativity in all its dimensions by Kamal Abul Magd in *Iza a wal Television*, March 7, 1992.

20 K. Abul Magd, *A Contemporary Islamic Vision: Statement of Principles*, Cairo: Dar al Sharuq, 1991, p. 13.

21 See B. Moore, Jr., *The Social Origins of Dictatorship and Democracy: Lord and Peasant in the Making of the Modern World*, Boston: Beacon Press, 1966, p. 144.
22 For a detailed treatment of this positive record on behalf of democratic goals, see my *Islam without Fear*, op. cit.
23 See R. Khalidi, *Resurrecting Empire*, Boston: Beacon Press, 2004.
24 J. Dewey, *The Public and Its Problems*, New York: H. Holt and Company, 1927, p. 84.
25 Ibid., pp. 148–49.
26 For a detailed discussion of the Kefaya movement that brings out the role of the *Wassatteyya* activists, see M. Shorbagy, "Understanding Kefaya: The New Politics in Egypt," *Arab Studies Quarterly*, January 2007. For the background and record of activities of the Wassat Party, see *Islam without Fear*, pp. 192–98, 200–10.
27 Both the mainstream and opposition press reported extensively on the Habib statement and the ensuring controversy from January 16–31, 2007. The best general coverage is in *al Masri al Yaum*, while the Wassat party interventions are highlighted in *al Araby*. For a critique of the reporting itself, see Fahmy Huwaidy, *al Ahram*, January 23, 2007.
28 See the discussion in E. Said, *Covering Islam*, New York: Pantheon Books, 1981.
29 A. S. Tamimi, *Rachid Ghannouchi: A Democrat within Islamism*, Oxford: Oxford University Press, 2001.
30 Surah 49: 13.

Bibliography

Abul Magd, K., *A Contemporary Islamic Vision: Statement of Principles*, Cairo: Dar al Sharuq, 1991.

Al Wafd, September 13, 1996.

Baker, R. W., *Islam without Fear: Egypt and the New Islamists*, Cambridge: Harvard University Press, 2006.

Brown, L. C., "The Dream Palace of the Empire: Is Iraq a 'Noble Failure'?" *Foreign Affairs*, September/October 2006.

Dewey, J., *The Public and Its Problems*, New York: Henry Holt and Company, 1927.

Hamzawy, A., *The Key to Arab Reform: Moderate Islamists*, Carnegie Endowment Policy Brief 40, 2005.

Huwaidy, F., *Al Ahram*, January 23, 2007.

Iza a wal Television, March 7, 1992.

Johnson, C., *The Sorrows of Empire: Militarism, Secrecy, and the End of the Republic*, New York: Henry Holt and Company, 2005.

Kepel, G., *The War for Muslim Minds*, Cambridge: Belnap Press, 2004.

Khalidi, R., *Resurrecting Empire*, Boston: Beacon Press, 2004.

Kirkpatrick, J., "Dictatorships and Double Standards," *Commentary*, November 1979.

Mamdani, M., *Good Muslim, Bad Muslim*, New York: Pantheon Books, 2004.

Moore, Jr. B., *The Social Origins of Dictatorship and Democracy: Lord and Peasant in the Making of the Modern World*, Boston: Beacon Press, 1966.

Said, E., *Covering Islam*, New York: Pantheon Books, 1981.

Shorbagy, M., "Understanding Kefaya: The New Politics in Egypt," *Arab Studies Quarterly* 29, 2007.

Tamimi, A. S., *Rachid Ghannouchi: A Democrat within Islamism*, Oxford: Oxford University Press, 2001.Zunes, S., *Tinderbox: U.S. Middle East Policy and the Roots of Terrorism*, Monroe, Maine: Common Courage Press, 2003.

Part II

Case studies: Islamist movements and politics in the Middle East

3

ISLAMIST SOCIAL NETWORKS AND SOCIAL WELFARE SERVICES IN TURKEY

Jenny B. White

Since its founding in 1923, Turkey's militantly secular state has controlled Islamic education and effectively banned religious symbols from the public arena, including universities, the government, and civil service. However, beginning in the 1980s overtly Islamic political parties began to win local and national elections that put them in control of neighborhoods, cities, and eventually parliament. The present government is led by such an Islam-inspired party, the Justice and Development Party (known by its Turkish acronym AKP). There are many reasons for the rise of Islamic parties and Islamic movements in general in the 1980s.[1] I will focus here on the role of networks, particularly women's activism, in their success. I will also discuss the implications network styles have for liberalism and accommodation between Islamic groups and the state.

Political parties of all stripes have used Islamic language and connections to obtain votes since Turkey's first multiparty elections in 1950, and there have been overtly Islamic political parties in Turkey since the 1970s. However, the Turkish electorate as a whole has tended to vote center-right and early Islamic parties represented the interests of relatively small constituencies. The National Order Party under Necmettin Erbakan, for instance, represented provincial businessmen who felt left out of state-subsidized industrialization. A year after it was established, the party was closed down by the Turkish military during the 1971 coup, accused of violating the constitutional separation of politics and religion. This became the pattern as, one after the other, Islam-inspired political parties were closed down by the Constitutional Court or by the military. Erbakan founded the National Salvation Party in 1973, appealing primarily to constituents from the eastern and central Anatolian provinces. The party's message, however, was distinctly more radical and anti-systemic, openly attacking the secular system. That party too was closed down, as were all political parties during the 1980 coup.

In 1983, Erbakan's fortunes began to change when his new Welfare Party (WP) vastly expanded its voter base, appealing to the urban poor, the growing Islamist business community, young professionals with a consciously Islamic identity and doing business on the basis of Islamic principles, and large numbers of conservative women who previously had not been politically active. An Islamist intellectual movement provided ideological input.[2] The urban poor responded to WP's promise of social justice in part because their champion, the Turkish Left, had been decimated by the military after the coup.

The center-right government elected in the first post-coup elections opened Turkey's heavily state-guided economic system to global competition. Economic liberalization put money and increasing influence into the hands of conservative businessmen, who organized themselves into civic and Islamic organizations and began to pour money into politics, education, and the media.[3] Networks of politically engaged conservative businessmen and industrialists created and supported charitable organizations, funded scholarships, gender-segregated dormitories, and professional certification programs open to both men and women. The followers of the preacher Fethullah Gülen, for instance, pumped money into education by opening schools (with mostly non-religious curricula) both in Turkey and abroad, and into television, radio, and print media.[4] Wealthy and middle-class conservative men and women became increasingly visible in the streets of major cities and in the media. This created a popular image of an upwardly mobile devout population that the press called the new Islamic bourgeoisie and that increased their social capital and attracted professionals, intellectuals, and large numbers of women who aspired to be what was called "the new Islamic woman."[5]

The fortunes of the Islamists, that is, devout Muslims active in politics on the basis of their religious ideology, began to change in the 1990s. Although Islamist parties regularly were accused of undermining the secular nature of the state and closed down, they reemerged strengthened on the political playing field. In the 1994 local elections, WP doubled its 1989 votes, capturing almost half of the mayoral seats in provincial capitals and six of Turkey's 15 largest cities, including Istanbul and the capital Ankara. It is important to remember, however, that the center right won twice as many votes (42 percent compared to WP's 19 percent), but their vote was split between a number of parties. In the 1995 parliamentary elections WP won the largest number of seats (158 of 550), with 21 percent of the vote. WP was closed down in 1998, replaced by the Virtue Party (VP, closed in 2001), then by the Justice and Development Party (AKP).[6]

In 2002, the AKP came to power as a single-party government with only weak opposition in parliament and since then it has consolidated its power. The AKP is led by Recep Tayyip Erdogan, who displaced Erbakan as leader of the political Islamic movement and has moved the party's platform away from Islam and toward liberal democracy.

The key to the success of these Islamic parties was not religious radicalism. In a poll 41 percent of those who voted for WP defined themselves as secular,[7] and WP election propaganda avoided religious themes and images.[8] Contextual factors played an important role. In some ways, a vote for WP was a protest vote against the corruption and ineffectualness of the secular parties that had been in power. The new economy had led to rising and more visible inequality, and the Islamists talked about local economic injustice while other parties focused on more global issues. The media had been de facto deregulated as a result of cable and satellite availability. This led to more open discussion of religious issues and even the possibility of Islamic law, which previously had been forbidden. The government had relaxed rules about religious discussion in the 1980s in order to counter the influence of leftist ideologies.

A major reason for the success of WP (and, after it, VP and AKP), however, was its style of mobilizing supporters. The party perfected a face-to-face, personalized style of mobilizing "cells" of neighbors on the basis of local solidarities. In other words, in addition to the business-as-usual patron–client relations common to all political parties in Turkey, WP relied on networks and horizontal relations, that is, relations among neighbors. These personal networks were mediated by a system of associations, foundations, and informal organizations formally unconnected to a party. This formal disconnection from the party apparatus allowed activists to perceive themselves as part of a social movement, rather than as working for a particular party. It also allowed the system to continue to accumulate support even when a party was closed down. The networks made the Islamist movement independent of the party and encouraged the enthusiasm of activists, who saw this as "their" social movement.

Islamist activists were highly organized. Computerized lists and maps were maintained of all neighborhoods, with a neighborhood management commission and a party-assigned head observer who was responsible for about 300 people in a voting district. Under the head observer were additional observers, one for every 75 people. These activists were local people, living on the same street, sometimes one per street, and in effect created a continual interface between residents and the party. Whether or not the activists provided services in the name of the party, it was known that they were party members and credit for their neighborly assistance was informally attributed to the party. This seamless interface between party and people contrasted with the approach of secular parties that tended to assign party representatives to voting districts only around election time.

Male and female versions of this structure operated in tandem, with women interacting only with women. Male activists visited homes on weekends, when the men would be home, and women visited during the week, when generally only women were home. All the families in a district would be contacted and their concerns noted. They were told that the party wanted to help establish a community and to extend help, both material and moral.[9] Detailed computer records were kept that could be called up in the capital. Specific needs were relayed to local Islamic foundations that could call upon Islamic businesses or the municipality run by an Islamist party to ask for whatever was needed, whether food, coal, or a job. In 1986 WP established the first women's branches, but none of these segments – activists, women's branches, foundations, municipality – were formally connected. The system operated in some ways like the old Chicago or New York ward politics, but without the explicit link to the party, except through the municipality itself. If the party was closed down, the networks continued to operate.

The activists' job was to keep track of people's needs. They sent holidays cards, took care of the ill, organized weddings and funerals. The party would even help find a spouse, come up with a dowry, arrange childcare, and mediate in a marriage. People were given assistance whether or not they joined the party and whether or not the women covered their heads. In her book on Islamist women, Yeşim Arat discusses a strategy whereby Islamist women would target secular women in their area by offering guidance setting up the religious ceremonies required for life-cycle events. The activists hoped their offer of such needed expertise would result in an emotional link to the women that would reap political benefits down the road. Female activists also attended ladies' circles, savings clubs, and religious ceremonies like holiday Quran readings and funerals. In more elite neighborhoods, Islamist women would hold fashion shows of Islamic clothing in upscale locations.[10]

In this way, Islamic parties were able to mobilize large numbers of conservative women previously believed to be politically disengaged. The activities of these women are widely considered to be a major factor in the success of Islamist parties in the 1990s. Between 1995 and 1997 the women's branches in Istanbul alone recruited 219,601 new members, held 3,465 educational seminars and 1,572 conferences, and organized 14,231 home chats and 156,415 person-to-person talks, 18,628 tea chats, 22,460 complete neighborhood canvasses, 12,325 hospital visits, 2,656 weddings, and 750 engagements and circumcisions. They made 4,215 condolence visits, visited 3,740 newborns, 6,325 artisans, and 12,625 sick people. This is only a partial list of their activities.[11]

The cultural framework for such practices was *imece*, a tradition of collaboration and mutual assistance, much like barn-raising in the rural United States, where the community pitches in to help its members. In *imece*, the community is responsible for its individual members and debt is never reckoned. Thus, what Islamist activists did seemed less like party mobilizing and more like ideal communal and familial practice. The line between politics and social practice was further obscured by the fact that when activists visited homes they rarely engaged in overt political discourse, but rather brought up subjects that concerned the women (inflation, the price of food, and schooling for less well-off families; for wealthier families, the issues would be morality, alcoholism, prostitution, the corruption of national culture by westernization). The ultimate aim was to make or reinforce an emotional connection modeled on familial relations that would come to the credit of the Islamist movement and the party. Arat points out that the Islamist women were not making the personal political, but rather locating women's material concerns that were political in nature and transferring them into an explicitly political domain.[12]

With regard to actual material support, in my observations of Islamist network support activities in Istanbul in the 1990s, I concluded that the amount of assistance given to poor families was minimal.[13] In order to get used clothing, for instance, a family was required to get a certificate of poverty from the local headman (*muhtar*) and then was allowed to get used clothing or furniture only once. The foundation head explained to me that it was more desirable to help families become self-sufficient by finding the husband employment, rather than by allowing them to become dependent on charity. The only exceptions were widows and elderly women with no male family members, who were given continual assistance until a sponsor was found. Also, poverty was so widespread that the resources available to the activists were dwarfed by the needs of the population.

Nevertheless, unlike other parties, WP, VP, and later AKP were perceived by the population to be greatly supportive. Indeed, opposition parties accused them of using their services to buy votes. I believe this impression of largesse is due in part to the manner in which assistance was given through familial and neighborly *imece* connections, rather than overtly through the party. In other words, the party received credit even for acts of mutual assistance that would have occurred anyway between members of a community.

Implications for rights and interaction with the state

Since the 1980s, Islamist activism has engaged an entire new segment of the population, devout conservative men and women, with the state, beginning a process of mutual transformation. Over time, Islam-inspired parties have become more moderate, moving from Erbakan's radical ideological Islamism of the 1980s to AKP's devout social conservatism and liberal democratic reform agenda. Currently, AKP's agenda and discourse overlap to a large extent with those of secularists who wish to use reforms to curb the Turkish state's authoritarianism.[14] In its nine years in power, AKP has pushed through a raft of reforms to bring Turkey's laws and social and economic structures in line with those of the European Union as part of its accession process. For instance, the AKP government has greatly expanded women's rights and protections[15] and liberalized laws dealing with ethnic and religious minority rights, leading to friction with secular nationalists. The AKP gambit is to transform the state and its institutions into a liberal democracy based on individual rights. Potentially this would allow women to choose to cover their heads in public institutions like universities and parliament, where the practice is banned, with no interference from the state.

Despite these reforms, however, conservative discourse flips back and forth between reference to universal rights and community rights.[16] These are quite different in their implications, since rights given to community members are conditional upon their being bona fide members in good standing. In other words, in order to be a community member worthy of receiving support, one must conform to certain basic moral and behavioral ideals. This has implications for women in the party and the community.

Activist women I interviewed in the 1990s assumed that once the party was in power they would be given official status and authority. They have been disappointed. Although the AKP has sponsored more women for parliament than other parties, in interviews in the 2000s women activists and elite women Islamists complained to me that they continued to hit a glass ceiling. The liberal convictions that drove many of the Islamist women activists in the 1990s were contradicted by the communalist and patriarchal views of male activists, who were able to use Islam to buttress their exclusionary claims.[17] The informal and complementary structure of women's networking, while feeding into the parties' success, at the same time undermined women's claim to equality within the party. In some cases, women's political activism did enhance their autonomy in the home,[18] but in my observations activism more often seemed a temporary phenomenon, especially for poorer women. Political activism was part of the life cycle, with women drawn back into the patriarchal family system, with its relative lack of mobility and autonomy, when they married or bore a child. Conservative women's political engagement also was a regional phenomenon. Outside the big cities, particularly in the eastern provinces, women's activism was negligible because they were unable to move outside their home without male accompaniment.[19]

Berna Turam, in her study of the Gülen movement, an influential moderate Islamic movement of mostly middle-class membership, concludes that, despite their progressive discourse, the Islamists' aim has been to incorporate women into the public sphere without actually intending to empower them.[20]

Since 2002, political Islam has given way to powerful social and economic networks of pious Muslims that are ambiguously institutionalized. The Gülen movement, for instance, takes the form of independent foundations that do not appear to be Islam-related and, since they are foundations, do not have members. Gülenists claim to have no political or even Islamic agenda; rather they focus on education, job training, and business networks. The AKP has consolidated its networks along party lines so that wealth created through party policies flows to its members. Women are visible "in the shop window," as some observers have put it, but play almost no role in central decision-making or wealth accumulation in these networks. This mirrors women's minimal representation in political office and women's very low 24 percent participation rate in the labor market in 2009, down from 34 percent a decade earlier.[21]

Furthermore, with the rise of an Islamic bourgeoisie, Islam has been privatized as a personal expression of identity (Muslimhood in place of Islamism) and commercialized as a middle-class lifestyle, with pious gated communities and runway fashion shows of the latest modest (and not so modest) styles. Despite accusations by secularists that the headscarf is a political symbol, recent developments instead have depoliticized it. A middle-class veiling style (*tesettür*) has come to mean being (or looking) urban, modern, and upwardly mobile. These days, elite pious women, like their secular counterparts, are charged with reproducing their family's class status by furnishing their houses and arranging family activities in a way that exhibits proper middle-class taste and style.[22]

Paradoxically, the secularization of political Islam has been bad news for pious women, who had been in the forefront of political activism when an Islamist agenda was front and center, but have been silenced and sidelined in terms of decision-making and authority in the "non-Islamic" AKP and the "non-political" Gülen movement. The Islamist movement of the 1980s and 1990s gave women a cover for leaving their domestic roles, getting out the vote for religious (Islamic) freedom of thought and practice, and working for an Islamist party. Lara Deeb's discussion of Shi'i women's expressions of public piety in Beirut's southern suburbs and their prominent activism in Hizbullah's Women's Committee makes an interesting comparison.[23] It may well be that Hizbullah's embattled role and revolutionary structure allow (and need) women's activism, much as Turkey's Islamist parties did in the 1990s. It remains to be seen whether Hizbullah women retain their role in decision-making structures if the party ever loses its revolutionary function and consolidates its power within mainstream Lebanese politics.

Clark and Schwedler point out that women's participation within Jordan's Islamic Action Front party and Yemen's Islah party increased in the 1990s, when intraparty disputes or external challenges opened windows of opportunity for women, but then often decreased when those disputes were resolved. Neither party had policies for advancing women within the party, and support from male leaders for women's initiatives was inconsistent. Despite social liberalization and women's increasing participation in civil society in Lebanon and Yemen, neither Islamist party supported women's activism and instead they continued to criticize and slander women in prominent political positions.

Conclusion

Islamist success in Turkey is less a triumph of Islamic ideology or religious affiliation than a result of strategies of mobilization that relied on face-to-face networking, in effect mobilizing one person at a time. This occurred within a cultural framework that allowed the party to take credit for mutual assistance activities even if these were not initiated by the party. Assistance was couched in familial and community terms, even though behind the scenes it was highly organized. Lack of obvious links between activists and the party and lack of an overtly political message in personalized interactions further disguised the political nature of the interactions. Women activists were central in using these tactics to bring the Islamists to power.

Islamist political success has brought a mutual accommodation between Islamic conservatives and the state, in part through shared agendas with other sectors of the population, in part through an intensified civil society. The pragmatism of rule has moderated the ideological impetus of the movement away from systemic change and toward what one might call a creeping conservatism. Women are still highly visible symbols of Islamic success and remain in the public arena to mobilize followers. However, the pious community's emphasis on conservative communal and gender values, buttressed by patriarchal interpretations in Islam and by similar gender expectations in secular Turkish society, has hindered women's participation in the success of their movement on both a personal and political level. It has kept women out of positions of authority except within their own complementary female networks. As Islamist parties consolidate power and are absorbed into the male-dominated political system, women's revolutionary role in public mobilization becomes less important and is replaced by their visibility "in the shop window" as emblems of national or party virtues and middle-class values.

Notes

1 J. White, *Islamist Mobilization in Turkey: A Study in Vernacular Politics*, Seattle: University of Washington Press, 2002.

2 M. Meeker, "The New Muslim Intellectuals in the Republic of Turkey," in R. Tapper (ed.) *Islam in Modern Turkey: Religion, Politics and Literature in a Secular State*, London: I. B. Tauris, 1991, pp. 223–53.

3 H. Gülalp, "Globalization and Political Islam: The Social Base of Turkey's Welfare Party," *International Journal of Middle East Studies* 33 (3), 2001, 433–48.
4 H. M. Yavuz and J. L. Esposito (eds.), *Turkish Islam and the Secular State*, Syracuse, NY: Syracuse University Press, 2003.
5 A. Saktanber, "'We Pray Like You Have Fun': New Islamic Youth in Turkey between Intellectualism and Popular Culture," in D. Kandiyoti and A. Saktanber (eds.) *Fragments of Culture: The Everyday of Modern Turkey*, London: I. B. Tauris, 2002, pp. 254–76.
6 H. Gülalp, "Political Islam in Turkey: The Rise and Fall of the Refah Party," *The Muslim World* 89, 1999, 22–41.
7 F. Kentel, "L'Islam, carrefour des identités sociales et culturelles en Turquie: Le Cas de Parti de la Prospérité," *Cahiers d'études sur la Méditéranée orientale et le monde turco-iranien (CEMOTI)* 19, January–June 1995, 211–27. See also the survey by A. Carkoğlu and B. Toprak, *Türkiye'de Din, Toplum ve Siyaset*, Istanbul: Türkiye Ekonomik ve Sosyal Etüdler Vakfi, 2000.
8 A. Öncü, "Packaging Islam: Cultural Politics on the Landscape of Turkish Commercial Television," *Public Culture* 8, 1995, 51–71.
9 Y. Arat, *Rethinking Islam and Liberal Democracy: Islamist Women in Turkish Politics*, Albany: SUNY Press, 2005, p. 81.
10 Ibid.
11 Ibid., p. 73.
12 Ibid., pp. 81, 83.
13 White, op. cit., 2002.
14 B. Turam, *Between Islam and the State: The Politics of Engagement*, Stanford: Stanford University Press, 2007, p. 31.
15 European Stability Initiative (ESI), "Sex and Power in Turkey: Feminism, Islam and the Maturing of Turkish Democracy," Berlin/Istanbul, June 2, 2007.
16 J. White, "The Islamist Movement in Turkey and Human Rights," *Human Rights Review* 3, 2001, 17–26.
17 Arat, op. cit., p. 114.
18 Arat, op. cit., p. 133.
19 Arat, op. cit., p. 88.
20 Turam, op. cit., pp. 14–15.
21 World Bank and Turkish State Prime Ministry, "Female Labor Force Participation in Turkey: Trends, Determinants and Policy Framework," Washington, DC, 2009.
22 S. Ayata, "The New Middle Class and the Joys of Suburbia," in D. Kandiyoti and A. Saktanber (eds.) *Fragments of Culture*, London: I. B. Tauris, 2002, pp. 25–42.
23 L. Deeb, *An Enchanted Modern: Gender and Public Piety in Shi'i Lebanon*, Princeton: Princeton University Press, 2006.

Bibliography

Arat, Y., *Rethinking Islam and Liberal Democracy: Islamist Women in Turkish Politics*, Albany: SUNY Press, 2005.

Ayata, S., "The New Middle Class and the Joys of Suburbia," in D. Kandiyoti and A. Saktanber (eds.) *Fragments of Culture*, London: I. B. Tauris, 2002, pp. 25–42.

Çarkoğlu, A. and Toprak, B., *Türkiye'de Din, Toplum ve Siyaset*, Istanbul: Türkiye Ekonomik ve Sosyal Etüdler Vakfi, 2000.

Deeb, L., *An Enchanted Modern: Gender and Public Piety in Shi'i Lebanon*, Princeton: Princeton University Press, 2006.

European Stability Initiative (ESI), "Sex and Power in Turkey: Feminism, Islam and the Maturing of Turkish Democracy," Berlin/Istanbul, June 2, 2007.

Gülalp, H., "Globalization and Political Islam: The Social Base of Turkey's Welfare Party," *International Journal of Middle East Studies* 33, 2001, 433–48.

Gülalp, H., "Political Islam in Turkey: The Rise and Fall of the Refah Party," *The Muslim World* 89, 1999, 22–41.

Kentel, F., "L'Islam, carrefour des identités sociales et culturelles en Turquie: Le Cas de Parti de la Prospérité," *Cahiers d'études sur la Méditéranée orientale et le monde turco-iranien (CEMOTI)* 19, 1995, 211–27.

Meeker, M., "The New Muslim Intellectuals in the Republic of Turkey," in R. Tapper (ed.) *Islam in Modern Turkey: Religion, Politics and Literature in a Secular State*, London: I. B. Tauris, 1991, pp. 223–53.

Öncü, A., "Packaging Islam: Cultural Politics on the Landscape of Turkish Commercial Television," *Public Culture* 8, 1995, 51–71.

Saktanber, Ayşe, "'We Pray Like You Have Fun': New Islamic Youth in Turkey between Intellectualism and Popular Culture," in D. Kandiyoti and A. Saktanber (eds.) *Fragments of Culture: The Everyday of Modern Turkey*, London: I. B. Tauris, 2002, pp. 254–76.

Turam, B., *Between Islam and the State: The Politics of Engagement*, Stanford: Stanford University Press, 2007.

White, J. B., *Islamist Mobilization in Turkey: A Study in Vernacular Politics*, Seattle: University of Washington Press, 2002.

White, J. B., "The Islamist Movement in Turkey and Human Rights," *Human Rights Review* 3, 2001, 17–26.

World Bank and Turkish State Prime Ministry, "Female Labor Force Participation in Turkey: Trends, Determinants and Policy Framework," Washington, DC, 2009.

Yavuz, H. M. and Esposito, J. L. (eds.), *Turkish Islam and the Secular State*, Syracuse, NY: Syracuse University Press, 2003.

4

PATRONAGE, PRESTIGE, AND POWER

The Islamic Center Charity Society's political role within the Muslim Brotherhood

Janine Astrid Clark

In July 2006, in response to growing political tensions between the Muslim Brotherhood (MB) and the Jordanian regime, the Jordanian Ministry of Social Development (MOSD) and the Audit Bureau released a 1,700 page report detailing cases of financial corruption in the Islamic Center Charity Society (ICCS), the charity organization of the Jordanian MB. Citing issues ranging from the purchase of improper and overpriced equipment for the Islamic Hospital to the improper issuance of loans and hiring of consultants, the report was sent to the prosecutor general for review. The prosecutor general took swift action, freezing all the assets of the ICCS.[1] Shortly thereafter, the government appointed a committee to take over and run the affairs of the ICCS; it remains in control today. Well versed in the use of patronage to ensure political support, the government struck where it knew it would hurt the MB the most – its economic wing and source of patronage, employment, and recruitment. The government's actions against the ICCS brought the issue of extensive patronage within the ICCS into the glaring public light. While a growing body of literature has examined Islamic social-welfare institutions, few scholars have looked at the political significance of the patronage associated with Islamic social-welfare institutions.[2] What role did patronage play in the ICCS prior to its takeover? How did patronage impact the political leadership of the ICCS and the ICCS' role within the MB? Most importantly, what can the examination of patronage within the ICCS reveal about the role of individual and material interests in the decision-making processes of Islamist movements?

The ICCS offers a rare opportunity to examine an Islamic social-welfare institution from the perspective of its influence and role within the decision-making processes of an Islamist movement as a whole, in this case the Muslim Brotherhood. The ICCS is a legal entity and, unlike the social-welfare institutions of Hizbullah, for example, its leadership is elected (at least until 2006, when they were suspended) through public and transparent elections that are reported in the press. Based on interviews and archival research, this chapter argues that extensive networks of patronage were affiliated with the ICCS, granting the institution considerable political weight within the MB. The ICCS was more than just a turf over which different factions within the MB fought for control. Rather, a director's position within the ICCS or any of its associated projects was a source of prestige, authority, and patronage which directors could disperse to friends and family. Whoever controlled the ICCS gained all three and could translate these into a position in the MB or IAF respective *Shura* or executive councils and the consequent ability to wield influence within the MB/IAF. Even if an ICCS director did not hold a position within the MB or IAF's executive councils, he still wielded the ability to bring vast resources and networks of patronage to the table and therefore was a desired coalition partner for other internal factions. Just as importantly, the ICCS was a relatively independent power base from which a director, independently elected and representing a large and economically powerful institution, could voice his opinions, even those critical of the MB itself. For these reasons, the most contested elections within the MB prior to 2006 tended to be for the leadership of the executive boards of the ICCS institutions.

The field research for this study was conducted between 1996 and 2008.[3] In addition to its main headquarters, the author visited a total of fourteen ICCS branches, centers, and services or projects located in six different governorates. The selection of interview sites was controlled for size and location, including a balance between urban and rural locations, sites dominated by Jordanians of Jordanian descent and those of Palestinian descent, and those reflecting varying degrees of affluence. The author also interviewed government officials, journalists, and the leadership of the other non-governmental organizations familiar with the ICCS.

In order to situate the phenomenon of Islamism and social welfare within a broader context, the chapter begins by asking why the provision of social welfare appears to be central to Islamist political movements wherever they are found and regardless of to whom they are directed. After providing the historical background to the MB in Jordan, it then examines the ICCS in depth, its establishment, services, employment, and patronage. This discussion is followed by a look at recent elections in the ICCS. The chapter concludes with a discussion of the broader significance of the argument.

Why social welfare?

Whether the MB in Jordan, Hamas in Gaza, or Hizbullah in Lebanon, Islamist movements tend to be multi-faceted social movements with political, economic, and social activities. In almost all cases, Islamist movements began with a focus on social-welfare activities – concrete activities to address the needs of their surrounding populations. The centrality of social welfare provision to the appeal, popularity, and ethos of Islamist political movements lies in the indisputable importance of giving or assisting those less fortunate in Islam, the symbolic nature of these services in addressing issues of social justice that governments cannot or will not address, the activist element of social-welfare provision – putting Islam as a solution into practice – and, simultaneously, the seemingly apolitical nature of charity.

Social-welfare services offer Islamist movements several advantages, making them in many cases a higher priority than other services or institutions. The first of these is that charity, in the form of *zakat* (a form of tithe), and other types of donations, such as *sadaqa*, a voluntary form of social or financial assistance, are an important aspect of Islam. Serving the needy as an act of worship is a central belief in Islam. *Zakat* is one of the pillars of Islam and many Muslims, even non-practicing Muslims, regularly express their religiosity through charitable donations or volunteer efforts in a charity, particularly during Ramadan. Closely related to this point is the fact that charitable giving provides an agreed-upon "common denominator" – regardless of sect or interpretation of Islam, charitable giving is indisputable and not subject to differences of opinion in jurisprudence as to its practice. Charitable giving thus offers an easy and natural "entry point" for people into Islamist social-welfare institutions.

Politically, social-welfare institutions offer Islamists the opportunity to "activate" Islam. Within the Islamist worldview is an understanding of Islam as a comprehensive system encompassing all things material, spiritual, societal, individual, political, and personal. The Islamist project, therefore, is an attempt to create a seemingly seamless web between religion, politics, charity, and all forms of activism.[4] In this conceptualization, working for a charity, as does working for politics, becomes working for Islam. Indeed, it becomes incumbent upon Muslims to do so. As Islamist institutions, therefore, one of the intentions of social-welfare institutions is to activate or apply Islam, and working or volunteering for or donating to an Islamic social-welfare institution becomes a form of activism that is visible and can be emulated by everyone.

Islamic social-welfare institutions furthermore represent a concrete response to their governments' apparent neglect of the social welfare of those suffering under the negative impact of structural adjustment programs, austerity measures, and neo-liberal economic policies. In contrast to the withdrawal of the state, Islamic social-welfare institutions embody and politicize the principles of social justice so essential in Islam. An integral aspect of Islamist identity is the creation of alternative institutions to those of the state. In this regard, Islamic social-welfare institutions represent the foundations of an alternative society. They represent an ideological and practical alternative to the present system. Indeed, they are that ideology put into practice and central to the Islamist vision of a new society and Islamist identity.[5]

At the same time, within authoritarian states where Islamists may not be able to freely organize, Islamist social-welfare institutions are particularly important to the Islamist project due to their technically apolitical nature.[6] Donating to or working in an Islamic social-welfare institution are not in and of themselves political acts. Rather, the degree to which these acts are political largely depends on the degree of political significance each person attributes to his/her actions. While the acts of those who donate money or volunteer their time in an Islamic social-welfare institution may appear relatively similar, the meaning the donor or the volunteer attributes to their involvement may be significantly different. It may be a simple act of charity, a conscious effort to apply Islam to all aspects of one's life, or an act in opposition to the state by contributing towards the viability and superiority of the Islamic alternative. None of these acts requires that individuals state their political positions publicly. In the context of predominantly authoritarian regimes in the region, the ability of individuals to participate in activities without having to explicitly reveal their political views is crucial to the success of the institution, in this case the ICCS, in terms of its stated aims and goals, and to the recruitment process of the movement of which it is part.

Finally, as demonstrated on pp. 73–75, Islamic social-welfare institutions offer Islamist movements the opportunity to address the needs of the middle class – the backbone of political Islamism. While the ethos of social-welfare institutions may be to provide for the poor, they simultaneously offer jobs and services to the middle-class supporters of the movement, including its leadership.

The MB in Jordan

The government's freezing of the ICCS' substantial assets came amidst heightened security concerns in Jordan. That the MB became one of the primary targets of the security-conscious regime was a result not only of international and domestic events leading up to the prosecutor general's release of the report but also of the change in relations between the MB and the regime beginning in the mid-1990s. The report came at a time when MB relations with the regime had entered their most strained period historically. Little has changed today.

The MB in Jordan was established in 1945 by Haj 'Abd al-Latif Abu Qura, a Jordanian merchant who established the Jordanian MB after visiting the founder of the Egyptian MB, Hassan al-Banna, in Egypt.[7] The MB's initial activities focused on religious education and as early as the 1950s it began establishing its own schools. It soon also developed a political focus, and after the 1948 war with Israel began demanding the implementation of Islamic law (*shari'a*). Despite its overt politicization, both Jordan's first king, King Abdullah I (1921–51), and King Hussein (1953–99)[8] allowed the MB to survive and even flourish under Jordan's martial law (1957–89).[9] In return, the MB refrained from criticizing the monarchy or political system directly and largely limited itself to criticizing policies. In 1963, the MB established the ICCS in order to more effectively administer its growing number of charity activities. At the same time, it was active in professional association and labor union elections. In 1992, after King Hussein liberalized the country politically and re-introduced national elections, the MB formalized its political efforts and established the Islamic Action Front (IAF), an umbrella party of MB together with independent Islamists.[10] These institutions, the ICCS and the IAF, are the two primary organizations with which the MB formally engages with the Jordanian public. In addition, individuals representing the MB (often in the form of an Islamic list) continue to run in professional association and university council elections. The ICCS, the IAF, and their mother organization, the MB, are administratively and financially separate. Each has (or, in the case of the ICCS, had) their own elections, executive councils, and revenues. However, the memberships of all three overlap significantly, with familiar faces represented on two and, prior to 2006, potentially all three of their general assemblies and/or *Shura* (consultative) councils.

Political liberalization has served the MB well. Largely as a result of the deep social roots it planted prior to 1989, the ICCS remains one of the largest non-governmental organizations (NGOs) in the country and the largest Islamic NGO. Only the royal NGOs, those established by individual members of the royal family, rival it in size and budget.[11] Since 1989, Islamists' electoral success in the country's professional associations and university student councils has skyrocketed.[12] And the IAF consistently wins the largest number of seats of any political party in national elections. In 1989, MB candidates (running as independents, as political parties were still banned at the time) won 22 seats.[13] In 1993, a new national electoral law came into being that (not coincidentally) is biased against urban areas, the stronghold of political parties, and towards rural, tribal independents – the backbone of monarchical support.[14] Despite the new law (still in existence today), the newly created IAF won 16 seats in the 1993 and 17 seats in the 2003 parliamentary elections.[15] In 2007, however, the IAF dropped down to 6 seats.[16]

Beginning in the mid-1990s, MB–regime relations began to change. As they were armed with greater freedom of speech, an increasing number of political clashes developed between the two. The onset of these political tensions largely began with the MB's vehement opposition to Jordan's peace treaty with Israel, signed in 1994. With the Islamists leading an opposition that represented the entire political spectrum, the streets of Jordan witnessed increasingly large and violent demonstrations in protest against the treaty and the normalization of relations with Israel.[17] These demonstrations only intensified after September 11, 2001, in protest against American and Israeli policies and practices in Palestine, and American actions in Afghanistan and Iraq as part of the war on terror – and, most importantly, against Jordan's relations with, if not support for, these two states.

In response to the growing political instability, the regime and government resorted to greater authoritarian measures to silence critical voices. The abovementioned new electoral law is a case in point. It was designed expressly to hurt the IAF at the polls in order to ensure a compliant parliament – one that would approve the peace treaty with Israel. Similarly, among other measures, greater restrictions were imposed upon mosques, demonstrations, and the press. In 2001, King Abdullah II (1999–) suspended parliament and postponed the then upcoming November elections until June 2003.

Following 2003 and the resumption of parliament, Jordan's streets witnessed fewer and smaller demonstrations; however, international events and the regime's responses to them continued to fuel friction between the regime and the MB.[18] More to the point, the regime increasingly began to view the MB as a security threat.[19] Security fears have increased dramatically in the Kingdom due to a series of events, the most deadly of which was in November 2005 when suicide bombers simultaneously attacked three hotels in Amman, killing 60 people and injuring over 100. Prominent al-Qaeda leader Abu Musab al-Zarqawi was identified as the mastermind behind the attacks. In the new security-conscious environment, Hamas' victory at the polls in the Palestinian Authority elections a few months later triggered a fear of the "Hamasization" of the MB/IAF.[20] It was no coincidence that shortly thereafter, prior to the IAF and MB elections (in February and March of the same year, respectively), an article appeared in the government-controlled *al-Ra'y* newspaper with the headline "Is it true that Hamas will appoint the new Secretary General of the Islamic Action

Front?"[21] The government hoped to prevent Hamas doing this and the article appeared to be an attempt to make sure it didn't. In April 2006, tensions were further raised when Jordanian security forces announced the discovery of a large cache of hidden weapons and arrested 10 Hamas members for allegedly targeting sites throughout the Kingdom.[22] The final event that appears to have been the straw that broke the camel's back occurred in June 2006, following the killing of al-Zarqawi by coalition forces in Iraq. Four IAF members of parliament visited the family home of al-Zarqawi in the Jordanian city of Zarka to express their condolences. All four were immediately arrested for fueling national discord and inciting sectarianism under Jordan's penal code.[23]

The four members' actions triggered a series of unprecedented spontaneous pro-government demonstrations in support of the families of the victims of Amman's hotel bombings and against the actions of the MPs. Reflecting popular sentiment, the speaker of the parliament also demanded an official apology from the IAF to the people of Jordan and a clarification of its allegiance to the country and to the Hashemite monarchy (among other issues). The IAF refused. Seizing a moment of popular discontent with the MB, the government took aim at the MB's ICCS.[24]

Indeed, the ICCS soon came to lie at the heart of the struggle between the regime and the MB – with the MB at a decided disadvantage. Less than one month after the arrest of the four members, the report was sent to the prosecutor general.[25] On July 10, 2006, the ICCS board was suspended and a seven-member temporary committee was appointed to run the ICCS.[26] The general manager of the Islamic Hospital was removed and, approximately one year later, the temporary committee dissolved the elected board of the Islamic Hospital in Amman.[27] The 14 members who were identified in the prosecutor general's report were eventually brought in for questioning. The ICCS accused the government of political motivation, arguing that all issues of corruption either were false or were minor offences that had already been dealt with internally.[28] Charges against all 14 members of the ICCS mentioned in the report were dismissed for lack of evidence.[29] Today the administration of both the ICCS and the Islamic Hospital continues to lie in the hands of government-appointed committees.[30] Furthermore, the MB accuses the government of recruiting large numbers of new members to the ICCS' General Assembly, raising the membership from 350 to over 700.[31] While the government and some members of the temporary committee have argued that as it is a general assembly anyone in society may join it, the MB accuses the government of attempting to take control of the ICCS by recruiting hundreds of people close to the government into the General Assembly.[32] It furthermore accuses the government of attempting to change the structure of the ICCS.[33] Since the takeover, no meetings of the General Assembly have been called and ICCS elections (which would normally have been held at the end of 2007) have not been held.[34]

The ICCS and the middle class[35]

The ICCS is a nationally registered NGO with its headquarters located in Amman, close to the headquarters of the MB, and with branches and centers throughout the country. In total, it runs four branches, located in Zarka, Mafraq, Irbid, and Ramtha, and 55 centers. According to its website, the goals of the ICCS are fourfold: education and teaching, through the establishment of schools, kindergartens, and other educational organizations; medical and health care, through its hospitals and medical centers; productive and training projects to serve local communities; and financial aid to poor families and orphans.[36] Accordingly, within its centers the ICCS runs 2 hospitals, 15 medical clinics, 1 college, and 28 schools. The most important of these are the Islamic Hospital in Amman and the (smaller) Islamic Hospital in Aqaba, the al-Arqam school system, and the Islamic College in Zarka.

Established in 1982, the Islamic Hospital in Amman is one of the best in the country and has played a pioneering role in several areas of medical care. According to the Hospital's website, between 1982 and 2000 the number of patients admitted was 298,2931.[37] During the same period the total number of surgeries performed reached 127,151. The ICCS' Fund for the Sick and Poor, a fund providing subsidies to poor patients to offset the costs of their treatments at the Islamic Hospital, has assisted 58,056 medical cases to the tune of 5,738,197 JD since the Hospital's establishment in 2006.[38] The ICCS' medical clinics received 153,819 patients in 2005 alone and its schools had 12,062 registered students.[39] The Islamic College has approximately an additional 1,000 students.

The budget of the ICCS is commensurately large. In 2004–05, the budget was over 1 billion JD.[40] This amounted to approximately 1.4 billion US$ at the time.[41] Its expenses included 9,880,000 JD spent on services and items for the poor, 2,100,000 JD and 815,000 JD on orphans and poor families, respectively (both of which receive financial support on a monthly basis), and 100,000 JD distributed to 880 university students to help cover their educational fees.[42] One report puts the total amount dispersed by the ICCS in 2005 on scholarships, treatment bills, and other grants to its members and supporters at approximately 9,900,000 JD.[43]

A closer examination of the ICCS facilities and services reveals that, while catering to Jordan's poor, the ICCS also offers a second type of service that is directed towards the country's fee-paying middle class. Both services, furthermore, are provided by the professional middle class. Since its establishment, the MB predominantly has been a movement of the professional middle class, with the profile of the MB's membership today looking remarkably similar to that of approximately 60 years ago.[44] The composition of the members of the IAF's Founding Committee broken down according to profession, for example, reveals that a high percentage of members are white-collar professionals. Of the 353 founding members, 37.7 percent were professionals.[45] Twenty-four were university professors, 26 physicians, 22 engineers, 16 pharmacists, 25 lawyers, 17 managers, and 3 journalists.[46] The ICCS services thus address the needs of the MB's constituency. It offers services, employment, and patronage to Jordan's middle class, as a means to ensure both the functioning of the ICCS (securing donors and doctors, for example) and that the instrumental needs of the Islamist movement – the dissemination of the Islamist message and recruitment to the movement – are met.

The middle-class bias within the ICCS is most evident in the fee structures of its most prominent institutions, the Islamic Hospital, the Dar al-Arqam schools, and the

Islamic College. According to the 2008 price list of the Islamic Hospital in Amman, for example, a natural delivery of one child with no complications and requiring one overnight stay in a third-class room costs 230 JD. In contrast, the same delivery and overnight stay costs only 25 JD at al-Bashir Hospital, a public hospital located in poorer East Amman and catering to those on lower incomes.[47] This middle-class bias is not new. In 1998, the same services cost 190 JD in the Islamic Hospital and 18 JD at al-Bashir.[48] A similar situation exists in the ICCS schools. According to the ICCS Executive Report for 1998, only 93 out of the ICCS' 11,345 kindergarten, elementary, and secondary/high school students received scholarships designated for the poor and orphans; 11,252 students paid full tuition fees, ranging from approximately 120 JD/year for kindergarten to 545 JD/year in secondary school.[49] As in the case of the Islamic Hospital, these fees are comparable to competing private institutions in the country. In contrast, Jordan's poor households spend only 19.99 JD per capita per year on education.[50] Similarly, the fees at the ICCS' college in Zarka are higher than those at other private colleges in the city, ranging from a difference of 228 JD to 410 JD in annual fees depending on the college and program.[51]

That the ICCS caters to the middle class furthermore is reflected in the locations of the ICCS institutions. In other words, ICCS services are located where the ICCS can address the needs of MB's constituency. According to voting data, the IAF power base is concentrated in urban, central Jordan, predominantly in Amman and Zarqa,[52] and it is no coincidence that these are precisely the cities where the majority of ICCS centers are concentrated.[53] An overwhelming number of centers are located in Amman, Zarka, and Irbid. Twenty-one of the ICCS' 55 centers (two of these are the Islamic Hospital and the Fund for the Sick and Poor) are based in Amman.[54] At the same time, the country's poorest and least developed regions, Ma'an and Tafiela (scoring the lowest of all regions in the Human Development Index), have significantly fewer.[55] Ma'an only has two (an education center and an orphanage) and Tafiela one (this center contains an orphanage and a health center).[56]

Employment and nepotism in the ICCS

The ICCS does not just provide services to Jordan's middle class, it also provides employment to the middle class. By providing positions, often with better salaries, working hours, vacation time, and equipment than those in comparable hospitals, clinics, and schools found elsewhere, the ICCS is able to attract and maintain the necessary workforce to sustain itself.[57] Estimates place the number of full-time employees in the ICCS as high as 4,500 in 2006.[58] The majority of these employees are middle-class doctors, dentists, school teachers, and other professionals. In addition to the employment of middle-class professionals, there is also the "trickle down" employment of bus drivers, guards, messengers, cleaners, and maintenance personnel. However, those who benefit from the ICCS financially and otherwise extend far beyond the employees. The ICCS and its various branches and centers furthermore rely on a significant number of private contractors. An extensive number of businesses, ranging from printers who produce ICCS literature and brochures to caterers, have contracts with the ICCS.[59] In the mid-2000s, the Islamic Hospital in Amman alone worked with more than 300 contracted companies and establishments.[60] In addition, there are those businesses that do not have an official contract with the ICCS but are favored by the ICCS when their services are needed. These employment opportunities within the ICCS offered its directors a great deal of economic clout that they could use as they wished. Ultimately, a director was able to create large networks of patronage that worked in his interest and the interest of those he represented.

The hirings within the ICCS and contracts it made invariably went to MB members.[61] As Ziad Abu Ghanemeh, who twice served on the executive board of the ICCS, stated in 2004, it was not a secret that the ICCS was 90 percent Muslim Brothers.[62] Similarly, the former director of the Fund for the Sick and Poor (and one of the founders of the IAF) stated in a 2004 interview with the author that the projects of the ICCS, such as the Hospital, were overwhelmingly staffed by Muslim Brothers, and most commonly friends and family of the directors.[63] Rarely, he added, would a non-MB doctor, for example, be hired. In an interview with Quintan Wiktorowicz, he furthermore confirmed that as many as 90 percent of the employees at ICCS organizations were Muslim Brothers and that their hiring over more qualified non-Islamist candidates lowered the quality of services.[64] Observers furthermore cite examples of "creative job creation" in the ICCS according to which Brothers were paid salaries for positions or contracts that existed merely on paper.[65]

These practices of nepotism within the ICCS were and are defended by many Muslim Brothers and are not regarded as corruption per se. Brothers assert that the fact that the majority of people on the ICCS board were Muslim Brothers or IAF members was a source of pride not a crime. Others argue that it is natural that colleagues would want to work with those who have a similar ideology or with relatives. Similarly, others argue that the "on paper only jobs" within the ICCS, such as cultural advisor, or paid-in-full contracts for books that are never written, are not to be viewed as corruption, but rather as well-deserved rewards for people who devoted their entire lives to an organization.

Nevertheless, the MB has been concerned with the problem of nepotism in the ICCS since the 1990s. At that time, the MB began taking action to eliminate egregious hirings and to enforce the hiring of appropriately qualified people.[66] As a result, a general manager of the Dar al-Arqam school system was dismissed for his lack of qualifications and an ICCS manager was convicted of embezzlement.[67] The efforts to clean house, however, proved to be difficult given the significant economic resources that were at stake within the ICCS and a prevailing attitude among many Muslim Brothers that MB supporters should be rewarded for their contributions to the movement. Largely unnoticed by most observers is the fact that this nepotism often was reflected in the hiring of supporters of one faction within the MB over another in order to strengthen the clout of that faction or camp. These internal power struggles through the use of nepotism were regularly witnessed with the election of new ICCS directors.

ICCS elections

Until 2006, the ICCS was run by a nine-member board of directors elected by a general assembly of 360 members.[68] An examination of the ICCS elections, which occur every two years, offers significant insights into the MB, its internal dynamics, and the role of patronage. Indeed, prior to 2006, when they were suspended, ICCS elections tended to be highly contentious, even more so than those for the leadership of the MB or the IAF. To a certain extent, more was at stake. An elected position in the ICCS offered not only prestige but access to resources with which the directors could benefit their friends and families and which they could translate into political clout within the MB.[69] As a result, control of elections swung quite dramatically from one faction of the MB to another from election to election.

As an increasing number of scholars have noted, the MB and IAF are comprised of different factions or camps reflecting a range of opinions and interests.[70] Prominent Jordanian political analysts refer to several divisions within the movement, including ideological divisions, those according to different personalities and the interests or institutions they represent, and generational divisions.[71] Members, for example, differ in the degree to which they are pragmatic or reformist as opposed to legalistic in their interpretations of religious texts.[72] They furthermore differ in the degree to which they are willing to engage with the state – with participating in elections being one thing and serving on a royal commission, for example, another. Decisions within the MB/IAF are a result of the interplay between different factions depending on the larger political context and the issue at hand. Members who share the same stance on one issue, and may in fact appear as a hard and fast camp, commonly do not share the same views on other issues. Not all "hawks" (those who are viewed as taking an ideologically uncompromising position), for example, necessarily share similar views when it comes to whether or not to boycott elections, on the one hand, and whether or not the MB should support female candidacy, on the other. The relatively fluid nature of decision-making within the MB means that coalition-building is a key element of the process.

The divisions within the MB were made clear by the events of July 2006 following the Speaker of the House demanding an apology from the MB for the four members' expression of condolences to the family of al-Zarqawi. In late July, following a meeting with the prime minister, the MB leadership issued a statement in which it stressed its commitment to national principles, the constitution, and laws; prioritization of national interests over all other interests; allegiance to the king; condemnation of terrorism in all forms; and rejection of extremist Islamic thought. The internal MB reaction to the statement was dramatic. Eighteen out of the MB's 40-member *Shura* Council resigned their posts in protest over the leadership's perceived capitulation to the government, with no promises on the government's behalf to address the unresolved issues of the four jailed MPs and the ICCS. While all 18 eventually were convinced to withdraw their resignations, one of the fault lines within the movement was openly revealed.[73]

To a large extent the factions within the MB as a whole are reflected in all its associated institutions, including, prior to 2006, the ICCS.[74] ICCS elections represented heated contests between those who are regarded as more dovish or hawkish. The director general was a case in point, with each bi-yearly election exchanging a hawk for a dove or vice versa in the position.[75]

However, the ICCS elections did more than merely reflect the tensions and debates within the MB. The ICCS, and its director general in particular, represented an important player in the MB. Representatives of the ICCS have never had reserved seats in the *Shura* councils or executive councils of either the MB or the IAF.[76] For example, during the four years he served on the board of the ICCS, Ziad Abu Ghanemeh was never on the executive council of the MB. As a result, the ICCS did not automatically have any form of direct influence in the decision-making processes of the MB/IAF. However, ICCS directors did have what one political analyst referred to as "moral receipts" as a result of many years of working in the MB and ICCS.[77] Their long-term efforts in the organization garnered them a wide network or coalition of like-minded colleagues and supporters that they used to their benefit.

These networks were responsible for getting a director general or a director elected to the ICCS board or those of its projects, such as the Islamic Hospital's board. Unknown candidates were rarely, if ever, elected to the boards of the ICCS or its projects. Rather, those who were successful in the ICCS or Hospital elections were so as a result of an established network of supporters within the ICCS or the Hospital, where the elections were held, and within the MB at large, which the ICCS voters kept in mind. Plum positions within the ICCS were a result of networks and coalitions.[78]

Upon being elected to the ICCS board of directors, a director had a far greater chance of being elected to the *Shura* Council of the MB or IAF or even to their respective executive councils. A director brought his authority and networks to the *Shura* Council of the MB. As an elected board member of the ICCS or an ICCS institution, representing a network of personal, institutional, and financial interests, a director's opinion carried weight within any internal MB/IAF discussions, regardless of whether or not he technically was elected to the respective executive councils.[79] Armed with large voting members in his network and economic clout, through his ability to dispense jobs and contracts, he furthermore was a desirable coalition partner. Members who brought economic clout to the MB decision-making table, such as an MP or the director of the ICCS, brought with them authority and the ability to distribute positions and wealth. As one Islamist and journalist stated, they struck coalitions or understandings with other factions, uniting political interests and sometimes people sharing similar interpretations in regards to *shari'a*.[80]

The ICCS elections therefore represented a battle for an important political and economic power base from which the director could affect MB/IAF decisions regardless of whether or not he was in their respective executive councils. As Raif Najem stated in 2004, it was a fight over prestige, political power, and the ability to employ friends.[81] The political and economic stakes remained high even though the elected directors to the ICCS, including institutions such as the Islamic Hospital, did not (and do not) draw salaries for their work on the boards. It was full-time voluntary work. In addition, even if the director secured a seat on the *Shura* Council of the MB or IAF as a result of his position in the ICCS, these councils only met twice in the year and did not play a daily role in decision-making.[82] The power of the directorship lay far beyond any formal position the director held in the MB.

Positions within the directorate of the ICCS also offered a podium from which directors could speak out. In fact, as they were elected positions, many analysts argue that directors had greater freedom of expression than other Muslim Brothers not affiliated with the ICCS. Ziad Abu Ghanemeh provides a case in point. In 1997, the IAF decided to boycott the national elections in protest against the 1993 electoral laws and the growing authoritarian measures in the country. Several prominent MB spoke out against the boycott (or indeed ran in the elections despite the boycott), all of whom were tried in an internal MB court and ejected from the organization.[83] Ziad Abu Ghanemeh similarly opposed the boycott and contested the MB decision using his pen in the public press. While Abu Ghanemeh also was kicked out of the MB, he retained his then position as Director of Public Relations for the Islamic Hospital.[84] As it was an elected position, only the General Assembly that elected him could determine whether or not he would be forced to end his term early. Ultimately, his network of supporters, much of which was held together by patronage, made no move to force his resignation. The MB could not fire him from his position, granting him an important de facto podium within the MB from which to announce his independent views and directly influence the thinking of others.

The economic and political significance of the ICCS, and specifically the political role that patronage played, was most evident during the 2003 ICCS elections.[85] The hotly contested elections brought Daoud Qojak, a former IAF MP considered an ideological hawk within the MB, to power as director general of the ICCS. Upon taking his seat in January 2004, Qojak and the newly elected board under him fired a total of 400 ICCS employees. The 400 had been appointed to the various advisory committees of the ICCS, such as economic, social, and medical committees – positions directly involved in the management of the ICCS and its institutions (including investment management). Unsurprisingly, all 400 of these employees had been hired by the former administration two years earlier under Kandil Shaker, an ideological dove within the MB.[86] Shaker himself had also undertaken some political housekeeping upon his election and as a result had eliminated many hawks from the ICCS.[87] Under Qojak, the issue had come full circle and the hawks regained their positions.

The 2003 elections were not the only contested ICCS elections. In fact, elected positions within the ICCS were so valued that members and candidates more than once turned to the state for assistance in resolving the regular electoral disputes that appeared to occur. During the 2002 elections, Mahmoud Abu Ghanemeh (the son of Ziad Abu Ghanemeh) lost to Ibrahim Masoud by a margin of only one vote. Mahmoud Abu Ghanemeh contested the election results based on improper supervision of the elections, specifically the vote-counting, by the Ministry of Social Development.[88] He eventually took the case to Jordan's Court of Higher Justice and won, and took his seat on the ICCS board.[89] It is worth remembering that this was an unpaid position.

Similarly, the election of four members of the 2006–08 board was contested in April 2006 as a result of a conflict of interest related to their private businesses.

Indeed, it was in response to ICCS members' complaints in regards to these four members that the Ministry of Social Development, with which the ICCS is registered, established a joint committee with the Audit Bureau in order to determine if the accusations were valid. These very complaints eventually provided an opportunity for ICCS assets to be frozen later that year.

Conclusions

As the case of the ICCS demonstrated, Islamist institutions are sites of conflict and competition. Rather than being the homogenous and unified entities that they are often assumed to be, Islamist movements are comprised of numerous interests – political, economic, social, institutional, and religious. Patronage plays a large role in determining which interests (or which combination of interests) win out. Far from being ideologically driven, decisions made by Islamist movements and parties reflect a variety of internal and external factors, including material interests. Indeed, the case study confirms the "context-dependent" nature of Islamist movements. A variety of factors influence decision-making processes within Islamist movements, including individual and material interests; how these factors come together often is not predictable, but rather the fluid outcome of personalities and coalitions. Within this context, those who have large networks are particularly influential.

The heated and contested elections within the ICCS prior to its takeover reflect and demonstrate the influence of the directorship positions within the ICCS and specifically the interconnectedness of patronage and the politics and direction of the MB. Large networks of patronage within the MB were pivotal in translating positions in the ICCS into political clout. The ICCS was neither subservient to the MB nor merely a mirror of larger political fault lines. Rather it was an important and relatively independent economic and political player within the MB – both in its own role and particularly in the context of the coalescing coalitions that are formed and broken in the process of decision-making within the MB and IAF. It is little wonder that the government sought to take control of it and that it remains reluctant to allow the resumption of ICCS elections.

At present, it is still unclear what the long-term impact of the government's takeover of the ICCS will be on the MB. At the grassroots level, little has changed. The individual centers continue to be run as previously. However, the accusations of fraud and corruption no doubt played a role in the abysmal performance of the IAF in the 2007 parliamentary elections – as did the deep divisions between streams within the MB/IAF. Furthermore, as stated above, the government has yet to call elections for the ICCS. When it does, the votes of the newly expanded General Assembly will have a profound impact both on the ICCS and on the MB itself.

Notes

1 In response to complaints of suspected administrative and financial irregularities in the ICCS, MOSD forced four members of the elected ICCS executive board directly linked to the complaints to step down from their positions. The four members were replaced

via new elections within the ICCS. At the same time, MOSD transferred the complaints file to the joint MOSD–Audit Bureau committee that eventually froze the ICCS' assets and replaced its entire board with a temporary government-appointed committee (see p. 73). *Al-Ghad*, March 16, 2006; *Al-Ghad*, June 22, 2006; *Al-Ghad*, June 28, 2006 (in Arabic).

2 D. Sullivan, *Private Voluntary Organizations in Egypt: Islamic Development, Private Initiative, and State Control*, Gainesville: University Press of Florida, 1994; A. Kandil and S. Ben Nefissa, *Civil Associations in Egypt*, Cairo: Al-Ahram Centre for Political and Strategic Studies, 1994 (in Arabic); D. Singerman, *Avenues of Participation: Family, Politics, and Networks in Urban Quarters of Cairo*, Princeton: Princeton University Press, 1995; J. Clark, "Islamic Social Welfare Organizations in Cairo: Islamization from Below?" *Arab Studies Quarterly* 17, 1995, 11–28; J. Clark, *Islam, Social Welfare, and the Middle Class: Networks, Activism, and Charity in Egypt, Yemen and Jordan*, Bloomington: Indiana University Press, 2004b; J. Clark, "Social Movement Theory and Patron-Clientelism: Islamic Social Institutions and the Middle Class in Egypt, Jordan and Yemen," *Comparative Political Studies* 37, 2004c, 1–28; J. Clark, "Islamist Women in Yemen: Informal Nodes of Activism," in Q. Wiktorowicz (ed.) *Islamic Activism: A Social Movement Theory Approach*, Bloomington: Indiana University Press, 2004a, pp. 164–84; J. Clark, "FBOs and Change in the Context of Authoritarianism: The Islamic Center Charity Society in Jordan," in G. Clarke and M. Jennings (eds.) *Development, Civil Society and Faith-based Organizations: Bridging the Sacred and the Secular*, New York: Palgrave Macmillan, 2008; Q. Wiktorowicz, *The Management of Islamic Activism*, Albany: SUNY Press, 2001; E. Harmsen, "Islamic Voluntary Welfare Activism in Jordan," *ISIM Newsletter* 13, 2003, 30–31.

3 The primary field work for this research was conducted between 1998 and 2002. Between 2003 and 2006, and again in 2011, the author further updated the research on the ICCS and conducted additional interviews. The original research forms the basis of Clark, *Islam, Social Welfare, and the Middle Class*; Clark, "Social Movement Theory and Patron-Clientelism"; Clark, "Islamist Women in Yemen." Parts of this chapter are based on an earlier version of the chapter Clark, "FBOs and Change in the Context of Authoritarianism."

4 Clark 2004b, op. cit., pp. 12–16; Clark 2004a, op. cit., pp. 168–69.

5 Clark 2004b, op. cit., p. 15.

6 Clark 2004b, op. cit., pp. 153–54; Clark 2004a, op. cit., p. 171.

7 M. Boulby, *The Muslim Brotherhood and the Kings of Jordan: 1945–1993*, Atlanta: Scholars Press, 1999; Clark 2004b, op. cit., pp. 84–89; J. Schwedler, *Faith in Moderation: Islamist Parties in Jordan and Yemen*, New York: Cambridge University Press, 2006, pp. 65–69.

8 Upon Abdullah's death, his eldest son, Talal, was crowned king, but he was forced to abdicate due to mental illness. Talal's son, Hussein, was proclaimed king in 1952, but as he was under the legal age to rule he was enthroned on May 2, 1953. When Hussein died in 1999, his eldest son, Abdullah II, came to power.

9 The MB was established under the patronage of King Abdullah I. Beginning with its establishment, it was consistently granted numerous advantages over other political groups. This privileging was most evident when in 1953 the MB was re-designated from a charitable society to a "general and comprehensive Islamic committee." The re-categorization enabled it to operate freely and for all intents and purposes to engage in political activities while other political organizations could not. This relationship between the MB and the monarchy was the result of several mutually beneficial factors. Both King Abdullah I and King Hussein shared the view that bringing the MB into the open (and under the close scrutiny of the state) by legalizing it was an important element in preventing the MB from engaging in violence, as the Jordanian MB's mother organization in Egypt had (Boulby, op. cit., p. 46). In addition, the monarchy and the MB shared a mutual antipathy for rising pan-Arab nationalism (Schwedler 2006, op. cit., pp. 42–43). The expansion of the MB, it was believed, could undermine the popularity of pan-Arab nationalism. Finally, the monarchy could reinforce its own religious legitimacy (based on its lineage in the tribe of Prophet Mohammed) and support base by granting the MB royal patronage

(Boulby, op. cit., p. 46; H. Hourani, T. Awad, H. Dabbas, and S. Kilani, *Islamic Action Front Party*, 1st edition, translated by S. Kilanhi, Amman: Al-Urdun al-Jadid Research Center, 1993, pp. 13–14; S. Bar, *The Muslim Brotherhood in Jordan*, Tel Aviv: The Moshe Dayan Center for Middle Eastern and African Studies/Tel Aviv University Press, 1998, p. 32; Wiktorowicz, op. cit., pp. 95–101; Schwedler 2006, op. cit., pp. 65–66).

10 Dominated by the MB members, the IAF is considered the party of the MB.

11 Established by the state, the General Union of Voluntary Societies, an umbrella NGO of all charitable NGOs, is technically the largest NGO.

12 U. K. Hamayil, "Institutional Characteristics of the Jordanian Professional Associations," in W. Knowles (ed.) *Professional Associations and the Challenges of Democratic Transformation in Jordan*, Amman: Al-Urdun al-Jadid Research Center, pp. 66–67.

13 Boulby, op. cit., pp. 73, 104; M. Mufti, "Elite Bargains and the Onset of Political Liberalization in Jordan," *Comparative Politics* 32, 1999, 110; L. S. Adams, "Political Liberalization in Jordan," *Journal of Church and State* 38, 1996, 511; L. Tal, "Dealing with Radical Islam," *Survival* 37, 1995, 139–56; H. Freij and L. Robinson, "Liberalization, the Islamists, and the Stability of the Arab State: Jordan as a Case Study," *Muslim World* 136, 1996, 1–32.

14 C. Ryan, *Jordan in Transition*, Boulder: Lynne Rienner Press, 2002, pp. 26–30; R. Lucas, *Institutions and the Politics of Survival in Jordan*, Albany: SUNY Press, pp. 72–85.

15 The IAF boycotted the 1997 elections.

16 For a discussion of the 2007 parliamentary elections and their significance, see M. Abu Rumman, *The Muslim Brotherhood: In the Jordanian Parliamentarian Elections 2007: A Passing "Political Setback" of Diminishing Popularity?* Amman: Friedrich Ebert Stiftung, 2008.

17 J. Schwedler and J. Clark, "Who Opened the Window? Women's Struggle for Voice within Islamist Political Parties," *Comparative Politics* 35, 2003; D. Kornbluth, "Jordan and the Anti-Normalization Campaign, 1994–2001," *Terrorism and Political Violence* 14, 2002; M. Lynch, "Jordan's Identity and Interests," in S. Telhami and M. Barnett (eds.) *Identity and Foreign Policy in the Middle East*, Ithaca: Cornell University Press, 2002; M. Lynch, *State Interests and Public Spheres*, New York: Columbia University Press, 1999; P. Scham and R. Lucas, "'Normalization' and 'Anti-Normalization' in Jordan," *MERIA* 5, 2001; A. Abu-Odeh, *Jordanians, Palestinians and the Hashemite Kingdom in the Middle East Peace Process,* Washington, DC: United States Institute of Peace, 1999; M. Hamarneh, R. Hollis, and K. Shikaki, *"Jordanian–Palestinian Relations: Where To?"* London: The Royal Institute of International Affairs, 1997; L. Brand, "Palestinians and Jordanians: A Crisis of Identity," *Journal of Palestine Affairs* XXIV, 1995.

18 In 2011, tensions flared again with the momentous changes throughout North Africa and the Middle East.

19 For an overview of changing relations between the MB and the regime, see Abu Rumman 2008, op. cit., chs. 2 and 3.

20 These concerns appeared confirmed when, subsequent to the elections, IAF MP and leader of the Islamist bloc in parliament Azzam al-Huneidi posted on the IAF website that the IAF was ready to take power after the next parliamentary elections by winning the majority of seats.

21 *Al-Ra'y*, March 7, 2006 (in Arabic).

22 The MB/IAF accused the government of fabricating the event.

23 Of the four, three were tried; one was acquitted and the other two were given limited jail sentences.

24 In response to the government's release of the 1,700 page report, the MB, along with other opposition parties, issued a statement accusing the government of attempting to eliminate the ICCS. The statement also demanded that the government abrogate the Wadi Araba peace treaty with Israel, cease supporting the invasion of Iraq and cease supporting Israel, end its opposition to Hamas (expelled from Jordan in 1999), and release the four MPs who visited the family of al-Zarqawi. It further accused the government of being a puppet of US President George W. Bush (*Al-Hayat*, 4 July 2006 (in Arabic); see also: K. Sowell, "Jordan–Muslim Brotherhood Conflict Heats up after

Zarqawi Homage," http//inbrief.threatswatch.org/2006/07/jordanmuslim-brotherhood-cpnfl/; Deutsche Presse-Agentur, "Jordan Moves against Brotherhood's Financial Arm," July 5, 2006; NGO Watch, "Jordanian Officials Probe Charity's Financial Dealings," July 7, 2006; *Al-Hayat*, July 4, 2006 (in Arabic).

25 In 2006, the government also referred three other cases of corruption by major Jordanian entities to the prosecutor general – the Jordan Magnesia Company, the General Union for Voluntary Societies, and former and present officials of the Ministry of Municipal Affairs.

26 *Jordan Times*, July 11, 2006; *Al-Ghad*, July 11, 2006 (in Arabic).

27 Interview with Dr. Ahmed Essa Al-Balasmeh, member of the Temporary Committee, Amman, March 25, 2008. See *Al-Ghad*, September 27, 2007 (in Arabic).

28 *Al-Ghad*, September 27, 2006; *Al-Ghad*, January 2, 2007; *Al-Ghad*, April 17, 2007 (in Arabic).

29 Interview with Dr. Ahmed Essa Al-Balasmeh, member of the Temporary Committee, Amman, March 25, 2008. The Temporary Committee also conducted its own investigations and found all accusations to be false.

30 The government's appointments also included some Muslim Brothers in addition to representatives of MOSD and other sectors of the state and society. Interview with Dr. Ahmed Essa Al-Balasmeh, member of the Temporary Committee, Amman, March 25, 2008. See *Al-Ghad*, July 12, 2006 (in Arabic).

31 Interview with Jamil Abu Bakr, Muslim Brother, Amman, March 23, 2008; interview with Dr. Ahmed Essa Al-Balasmeh, member of the Temporary Committee, Amman, March 25, 2008. See *Al-Ghad*, April 17, 2007 (in Arabic).

32 *Al-Ghad*, April 17, 2007; *Al-Ghad*, January 2, 2007 (in Arabic).

33 *Jordan Times*, March 9, 2010.

34 Interview with Dr. Ahmed Essa Al-Balasmeh, member of the Temporary Committee, Amman, March 25, 2008. The ICCS formed a follow-up committee to pursue the issue of elections (interview with Dr. Ahmed Essa Al-Balasmeh, member of the Temporary Committee, Amman, March 25, 2008). See *Al-Ghad*, September 27, 2006 (in Arabic); *Jordan Times*, June 26, 2009. The MB also accuses the government-appointed management of financial irregularities. See *Jordan Times*, June 26, 2009.

35 For an earlier version of this section, see Clark 2008, op. cit.

36 www.islamicc.org.

37 http://www.islamic-hospital.org/english/index.htm.

38 *Al-Arab Al-Youm*, July 1, 2006 (in Arabic). Ziad Abu Ghanemah estimates that the Fund spends over 500,000 JD each year. Interview with Ziad Abu Ghanemeh, ICCS, Amman, January 20, 2004.

39 *Al-Arab Al-Youm*, July 1, 2006 (in Arabic).

40 *Al-Hayat*, July 4, 2006 (in Arabic).

41 During this time period, 1 JD was approximately .73 British pounds or 1.04 euros or 1.41 US$.

42 *Al-Arab Al-Youm*, July 1, 2006 (in Arabic). Since 1963, the ICCS has sponsored over 8,500 orphans (www.islamicc.org).

43 This amounts to 14 million US dollars (Deutsche Press-Agentur, 2006).

44 Boulby, op. cit., pp. 37–38, 50–58, 103; Clark 2004b, op. cit., pp. 86–87.

45 These figures do not include the many businesspeople and salaried employees in the IAF.

46 Azm, A., "The Islamic Action Front Party," in H. Hourani (Ed.) *Islamic Movements in Jordan*, Amman: Al-Urdun Al-Jadid Research Center, 1997, pp. 101–03; M. Moaddel, *Jordanian Exceptionalism*, New York: Palgrave, 2002, pp. 121–22; Clark 2004b, op. cit., p. 17.

47 The first- and second-class rooms at the Islamic Hospital for the same services cost 350 JD and 270 JD, respectively. Prices were obtained March 26, 2008. The exchange rate at this point was 1 JD = 1.421 US$.

48 Clark 2004b, op. cit., pp. 100–01.

49 Ibid., p. 103.

50 Ibid., p. 103.

51 Ibid., p. 105.
52 The IAF also has strong representation in Palestinian refugee camps, particularly Baqa'a Camp, outside Amman (Clark 2004b, op. cit., p. 89).
53 While the charitable NGO community in general is evenly distributed between rural and urban communities, the Islamic NGO community (comprising Islamic charitable and cultural NGOs) tends to be located in urban centers only (Wiktorowicz, op. cit., pp. 86–87; Clark 2004b, op. cit., pp. 98–99).
54 This is not to deny the hidden poverty in Amman. According to the World Bank, Amman has the lowest incidence of people living in the poorest decile of the population but the second-highest distribution nationwide (Clark 2004b, op. cit., p. 99).
55 *Jordan Human Development Report: Building Sustainable Livelihoods*, Amman: Ministry of Planning and International Cooperation, the UNDP; JOHUD/Queen Zein Al Sharaf Institute for Development, 2004, 1, 20. These areas are predominantly agriculturally based – a sector that has witnessed an ongoing decline in labor productivity (I. Saif, "Employment Poverty Linkages and Policies for Pro-Poor Growth in Jordan (1990–2003)," International Labor Organization, forthcoming). Amman scores the country's highest levels in the Human Development Index (HDI).
56 http://www.islamicc.org.
57 Clark 2004b, op. cit., pp. 103, 106.
58 *Jordan Times*, July 10, 2006. According to *Al-Arab al-Youm*, the number of employees is lower. In 2006, it states, the ICCS had approximately 3,400 full-time employees (*Al-Arab Al-Youm* July 1, 2006 (in Arabic)).
59 Those who control the boards of directors of Jordan's professional associations also are in a position to bestow considerable patronage in the form of contracts to various companies for printing, room rentals, and the like.
60 http://www.islamic-hospital.org/english/index.htm.
61 Non-Islamists also work within the ICCS (Clark 2004b, op. cit., pp. 36–38).
62 Interview with Ziad Abu Ghanemeh, ICCS, Amman, January 20, 2004.
63 Interview with Ra'if Nijim, former Director of the Fund for the Sick and Poor, Amman, January 25, 2004.
64 Wiktorowicz, op. cit., pp. 107–08; Clark 2004b, op. cit., p. 105.
65 Interview with Ibrahim Ghoreibeh, *Al-Ghad* newspaper, Amman, January 12, 2004.
66 Interview with Mohammad Abu Rumman, *Al-Ghad* newspaper, Amman, May 11, 2006; interview with Mohammed Najjar, *As-Sabeel* newspaper, Amman, January 19, 2004; interview with Ibrahim Ghoreibeh, *Al-Ghad* newspaper, Amman, January 12, 2004.
67 Interview with Mohammed Najjar, *As-Sabeel* newspaper, Amman, January 19, 2004; interview with Ibrahim Ghoreibeh, *Al-Ghad* newspaper, Amman, January 12, 2004. The author was not able to verify these events with the ICCS itself.
68 Clark 2004b, op. cit., p. 92. See also *Al-Arab Al-Youm* July 1, 2006 (in Arabic). The members of the general assembly are not exclusively Muslim Brothers, although the Brothers dominate.
69 Interview with Ra'if Nijim, former Director of the Fund for the Sick and Poor, Amman, January 25, 2004.
70 M. Abu Rumman, "The Muslim Brothers Following the Boycott of the 2010 Elections: Redrawing the Political Role of the Movement," Amman: Center for Strategic Studies, University of Jordan, 2011; Abu Rumman 2008, op. cit.; J. Clark, "Questioning Power, Mobilization, and Strategies of the Islamist Opposition: How Strong Is the Muslim Brotherhood in Jordan?" in H. Albrecht (ed.) *Contentious Politics in the Middle East: Political Opposition under Authoritarianism*, Gainesville: The University of Florida Press, 2010; Schwedler and Clark, op. cit.; Schwedler 2006, op. cit., pp. 158–59.
71 Interview with Samih Ma'ita, journalist, Amman, February 7, 2004; interview with Ibrahim Ghoreibeh, *Al-Ghad* newspaper, Amman, January 12, 2004; interview with Hilmi Asmar, journalist, Amman, January 15, 2004.
72 Schwedler and Clark, op. cit.

73 Mohammad Abu Rumman argues that the divisions within the movement over the MB's relationship to the regime and, consequently, its strategies when dealing with the regime, have exposed what he calls a "Fourth Trend" within the MB that also strongly sympathizes with Hamas and advocates greater ties with Hamas (Abu Rumman 2008, op. cit.).
74 Interview with Majid Tobeh, *Al-Ghad* newspaper, Amman, February 8, 2004.
75 Ibid.
76 Interview with Ra'if Nijim, former Director of the Fund for Sick and Poor, Amman, January 25, 2004.
77 Interview with Hilmi Asmar, journalist, Amman, January 15, 2004.
78 Ibid.
79 Interview with Samih Ma'ita, journalist, Amman, February 7, 2004, January 10, 2004; interview with Ibrahim Ghoreibeh, *Al-Ghad* newspaper, Amman, January 12, 2004; interview with Hilmi Asmar, journalist, Amman, January 15, 2004.
80 Interview with Hilmi Asmar, journalist, Amman, January 15, 2004; interview with Samih Ma'ita, journalist, Amman, January 10, 2004.
81 Interview with Ra'if Nijim, former Director of the Fund for Sick and Poor, Amman, January 15, 2004.
82 The *Shura* councils may be called in for extraordinary sessions, sometimes meeting a total of three or four times per year.
83 Schwedler 2006, op. cit., p. 201.
84 Interview with Majid Tobeh, *Al-Ghad* newspaper, Amman, February 8, 2004; interview with Samih Ma'ita, journalist, Amman, February 7, 2004.
85 See I. Ghoreibeh, "The Islamic Center Associations: Where To?" *Al-Ghad*, July 12, 2006 (in Arabic).
86 Interview with Majid Tobeh, *Al-Ghad* newspaper, Amman, February 8, 2004.
87 *Al-Majd*, January 28, 2004 (in Arabic); *Al-Dustur*, January 29, 2004 (in Arabic); interview with Majid Tobeh, *Al-Ghad* newspaper, Amman, February 8, 2004. Qojak's actions ultimately lead to a sit-in of ICCS members protesting the dismissals. While both *al-Dustour* and *al-Majd* newspapers reported the sit-in, the MB denied it occurred.
88 Interview with Ziad Abu Ghanemeh, ICCS, Amman, January 20, 2004; interview with Ibrahim Ghoreibeh, *Al-Ghad* newspaper, Amman, January 12, 2004.
89 Interview with Ibrahim Ghoreibeh, *Al-Ghad* newspaper, Amman, January 12, 2004; interview with Ziad Abu Ghanemeh, ICCS, Amman, January 20, 2004; interview with Majid Tobeh, *Al-Ghad* newspaper, Amman, February 8, 2004.

Bibliography

Abu-Odeh, A., *Jordanians, Palestinians and the Hashemite Kingdom in the Middle East Peace Process*, Washington, DC: United States Institute of Peace, 1999.

Abu Rumman, M., "The Muslim Brothers Following the Boycott of the 2010 Elections: Redrawing the Political Role of the Movement," Amman: Center for Strategic Studies, University of Jordan, 2011.

Abu Rumman, M., *The Muslim Brotherhood: In the Jordanian Parliamentarian Elections 2007: A Passing "Political Setback" of Diminishing Popularity?* Amman: Friedrich Ebert Stiftung, 2008.

Adams, L. S., "Political Liberalization in Jordan," *Journal of Church and State* 38, 1996, 507–28.

Azm, A., "The Islamic Action Front Party," in H. Hourani (ed.) *Islamic Movements in Jordan*, Amman: Al-Urdun Al-Jadid Research Center, 1997.

Bar, S., *The Muslim Brotherhood in Jordan*, Tel Aviv: The Moshe Dayan Center for Middle Eastern and African Studies/Tel Aviv University Press, 1998.

Boulby, M., *The Muslim Brotherhood and the Kings of Jordan: 1945–1993*, Atlanta: Scholars Press, 1999.

Brand, L., "Palestinians and Jordanians: A Crisis of Identity," *Journal of Palestine Affairs* XXIV, 1995, 46–61.

Clark, J., "Questioning Power, Mobilization, and Strategies of the Islamist Opposition: How Strong Is the Muslim Brotherhood in Jordan?" in H. Albrecht (ed.) *Contentious Politics in the Middle East: Political Opposition under Authoritarianism*, Gainesville: University of Florida Press, 2010.

Clark, J., "FBOs and Change in the Context of Authoritarianism: The Islamic Center Charity Society in Jordan," in G. Clarke and M. Jennings (eds.) *Development, Civil Society and Faith-based Organizations: Bridging the Sacred and the Secular*, New York: Palgrave Macmillan, 2008.

Clark, J., "Jordan," in T. Archer and H. Huuhtanen (eds.) *Islamist Opposition Parties and the Potential for EU Engagement*, Helsinki: The Finnish Institute of International Affairs, 2007.

Clark, J., "Islamist Women in Yemen: Informal Nodes of Activism," in Q. Wiktorowicz (ed.) *Islamic Activism: A Social Movement Theory Approach*, Bloomington: Indiana University Press, 2004a.

Clark, J., *Islam, Social Welfare, and the Middle Class: Networks, Activism, and Charity in Egypt, Yemen and Jordan*, Bloomington: Indiana University Press, 2004b.

Clark, J., "Social Movement Theory and Patron-Clientelism: Islamic Social Institutions and the Middle Class in Egypt, Jordan and Yemen," *Comparative Political Studies* 37, 2004c, 1–28.

Clark, J., "Islamic Social Welfare Organizations in Cairo: Islamization from Below?" *Arab Studies Quarterly* 17, 1995, 11–28.

Clark, J. A. and Schwedler, J., "Who Opened the Window? Women's Activism in Islamist Parties," *Comparative Politics* 35, 2003, 293–312.

Deutsche Presse-Agentur, "Jordan Moves against Brotherhood's Financial Arm," July 5, 2006.

Freij, H. and Robinson, L., "Liberalization, the Islamists, and the Stability of the Arab State: Jordan as a Case Study," *Muslim World* 136, 1996, 1–32.

Ghoreibeh, I., "The Islamic Center Associations: Where To?" *Al-Ghad*, July 12, 2006 (in Arabic).

Hamarneh, M., Hollis, R., and Shikaki, K., *Jordanian–Palestinian Relations: Where To?* London: The Royal Institute of International Affairs, 1997.

Hamayil, U., "Institutional Characteristics of the Jordanian Professional Associations," in W. Knowles (ed.) *Professional Associations and the Challenges of Democratic Transformation in Jordan*, Amman: Al-Urdun al-Jadid Research Center, 2000.

Harmsen, E., "Islamic Voluntary Welfare Activism in Jordan," *ISIM* Newsletter 13, 2003, 30–31.

Hourani, H., Awad, T., Dabbas, H. and Kilani S., *Islamic Action Front Party*, 1st edition, translated by Sa'eda Kilanhi, Amman: Al-Urdun al-Jadid Research Center, 1993.

Jordan Human Development Report: Building Sustainable Livelihoods, Amman: Ministry of Planning and International Cooperation, the UNDP; JOHUD/Queen Zein Al Sharaf Institute for Development, 2004.

Kandil, A. and Ben Nefissa, S., *Civil Associations in Egypt*, Cairo: Al-Ahram Centre for Political and Strategic Studies, 1994 (in Arabic).

Kornbluth, D., "Jordan and the Anti-Normalization Campaign, 1994–2001," *Terrorism and Political Violence* 14, 2002.

Lucas, R., *Institutions and the Politics of Survival in Jordan*, Albany: SUNY Press, 2005.

Lynch, M., "Jordan's Identity and Interests," in S. Telhami and M. Barnett (eds.) *Identity and Foreign Policy in the Middle East*, Ithaca: Cornell University Press, 2002.

Lynch, M., *State Interests and Public Spheres*, New York: Columbia University Press, 1999.

Moaddel, M., *Jordanian Exceptionalism*, New York: Palgrave, 2002.

Mufti, M., "Elite Bargains and the Onset of Political Liberalization in Jordan," *Comparative Politics* 32, 1999, 100–29.

NGO Watch, "Jordanian Officials Probe Charity's Financial Dealings," July 7, 2006.

Ryan, C., *Jordan in Transition*, Boulder: Lynne Rienner Press, 2002.

Saif, I., "Employment Poverty Linkages and Policies for Pro-Poor Growth in Jordan (1990–2003)," International Labor Organization, forthcoming.

Scham, P. and Lucas, R., "'Normalization' and 'Anti-Normalization' in Jordan," *MERIA* 5, 2001, 54–70.

Sowell, K., "Jordan–Muslim Brotherhood Conflict Heats up after Zarqawi Homage," http//inbrief.threatswatch.org/2006/07/jordanmuslim-brotherhood-cpnfl/.

Schwedler, J., *Faith in Moderation: Islamist Parties in Jordan and Yemen*, New York: Cambridge University Press, 2006.

Schwedler, J., "More than a Mob," *Middle East Report* 226, 2003, 18–23.

Schwedler, J. and Clark, J., "Who Opened the Window? Women's Struggle for Voice within Islamist Political Parties," *Comparative Politics* 35, 2003, 293–312.

Singerman, D., *Avenues of Participation: Family, Politics, and Networks in Urban Quarters of Cairo*, Princeton: Princeton University Press, 1995.

Sullivan, D., *Private Voluntary Organizations in Egypt: Islamic Development, Private Initiative, and State Control*, Gainesville: University Press of Florida, 1994.

Tal, L., "Dealing with Radical Islam," *Survival* 37, 1995, 139–56.

Wiktorowicz, Q., *The Management of Islamic Activism*, Albany: SUNY Press, 2001.

5

THE RELIGIOUS DIMENSION OF ISLAMISM

Sufism, Salafism, and politics in Morocco

Henri Lauzière

Of the difficulties inherent in the study of Islamism, none appears to be as elementary, and yet as frustrating, as the issue of typology. The various labels that have emerged over the years show that scholars have struggled to explain why they would assign certain Muslims to an analytical category. They have also struggled to find an appropriate label for that category and agree on its definition. While "Islamism" and "Islamists" have become the most widely accepted labels, differences persist in the West as well as in the Muslim world. While many Islamists now refer to themselves as *islāmiyyūn*, the Arabic term for "Islamists," others reject such labels, which they consider exogenous and unwarranted. Instead, they may choose a broader and less exclusive category such as "the Islamic movement" (*al-ḥaraka al-islāmiyya*), thus suggesting that there is no such thing as "Islamism" and that it would be wrong to single it out and stigmatize it.[1]

Although most analysts agree that Islamists are unique enough to be distinguished from other Muslims, capturing this distinction remains a challenge. What exactly is Islamism and what are its defining characteristics? What actions or thoughts qualify someone as an Islamist? There is generally no consensus on the answers to these questions because Islamism is a category whose contours are shaped by analytical expediency.[2] Therefore, its definition often depends on one's interests, goals, or vantage point. For example, when scholars talk about "political Islam" instead of "Islamism," they often signal their inclination to put politics above religion. In many cases, this is a perfectly understandable decision. Political scientists, among others, are first and foremost interested in political issues and do not usually examine theology or spirituality for its own sake. As a result, some approach Islamism as primarily a political phenomenon whose religious dimension is tangential. While they may acknowledge that Islamism has a religious basis, they do not think that this aspect requires further scholarly investigation, especially if it takes the analyst away from what they regard as truly significant matters such as political thoughts, platforms, or actions.

Problems can occur, however, if this political approach is taken for granted and passes as canonical. In a 2002 typological article, for instance, one scholar who set out to clarify the basic terms and definitions pertaining to Islamism – or political Islam – invoked the authority of a substantial body of literature to clarify the issue for the benefit of a broad audience of scholars, policymakers, and general readers. His typology, however, turned the political approach into a benchmark. The author's position was encapsulated in his statement that "Politics lies at the heart of Islamism, which ultimately has far more to do with power than with religion."[3] While the first part of this statement is undeniable, the second raises a complex issue that is difficult to resolve and that empirical research does not always validate.[4] This tendency to conceive of Islamism as *political* Islam can easily become an analytical straitjacket because it advises against researching, noticing, or even asking questions that appear nonpolitical. This is not to say that political considerations are secondary, nor does it deny that Islamism is a politicized understanding of Islam. In fact, many of the studies that deemphasized the religious aspect of Islamism proved insightful because they either overcame religious essentialism or drew enlightening parallels between Islamism and secular ideologies.[5] Yet, it would be counterproductive to assume *ipso facto* that political factors alone define Islamism, or that a better understanding of this phenomenon depends on our putting aside its religious dimension. The danger in allowing political concerns to dictate a normative definition of Islamism is that it invites analysts to minimize or even disregard religious discourses that may prove enlightening. In recent years, this political conceptualization has led some scholars to claim that Muslim activists who do not focus strictly on the notion of the Islamic state should not be considered Islamists – as though a real Islamist could not conceivably emphasize spiritual matters.[6]

Evidence suggests that we have much to gain from taking religion into consideration when studying Islamism. Scholars applying social movement theory to the study of Islamism – whether they analyze religious discourses from a framing or a dialogic perspective – have recently demonstrated the extent to which religious factors can contribute to the success or failure of Islamist groups.[7] Moreover, the sociology of religion has long maintained that raising questions about the genuineness of faith, or the possible ideological motivations behind it, is no reason to disregard religious beliefs and practices. Even if considered a political tool, a smokescreen, or a false consciousness in the Marxist sense, religion remains a social reality that cannot be ignored. Marx's intellectual *tour de force* was precisely to bring religion into the spotlight as an object of study while trying to deny its significance.[8]

Taking religion into consideration is particularly important in the study of Islamism in Morocco, a country where religious discourse is often as important as political discourse in explaining why some Islamist groups have had more appeal than others (especially outside the electoral scene), or why they have adopted different forms of activism. Thus, an overly political definition of Islamism would be unnecessarily restrictive. To claim that Islamism is more about power than religion would only reduce our chances of understanding why, for instance, a movement such as Morocco's al-ʿAdl wa-l-Ihsan (Justice and Benevolence) continues to thrive despite its refusal to take part in active politics.[9] One cannot fully account for the success of al-ʿAdl wa-l-Ihsan without addressing the fact that the movement resorts to a Sufi-inspired vocabulary and practices.[10] As an Islamist movement that pledges to impart spiritual knowledge to its militants, al-ʿAdl wa-l-Ihsan can afford to stay away from electoral politics without losing its *raison d'être* and prominence, whereas the same approach would have negative consequences for other Islamist groups in the country, such as the Party of Justice and Development (PJD). Al-ʿAdl wa-l-Ihsan does not eschew electoral politics because of religious considerations – on the contrary this appears to be a rational political choice – but the distinctive Sufi-inspired religious character of al-ʿAdl wa-l-Ihsan makes it easier for the movement to follow a different path.[11]

The remainder of this chapter will further develop the idea that in the case of Morocco religion helps us to better understand the nature of Islamist politics and comprehend how movements fare in their political milieu, how they manage to cope with unexpected setbacks, and how easily they can negotiate their public image. More specifically, this study will attempt to demonstrate that al-ʿAdl wa-l-Ihsan has benefited from a subtle shift in the way Sufism is perceived. For over a century, most Islamic reformers and activists in the Muslim world regarded Sufism with suspicion. Not only did they doubt its religious soundness, they often portrayed it as a superstitious and thus inept expression of Islam that obstructed progress and prevented the advent of an Islamic modernity. However, as definitions of modernity evolved, some segments of society began challenging the old concept of Sufism. In Morocco, the shift has clearly gained momentum in recent years, especially since the terrorist attacks in Casablanca in May 2003 perpetrated by the proponents of so-called "jihadist Salafism" (*al-salafiyya al-jihādiyya*).[12] Increasingly, Sufism is taking on a positive, progressive, and "modern" connotation. In these circumstances, the spiritual and Sufi-inspired dimension of al-ʿAdl wa-l-Ihsan has proven beneficial. Because of its atypical religious stance and its uneasy relationship with Salafi Islam, this movement found itself in a better position to weather the consequences of May 2003 than other Moroccan Islamist groups.

Why religious discourse matters in Morocco

Moroccan Islamists have always faced a unique constraint. Unlike their counterparts in the rest of the Muslim world, they must struggle to find their niche in a system where the king derives his legitimacy from being both a political and a religious leader. Morocco is thus an exception: no other Muslim country enshrines constitutional articles that define the head of state as the Commander of the Faithful whose person is deemed sacred. This oft-quoted detail remains important when considered from the perspective of a religious economy in which proponents of various forms of Islamic religiosity struggle for followers and authority.[13] Whether Moroccan Islamists believe in the alleged religious stature of the Commander of the Faithful is a secondary issue; they must – willingly or unwillingly – acknowledge him as an active participant in this economy, if only to question his status as *amīr al-mu'minīn*. As long as the king is a key player in the religious sphere, Islamists have little choice but to compete or negotiate with him. In other words, because the monarch claims both religious and temporal leadership, the religious sphere in Morocco has never been up for grabs.

The fact that the king uses the title Commander of the Faithful does not mean that all Moroccans truly consider his person sacred, nor does it mean that Moroccan Islamists are doomed to fail. Rather, it means that Moroccan Islamists must contend with an additional and powerful rival and cannot expect to challenge state authority by simply invoking religion. There are both religious and political hurdles.

The religious sphere in Morocco, as in other Muslim countries, includes multiple dimensions of Islam that either overlap or oppose one another. Expressions of Sufism, Salafism, and Malikism, which are not always mutually exclusive, can further vary depending on the religious ethos through which one approaches them. In a way, the monarch has a stake in each of these dimensions and is careful to associate himself with, and cater to, all of them. Leaving a part of the religious sphere unattended would be a weakness that potential opponents could exploit. Thus, the king is simultaneously a player and a regulator in the religious space. In keeping with a strategy established by his grandfather in the late 1950s and refined under Hasan II, Muhammad VI either recognizes or tolerates competing religious groups and arbitrates between them. This creates asymmetric competition between the dominant king, who holds political power and is able to use the various aspects of his religious repertoire, on the one hand, and all remaining religious players, on the other hand, be they political or nonpolitical.

In this intricate context filled with constraints, any feature that sets a player apart from its competitors is potentially significant. Because many studies of Islamism focus on politics, there is a tendency to assume that the only meaningful distinctions are political – between "moderate" and "radical" Islamists. From that point of view, Islamists mainly differentiate themselves in their stance on political violence, their degree of pragmatism, and their willingness to accept political accommodation and the democratic process.[14] While political thoughts and attitudes are significant, they are not the only elements that help distinguish Islamists in Morocco. Differences concerning religiosity, religious epistemology, and the fundamental principles of Islam, which are often of little or no interest to students of Islamism, are also significant. Not only can they enhance the visibility of a movement, but they affect its viability and, ultimately, its level of success.

On a nonpolitical level, the two ideal-types that best represent each end of the Islamic spectrum in Morocco are the Sufis, on the one hand (such as the Qadiriyya-Butshishiyya order), and the purist Wahhabi-inspired Salafis, on the other hand (such as the association al-Daʿwa ila al-Qur'an wa-l-Sunna headed by Muhammad al-Maghrawi in Marrakech).[15] There are, of course, multiple positions between these two ends of the spectrum, but politics is not necessarily a critical factor in defining them. Because both ideal-types hardly articulate any political discourse, the issue that truly distinguishes Sufis from purist Salafis is their approach to religious knowledge and fulfillment. Although it is often overlooked, this issue is germane to Islamism, regardless of its political flavor. To ask where Islamists stand on political issues only sheds light on one facet of the phenomenon. As it turns out, their position on religious issues can be just as relevant.

The majority of Moroccan Islamist groups gravitate towards Salafism and its religious methodology, though their involvement in politics usually prevents them from meeting the standards of orthodoxy and orthopraxy set by truly purist Salafis.[16] Such is the case with the PJD and its rearguard, the Movement for Unity and Reform (MUR), with which many PJD members are affiliated. However, the movement with the most idiosyncratic religious discourse is indisputably al-ʿAdl wa-l-Ihsan, located on the other half of the spectrum, closer to Sufism. Its leader, ʿAbd al-Salam Yasin, is not the first thinker to have incorporated Sufi elements into Islamism, but his achievements have overshadowed all others.[17] A former Sufi, Yasin left the Butshishiyya order, embraced Islamism in 1972, and established one of Morocco's largest and most structured organizations. Although he is no longer affiliated with an established Sufi order (*ṭarīqa*), he never fully abandoned the spirit of Sufism. No other Islamist intellectual has emphasized spirituality and Sufi-inspired ideas to a comparable extent. In terms of typology, however, Yasin should not be considered a Sufi per se. His thoughts and political agenda are clearly in the realm of Islamism: through his institutions, he promotes a non-violent but holistic uprising (*qawma*) aimed at changing people's ideas and behavior, so that major transformations can take place in the social and political spheres as well. The ultimate objective is the emergence of a novel, just, and equitable form of Islamic polity throughout the Muslim world.[18] Yasin is an idealist who challenges the status quo in an Islamist fashion, through an ambitious project inspired by the pioneers of Islamism in the twentieth century such as Mawdudi, al-Banna, and Qutb. Thus, branding him a mere Sufi would be inaccurate, especially since Yasin himself denies being one.[19] At best, one may view him as the leader of an Islamist movement that operates, to a certain extent, like a Sufi order.

It is important not to underestimate the originality of Yasin's religious discourse – and therefore its role as a distinguishing feature in the religious sphere – by claiming that it is one of many mystical voices. Admittedly, Yasin's spiritual teachings have much in common with those of major Sufi shaykhs. In that sense, his religious discourse may indeed appear unexceptional. However, such a characterization is misleading and can be sustained only if Yasin's religious discourse is isolated from his political ideology. When the two are combined, they create a synthesis unusual enough to challenge our standard concepts of Islamism as well as our understanding of the relationship between Sufism and politics. Rüdiger Seesemann correctly points out that even when Sufis hail the merits of shunning temporal power, few of them actually avoid associating with the political class.[20] Nevertheless, because Yasin is a Sufi-inspired Islamist and not an actual Sufi, his objectives transcend any consideration of an association or a rapprochement with those who hold power. As a result, al-ʿAdl wa-l-Ihsan and its leader cannot be categorized in any of the existing theoretical models concerning the contemporary attitude of Sufis *vis-à-vis* political power. For example, Yasin and his movement do not simply use Sufi ideas and structures to counterbalance the power of the state and encourage civil society, as occurred in Senegal.[21] Nor is the state trying to co-opt them in order to gain the support of their members in exchange for various benefits, as the Islamist regime in the Sudan strove to do with local Sufis.[22] Moreover, Yasin and his followers are different from militant Sufis such as the al-Ahbash in Lebanon, who entered the political scene in reaction to the rise of Islamism.[23] In short, because Yasin and his movement lie at the confluence of Islamism and

Sufism, their religious and political discourses reinforce each other's distinctive character and together they break common patterns.[24]

The Sufi gamble

Until recently, there were three main reasons why Sufi-inspired ideas were key to al-ʿAdl wa-l-Ihsan's position on the political chessboard. First, of all the aspects of Islam on which the Moroccan monarchy is able to capitalize, Sufism is arguably the one that King Hasan II emphasized the least from the 1960s to the 1990s. Second, Sufism provides a source of pious authority the opponents of the status quo can tap into. Yasin often highlights the fact that besides their role as spiritual educators, the great Sufis of the past also "settled disputes and interceded with the rulers on behalf of the oppressed."[25] Indeed, various Sufis from the pre-modern and modern periods figure on Yasin's list of illustrious men who embody Islamic resistance against oppressive rule. He mentions al-Yusi (d. 1691), well-known in Moroccan hagiographical literature for having confronted Sultan Mawlay Ismaʿil; ʿAbd al-Qadir al-Jaza'iri (d. 1883), who fought the French colonial army in Algeria; the shaykhs of the Sanusi order in Libya, who led the resistance against Italian colonialism; and the mahdi of the Sudan (d. 1885), who fought Anglo-Egyptian forces at the time of British colonial ascendancy.[26] Third, Sufism remains a significant dimension of Moroccan Islam that resonates with many citizens from different social backgrounds. Still, because of the Salafi underpinnings of their ideology, most Islamist movements – including the PJD, the MUR, and their forerunners – dismissed Sufism. Thus, they allowed Yasin and al-ʿAdl wa-l-Ihsan the privilege of using Sufi-inspired ideas to mobilize individuals, structure their actions, and address political questions.

The decision of the other Islamists to oppose Sufism was a bold one. Not only did they surrender a source of authority to ʿAbd al-Salam Yasin, but they chose stringent reformism over a perspective with wider popular appeal. Sufism has been a perplexing issue for Moroccan Islamic activists since the beginning of the twentieth century. Even its most devoted critics sometimes had to acknowledge it out of populism or nationalism. ʿAllal al-Fasi (d. 1974), the country's foremost modernist reformer and nationalist, spent years trying to steer his fellow citizens away from Sufism under the French Protectorate. Yet Sufism was so deeply rooted in Morocco's religious identity that in the end al-Fasi preferred to turn it into a national symbol. In one of the articles devoted to this issue, he encouraged the study of the Sufi past because "it sheds light on one of the most important aspects of Moroccan thought and it is our country's contribution *('aṭā')* to the field of Qur'anic philosophy."[27] In another text dating from the late 1940s, al-Fasi tried to resolve an issue that divided the nation by arguing that the virtues of Sufism had predisposed Moroccans to accept Salafism, which al-Fasi loosely defined as a scripturalist but rational, humanistic, and progressive understanding of Islam. The simplicity of Morocco's mystical instincts, he claimed, had favored the transition from mysticism to the pure and equally uncomplicated scriptural approach of the Salafis.[28] In other words, because Moroccans were such good Sufis, they willingly embraced Salafism.

Despite this rather unusual argument, al-Fasi did not want to rehabilitate Sufism per se, and he certainly did not think that it was a proper Islamic response to the challenges posed by modernity, the West, and post-colonialism. Yet he was forced to admit that Sufism was a fundamental aspect of the Moroccan religious heritage and that it was politically unwise to condemn it outright.[29]

ʿAbd al-Salam Yasin came to a similar conclusion; unlike al-Fasi, however, he made Sufism the cornerstone of his ideology. His decision to openly merge Sufi-inspired ideas with Islamism was also a risky one. On a popular level, Yasin did benefit from his reappropriation of Sufism, but he sometimes carried it so far that it undermined his credibility in the eyes of those who were either insensitive to mysticism or had Salafi inclinations. Over the years, the francophone and secular Moroccan press regularly scoffed at Yasin's mystical visions (*ru'an*) and alleged supernatural exploits, such as the rumors concerning his gift of ubiquity.[30] Mainstream Islamists followed suit and, from a religious point of view, kept discrediting the Sufi-inspired side of Yasin's thought. This external pressure has been a constant thorn in the side of al-ʿAdl wa-l-Ihsan, forcing Yasin to devote much of his literary output to justifying his religious stance. In the crowded religious sphere of Morocco, where Islamist movements have little room to compete for constituents, it is vital to respond adequately to theological critiques, regardless of how technical they may be.[31]

In at least one instance, disagreements about the mystical nature of Yasin's leadership contributed to dissent within his own movement. Muhammad al-Bashiri (d. 1999), one of Yasin's main collaborators and a senior member of al-ʿAdl wa-l-Ihsan's Guidance Council (*majlis al-irshād*), left the party in 1999, just before his untimely death. His departure was unsettling and revealed the tensions that had been building up within al-ʿAdl wa-l-Ihsan for some time. Not only was al-Bashiri Yasin's right-hand man, he also represented the small Salafi-inclined wing of the movement. Commentators disagree on the motives behind his break with Yasin. Some close to al-Bashiri have suggested that he disapproved of Yasin's growing tendency toward arbitrary leadership, whereby he allowed his daughter Nadia to rise in the ranks of al-ʿAdl wa-l-Ihsan without following proper procedures.[32] Others claim that al-Bashiri left because he disapproved of Yasin's refusal to take part in the electoral process.[33]

There is no doubt that al-Bashiri broke away from al-ʿAdl wa-l-Ihsan because of frustrated personal and political ambitions. However, he related those frustrations to Yasin's Sufi inspiration. Al-Bashiri did not approve of the leader's emphasis on spiritual authority based on prophetic visions and dream interpretations. In declarations he later made to the Moroccan press, al-Bashiri claimed that Yasin had unnecessarily increased his reliance on Sufism between the 1980s and the late 1990s. As a result, he crossed a line and started posing as a Saint-Guide (*al-walī al-murshid*) rather than a Guide-in-Chief (*al-murshid al-ʿāmm*), Yasin's official title, which is commonly translated as "Supreme Guide." A Saint-Guide, al-Bashiri added, is someone who cannot conceivably be mistaken and whose decisions are therefore unquestionable.[34] Al-Bashiri's objections did not revolve around theological minutiae per se, but he could not dissociate Yasin's Sufi-inspired religious discourse from the structural and political evolution of al-ʿAdl wa-l-Ihsan. According to him, the former had a detrimental impact on the latter.

On the whole, however, the inspiration from Sufism appears to have been powerful enough to prompt the Moroccan government to neutralize the fundamental aspects of Yasin's religious ideas by making them part of official Islam. In 2001, the Ministry of Awqaf and Religious Affairs published the text of a conference on Salafi Sufism (*al-taṣawwuf al-salafi*) that the minister had delivered at the Royal Palace in Rabat.[35] Surprisingly, it was a trilingual edition – in Arabic, French, and English – clearly aimed at an audience as wide as that of Yasin, whose writings have also been published in these three languages. The content itself is no less surprising. Anyone familiar with Yasin's writings cannot fail to notice a striking similarity between the Ministry's booklet and a larger book entitled *al-Ihsan*, which Yasin had originally written in the 1980s but could not formally publish in its entirety until 1998.[36] In the text of his allocution, the Minister of Awqaf and Religious Affairs discusses the same issues, uses the same categories of "Salafi Sufism" and "philosophical Sufism" that Yasin had previously emphasized, and, like Yasin, concludes that Salafi Sufism is moderate, perfectly valid, and orthodox.

One may argue that, through the minister, the monarchy was merely reaffirming its time-honored stance on Sufism. Indeed, the monarchy had never been opposed to Sufism, Salafism (as defined by al-Fasi and the Moroccan Islamic modernists from the 1940s onward), or a moderate combination of both; however, it had never cared to officially articulate its views in terms of "Salafi Sufism" before. The timing of this publication and the ideas contained in it suggest that the monarchy intended to duplicate a major aspect of Yasin's religious discourse and pass it as its own. This would be consistent with the monarchy's strategy of encroaching upon the religious sphere by preventing a political opponent – in this case Yasin – from being the sole beneficiary of a particular interpretation of the Islamic heritage. Needless to say, the monarchy would not have tried to stymie Yasin if it did not believe that his Sufi-inspired ideas were competitive in the religious sphere and could translate into political gains.

Axiological reversal

Due to a subtle shift in religious values in recent years, there now seems to be a fourth reason why Yasin's Sufi-inspired ideas are key to the politics of al-ʿAdl wa-l-Ihsan. As mentioned in the introduction (p. 90), Sufism enjoyed limited support from Islamists and their early twentieth-century precursors. Individual and regional differences notwithstanding, most twentieth-century Islamic reformers saw Sufism as a form of piety fraught with superstitions and religious innovations. Not only was it one of the main causes of Muslim decline, they argued, it also hindered the renaissance of Islamic society. Sufism was seen as cultivating passivism, discouraging Muslims from becoming active in the public sphere, and even preventing them from accepting modern scientific advances and technologies. Rashid Rida (d. 1935), the great proponent of Islamic modernist reform in Egypt, lamented that Sufis were giving Islam a bad name: they prevented Europeans from seeing its true, progressive, and rational nature.[37] Worse, Sufism had also paved the way for colonialism. Rida recalled how the warnings about French encroachment in North Africa issued in his journal *al-Manar* fell on deaf ears. Moroccans were so imbued with Sufism, he remarked, that they naively preferred to seek protection from their national saint, Mawlay Idris (d. 791).[38]

Despite the efforts of Hasan al-Banna in Egypt and especially Saʿid Hawwa (d. 1989) in Syria to salvage aspects of Sufism, Islamists largely embraced Rida's critical views.[39] Most deemed mysticism at odds with an instrumental-rational concept of Islamic modernity. What mattered to Islamists first and foremost was the rational, systematic, and pragmatic dimension of religion. Thus, they used to support an Islamic version of political modernity that envisioned an organic sociopolitical order superior to modern Western polities in every respect: governance, justice, economics, ethics, and faith. The more Islamists conceived of their ideology as an Islamic version of the Western utopia of a triumphant modernity, the more likely they were to regard Sufism with suspicion.[40] To paraphrase a famous slogan, Islam was the solution because it was an inherently rational religion capable of ushering Muslims into the ultimate kind of modernity. To be sure, Islamic definitions of this modernity varied and changed over time, just as they did in the West. Yet Sufi approaches to religion remained on the losing end so long as instrumental-rationalist Islamists concurred with Western instrumental-rationalist ideas about the pre-modern character of mysticism and esoteric knowledge.

As serious reevaluations of the notion of modernity gained momentum in the West after the Second World War, the waning of instrumental-rational certitudes opened the door to a reappraisal of previously degraded forms of religion. Whether scholars call this newest paradigm high modernity, late modernity, or ultramodernity, it does not imply that previous models are being jettisoned. As Jean-Paul Willaime put it, "Ultramodernity is still modernity, but it is a disenchanted, problematised and self-relativised modernity."[41] The full implications of this phenomenon are too vast to be discussed here, but ultramodernity did encourage a renewed interest in mysticism in general. In the West, sociologists have noted that new religious trends favor experience and faith over ritual, emphasize spiritual growth, and stress intuitive knowledge over exoteric scriptural knowledge.[42] Ultramodernity thus set the stage for the rehabilitation of Sufism and its gradual reconciliation with the notion of modernity. In this new context, Rashid Rida's old fear that Sufism may cause rationalist Westerners and Westernized elites to denigrate Islam no longer seems as *apropos* as it did in the early twentieth century.

In 1992, commenting on the Islamists and their overall lack of awareness of the latest intellectual debates in the West, Ernest Gellner remarked: "[they] are not very much concerned with our relativists. I doubt whether they give them a great deal of thought."[43] The truth is that some of them did. In 1998, ʿAbd al-Salam Yasin used Western critics of modernity to write the most original claim in support of mysticism ever written by an Islamist.[44] The book, written in French, claims that the best remedy to the crisis of modernity is the largely spiritual, Sufi-inspired interpretation of Islam that had become the hallmark of al-ʿAdl wa-l-Ihsan. Yasin's argument simultaneously built on and reacted against ultramodernity. He was aware that some Western thinkers were turning the tide of intellectual history and that the age of hegemonic rationalist utopias was virtually over. He was also aware that, in those circumstances, the supra-rational or intuitive dimension of mystical knowledge could be imbued with greater credibility. This is what Yasin had in mind when he claimed: "One day, the 'post-post-period' will be Islamic."[45]

But while ultramodernity created favorable conditions for the rehabilitation of Sufism and Sufi-inspired ideas, studies have shown that it also favored purist Salafism and other forms of "neo-fundamentalism," to use Olivier Roy's expression.[46] What, then, allowed Yasin's atypical Islamist discourse to gain a competitive edge in the religious landscape of Morocco? Why does one find indications that his Sufi-inspired ideas elicited more positive responses than the Salafi-inspired ideas of his Islamist competitors in the past few years? Terrorism is certainly part of the answer. Despite criticism of the alleged non-modern character of Sufism, its Moroccan proponents have at least enjoyed the reputation of being peaceful and more tolerant of religious diversity than the Salafis.[47] This essentialist representation of the Sufi, however, does not always correspond to reality: Sufis can be – and have been – violent, even in recent times.[48] Nonetheless, this representation is often taken for granted, and a Sufi-inspired Islamist like Yasin has been able to benefit from that. In an unexpected and indirect way, his Sufi gamble proved particularly rewarding from 2003 onward, when the conflation of violence with Salafism in some of the Moroccan media put pressure on most major Islamists. Not only did Yasin avoid the ensuing wave of criticism because of his religious stance; the crisis allowed him and his collaborators to play the Sufi card in an attempt to enhance the reputation of al-ʿAdl wa-l-Ihsan. In other words, the backlash against homegrown Moroccan terrorism momentarily heightened the axiological reversal by suggesting that Sufi-inspired ideas were ethically superior to – and not merely on a par with – Salafi-inspired ones.

It is interesting to note that the transition was rather abrupt. Two days prior to the terrorist attacks of May 16, 2003 in Casablanca that killed forty-five people in a series of explosions, one of the major francophone newspapers in Morocco published a short article on the virtues of Sufism, which the author presented as a bulwark against all forms of Islamism, including the Sufi-inspired ideology of al-ʿAdl wa-l-Ihsan.[49] The events of 9/11 had cast a shadow on Islamism in general, but the particulars of Yasin's religious discourse were not yet sufficient to protect him and his movement from criticism.

The shock of May 2003 changed that situation. First, the terrorist attacks had been perpetrated by local maverick Salafis linked to a religious trend dubbed "jihadist Salafism" (*al-salafiyya al-jihādiyya*). For decades, Salafism in Morocco had been primarily associated with the nationalist religious figures that opposed French and Spanish colonialism from the perspective of Islamic modernism, such as ʿAllal al-Fasi and ʿAbdallah Guennoun (d. 1989). These self-styled Salafis of a previous era were committed patriots whose religious and political contributions to independent Morocco were undeniably positive. However, they conceptualized Salafism in a loose and somewhat peculiar fashion of which purist Salafis in Morocco and elsewhere could not approve. In the wake of May 2003, Moroccans were suddenly confronted with the meaning of Salafism predominant in the rest of the Muslim world. This purist type of Salafism was closer to Wahhabi Islam; its center of gravity was in Saudi Arabia, where many of its Moroccan advocates had studied. It was also much less tolerant of the religious traditions dear to many Moroccans, including the Maliki school of law, Ash'ari theology, and, of course, Sufism. Second, May 2003 suggested that this form of Salafism could degenerate into jihadist violence. As a result, Moroccans' suspicions turned to all groups and individuals associated with, or remotely connected to, purist Salafism and its epistemology. The detention and highly publicized trial of several Wahhabi-inspired Salafis accused of propagating religious extremism and promoting violence put Salafi-inclined activists of all shades in a delicate position.[50]

This conjuncture provided al-'Adl wa-l-Ihsan with an opportunity to use its atypical religious discourse for political advantage. Until May 2003, mainstream Moroccan Islamists, including leaders of the PJD and the MUR, had boasted their affinities with purist Salafi Islam. Following the events of Casablanca, however, genealogical and methodological links with this type of Salafism became a political drawback, whereas popular appreciation of religious discourses located toward the other end of the Islamic spectrum increased proportionally. In that context, the religious dimension of Islamism took on a particular relevance.

Though non-violent and less purist than the Wahhabi-inspired Salafi preachers under trial, the leaders of the PJD and the MUR faced an unprecedented wave of criticism. The Moroccan press regularly accused the PJD of having an ambivalent religious discourse that could lead to extremism.[51] Commentators suggested that the party was an accomplice of the *salafiyya jihādiyya* and some ministers even asked for its dissolution.[52] The party thus found itself in a very uncomfortable situation: both its credibility and its popular appeal were undermined. To remedy the problem, the PJD distanced itself from its more openly rigorist and Salafi-oriented rearguard, the MUR. The two organizations continued to work in symbiosis behind the scenes, but the leaders of the PJD felt the need to publicly establish a clear distinction between the political party and its sister organization and to reiterate that the former was independent of the latter.[53] Nevertheless, the wave of criticism forced the PJD to keep a lower profile on the political scene, which ran against its very *raison d'être*. The election of Sa'd al-Din al-'Uthmani as Secretary-General in the spring of 2004 was intended to cast the party in a more favorable light. A psychiatrist by training, al-'Uthmani (b. 1956) provided the PJD with a younger, more modern, and conciliatory image. Still, the events of May 2003 clearly slowed the party's progress.

The MUR also found itself in the line of fire because of its Salafi orientation. Prior to the terrorist attacks, its newspaper *al-Tajdid* had lent support to the purist strand of Salafism in Morocco. Defending Hasan al-Kattani, a conservative Salafi educated in Saudi Arabia and Jordan and based in Salé, who had been arrested in February 2003, the newspaper claimed that anyone who questioned al-Kattani's creed – or the creed of the most towering figures associated with purist Salafism, such as Muhammad ibn 'Abd al-Wahhab (d. 1792) and Nasir al-Din al-Albani (d. 1999) – was either a hypocrite or someone with little religious knowledge.[54] By May 2003, however, such bold affirmations became too compromising and compelled the leaders of the MUR to justify the association's religious stance. One interesting example comes from a book published in Casablanca in 2004 by Ahmad al-Raysuni (b. 1953), a former leader of the MUR who moved to Saudi Arabia in 2006. In one section of his book, al-Raysuni downplays the organization's connection to Salafism. He claims that no Muslim would ever object to being branded a Salafi because being associated with the pious ancestors (*salaf*) is an honor; yet he also contends that Muslim activists seldom use the labels "Salafi" and "Salafism." According to him, Western scholars and outsiders are generally responsible for imposing these labels on Muslims, either for typological purposes or to denigrate them.[55] For this reason, al-Raysuni refrains from claiming Salafi labels for the MUR or for himself.

Al-Raysuni's argument is highly unusual and betrays his attempt to counter the negative connotation of Salafism after May 2003. Historically, Islamists have often tried to underscore their Salafi identity or at least to argue that they fell within the pale of Salafism. Al-Raysuni, however, goes in the other direction. He is right when he says that Western scholars and outsiders use the term "Salafism" *ad lib*, and it is true that Western scholars played a key role in the elaboration of a questionable conceptual package that conflates Salafism and Islamic modernist reform in general, but it is preposterous to pretend that Muslim activists seldom call themselves Salafis or use the term *salafiyya*.[56] In Morocco and elsewhere, these labels are now as commonplace as they are self-ascribed. Purist Salafis, for instance, use them systematically and insist that they are an authentic part of Islamic vocabulary. Nasir al-Din al-Albani, the same scholar that the MUR cited as an authority in February 2003, even decreed that it is mandatory for all true Salafis to call themselves Salafis.[57]

Throughout the crisis, al-ʿAdl wa-l-Ihsan remained largely free of criticism. As a Sufi-inspired organization that does not receive outside funding, it avoided the kind of public scrutiny other Islamist movements were subjected to.[58] Yasin and his organization were not only further from purist Salafism on the religious spectrum, they also had a history of tense relations with its supporters. A year after the events of Casablanca, a leading Moroccan analyst claimed that Morocco was lucky to have al-ʿAdl wa-l-Ihsan because it served as a bulwark against rigorist, Wahhabi-inspired Salafis. He remarked that Muhammad al-Fizazi, a purist Salafi preacher who stood trial and was condemned in the wake of May 2003, had previously condemned Yasin, his Sufi-inspired religious discourse, and his organization.[59] The clear antagonism between purist Salafis and Yasin proved beneficial to the latter and enhanced the reputation of his movement. Speaking on behalf of al-ʿAdl wa-l-Ihsan, Yasin's daughter Nadia did not hesitate to play the Sufi card. To an American journalist, she claimed that those who carried out the 2003 terrorist attacks were Wahhabis through whom the state had once hoped to counterbalance al-ʿAdl wa-l-Ihsan, adding: "[The authorities] will realize that we're the loyal opposition and against destabilization. Already they understand that our program for political change is based on spirituality, acts of faith and [is] close to the Sufi program."[60]

The state's response to the terrorist attacks also took some pressure off al-ʿAdl wa-l-Ihsan and validated certain aspects of its religious discourse. From the onset, the king and the Ministry of Awqaf and Religious Affairs turned their attention to purist Salafism, which they branded an "imported" form of Islam. This elevated the status of al-ʿAdl wa-l-Ihsan, on the opposite side of the religious spectrum. Indeed, the

Palace renewed its commitment to Sufism and its major orders, which were already important assets in the Kingdom's foreign policy with West African countries. Official references to Sufism as a pillar of Moroccan Islam became prominent enough that in 2005 the MUR publicly questioned the soundness of the position of the Ministry of Awqaf and Religious Affairs on this issue.[61] On its Arabic website, the Ministry responded by reasserting the religious validity of Sufism and its positive impact on Moroccan society.[62] Since then, the monarchy has also sponsored the Fes Festival of Sufi Culture and the Marrakech World Festival of Sufi Music and Meetings – also known as Samaâ Marrakech – both of which began in 2007. These international festivals, which celebrate the authenticity and centrality of Sufism in Moroccan Islam (the former presents Morocco as a "land of Sufism"), have provided the monarchy with additional opportunities to promote Sufism as a wellspring of tolerance and an antidote against hatred and extremism.[63]

While the authorities concentrated on counterbalancing purist Salafism and its potential excesses, al-ʿAdl wa-l-Ihsan and its leading militants remained quite visible. At times, they were even daring. Several events suggest that the movement's confidence was on the rise: proselytizing activities increased and Nadia Yasin confronted the monarchy in 2005 when she declared that she favors a republican system in Morocco. In May 2006, the police arrested about 300 members of al-ʿAdl wa-l-Ihsan – most of whom were immediately released – probably to remind the movement to curb its ambition.[64] Nonetheless, al-ʿAdl wa-l-Ihsan may have mismanaged the credibility it acquired after the events of May 2003. Much has been written in the past few years about a highly publicized vision ʿAbd al-Salam Yasin reportedly had, which foretold that the *qawma* (uprising) would occur before the end of 2006. This renewed emphasis on dreams and visions exposed the movement to criticism, especially when it became obvious that the supernatural prediction was erroneous. In a sudden turn of events, the secular and the Islamist press united in their condemnation of Yasin and his movement. The MUR, in particular, seized the opportunity to portray itself as a more reasonable religious player than al-ʿAdl wa-l-Ihsan. In numerous written admonitions, its newspaper lamented Yasin's lack of seriousness, accusing him of impeding critical thinking and tarnishing the reputation of Islamism as a whole through the mystical excesses of his religious discourse.[65] It is not clear that al-ʿAdl wa-l-Ihsan has fully recovered, politically and religiously, from this tactical error. In February 2011, the movement's spokesman, Fathallah Arsalan, still had to explain why the *qawma* has not happened yet and whether Yasin's prediction was still valid.[66]

Conclusion

The case of Morocco suggests that religious discourses have a noticeable impact on the evolution and political success of Islamist movements. By assuming that the definitions of Islamism that focus too closely on politics are normative, one may disregard an equally important dimension of the phenomenon. As recent Moroccan history demonstrates, a movement's position on the religious spectrum can greatly affect its political stance. Yet because these are variables that do not occur on the political spectrum, they will likely escape the attention of observers who classify Islamist movements solely on the basis of their political agenda or degree of political moderation (or extremism). In the Moroccan religious landscape, al-ʿAdl wa-l-Ihsan possesses a distinctive religious discourse that draws its inspiration from Sufism. Besides the monarch, its main rivals are Islamist groups of Salafi persuasion such as the PJD and the MUR. Whereas for many decades Salafism had been considered more "modern" than Sufism, the gradual redefinition of modernity in the West created conditions in which the spiritual message of al-ʿAdl wa-l-Ihsan was able to gain prominence. After the terrorist attacks of May 16, 2003 in Casablanca, ʿAbd al-Salam Yasin's movement took advantage of an apparent axiological reversal whereby Salafism lost some of its positive connotation in Morocco. As a result, al-ʿAdl wa-l-Ihsan gained some leverage and, for the most part, fared much better than its Salafi-oriented rivals throughout the 2003 crisis and its aftermath.

Notes

1 Ahmad al-Raysuni, *al-Haraka al-islamiyya al-maghribiyya: suʿud am uful?* Casablanca: Matbaʿat al-Najah al-Jadida, 2004, p. 17.

2 There are nonetheless excellent working definitions of Islamism such as that of Roxanne Euben and Muhammad Qasim Zaman, whose nuanced analysis reminds us of the difficulty of drawing sharp typological lines between Islamists and other Muslims. See their introduction to Roxanne L. Euben and Muhammad Qasim Zaman (eds.), *Princeton Readings in Islamist Thought: Texts and Contexts from al-Banna to Bin Laden*, Princeton: Princeton University Press, 2009, pp. 1–46.

3 Guilain Denoeux, "The Forgotten Swamp: Navigating Political Islam," *Middle East Policy* 9, June 2002, p. 63.

4 The late political scientist Nazih Ayubi's broad perspective and careful attention to the religious elements of Islamism allowed him to admit that "political Islam" is not always so political. Nazih Ayubi, *Political Islam: Religion and Politics in the Arab World*, London: Routledge, 1991, p. 131. More recently, Raymond Baker underlined how the New Islamists in Egypt insist on dissociating themselves from political Islam and its proponents, whose sole concern appears to be political power. In that context, it becomes rather difficult to use "Islamism" and "political Islam" interchangeably. See Raymond William Baker, *Islam Without Fear: Egypt and the New Islamists*, Cambridge, MA: Harvard University Press, 2003, pp. 175–76.

5 See Fred Halliday, "The Politics of 'Islam': A Second Look," *British Journal of Political Science* 25, July 1995, 399–417.

6 This is a debatable assumption behind the notion of post-Islamism, which is an otherwise very stimulating concept. See Olivier Roy, *Globalized Islam: The Search for a New Ummah*, New York: Columbia University Press, 2004, p. 3.

7 A stimulating study that features the dialogical perspective is Cihan Z. Tugal, "The Appeal of Islamic Politics: Ritual and Dialogue in a Poor District of Turkey," *Sociological Quarterly* 47, 2006, 245–73.

8 See Shmuel Trigano, *Qu'est-ce que la religion? La Transcendance des sociologues*, Paris: Flammarion, 2001, pp. 117–19.

9 Nadia Yasin, the daughter of al-ʿAdl wa-l-Ihsan's founder and leader ʿAbd al-Salam Yasin, defines the movement's political action negatively: "No to violence, no to clandestine action, no to external funding." She claims that the movement's political action is limited to education; it eschews both elections and armed revolution. See http://oumma.com/Notre-projet-se-resume-a-l (last accessed September 28, 2007).

10 For further details, see Henri Lauzière, "Post-Islamism and the Religious Discourse of ʿAbd al-Salam Yasin," *International Journal of Middle East Studies* 37, May 2005, 241–61.

11 It must be noted that al-ʿAdl wa-l-Ihsan is still a technically illegal but tolerated association that has never been authorized to participate in formal politics. But even if the Moroccan Ministry of the Interior were to allow the movement to form a political party – which is not impossible – the leadership of al-ʿAdl wa-l-Ihsan might still choose to eschew electoral politics to preserve the movement's credibility and independence, especially since political participation would entail compromises and the recognition that the current rules of the political game are acceptable. Hence, al-ʿAdl wa-l-Ihsan might prefer to continue playing the role of the "virtuous outsider" capable of criticizing the status of the monarch, the weakness of the Chamber of Representatives (the lower house of the Parliament), and the legitimacy of the electoral process, which the Palace continues to control. One could therefore argue that al-ʿAdl wa-l-Ihsan has little to gain and more to lose by getting involved in electoral politics. Conversely, it may have more to gain and little to lose by staying on the sidelines, which it can afford to do. This seems to be the logic behind the declaration of Hasan Binnajih, a member of al-ʿAdl wa-l-Ihsan's political office (*dā'ira siyāsiyya*), who in March 2011 speculated that the movement could form a political party while still refusing to participate in elections. See Tahar Abou El Farah, "Al Adl Wal Ihsanne bientôt parti politique reconnu?" *La Vie éco*, March 14, 2011. Available at: www.lavieeco.com (last accessed March 17, 2011).

12 In the Moroccan context, the authorities and the press are largely responsible for the popularity of this label.

13 A good presentation in a Christian context is Laurence R. Iannaccione, "The Consequences of Religious Market Structures: Adam Smith and the Economics of Religion," *Rationality and Society* 3, April 1991, 156–77.

14 Ray Takeyh and Nikolas K. Gvosdev, *The Receding Shadow of the Prophet: The Rise and Fall of Radical Political Islam*, Westport: Praeger, 2004, pp. 68–73.

15 I use the expression "purist Salafism" to describe the quietist but religiously uncompromising Salafi movement whose primary focus is to "purify" Islam from all forms of innovations and heresies, be they real or conjectural. Because Moroccan scholars and analysts often refer to this form of Salafism as *al-salafiyya al-wahhābiyya*, I will at times use the expression "Wahhabi-inspired Salafism."

16 In a 2004 interview, Muhammad Yatim, a leading member of the MUR, declared his movement's attachment to the Maliki school of law, which is dominant in Morocco. Yet at the same time he dismissed Maliki jurisprudence, arguing that Malik was a *salaf* who did not require anyone to follow his opinions but rather urged Muslims to search for the truth by returning to the Qur'an and the Sunna. This rather convoluted statement, whereby Yatim strove to strike a balance between the traditional Maliki identity of Morocco and the requirements of Salafi Islam, could hardly satisfy purist Salafis. See ʿAbd al-Hakim Abu al-Lawz, *al-Harakat al-salafiyya fi-l-Maghrib (1971–2004): bahth anthrubuluji susiyuluji*, Beirut: Markaz Dirasat al-Wahda al-ʿArabiyya, 2009, p. 395.

17 Henry Munson, Jr., *Religion and Power in Morocco*, New Haven: Yale University Press, 1993, pp. 153–58.

18 ʿAbd al-Salam Yasin, *Rijal al-qawma wa-l-islah*, n.p.: Manshurat al-Safa' li-l-Intaj, 2001, pp. 7, 30–32, 52–53.

19 Idem., *al-Ihsan*, Casablanca: Matbuʿat al-Ufuq, 1998, pp. 7, 23.

20 Rüdiger Seesemann, "Between Sufism and Islamism: The Tijaniyya and Islamist Rule in the Sudan," in Paul L. Heck (ed.) *Sufism and Politics*, Princeton: Markus Wiener, 2007, p. 32.

21 Leonardo A. Villalon, *Islamic Society and State Power in Senegal: Disciples and Citizens in Fatick*, Cambridge: Cambridge University Press, 1995.

22 Seesemann, op. cit., pp. 23–57.

23 A. Nizar Amzeh and R. Hrair Dekmejian, "A Sufi Response to Political Islamism: The Al-Ahbash of Lebanon," *International Journal of Middle East Studies* 28, May 1996, 217–29.

24 A study by Leonardo Villalon suggests that the distinctions between Sufi activists and Islamists in Senegal are becoming increasingly blurred. Yet there is little evidence that a systematic intellectual attempt at combining Sufism with Islamism – as Yasin did – is

taking place in that country. Leonardo A. Villalon, "Senegal: Shades of Islamism on a Sufi Landscape," in William F. S. Miles (ed.) *Political Islam in West Africa: State–Society Relations Transformed*, Boulder: Lynne Rienner, 2007, pp. 161–82.

25 Yasin, *Rijal*, p. 94.

26 Ibid., pp. 111–12.

27 ʿAllal al-Fasi, *al-Tasawwuf al-islami fi-l-Maghrib*, Rabat: Mu'assasat ʿAllal al-Fasi, 1998, p. 6.

28 Idem., *al-Harakat al-istiqlaliyya fi-l-maghrib al-ʿarabi*, 5th edition, Rabat: Mu'assasat ʿAllal al-Fasi, 1993, p. 133.

29 Al-Fasi was not the only modernist reformer of his generation to allow a qualified return to Sufism. His Moroccan colleague Mukhtar al-Susi (d. 1963), whose father was a Sufi shaykh, never considered himself a Sufi; but he recorded and documented the oral history of Sufi orders and admitted that pure mysticism could be a source of truth. See Hassan Rachik, "La Science est une chasse: Aperçu sur la pensée de Mokhtar Soussi," in Abdou-Filaly Ansari and Mohamed Tozy (eds.) *Penseurs maghrébins contemporains*, Tunis: Cérès, 1993, pp. 262–65.

30 Yasin is said to have visited some followers in the city of Fes while physically remaining in Salé. See Taïeb Chadi, "Les Mystères d'une machine," *Maroc Hebdo International*, 507, April 2002, 5.

31 For an example of how some religious detractors criticize Yasin on issues of creed and religious epistemology, see Abu ʿAbd al-Rahman Dhu al-Fiqar, *Mashayikh al-sufiya: al-inhiraf al-tarbawi wa-l-fasad al-ʿaqadi*, Rabat: Abu ʿAbd al-Rahman Dhu al-Fiqar, 2004.

32 Karim Boukhari, "Qui est vraiment Abdeslam Yassine?" *Tel Quel* 168, March 2006. Available at: www.telquel-online.com/168/couverture_168_1.shtml (last accessed October 15, 2007).

33 Ahmed Chaarani, *La Mouvance islamiste au Maroc: Du 11 septembre 2001 aux attentats de Casablanca du 16 mai 2003*, Paris: Karthala, 2004, p. 267.

34 Muhammad Darif, *al-Islamiyyun al-maghariba: hisabat al-siyasa fi-l-ʿamal al-islami, 1969–1999*, Casablanca: Manshurat al-Majalla al-Maghribiyya li-ʿIlm al-Ijtimaʿ al-Siyasi, 1999, p. 296.

35 ʿAbd al-Kabir al-Mudaghghari, *al-Tasawwuf al-salafi*, Rabat: Wizarat al-Awqaf wa-l-Shu'un al-Islamiyya, 2001.

36 Yasin, *al-Ihsan*, p. 7.

37 Muhammad Rashid Rida, *Tafsir al-Qur'an al-hakim al-shahir bi-Tafsir al-Manar*, 2nd edition, Cairo: Dar al-Manar, 1947, 10, pp. 423–24.

38 Jacques Jomier, *Le Commentaire coranique du Manâr: Tendances modernes de l'exégèse coranique en Égypte*, Paris: G.-P. Maisonneuve et Cie., 1954, p. 257. See also Rida, op. cit., 10, p. 446.

39 Al-Banna used the expressions "correct Sufism" (*al-taṣawwuf al-ṣaḥīḥ*) and "religious Sufism" (*taṣawwuf dīnī islāmī*). See *Jaridat al-Ikhwan al-Muslimin* 1, 1, June 1933, p. 9. On Hawwa, see Itzchak Weissman, "Saʿid Hawwa and Islamic Revivalism in Baʿthist Syria," *Studia Islamica* 85, 1, February 1997, 138–43.

40 The expressions "classical modernity" and "triumphant modernity" are from Alain Touraine, *Critique de la modernité*, Paris: Fayard, 1992, pp. 15, 21–25, 85–86.

41 Jean-Paul Willaime, "Religion in Ultramodernity," in James A. Beckford and John Walliss (eds.) *Theorising Religion: Classical and Contemporary Debates*, Aldershot: Ashgate, 2006, p. 79.

42 Lorne L. Dawson, "Anti-Modernism, Modernism, and Postmodernism: Struggling with the Cultural Significance of New Religious Movements," *Sociology of Religion* 59, 1998, pp. 138, 140–42, 148–49.

43 Ernest Gellner, *Postmodernism, Reason and Religion*, London: Routledge, 1992, p. 74.

44 ʿAbd al-Salam Yasin, *Islamiser la modernité*, Rabat: al-Ofok Impressions, 1998. For more details, see Lauzière, op. cit., pp. 252–54.

45 This quote is taken from the English translation of the book. Abdessalam Yassine, *Winning the Modern World for Islam*, translated by Martin Jenni, Iowa City: Justice and Spirituality Publishing, 2000, p. 9.

46 Roy, pp. 148–49.
47 Mark Sedgwick, *Islam & Muslims: A Guide to Diverse Experience in a Modern World*, Boston: Nicholas Brealey Publishing, 2006, p. 46.
48 Marc Gaborieau, *Le Mahdi incompris: Sayyid Ahmad Barelwî (1786–1831) et le millénarisme en Inde*, Paris: CNRS Éditions, 2010; Roman Loimeier, "Sufis and Politics in Sub-Saharan Africa," in Heck, op. cit., p. 92.
49 Abdellah Chankou, "Soufisme contre islamisme," *Aujourd'hui le Maroc*, 384, March 14, 2003. Available at: www.aujourdhui.ma/societe-details32783.html (last accessed March 2, 2007).
50 Abdellatif El Azizi, "Le Procès de la Salafia," *Maroc Hebdo International* 569, August–September 2003, 9.
51 Jean-Claude Santucci, "Le Pouvoir à l'épreuve du choc terroriste: Entre Dérives autoritaires et tentation de l'arbitraire," *Annuaire de l'Afrique du Nord* 41, 2003, 243.
52 Khadija Mohsen-Finan and Malika Zeghal, "Opposition islamiste et pouvoir monarchique au Maroc: Le Cas du Parti de la Justice et du Développement," *Revue française de science politique* 56, February 2006, 108.
53 Abdellah Chankou, "Le PJD dos au 'MUR' fait son mea culpa," *Aujourd'hui le Maroc* 415, June 26, 2003. Available at: www.aujourdhui.ma/couverture-details34218.html (last accessed August 10, 2007).
54 See the short article entitled "Yaqaza mufaji'a" in *al-Tajdid*, February 7, 2003. Available from the newspaper's archive at: www.attajdid.ma (last accessed October 17, 2007).
55 Al-Raysuni, op. cit., p. 24.
56 On the flawed assumption that Islamic modernists such as Jamal al-Din al-Afghani and Muhammad ʿAbduh were Salafis and proponents of a religious orientation called Salafism, see Henri Lauzière, "The Construction of *Salafiyya*: Reconsidering Salafism from the Perspective of Conceptual History," *International Journal of Middle East Studies* 42, August 2010, 369–89.
57 Muhammad Nasir al-Din al-Albani, "Masa'il wa ajwibatuha," *al-Asala* 2, 9, 1994, 89–90.
58 Youssef Chmirou, "La Patte blanche de Yassine," *Maroc Hebdo International* 563, June 2003, 10.
59 Mohamed Darif, "La 'Salafya jihadia' en questions," *La Vie éco* (special supplement), May 14, 2004, xiv.
60 Quoted in Marvine Howe, *Morocco: The Islamist Awakening and Other Challenges*, New York: Oxford University Press, 2005, p. 344.
61 Maʿadh al-Matiri, "Khurafa fi mawqiʿ Wizarat al-Awqaf wa-l-Shu'un al-Islamiyya," *al-Tajdid*, November 16, 2005. Available through the newspaper's online archive at: www.attajdid.ma (last accessed February 7, 2007).
62 See www.habous.gov.ma/ar/detail.aspx?id=1801&z=254 (last accessed February 7, 2007).
63 The program of the 2007 edition of the Fes Festival of Sufi Culture quotes telling excerpts from a declaration by King Muhammad VI. The declaration was originally intended for the participants of the International Meeting of Sidi Chiker, which the Ministry of Awqaf and Islamic Affairs created in 2004 to promote Sufism and establish stronger links with Sufis worldwide. The program is available under "archives" at: www.festivalculturesoufie.com (last accessed March 26, 2011).
64 Majdouline El Atouabi, "La Guerre d'usure de Yassine," *Maroc Hebdo International* 701, June 2006, 14–15.
65 See Muhammad al-Hamdawi, "Risalat nash min Harakat al-Tawhid wa-l-Islah ila Jamaʿat al-ʿAdl wa-l-Ihsan," *al-Tajdid*, January 24, 2006. See also the third article in a series of five by Muhammad al-Sahabi, "Jamaʿat al-ʿAdl wa-l-Ihsan: ma liha wa ma ʿalayha," *al-Tajdid*, April 26, 2006. These texts are available through the newspaper's online archive at: www.attajdid.ma (last accessed May 31, 2007).
66 Ahmad Najim, "Fathallah Arsalan: ma yajmaʿuna bi-l-ʿilmaniyyin akthar mimma yufarriquna," February 10, 2011. Available at: www.elaph.com (last accessed March 17, 2011).

Bibliography

al-Albani, M., "Masa'il wa ajwibatuha," *al-Asala* 2, 1994.

al-Banna, H., *Jaridat al-Ikhwan al-Muslimin* 1, 1, June 1933.

al-Fasi, A., *al-Tasawwuf al-islami fi-l-Maghrib*, Rabat: Mu'assasat ʿAllal al-Fasi, 1998.

al-Fasi, A., *al-Harakat al-istiqlaliyya fi-l-maghrib al-ʿarabi*, 5th edition, Rabat: Mu'assasat ʿAllal al-Fasi, 1993.

al-Fiqar, A., *Mashayikh al-sufiya: al-inhiraf al-tarbawi wa-l-fasad al-ʿaqadi*, Rabat: Abu ʿAbd al-Rahman Dhu al-Fiqar, 2004.

al-Hamdawi, M., "Risalat nash min Harakat al-Tawhid wa-l-Islah ila Jamaʿat al-ʿAdl wa-l-Ihsan," *al-Tajdid*, January 24, 2006.

al-Lawz, A., *al-Harakat al-salafiyya fi-l-Maghrib (1971–2004): bahth anthrubuluji susiyuluji*, Beirut: Markaz Dirasat al-Wahda al-ʿArabiyya, 2009.

al-Matiri, M., "Khurafa fi mawqiʿ Wizarat al-Awqaf wa-l-Shu'un al-Islamiyya," *al-Tajdid*, November 16, 2005.

al-Mudaghghari, A., *al-Tasawwuf al-salafi*, Rabat: Wizarat al-Awqaf wa-l-Shu'un al-Islamiyya, 2001.

al-Raysuni, A., *al-Haraka al-islamiyya al-maghribiyya: suʿud am ufu1?* Casablanca: Matbaʿat al-Najah al-Jadida, 2004.

al-Sahabi, M., "Jamaʿat al-ʿAdl wa-l-Ihsan: ma liha wa ma ʿalayha," *al-Tajdid*, April 26, 2006.

Amzeh, A. N. and Dekmejian, R. H., "A Sufi Response to Political Islamism: The Al-Ahbash of Lebanon," *International Journal of Middle East Studies* 28, 1996.

Ayubi, N., *Political Islam: Religion and Politics in the Arab World*, London: Routledge, 1991.

Baker, R. W., *Islam without Fear: Egypt and the New Islamists*, Cambridge, MA: Harvard University Press, 2003.

Beckford, J. A. and Walliss, J. (ed.) *Theorising Religion: Classical and Contemporary Debates*, Aldershot: Ashgate, 2006.

Boukhari, K., "Qui est vraiment Abdeslam Yassine?" *Tel Quel* 168, 2006.

Chaarani, A., *La Mouvance islamiste au Maroc: Du 11 septembre 2001 aux attentats de Casablanca du 16 mai 2003*, Paris: Karthala, 2004.

Chadi, T., "Les Mystères d'une machine," *Maroc Hebdo International* 507, 2002.

Chankou, A., "Le PJD dos au 'MUR' fait son mea culpa," *Aujourd'hui le Maroc* 415, June 26, 2003.

Chankou, A., "Soufisme contre islamisme," *Aujourd'hui le Maroc* 384, March 14, 2003.

Chmirou, Y., "La Patte blanche de Yassine," *Maroc Hebdo International* 563, 2003.

Darif, M., "La 'Salafya jihadia' en questions," *La Vie éco* (special supplement), May 14, 2004.

Darif, M., *al-Islamiyyun al-magharibа: hisabat al-siyasa fi-l-ʿamal al-islami, 1969–1999*, Casablanca: Manshurat al-Majalla al-Maghribiyya li-ʿIlm al-Ijtimaʿ al-Siyasi, 1999.

Dawson, L. L., "Anti-Modernism, Modernism, and Postmodernism: Struggling with the Cultural Significance of New Religious Movements," *Sociology of Religion* 59, 1998.

Denoeux, G., "The Forgotten Swamp: Navigating Political Islam," *Middle East Policy* 9, 2002.

El Atouabi, M., "La Guerre d'usure de Yassine," *Maroc Hebdo International* 701, 2006.

El Azizi, A., "Le Procès de la Salafia," *Maroc Hebdo International* 559, 2003.

El Farah, T. A., "Al Adl Wal Ihsanne bientôt parti politique reconnu?" *La Vie éco*, March 14, 2011.

Euben, R. and Zaman, M. Q. (eds.), *Princeton Readings in Islamist Thought: Texts and Contexts from al-Banna to Bin Laden*, Princeton: Princeton University Press, 2009.

Filaly-Ansari, A. and Tozy, M. (eds.), *Penseurs maghrébins contemporains*, Tunis: Cérès, 1993.

Gaborieau, M., *Le Mahdi incompris: Sayyid Ahmad Barelwî (1786–1831) et le millénarisme en Inde*, Paris: CNRS Éditions, 2010.

Gellner, E., *Postmodernism, Reason and Religion*, London: Routledge, 1992.

Halliday, F., "The Politics of 'Islam': A Second Look," *British Journal of Political Science* 25, 1995.

Heck, P. (ed.), *Sufism and Politics*, Princeton: Markus Wiener, 2007.
Howe, M., *Morocco: The Islamist Awakening and Other Challenges*, New York: Oxford University Press, 2005.
Iannaccione, L. R., "The Consequences of Religious Market Structures: Adam Smith and the Economics of Religion," *Rationality and Society* 3, 1991.
Jomier, J., *Le Commentaire coranique du Manâr: Tendances modernes de l'exégèse coranique en Égypte*, Paris: G.-P. Maisonneuve et Cie, 1954.
Lauzière, H., "The Construction of *Salafiyya*: Reconsidering Salafism From the Perspective of Conceptual History," *International Journal of Middle East Studies* 42, 2010.
Lauzière, H., "Post-Islamism and the Religious Discourse of ʿAbd al-Salam Yasin," *International Journal of Middle East Studies* 37, 2005.
Miles, W. F. S. (ed.), *Political Islam in West Africa: State–Society Relations Transformed*, Boulder: Lynne Rienner, 2007.
Mohsen-Finan, K. and Zeghal, M., "Opposition islamiste et pouvoir monarchique au Maroc: Le Cas du Parti de la Justice et du Développement," *Revue française de science politique* 56, 2006.
Munson, H., Jr., *Religion and Power in Morocco*, New Haven: Yale University Press, 1993.
Najim, A., "Fathallah Arsalan: ma yajmaʿuna bi-l-ʿilmaniyyin akthar mimma yufarriquna," February 10, 2011.
Rida, M. R., *Tafsir al-Qur'an al-hakim al-shahir bi-Tafsir al-Manar*, 2nd edition, Cairo: Dar al-Manar, 1947.
Roy, O., *Globalized Islam: The Search for a New Ummah*, New York: Columbia University Press, 2004.
Santucci, J., "Le Pouvoir à l'épreuve du choc terroriste: Entre Dérives autoritaires et tentation de l'arbitraire," *Annuaire de l'Afrique du Nord* 41, 2003.
Sedgwick, M., *Islam & Muslims: A Guide to Diverse Experience in a Modern World*, Boston: Nicholas Brealey Publishing, 2006.
Takeyh, R. and Gvosdev, N. K., *The Receding Shadow of the Prophet: The Rise and Fall of Radical Political Islam*, Westport: Praeger, 2004.
Touraine, A., *Critique de la modernité*, Paris: Fayard, 1992.
Trigano, S., *Qu'est-ce que la religion? La Transcendance des sociologues*, Paris: Flammarion, 2001.
Tugal, C. Z., "The Appeal of Islamic Politics: Ritual and Dialogue in a Poor District of Turkey," *Sociological Quarterly* 47, 2006.
Villalon, L. A., *Islamic Society and State Power in Senegal: Disciples and Citizens in Fatick*, Cambridge: Cambridge University Press, 1995.
Weissman, I., "Saʿid Hawwa and Islamic Revivalism in Baʿthist Syria," *Studia Islamica* 85, 1997.
www.festivalculturesoufie.com (accessed March 26, 2011).
www.habous.gov.ma/ar/detail.aspx?id=1801&z=254 (accessed February 07, 2007).
"Yaqaza mufaji'a," in *al-Tajdid*, February 7, 2003. Available from the newspaper's archive at: www.attajdid.ma (accessed October 17, 2007).
Yasin, A., *Rijal al-qawma wa-l-islah*, n.p.: Manshurat al-Safa' li-l-Intaj, 2001.
Yasin, A., *Islamiser la modernité*, Rabat: al-Ofok Impressions, 1998.
Yasin, N., "Notre Projet se résume à l'appellation de notre mouvement: Justice et Spiritualité," Bagnolet, France: Oumma, 2007. Available at: http://oumma.com/Notre-projet-se-resume-a-l (last accessed September 28, 2007).
Yassine, A., *Winning the Modern World for Islam*, translated by Martin Jenni, Iowa City: Justice and Spirituality Publishing, 2000.

6

THE MUSLIM BROTHERHOOD – BETWEEN EVANGELIZING AND POLITICS

The challenges of incorporating the Brotherhood into the political process

Amr Elshobaki

Introduction

Ever since its foundation in 1928 by Hassan al-Banna the Muslim Brotherhood has been in an almost constant state of conflict with the political authorities. Although its intensity has varied, this confrontation was a consistent feature of the political scene of the last century, and continued until the ouster of Hosni Mubarak from office on February 11, 2011. Now that the "January 25 Egyptian revolution" has succeeded in removing Mubarak from power, the Brotherhood has established a political party, the Freedom and Justice Party. With the founding of the group's first legally established political party in June 2011, the possibility now exists for the group to overcome some of the tensions that have existed since its inception.

The Brotherhood's historical journey is that of the Egyptian political system itself. The organization grew under the monarchy and a period of quasi-liberal rule, clashed with the Nasserite authorities, reached a truce with the Sadat regime, and was subjected to a policy of partial inclusion (or partial exclusion) under Mubarak.

The organization is now more than 80 years old, years that have packed in a rich legacy of generational, intellectual, and political diversity, generating debate both over and within the Brotherhood. Following the 1952 revolution, the Brotherhood engaged in a bitter struggle with Abdel Nasser's regime. With its members suffering inside prisons and detention camps, the organization developed a siege mentality, and for the duration of Sadat's presidency – which began with the release of Brotherhood members and ended with their re-arrest – the group withdrew from public life. The organization's flexible political and intellectual stance has allowed it to espouse a largely inclusive vision of Islam and its role in society. Its approach allows it to accommodate members across the spectrum of Islamic activism: politicians and preachers, parliamentarians and clergy, Sufis and revolutionaries. The Brotherhood's leadership has included both Hassan Al-Hodeibi, a conservative judge, and the radical ideologue Sayyid Qutb.

This organizational diversity mirrors the variety of the various political regimes that the group has dealt with and opposed. Indeed, it is perhaps the only political organization that deserves to be called a "witness to history." The evolution of the Brotherhood can be summarized as consisting of three main stages. The first two are historical experiences, while the third is projected and concerns the post-Mubarak period.

The founding Brothers: the beginnings of the Society of Muslim Brothers

The Society of Muslim Brothers was founded by Sheikh Hassan al-Banna in the city of Ismailia in 1928. Almost from its inception it has remained one of the largest political organizations in Egypt and the region. It has successfully varied its tactics to meet the different challenges it has faced, oscillating between rapid progress and patient immobility, attack and defense, and dialogue and confrontation. This strategic flexibility reflects remarkable organizational capabilities that have enabled it to endure and thrive under monarchy and republic alike.

Commentators often express surprise that the Muslim Brotherhood has managed to maintain its organizational structure intact, or that contemporary Brothers are able to coexist despite the clear intellectual and generational divisions within the group.

General features of the Muslim Brotherhood

Al-Banna himself defined the Brotherhood within a broad framework resistant to easy categorization: "Brothers, you are not a charitable organization, nor a political party, nor an institution founded to achieve some narrow purpose. You are a new spirit coursing through the heart of the *umma*, animating it with the word of Allah; a new light breaking, scattering the darkness of materialism through knowledge of Allah; a ringing voice repeating the Prophet's call. It is right and proper to feel that you have taken up the burden others have relinquished."[1] Al-Banna himself had observed the infighting and weaknesses of the pre-1952 political scene in Egypt and had little sympathy for political parties or factionalism: "Gentlemen, I believe that Islam – which is above all else the religion of unity, contentment, true brotherhood and sincere fellowship between all men, not to mention the creed of a united *umma* and people – is neither content nor compatible with the party system ... Our one hope is that these parties be disbanded and a single national body formed to lead the *umma* to victory in accordance with the teachings of the Noble Quran."[2]

The founding Brothers' default position was one of non-violence and peaceful evangelism, but this did not preclude the existence of a minority trend with a preference for violence, which – as in the case of the "special organization" (*al tanzim al khaas*) – it occasionally acted on. Consequently, the decision to construct a broad-based and varied organization was not an arbitrary one, nor was it due to a desire to attract the maximum possible number of members and supporters. It was a reflection of the group's integrated vision of its organizational structure and political outlook. In contrast to the monolithic image many have of the group, its overarching structure includes a number of narrower channels (and lower levels of membership) that allow individual members to carry out their organizational role in a precise and defined manner.

A complex organizational structure

The Brotherhood was careful to construct its organization along highly complex and precise lines incorporating a variety of different structural levels, each of which has its own program of religious and doctrinal education. This complexity sets it apart from other political and religious organizations. This structure can be broken down into three main levels.

One: Organizational levels

The Brotherhood has been careful to ensure that recruitment takes place on more than one level. Hassan al-Banna touched on this issue in *Mudhakkirat Al-Da'wa wa-l-Da'iyya*, when he spoke of the need for Brotherhood offices and agencies to provide members with a psychological education that conformed to their principles, and that to realize this goal there would be three different grades of membership:[3]

1. *General membership*: Open to any Muslim deemed acceptable by the leadership of the *da'ira* [local Brotherhood lodge or district]. He must declare that he is prepared to live a righteous life and sign an enrollment form [*istimarat al-ta'aruf*]. A member of this rank is known as an Assistant Brother [*akh musa'id*].
2. *Brotherhood membership*: Open to any Muslim deemed acceptable by the leadership of the *da'ira*. In addition to the procedures for general membership he must give a pledge of allegiance and promise to "safeguard the faith." A member of this rank is known as an Affiliated Brother [*akh muntasib*].
3. *Working membership*: Open to any Muslim deemed acceptable by the leadership of the local *da'ira*. In addition to the duties and procedures of Brotherhood enrollment, the applicant must provide all personal data requested by the group, study Brotherhood doctrine, attend weekly Quran groups and meetings of the *da'ira*, pledge to speak in classical Arabic whenever possible, educate and inform himself about general social (not political) issues, and memorize 40 sayings of the Prophet [*hadith*]. A member of this rank is known as a working Brother [*akh 'amil*].

Al-Banna mentions a fourth degree of membership that, significantly, he insists should be kept separate from the three degrees mentioned above. He refers to this degree as *jihadi* membership. *Jihadi* membership is restricted to working Brothers who have demonstrated commitment to their duties to the Guidance Bureau. Their duties include: adhering to Prophetic *sunna*, praying at night, avoiding empty pleasures and all forms of non-Islamic worship and interactions, making a financial contribution to the Guidance Bureau and the Preaching and Advice Fund (*sunduq al-da'wa wa-l-wasiyya*) through a bequest to the Muslim Brotherhood, performing good deeds and rejecting sinful acts, carrying the Holy Book to remind him of his duty to the Quran, and, finally, undergoing a period of indoctrination at the Guidance Bureau. A member of this rank is known as a *mujahid*.[4]

The existence of different forms of membership and recruitment within the Brotherhood is highly significant. Even though all members may declare their loyalty to a single authority, the gulf between the duties and outlook of the assistant and affiliate members, on the one hand, and the *mujahid*, on the other, is vast.

Two: The indoctrination of Brotherhood cadres

Just as with recruitment, this takes place on a number of levels. Examining the weekly and monthly activities program drawn up at the 1938 conference it is clear that this document is an expression of the varied and complex vision of the Brotherhood cadres' doctrinal education. The Guidance Bureau (i.e., the leadership level within the organization) has suggested that members set a number of days per month to implement the following program:

- *day of counsel*: during which members advise their neighbors on what is acceptable and forbidden and exhort them to do good;
- *day of the afterlife*: during which members visit graveyards to give sermons and remember the life to come;
- *clinic day*: during which members visit sick and ailing Muslims;
- *day of acquaintance*: to increase the bonds of friendship between members.

These peaceful activities, with their social and moral focus, are set alongside a set of more rigorous duties, described as the three pillars of the Brotherhood's weekly activities:

- *study night*: set aside for studying the General Guide's weekly lesson;
- *squad night*: preparing for hardship and self-denial in the path of God;
- *camp day*: training and preparation for Holy War, by which the Brotherhood means everything that leads to the creation of an Islamic army and that is required for the realization of their ultimate goals.

Three: Embodiment

The third level is better described as an embodiment, or the fruit of the first two levels, and is represented by the dualism of the private and the public, a dualism that dominated the Brotherhood Movement from 1938 (i.e. following the outbreak of violence in Palestine) through the end of Nasser's presidency. This dualism found its clearest expression in the secret organization that functioned alongside the official Muslim Brotherhood movement and was known to members as the special organization (*al-tanzim al-khass*), and to outsiders as the secret organization (*al-tanzim al-sirri*, or secret apparatus).

According to Mahmoud Abdel Halim, one of its founders, the Brotherhood decided to create the special organization in 1940, and its members were successfully incorporated into the main body of the Brotherhood over the course of the next eight years, despite holding doctrinal beliefs that were often at odds with the educational and indoctrination process undergone by regular members of the movement.[5] However, changes in the internal social and political environment, and the outbreak of war in Palestine, caused latent divisions between cadres of the Brotherhood's private and public organizations to erupt into open confrontation.

In the first part of his book, Abdel Halim describes the structure and duties of the special organization as follows:

- Members were divided between different *usra* [literally, family: organizational subdivision] linked by a chain of command. Members participated in all forms of public preaching activities.
- Intense, in-depth study of the concept of *jihad* in Islam i.e., in the Quran, the Prophetic *sunna* and *hadith* and Islamic history. Members must also observe all forms of prayer, worship, and fasting.
- Training for physically arduous tasks.
- Training on the dissemination of literature.
- Training in encryption techniques.
- Weapons training.
- Heavy emphasis on obedience and loyalty, self-discipline, and secrecy.[6]

In *The Society of the Muslim Brothers*, Richard Mitchell noted that between late 1942 and early 1943 a unit was created within the Brotherhood known internally as the special organization and by outsiders as the secret apparatus. His choice of dates is probably accurate, although this refers to the date the unit was created and not the point at which the idea of such a unit was first discussed.[7]

With the outbreak of the war in Palestine the secret apparatus stepped up its campaign of violence against regime figures and politicians. In doing so it successfully undid two decades of work by the founding Brothers, switching the group's focus from confronting the Zionist occupation to direct conflict with the political authorities in Egypt. Prime Minister Mahmoud Fahmi Al-Naqrashi was assassinated by young members of the organization, a trend that continued after the "1952 revolution" with the attempted assassination of President Gamal Abdel Nasser in 1954.

It was at this point that the Brotherhood exited the framework of legitimate political participation, its evangelizing mission, and its social activism, despite the fact that Nasser was careful to incorporate some of its members into Al-Azhar, the religious endowments system, and the institutions of state (e.g. Al-Baqouri, Sheikh of Al-Azhar, was a member of the Brotherhood, as were many senior members of the religious endowments system, like Sheikh Mohammed Al-Ghazali and Sheikh Sayyid Sabiq).

On his accession to the presidency, Sadat released the Brotherhood's leaders from prison, but throughout the 1970s the Brotherhood was politically and socially inactive, with the exception of student activism. As a result it became cocooned in closed ideological frameworks within which it conducted intellectual and doctrinal debates entirely divorced from the realities of Egyptian society and political issues. The silence was broken by the group's public rejection of the Camp David agreement, prompting Sadat to re-arrest the Brotherhood's leadership in the notorious crackdown of September 1981.

The legacy of the founding period

In the period between 1928 and the outbreak of war in 1948 the Brotherhood was primarily an evangelizing organization whose activities were religious and social in nature. Even as membership swelled throughout Egypt's various provinces, politics – in its modern sense – was largely absent from the Brotherhood's discourse. The organization's size vastly outweighed its political strength: prior to the 1952 revolution, the Brotherhood never gained a single parliamentary seat. The reasons for this are largely due to the group's structure and intellectual priorities, but it should be noted that they were competing in a political environment that offered genuine competition. For example, the liberal agenda of the Wafd Party, which was demanding national independence and a civil constitution, appealed to wide swathes of the Egyptian people.

Dualities within the Brotherhood's organizational structure enabled it to successfully assimilate reformist and extremist elements, Sufis and revolutionaries, political activists, preachers espousing a moral discourse, and individuals working in the social sphere. But although al-Banna's melting-pot managed to unite these disparate elements into one organizational structure and political discourse during two decades of political stability (i.e., between 1928 and 1948), changes in the political environment threw the Brotherhood into disarray, leaving it incapable of functioning with its former efficiency, especially during periods of confrontation with the regime, when its carefully constructed unity fell apart.

Amending the founders' legacy

In the course of the last three decades the Muslim Brotherhood has undergone a number of changes and transformations, yet it has managed to preserve the essence of Hassan al-Banna's message: that the Brotherhood's mission, its call, should embrace all areas of one's life, social, spiritual, political, and cultural. Islam, in the view of al-Banna and his adherents, is a comprehensive religion, an ultimate point of reference on which to instigate a renaissance in the *umma*.

As the world changed, the Brotherhood stuck close to al-Banna's ideas, while openly endorsing multi-party politics and declaring its support for democracy as a means of allowing competition between different political forces. However, it never abandoned its faith in blending religious evangelizing with political activism. Over the course of more than eight decades the Brotherhood has been able to preserve its organizational structure, despite the assassination of its founder in 1949. The loss of al-Banna had no immediate impact on his vision of a primarily socio-religious group with a secondary political role (i.e., an evangelizing group or Islamic institution rather than a political party per se). At least initially, this understanding dominated the organization's structure, although in recent years it has given ground to a more political mentality, which sees the opportunity to work with – not abolish – the traditional evangelizing culture in reshaping the Brotherhood's image. Although it preserved the same multifaceted approach as before, it offered new dualities in place of the old division between violence and peace that had dominated its organizational mentality from the outbreak of the 1948 War until the mid-1960s.

In the early 1970s elements claiming to represent al-Banna's legacy renounced the use of violence in all its forms, attempting to make the peaceful discourse espoused by the majority of members the sole discourse within the organization. The group retained its old dualist mentality, its discourse and activities dominated by the interrelationship between the group's evangelizing and political activities. Compared with the 1940s, however, the political component was given much greater prominence. From the very beginning of the 1980s this new "Brotherhood of politics" plunged into politics enthusiastically, entering the 1984 and 1987 parliamentary elections and achieving impressive results. It also succeeded in using democratic processes to gain and maintain control of the most important professional syndicates in Egypt throughout the 1980s, before making a comeback in the early 2000s through a heavy presence in the Lawyers' Syndicate and two seats in the Journalists' Syndicate. In 2000, the Brotherhood won 17 parliamentary seats, a figure that leapt to 88 following the 2005 elections.

Throughout this period the group was obsessed with the question of how to manage the relationship between their interpretations of the sacred religious text and the pragmatic demands of the social and political reality in which it operated. For the first time in its history, the Brotherhood entered elections in alliance with other groups. In 1984 it joined forces with the Wafd Party, while in 1987 it formed the backbone of what was known as the "Islamic Alliance," with the Labor and Liberal Parties. In 2000 and 2005 Brotherhood members entered the parliamentary elections as independent candidates. The alliances formed with other political parties allowed – or rather compelled – the Brothers to recognize concepts such as the sovereignty of the people and the authority of the constitution. For the first time the Brotherhood presented a political program that, despite its generalizing nature and references to Islam as an ultimate authority, could be characterized as civil in nature.

This newly won experience directly impacted the Brotherhood's political discourse and its propaganda, generating a new Brotherhood approach entirely distinct from the organization's direction under the monarchy, Nasser, and Sadat.

It would be an exaggeration to claim that the Brotherhood of the 1980s had fully assimilated the concepts of democracy, or that it had managed to disassociate the religious from the political in its discourse. What we can say is that politics had come to occupy a far larger share of the organization's priorities and concerns. This is in direct contrast to the Brotherhood's activities under the monarchy, when its essentially peaceful message was propagated through social activities and calls for religious and moral standards of behavior entirely divorced from concepts of modern political activism.

Nevertheless, the problem – indeed, the organization's greatest problem – of the interaction between the sacred and the civil, the political and the moral, remained unresolved during the Mubarak era, making it very difficult to describe the organization as either a political movement or an evangelizing society. Many of the group's members had joined up because they viewed it as a religious society for good, pious people who adhered to the rules and values of Islam. These members have little or no political experience.

Creating a clear separation between the religious and the political would allow the "Brotherhood of the Third Millennium" to transform itself into a civil political organization seeking to attain power peacefully in accordance with democratic principles. Rather than a society that aims to reform people by calling on them to adhere to religious teachings and imagines that political power can be attained by means of a moralizing manifesto for the guidance of the masses (however much it has benefited from modern civil institutions such as parliament and the syndicates in the pursuit of religious and moralizing goals), a clear separation between religious and political functions would facilitate the organization's transformation into a political party. Although it is still too early to determine whether the establishment of the Freedom and Justice Party in June 2011 will fully produce such a separation (between the religious and political functions of the Brotherhood), the mere fact that the organization now has a legally established political party entitled to participate in formal politics makes such a transformation possible.

The Brotherhood previously attributed its failure to resolve the issue of its political identity to the fact that under the Mubarak regime it was not recognized as a legitimate political party in accordance with the legal principles that applied to all non-violent political forces in Egypt. The organization believes that questions over its failure to distinguish its religious discourse from its political message should be directed toward a political environment that refused to legally recognize the group, and not to the organization itself. Its reluctance to abandon its commitment to the absolute unity between the religious and political can be interpreted as a form of self-defense, or perhaps defensiveness, allowing the group to portray its opponents as hostile either to Islam or to pious Muslims, which in turn won the organization the sympathy of broad swathes of the public.

Towards a second foundation of the Muslim Brotherhood

Despite changes in its approach and priorities, until recently the Brotherhood remained a prisoner of its dual loyalties to evangelizing and political activism, split between defending the faith and propagating the call to Islam and its political and party-political activism. The Brotherhood's longevity can be attributed to its unique intellectual and organizational capabilities that set it apart from the majority of Egypt's political forces. Its inclusive discourse, administrative efficiency, and organizational precision have facilitated the spread of its religious and political messages, while its provision of numerous social services to Egyptian citizens turns its opponents, whether from the government or the opposition parties, green with envy.

The irony is that this illegal group – or "banned group," as the Mubarak government preferred to term it – managed to attract 20 percent of the vote in the 2005 legislative elections, ten times more than the combined vote received by the three opposition parties represented in parliament at the time (i.e., the Wafd Party, six seats; the Tagammuʿ Party, two seats; the Ghad Party, one seat). So, if the Brotherhood could win as many seats as a banned organization does this mean it will sweep elections now that the Freedom and Justice Party has been legalized? In the case of any other political movement, the answer would be simple, but with the Brotherhood matters are infinitely more complex. To begin with, much of its organizational rigor and ability to control its membership stem from the fact it is an evangelizing-political group that exploited its illegal status to maintain discipline and obedience in its ranks.

Since it was unable to confront the Egyptian state under Mubarak, with its attendant army of bureaucrats, security agencies, and capacity for violence and intimidation, the Brotherhood previously confined itself to a discourse of tribulation and oppression that formed an important component of many of its members' political and doctrinal education. Brotherhood leaders first deployed this discourse following the waves of arrests under Nasser's revolutionary regime, using it to encourage obedience in the ranks. Maintaining and reinforcing the group's unity seemed to be an end in itself.

Given Mubarak's undemocratic regime and the heavy-handedness of the state's security services, it seems unfair to expect the group could have initiated unilateral intellectual, organizational, and political reform without any chance of being allowed to establish a political party capable of competing in a democratic environment, especially since such reforms would likely have fragmented the Brotherhood. The Mubarak regime and leaders of the opposition must share responsibility for the precipitous decline in Egyptian political life in the previous decades.

The undemocratic environment of the Mubarak era played an important part in the Brotherhood's reluctance to establish a political party, not least because the concept of political "legitimacy" that existed created parties which, due to restrictions placed on them by the security services and the errors of their own leadership, were marginal groups with no real support base. However, equally relevant is that by starting its own political party during the Mubarak period the Brotherhood would have found itself facing a number of challenges, some of which it faces today.

The first challenge

How is the group to deal with its founding values? These values have been effective and influential while the group has been in opposition, but there is no guarantee that they will remain unaffected now that the organization can operate more freely, let alone if it were to gain power. Indeed, now that the Brotherhood has formed a political party, it will have to operate in the full glare of the media spotlight for the first time, with its leadership granted airtime on satellite channels alongside its political opponents. It will also have to open its doors to Christians as well as Muslims, the irreligious as well as the devout, and as it does so the membership, recruitment methods, and the discourse of the new political party will likely start to split away from the strict adherence to religious ritual and values prescribed by the Brotherhood's founders.

The group's religious mission was one of the principal sources of its structural integrity and strength. The Brothers do not engage in public life simply to achieve political and democratic reform, but also, and more importantly, to please God. They do not vote for Brotherhood candidates in elections simply to exercise their political rights, but because not to do so would amount to a sin of omission: passing up the chance to do a good deed that would bring them closer to God.

The second challenge

The second challenge is linked to the Brotherhood's ideology, which remains based on a doctrine of Islam's comprehensive nature even as the rest of the world – with the collapse of the Soviet Union and the Socialist bloc – moves away from all-embracing ideologies to embrace partial or "soft ideologies."

Major political doctrines are founded on ideas that seek to create revolutionary or "socialist man" and engineer society and individuals to fit into rigid, pre-constructed molds. These ideas have fallen by the wayside, and with them a whole way of thinking.

Much of the Brotherhood's intellectual output belongs to this generalizing ideological approach. For many years, the organization saw its position as distinct from other major ideologies on the grounds that it derived its ideas and principles from religion and a sacred Islamic doctrine. However, the reality of political engagement has transformed this doctrinal inflexibility into a reliance on more flexible political thought and practice. It is this change that necessitates a second foundation for the Brotherhood, establishing an organization that is aware that patterns of thought and group indoctrination based on faith in a universal Islam are incompatible with modern democratic political systems. In order for the organization to progress, therefore, it is vital that the Brotherhood (and especially the Freedom and Justice Party) understand that it is operating in a new era of democratic values and principles. It has an historic opportunity to embrace what are sometimes known as "soft ideologies," which are characterized by a flexible approach to the details of lived experience. Such a move would provide the Brotherhood with a realistic understanding of the international environment and the balance of power on the world stage.

The third challenge

The Muslim Brotherhood is first and foremost an oppositional entity. As long as it remains in opposition to power it will remain prisoner of the purely religious values and isolationist approach of its founder Hassan al-Banna. These values and principles remain influential as long as the group is in opposition, but once in power it is unlikely that this religious element will be enough to preserve the integrity of the rulers. This is the ostensible function of a democratic system capable of legal and constitutional oversight of those in power.

Religious values alone are insufficient for the task of governing a country or understanding the nature of regional and international challenges. In fact, the evidence would seem to suggest that a religious movement can only flourish in power in the absence of the modern safeguards established by advanced democracies.

The idea of an international or U.S. conspiracy against Islam, the Muslim world, and Islamic movements advanced by the Brotherhood and other movements does not stand up to scrutiny let alone academic analysis. For example, claims that the Hamas government failed because of international sanctions and double standards reflect an incomplete, if not faulty, reading of the international and regional environment. The real question that these Islamic movements need to answer is: How do they intend to successfully challenge American and Western hegemony? How can moderate Islamic movements such as the Brotherhood create a place for themselves, and actively participate, in the international order?

There are no inherent or "genetic" reasons why the Brotherhood should not wholeheartedly embrace democracy. However, democratic politics will present the organization with an entirely new set of challenges, solutions to which will only be forthcoming in a fully democratic environment that is, as yet, non-existent in the Arab world.

The fourth challenge

From 1954 until 2011, the Muslim Brotherhood operated outside the framework and legacy of the civil Egyptian state and the republican system. Indeed, much of the time it represented the antithesis of this civil culture, persecuted by security services that saw it in a stereotypical and negative light, a misapprehension exacerbated by the security services' own exaggerated claims and the Brotherhood's own mistakes. Normalization of relations between the state and the Brotherhood will be no easy matter, but there is no alternative if the process of peaceful integration is to succeed, especially in light of the Brotherhood's internal culture developed in opposition – often violent – to previous regimes, the state, and the nationalist movement. The Brotherhood remained outside the nationalist movement of the 1930s and 1940s and clashed with the newly established republican regime during the 1950s and 1960s. The time has come for the Brotherhood to participate in the future of the country.

This problem is not unique to Egypt. Hamas, too, comes from outside the Palestinian nationalist movement (embodied by the PLO), and it too must seek some form of intellectual integration into this heritage before it can be accepted politically. The Brotherhood was a bitter opponent of Nasser's regime, but this does not logically entail opposition to the republican system, the civil constitution, and the discourse of national liberation, as all of this can be reformulated and Islamized.

A political party for the Brotherhood: deferred challenges

What if the Brotherhood were able to overcome the four challenges listed above, or at least some of them, with the establishment of the Freedom and Justice Party, ostensibly a civil political party that recognizes the republican system and the civil constitution and unconditionally accepts the rotation of power and the right of all political forces, including secularists and communists, to form independent parties? On the one hand, this would constitute a huge step towards bolstering democracy in Egypt and, on the other, it would encourage the Brotherhood to effect a permanent separation between the religious and the political.

Incorporating a non-violent Islamist movement like the Muslim Brotherhood into the process of democratic development is a subject that deserves the attention of researchers and academics, as well as considerable political courage on the part of those who recognize that successful democratic reform in the Arab world depends, in part, on finding a solution to the question of political Islam. Marginalizing these groups, a tactic whose inadequacy has been exposed repeatedly over the last 80 years, is not the solution. Incorporating non-violent political Islam into the process of democratic development is much more than a solution to this deep-seated historical dilemma. It would also serve to involve large segments of society in the political process. With the guidance of the Brotherhood's organizational structure and its role in Egyptian syndicates and professional associations, Brotherhood members and supporters would be encouraged to participate in elections, join political parties, and respect the verdict of the ballot box.

The modernization of non-violent political Islam means, in essence, encouraging Islamists to adopt the rules and concepts of democratic practice. The creation of democratic Islamist movements would also better enable Islamists to confront domestic challenges of corruption and despotism and the foreign policy challenges posed by the Israeli occupation of Palestine and U.S. policies in the region. Islamists must be capable of resisting these policies using non-violent and democratic approaches based on international law, a tool the George W. Bush administration (2000–09) monopolized, manipulated, and imposed on the world according to its own warped interpretation.

The truth is that constructing a genuine democratic project in Egypt is doomed to failure without the assimilation of non-violent political Islamic movements. After all, including the Muslim Brotherhood in the process of democratic development is about reintroducing politics into public life and reviving Egypt's other parties, both new and old, which will be keen to develop their own discourse and recruit the cream of Egypt's political talent to tackle the political challenge posed by the Brotherhood's own cadres. The successes recorded by other Islamic-based movements, such as Turkey's Justice and Development Party, stem from an absolute separation of the religious and the political. Their successes are evaluated solely in terms of their economic and political achievements and not the popular appeal of their religious slogans or the "truth" of their ideological authority. Ultimately, the movement will be judged on its material achievements alone.

The significance of the Turkish model, or rather the irony, is that the country's secular political forces – which traditionally fought to give Turkey a "European face" – have become the least democratic and the most reluctant to join the European Union. At the same time, those parties with Islamic roots are currently the keenest proponents of democratic reform and enthusiastic cheerleaders for EU membership and the adoption of "European" values such as democracy and respect for human rights. It may not be perfect, but Turkey's democratic environment has been instrumental in facilitating the transformation of traditional Islamists into "conservative democrats" (as they call themselves) who place their formidable social and political capabilities at the service of progress and democracy. Their opponents, meanwhile, stay entrenched behind secularist slogans that provide the flimsiest cover for their authoritarian tendencies. It is therefore of the utmost importance to find a new way of dealing with non-violent Islamism, based on legal and civil rules for regulating political activism and the process of democratic development. These regulations will allow the Islamists' potential to be released, harnessing their organizational and political capabilities, encouraging other political players to evolve and reshape their intellectual and political positions so as to be able to compete effectively with the forces of moderate Islam.

The transformation of the Brotherhood into a civil political movement requires a democratic system and the presence of other political forces to compete with it for the electorate's approval and to hold the group accountable for its actions. Such an environment might inevitably engender a split in the organization between an evangelizing religious group that calls for moral rectitude and piety and a genuine political party. Although it is still too early in the post-Mubarak period to determine whether or not this will actually happen, now – at least – this possibility exists.

Notes

1 H. Al Banna, "The First Letter: Between "Yesterday and Today," in *Collection of Letters of Hassan Al Banna*, Cairo: Dar Al-Shehab edition, n.d., p. 144 (in Arabic).
2 H. Al Banna, "In the Muslim Brotherhood Students' Conference," in *Collection of the Letters of Hassan Al Banna*, pp. 180–81 (in Arabic).
3 H. Al Banna, *Diaries of Preaching and the Preacher*, Cairo: The Islamic Publishing and Distribution House, 1986 (in Arabic).
4 Ibid., pp. 220–21.
5 Mahmoud Abdel Halim, *The Muslim Brotherhood: Events that Made History*, 1st edition, Cairo: Dar Al-Daʿwa, 1979, pp. 258–59 (In Arabic).
6 Ibid., pp. 258–59.
7 R. Mitchell, *The Society of Muslim Brothers*, 2nd edition, Cairo: Madbouli Publishing House and Bookshop, 1985, p. 58 (Arabic edition).

Bibliography

Al Banna, H., *Collection of Letters of Hassan Al Banna*, Cairo: Dar Al-Shehab edition, n.d. (in Arabic).
Al Banna, H., *Diaries of Preaching and the Preacher*, Cairo: The Islamic Publishing and Distribution House, 1986 (in Arabic).
Halim, Mahmoud Abdel, *The Muslim Brotherhood: Events that Made History*, 1st edition, Cairo: Dar Al-Daʿwa, 1979 (in Arabic).
Mitchell, R. *The Society of Muslim Brothers*, 2nd edition, Cairo: Madbouli Publishing House and Bookshop, 1985 (Arabic edition).

7

POLITICAL *DA'WA*

Understanding the Muslim Brotherhood's participation in semi-authoritarian elections

Samer S. Shehata[1]

Introduction

The Egyptian Muslim Brotherhood has a long history of electoral participation, competing in every legislative election since 1984, with only one exception. Under the Mubarak regime (1981–2011), Brotherhood candidates stood in elections for the People's Assembly, the lower house of parliament, in 1984, 1987, 1995, 2000, 2005, and 2010. Only in 1990, when all political parties except the leftist Tagammu' Party boycotted the vote, did the Brotherhood refrain from electoral participation.[2]

What makes this surprising is that during Hosni Mubarak's rule Egyptian elections were regularly characterized by widespread electoral fraud, including ballot-stuffing, biased electoral administration, vote-buying, regime coercion against opposition supporters and candidates, and violence, often on the part of the regime against its opponents. As a result, elections in Egypt provided neither an opportunity to come to power through the ballot box nor a mechanism for opposition parties and groups to influence policy. Despite these limitations and the significant costs associated with electoral participation, the Muslim Brotherhood consistently participated in parliamentary elections.

Why did Egypt's most popular opposition group participate in elections that were neither free nor fair? Why did the Brotherhood contest elections that provided no chance of coming to power through the ballot box? This chapter addresses these and other related questions by analyzing the Brotherhood's past electoral participation.[3]

I argue that elections in semi-authoritarian regimes often provide *moments of opportunity* to publicly engage in politics for opposition groups that otherwise face serious restrictions on political activity, including certain types of activities that usually cannot be undertaken in such polities.[4] For the Muslim Brotherhood, electoral participation (and, later, membership in parliament) served as a mechanism to propagate its ideas and disseminate its ideology to wider segments of society. I call this political *da'wa*. The word has specific religious (Islamic) connotations, but here I use it to describe the Brotherhood's efforts to use both elections and parliament to communicate its *political message*. Therefore, political *da'wa* is a form of electoral participation in semi-authoritarian regimes where participating in elections is not primarily about winning seats, influencing policy, or controlling resources, but rather disseminating a group's message and expanding its influence, with the ultimate goal of affecting social and political change. Thus, for the Muslim Brotherhood electoral participation was its own reward, irrespective of whether elections were free or fair or opposition candidates won parliamentary seats.

The significance of such questions extends far beyond Egypt and Islamist political movements. "Authoritarian elections" are increasingly the subject of scholarly attention. And Islamist movements in the Middle East (and elsewhere) have frequently participated in "limited," "controlled," or "authoritarian elections" (e.g., Morocco's Justice and Development Party and Jordan's Islamic Action Front, among others). Yet the question of *why* popular opposition groups (Islamist and non-Islamist) contest such elections remains insufficiently examined. I hope my analysis of the Muslim Brotherhood's electoral participation under the Mubarak regime contributes to answering more general questions about electoral participation in non-democratic regimes, despite important differences between cases.[5]

Egyptian elections

In the past, Egyptian elections were regularly far from free or fair, and at times they were simultaneously farcical and tragic. In addition to significant problems in electoral administration (e.g., including notoriously inaccurate voter registration lists),[6] elections in Egypt have consistently been characterized by different types of electoral fraud.[7]

In 2005 balloting, for example, after the Muslim Brotherhood candidate Hazem Abu Ismail was declared the winner in Cairo's Dokki neighborhood by the state press, the government announced entirely different results the following day, awarding the seat to long-time Mubarak-regime insider Amal Othman.[8] Othman was a regime stalwart who was first appointed Minister of Social Affairs by Anwar Al Sadat in 1977. She served in parliament from 1984 until Mubarak's departure in 2011 and was said to be close friends with Suzanne Mubarak, the former president's wife.

In round two of the 2005 elections, the regime employed brute force and blatant electoral fraud in the Delta town of Damanhour to install ruling party ideologue Mustapha El Fikki in parliament.[9] Days later a senior judge responsible for supervising the district's vote penned a long testimonial on the front page of the country's leading independent newspaper describing the electoral fraud she witnessed.[10] Judge Noha El Zeini recounted how officials from the Interior Ministry and State Security Investigations altered the election results. Over one hundred other judges who supervised voting in Damanhour supported her testimony.[11] El Zeini provided the actual results (approximately 7,000 votes for El Fikki, compared with 25,000 votes for his opponent) and declared Gamal Hishmat to be the legitimate winner. Hishmat is a popular Muslim Brotherhood figure and the district's former representative (the official results gave El Fikki 22,982 votes, or 50.21 percent of the total vote). Rather than isolated cases, however, these are simply two of the most well-known examples of recent electoral fraud.

I myself witnessed electoral fraud in Mansoura, the capital of Daqahilayyah governorate, during the third round of the 2005 elections. I watched as the regime's Central Security Forces (CSF) blocked thousands of voters from entering polling stations. CSF personnel also prevented the district's two Muslim Brotherhood candidates, Yussri Hani and Saber Zaher, from casting their ballots. Similar scenes were widely reported throughout the country during the third round of voting in 2005.[12]

Violence has also been a recurring feature of Egyptian elections. Intimidation and other forms of coercion have been used by supporters of competing candidates against their rivals, and in some cases violence has a familial or clan basis. The use of knives, metal chains, guns, and other weapons during elections has been widely reported by the press and is unfortunately not uncommon.[13] Such reports have also been well documented by election monitors, who themselves have been frequent victims of election violence.[14]

Mubarak's ruling party candidates sometimes employed thugs (*baltagaya*) wielding these weapons to intimidate opposition supporters, often with the regime's tacit approval. Government security forces were also frequently deployed across the country to physically engineer electoral outcomes. This often entailed thousands of CSF personnel using tear gas, rubber bullets, and live ammunition in order to prevent citizens from voting.[15]

The 1995 legislative elections were particularly violent, with over 50 deaths and hundreds of injuries.[16] The 2000 polls were somewhat less violent. Approximately 10 people died during those elections, although analysts and human rights groups noted that the type of violence shifted from violence between supporters of rival candidates to state-directed violence against citizens and would-be voters.[17] The 2005 balloting was also bloody. At least 13 people were killed and hundreds of others were injured during the elections.[18] And the 2010 parliamentary elections were considered among the most fraudulent in Egyptian history.[19]

Why did Egypt's most popular opposition group participate in elections that were consistently rigged and marred by violence? Why did the Muslim Brotherhood "compete" in elections that lacked integrity?

Costs and risks of electoral participation

These questions become even more vexing when we recognize that there were also significant costs associated with the Brotherhood's electoral participation. In addition to the ordinary financial expenses needed to mount effective campaigns (e.g., the resources required to finance events, rent offices, employ staff, and produce campaign advertisements) and the organizational challenges involved in running campaigns, the Brotherhood paid a higher price for its electoral participation. Brotherhood leaders and members regularly became targets of regime repression around election time.[20] Brotherhood candidates and supporters were routinely detained and sometimes imprisoned in pre-election raids (see Table 7.1).[21] This type of repression, or "cost,"

TABLE 7.1 Estimates of number of Brothers arrested before elections, 2000–10

Election year	*Number of Brothers arrested before elections*
2000	1,600
2005	800 +
2008 (municipal)	831 +
2010	1,206

Source: Human Rights Watch, *Elections in Egypt: State of Permanent Emergency Incompatible with Free and Fair Vote*, 2010, pp. 7–8.

was intended to curtail the organization's ability to challenge the regime effectively in the electoral arena.[22]

There were also different types of risks involved in standing against the regime in elections. Competing against ruling party candidates could provoke the regime's wrath, generating even greater repression against the organization as a whole. This is particularly important for the Muslim Brotherhood because it is engaged in many different types of activities in addition to formal politics. The Brotherhood is a large and multifaceted religious and social welfare organization with dozens of affiliated organizations across the country, including publishing houses, schools, medical clinics, and various charities. These social welfare functions are an integral part of the Brotherhood's mission and identity. Challenging the Mubarak regime in the electoral arena placed all of these activities at risk.

There are also unique risks involved in participating in "authoritarian elections." Some claim that contesting such elections can serve to legitimate semi-authoritarian governments. Members of the Brotherhood have argued that standing in "sham elections" contributed to the Mubarak regime's façade democracy. Such elections are a "show" or "theater," they argued, staged largely for foreign consumption. Taking electoral politics seriously only benefited the regime and cost the Brotherhood dearly. Others, including some members of the Brotherhood's Guidance Office,[23] argued that the costs of participating in such elections far outweighed the benefits.[24]

These concerns were echoed by members of the general public. Egypt's leading independent newspaper (*Al Masry Al Youm*) allows readers to post responses to articles on the paper's website. In response to a January 12, 2009 article about Brotherhood parliamentarians protesting the 2008–09 Gaza War, a reader named Ahmed Farid posted the following comment:

> I ask why don't the Brotherhood members and the independents and opposition [members of parliament, or MPs] submit their resignations from the People's Assembly as long as they are not taken seriously and they are accused of treason and being proxies for foreign powers and none of their requests (for information) and interpellations are answered, so what is the benefit of their sitting [in the Assembly] and what is their purpose unless they are there as part of a deal with State Security to beautify the [face of the] regime and these are roles that are scripted for them to fool the people and I swear that we are without

> representatives in our district – Aga – and this is better because we do not feel any role [effectiveness] for the member of the People's Assembly so get rid of it and enough pretending.[25]

Such skepticism about the effectiveness of Brotherhood parliamentarians and the Egyptian parliament was not altogether uncommon. Intellectuals have also voiced similar concerns. For example, in 2008 Heba Raouf Ezzat, a Cairo University professor and prominent Islamist thinker, suggested that the entire Brotherhood parliamentary bloc should resign because they could not effectively operate in an authoritarian political system where the ruling party was unwilling to give up power. Ezzat also wrote that the presence of Brotherhood representatives in parliament benefited the regime more than the nation.[26]

The prize

The Brotherhood's electoral participation appears even more puzzling when one realizes that what was at stake was membership in a largely toothless parliament.[27] In other words, if Brotherhood candidates emerged victorious after suffering through electoral battle (including the likelihood of violence and electoral fraud), what they "won" turned out to be membership in an impotent, "rubber-stamp" legislature: what Jennifer Gandhi and Adam Pzeworski have described as "legislatures [that] do not legislate."[28]

In Egypt, as in other semi-authoritarian regimes, many considered the parliament to be "décor," an empty shell devoid of real power that primarily functioned to mask the authoritarian character of rule. Real power, including legislative power, was overwhelmingly concentrated in the executive, and in the case of Mubarak's Egypt, in the person of the president. The People's Assembly functioned neither as an independent institution nor as a check on executive authority.[29]

Further contributing to the puzzle of the Brotherhood's electoral participation was the fact that the organization never fielded enough candidates to potentially achieve a parliamentary majority. The Brotherhood never ran more than 165 candidates in elections for a 454-person Assembly.[30] Therefore, even if *all* Brotherhood candidates miraculously managed to win, something extremely unlikely in elections that were neither free nor fair, it still would not have held sufficient seats to pass or block legislation.

Complicating matters still further is the fact that if Brotherhood candidates were elected to the People's Assembly they would eventually face constituents who would likely make demands of them as parliamentarians. Constituents could ask for different types of assistance, ranging from help securing employment and housing to assistance dealing with the government bureaucracy. Brotherhood MPs who wanted to be reelected would face pressures from district residents, who would ask, "What have you done for me?" and "How have I benefited from your membership in the People's Assembly?" This is particularly true in Egypt (and in authoritarian states more generally), where voting has been described as "clientelistic": that is, many voters cast their ballots based on what candidates offer them in terms of government and other services. In a Middle Eastern context, some have described this as "voting for *wasta*" or "voting for services."[31]

Muslim Brotherhood parliamentarians would potentially confront such pressures in a hostile political environment: one where Mubarak's ruling party (and government) would likely attempt to prevent them – for political reasons – from being effective "service providers."[32] Faced with such high costs and significant risks, why participate in elections that are unlikely to yield the expected benefits of electoral participation?

The existing literature

There is a vast political science literature about political parties and elections, most of which concerns democratic political systems in Europe and the United States.[33] As such it provides limited insight into electoral participation in non-democratic regimes. A great deal of this literature assumes that parties are "vote-seeking" (or "vote-maximizing"), "office-seeking," and/or "policy-or-influence seeking" organizations.[34] Much of the debate in the literature focuses on which of these attributes (or which combination) most accurately characterizes political parties and their behavior.

Recently there has been growing interest in elections in non-democratic regimes (e.g., "authoritarian elections").[35] Most of the attention has focused on the relationship between "authoritarian elections" and democratization (i.e., whether such elections can contribute to democratization or whether they serve to reproduce, and thereby prolong, authoritarian regimes).[36] Scholars have also explored voting behavior (e.g., who votes and for whom) and the function of elections in such regimes. The question of *why* opposition parties participate in "authoritarian elections" has received less attention.

Much of the recent literature on "authoritarian elections" concludes that they are contests over access to state resources (e.g., clientelism). Voters in such situations are said to cast their ballots for candidates (and parties) who can deliver "the goods" (e.g., government services). Implicit in these conclusions is an understanding of why candidates and parties compete in such elections: "candidates vie for the privilege of acting as intermediaries in patron–client relations."[37]

While membership in parliament does confer some access to resources, such explanations provide little insight into the Muslim Brotherhood's past electoral participation.[38] Moreover, like many other Islamist organizations, the Brotherhood already derives influence from various forms of social service provision. The Brotherhood's calculus for participating in "authoritarian elections" is surely different.

A few studies have endeavored to directly address the subject of Islamist electoral participation. For example, Abdulkader Sinno and Ahmed Khanani have recently attempted to present a general explanation of the phenomenon.[39] They argue that the "quality of the political opening" and the "organizational structure" of Islamist parties explain why some Islamist parties participate while others do not.[40]

While their focus on "organizational structure" is astute, their "prediction" that Islamist organizations participate in elections "depending on the quality of the electoral opening and their ability to benefit from it" is neither revealing nor unexpected.[41] More importantly for our purposes, their focus is different from my own. Sinno and

Khanani are concerned with explaining *when* Islamists participate rather than *why* they participate (or, stated differently, *how* Islamists benefit from electoral participation).[42] The real challenge is to explain how Islamists benefit from electoral participation, including participation in "authoritarian elections." Sinno and Khanani neither explain the actual benefits of electoral participation nor discuss the Egyptian case in any depth.

By contrast, Mona El-Ghobashy directly addresses the Muslim Brotherhood's electoral participation in detail. However, the questions she asks are different from my own. Rather than trying to determine why the Brothers participate in "limited" or "controlled" elections, she brilliantly examines the consequences of electoral participation for the group's organizational structure and thinking.[43]

Marina Ottaway and Amr Hamzawy have also written about Islamist electoral participation.[44] However, their primary focus is determining whether Islamists who participate in elections are "truly committed to democracy" (a frequent concern in the literature about Islamist political parties) and whether electoral participation leads to "moderation" (defined by the authors as moving from a religious and ideological focus to a policy focus).[45]

In fact, Ottaway and Hamzawy judge the benefits of electoral participation for Islamists to be "limited." "The poor payback of political participation presents Islamists with three major challenges," they write. Ottaway and Hamzawy do discuss the reputational benefits of limited electoral participation for Islamists (i.e., signaling to regimes and others that they are "responsible political actors"),[46] but the closest they come to discussing the "non-traditional" benefits of electoral participation elaborated here is when they state that "parliamentary and legislative activity allows them [Islamists] to … sustain the impetus of their popular base through the regular public broadcast of their demands."[47] Even this is quite different from the specific benefits of political *da'wa* outlined on pp. 127–130. Overall, the authors seem to accept a more traditional understanding of the supposed benefits of electoral participation, using democratic elections as a model. As a result they are unable to see that political *da'wa* is one of – if not *the* – primary benefit of electoral participation for Islamists such as the Muslim Brotherhood operating within "authoritarian elections."

Elections as moments of opportunity

Paradoxically, participating in "limited" or "controlled" elections turns out to be important for groups such as the Muslim Brotherhood for several reasons. Most importantly, elections in such contexts often provide *moments of opportunity* in otherwise politically repressive environments. Winning elections and getting into parliament, therefore, turns out to be only part of the story.[48] Elections and campaigns provide opportunities for groups that otherwise face serious restrictions on political activity to publicly engage in politics. Certain types of activities usually barred under such regimes (e.g., street marches, rallies, political meetings, opening campaign offices, displaying campaign banners and posters, and holding campaign events) are periodically tolerated before elections.[49]

This is likely the case because elections constitute a structural contradiction for semi-authoritarian regimes: they are a democratic mechanism in a semi-authoritarian system. Elections in such regimes are a contradiction between closed, semi-authoritarian politics and what elections are ostensibly about: political competition, contestation, and a mechanism for choosing leaders and deciding policy. The dilemma that confronts these regimes is reconciling the desire to appear democratic with the necessity of limiting real competition.[50] The "solution" appears to be allowing relatively more freedom – within limits – during election periods. As a result, the space of permitted political contestation in such regimes sometimes expands during election periods.

In Mubarak's Egypt, for example, certain forms of political activity that would normally not be permitted were tolerated around elections. Elections have entailed relatively more space for opposition groups, including the Muslim Brotherhood, to organize events, hold rallies and marches, distribute political material, and display posters and banners. Candidates have been allowed to "campaign" and thus "compete" in elections. And even though elections were also periods of increased repression against the Brotherhood, they were simultaneously periods of increased Muslim Brotherhood political activity.[51]

Therefore, electoral participation is often its own reward in semi-authoritarian regimes, irrespective of whether elections are free or fair or opposition candidates win seats in parliament.[52] Electoral participation in the form of campaigns often allows organizations such as Egypt's Muslim Brotherhood greater opportunities to engage in political activity that is usually prohibited.

Political *da'wa*

Electoral participation, including campaigning for office (and, later, membership in parliament) served as a mechanism for the Muslim Brotherhood to propagate its ideas and make itself known to wider segments of the public. I call this political *da'wa*. Of course, political campaigns are, in part, about presenting one's ideas and reaching out to voters. However, the Muslim Brotherhood has been tremendously adept at using campaigns and parliament to disseminate its ideology, to make itself heard in the media, and to connect with wider segments of society (and, in the process, to criticize the Mubarak regime and the political, economic, and social situation in the country). This is what I mean by political *da'wa*.

I use the term *da'wa* somewhat loosely. The word has specific religious (Islamic) connotations meaning "call," "invitation," "propagation," and especially "proselytizing" or "missionary activity." In fact, one of the Brotherhood's main activities is *da'wa*: spreading the message of Islam.[53] Here, I use the term to describe the Brotherhood's efforts to use elections and parliament to communicate its *political message*. In the context of semi-authoritarian regimes, and in the Brotherhood's situation more specifically, political *da'wa* becomes one of the primary goals – and benefits – of electoral participation and parliamentary membership.[54]

More generally, political *da'wa* is a form of electoral participation in semi-authoritarian regimes where participating in elections is not primarily intended to win seats, gain policy influence, or achieve state power. Rather, for some opposition groups participating in "limited" or "controlled" elections is viewed as an opportunity to increase contact with society, disseminate the group's message, and, ultimately, expand its influence.

This understanding of the Brotherhood's electoral participation was sometimes made explicit by the group's leaders, even if it was not obvious to most observers.[55] Mohamed Habib, the former Deputy Guide, expressed it most articulately in the following long quotation. Describing regime repression against the Brotherhood, Habib stated:

> In doing this they utilize specific methods and machinations: military trials, constitutional amendments, arrests etc ... the intention behind all this is to restrict the action of the Brotherhood and marginalize their role in political life. ... *For our part, we try, as much as is possible, through elections, to confront this strategy through contact with the public to exhibit our ideas and ambitions ... The elections provide us with a semi-legal and extraordinary avenue through which we can communicate with the people – this is our original mode of operation in that we are not so much competing to rule as we are pursuing to work with the masses, the people – with the goal to change their understandings, their mores, their impressions i.e., to change the political, economic, and social reality in the country.* When the issue of entry into the elections comes up and procurement of some specific gains ... whether it is in local council elections, in parliament or the Shura Council – *these are then utilized for more [increased] contact with people in that they provide a legal and constitutional umbrella for contact with the masses.* Additionally, there is also an attempt to change corruption and resist repression and other efforts. Consequently, quite apart from the question of whether we have procured gains from these elections or not, *the real gain has been the contact with the masses and the exhibition of our ideas and vision. ... We want the real picture to be put out: this is not competition for rule ... we are not competing for power. Rather we communicate with the masses to change their mores, impressions, visions, their political rearing ...* to raise their level of political consciousness in general to reveal to them the challenges, on the internal and external level, that face them.[56]

Habib makes it clear that the Muslim Brotherhood was not competing for power, nor was it competing for parliamentary seats. The primary purpose of electoral competition was to augment the organization's ability to connect with members of the general public: citizens, people, and the masses. Elections provided a "legal and constitutional" mechanism for doing so.

The Brotherhood used elections instrumentally for this purpose. For example, during elections Brotherhood candidates campaign much like others: they open offices if allowed, take campaign walks in their districts, shake hands and smile, meet potential voters, print campaign material, hold rallies, give speeches, and present their views to the public. What I call political *da'wa* also continues once inside parliament, when those fortunate Muslim Brotherhood candidates become Muslim Brotherhood parliamentarians.[57] And Brotherhood parliamentarians have been particularly skillful at using parliament (and their status as MPs) as a stage or platform to make their views heard, criticize the regime, publicize certain issues, and present themselves to the public as serious, responsible, sincere, hard-working, and reliable leaders.

With only 86 representatives in a 454-member assembly dominated by the regime's National Democratic Party (NDP) in the 2005–10 parliamentary session, Brotherhood MPs could neither pass nor block legislation.[58] Moreover, like legislative institutions in other semi-authoritarian regimes, the Egyptian People's Assembly did not function as an effective legislative body. Drafting legislation or even impacting policy was unlikely. In this context, regime constraints on the propagation of real policy made political *da'wa* the primary purpose of parliamentary membership.

For example, when Brotherhood MPs learned, without prior notice, on the evening of April 30, 2006 that NDP MPs were about to call for the renewal of the Emergency Law in parliament the following day, Brotherhood MPs prepared black sashes that read "No to Emergency" which they then wore in the Assembly the next day while the body voted on the law's renewal.[59] Brotherhood MPs were under no illusion that they could prevent the Emergency Law's extension, a central pillar of the regime's authoritarianism. In addition to voting against the renewal, wearing the sashes was an eye-catching symbolic protest. A picture of the Muslim Brotherhood parliamentary bloc dressed in black sashes emblazoned with "No to Emergency" appeared on the front page of the country's leading independent newspaper the following day.

Brotherhood parliamentarians employed sashes to similar effect on several other occasions. When the regime put two prominent pro-reform judges in front of a disciplinary hearing after they publicly denounced electoral fraud during the 2005 elections, approximately 20 Brotherhood MPs protested on the downtown Cairo street outside the courtroom where the proceedings took place, draped in sashes that read "The People's Representatives with Egypt's Judges." Similarly, on March 19, 2007, when the People's Assembly voted on the ruling party's proposed 34 amendments to the Egyptian constitution, the Muslim Brotherhood parliamentary bloc attended the session wearing sashes that read "No to the Constitutional Coup." The Brotherhood MPs raised bright yellow placards that stated "The Arab Republic of Egypt's Constitution – March 2007, Rest in Peace, For Personal Freedoms and Free Elections."[60] Pictures of Brotherhood parliamentarians holding the placards and draped in the sashes later appeared in the Egyptian press.

In addition to using the media to gain visibility for their political positions, the Brotherhood parliamentary bloc also demonstrated tremendous media savvy in presenting a favorable image of themselves, especially compared with the ruling party. For example, on September 23, 2006 the Brotherhood parliamentary bloc held internal elections to choose a chairman, deputy chairman, and a general secretariat.[61] The announcement of elections was made several days earlier and the balloting took place inside the People's Assembly. Brotherhood MPs invited the media and other parliamentarians to attend, including former parliamentary speaker Fathy Sorour, a leading NDP figure and regime symbol.[62] The elections were supervised by independent and opposition MPs using a transparent glass ballot box, and vote tallies were made public.[63] Sayyid Askar, the oldest Muslim Brotherhood parliamentarian, described the elections to the press as a "democratic celebration" and the developed meaning of Islamic *shura*.[64] The message the parliamentarians were sending was clear: unlike the Mubarak regime and its ruling party, the Brotherhood believes in elections and democracy, including internal democracy. The parliamentary bloc undertook similar internal elections in subsequent years.

Brotherhood MPs also used parliamentary membership to effectively undertake political *da'wa* in a number of other important ways. Two of these have been by opening district offices (and their associated community outreach programs) and through the parliamentary bloc's "media center."[65] Across the country, Brotherhood parliamentarians opened district offices, often opening multiple offices in different neighborhoods in a single district.[66] These offices provided a legal and semi-permanent presence for Brotherhood MPs – and, by extension, for the Brotherhood organization – to connect with local residents. They were also places where residents would come to present their problems and seek assistance; Brotherhood MPs and their office staff met with district residents and provided constituent services, one of the primary functions of Egyptian parliamentarians.[67] The importance of such offices cannot be overstated: they constituted a physical presence in the community, providing services to residents, engaging in outreach activities, and propagating the organization's message (through *da'wa* and action). District offices afforded the organization legal and institutional proximity to the populace to further engage in political *da'wa*.

Brotherhood parliamentarians also publicized their own accomplishments and activities as well as news of their districts through printed material, flyers, community newsletters, and websites.[68] For example, Hamdy Hassan and Hussein Ibrahim, MPs from Alexandria's Mina Al Basal district (2000–10), produced a colorful semi-regular newsletter about their community activities. The cover of the July 2006 issue carried a picture of Hassan, a medical doctor, examining a young boy as part of a "medical caravan" the parliamentarians organized for children in their district.[69] The newsletter, which contains pictures and text, also includes information about the parliamentary activities of both MPs (e.g., the interpellations submitted, questions posed to ministers, statements released), announcements about the district offices' future activities (e.g., computer training and English language classes, parties for district students who receive good grades), as well as basic information about the work of each office in the district (e.g., the number of residents who visited the offices, the number of requests for assistance registered, distribution of clothing, numbers of residents who participated in a women's and children's health program).[70] Of course, the newsletter also included the telephone numbers and addresses of the six offices the MPs opened in the Mina Al Basal district.

Additional benefits of electoral participation and parliamentary membership

The Brotherhood derived other benefits from participating in semi-authoritarian elections, many of which are directly related to political *da'wa*. Electoral participation and parliamentary membership can provide *reputational benefits* for Islamist groups such as the Muslim Brotherhood and other supposedly "radical" organizations.[71] Participating in elections demonstrates to the general public, the regime, and the international community that the Brotherhood is neither radical nor revolutionary, but willing to play within the existing political system, despite the rigged rules of the game.[72] Electoral participation became a demonstration of the group's commitment to peaceful political activity, despite regime repression and electoral manipulation.[73]

In fact, in Egypt and elsewhere, Islamists have made concerted efforts to limit their electoral participation so as not to threaten incumbent regimes. Islamist organizations have intentionally fielded fewer candidates than possible in order to signal their limited political aspirations: to be included in politics but not to dominate. In fact, "participation not domination" was one of the Brotherhood's slogans during the 2005 and 2010 elections.[74] And in the scheduled 2011 parliamentary elections, the first since Mubarak's ouster, the Brotherhood announced they would only compete for half of the parliamentary seats (although they first announced they would only compete for one third of parliamentary seats). They also announced they would not field a candidate in the next presidential election.[75]

The Muslim Brotherhood has also thought strategically about which districts and seats to contest. For example, in the 2005 legislative elections the group did not run candidates against Mubarak's sitting cabinet ministers. It calculated that competing against such high-profile regime symbols (and potentially defeating them) would unnecessarily embarrass the regime (and possibly lead to further repression).[76] Moreover, once in parliament, responsible participation and professional performance by Islamist MPs demonstrated that they took state institutions and their positions as parliamentarians seriously, often in contrast with MPs loyal to the regime.

Contesting elections and working in parliament also served as a rejection of the regime's claim that the Brotherhood was illegal (a "banned organization"). It was also an assertion of the group's right to participate in the political process.[77]

Participation in "authoritarian elections" also served as a vivid reminder to audiences, both foreign and domestic, that the Egyptian regime lacked electoral legitimacy. Contesting fraudulent elections exposed the regime as unpopular, based in great measure on violence and electoral manipulation. While exposing the regime's democratic façade, electoral participation simultaneously won the Brotherhood sympathy as a victim of electoral fraud and repression.

Membership in parliament also had its privileges. Both individual MPs and the Brotherhood as an organization benefited from having representatives in the People's Assembly. In Egypt, parliamentary membership provides MPs with "immunity" and some, although not complete, protection from the regime and its often arbitrary exercise of power. For example, Muslim Brotherhood MPs had more freedom of maneuver and movement than their colleagues in the Brotherhood, including the ability to travel abroad.[78] And despite the Mubarak regime's crackdown on the organization beginning in 2006, not a single Brotherhood MP was arrested.[79] Although the regime could harass parliamentarians, membership in parliament made repression against MPs more costly as a regime strategy.

Membership in parliament also provided connections and some access to state resources, and hence opportunities to serve constituents. Even though the regime was likely to limit the access of opposition MPs to government coffers, their status as parliamentarians provided connections to ministries and local officials that could potentially be useful for local residents.[80]

Participating in elections also afforded the Brotherhood some of the usual benefits of electoral participation: training and educating cadres and mobilizing members. Competing in national elections involved mobilizing thousands of members from across the country and actively including them in the group's political activities. Thus, elections allowed the Brotherhood to "mobilize the base."

Elections also provided opportunities for members to gain valuable political experience and skill. Members managed district campaigns, organized events, interacted with the public, disseminated a "message," and ran against other candidates. In the process, they learned about strategy, political communication, and gained organizational experience and skills. Brotherhood candidates who were elected to office benefited even more from participation: they "are educated [by this process] legally, media-wise, politically."[81] Essam El Erian, a member of the Brotherhood's Guidance Bureau who was twice elected to parliament (and is now a leading member of the Brotherhood's Freedom and Justice Party, established in July 2011) described it this way:

> to move from a distant observer to a position of a participant … this is an important thing. To move from a position of mere critic of the government to an accuser of the government – by legal and constitutional means – this is an important thing. To be transformed from a populist man to a statesman – to talk about the budget, statistics, policies, plans – this is a momentous thing. … So they [elected candidates] are transformed from people who talk about politics into actual politicians.[82]

El Erian also noted that a number of Brotherhood MPs (including the parliamentary bloc's deputy chairman) were previously elected to municipal councils, where they gained valuable experience.

Conclusion

Paradoxically, "limited elections" are often moments of opportunity for opposition groups and parties to engage in forms of politics that are usually prohibited in semi-authoritarian regimes. In such regimes, the space of politics often expands before elections, and certain types of activities that are usually not permitted are often tolerated during election periods. For groups such as Egypt's Muslim Brotherhood that usually face severe restrictions on political activity, elections provide opportunities (limited in time) to hold meeting and rallies, open campaign offices, reach out to citizens, and criticize the regime in harsher tones. Elections provide opportunities for political *da'wa*: to propagate the Brotherhood's message to society.

Electoral participation for the Brotherhood was therefore not about coming to power through the ballot box. Neither was it motivated by the desire to play a policy-making role. The Brotherhood is not primarily a "vote-seeking" (or "vote-maximizing"), "office-seeking," or "policy-or-influence-seeking" organization. Such an understanding of the group would be inaccurate. The logic of the Brotherhood's electoral and parliamentary participation was different. I have described it as political *da'wa*.

Electoral participation was one among a number of methods the group employed in a long-term "war of position" to gradually transform Egyptian society and politics. It is a method that reflects both the movement's philosophy and its time horizon; a strategy of gradual change from the bottom up, a generational endeavor in which electoral participation and parliamentary membership are means and not ends.[83]

This strategy also reflects the Brotherhood's conception of power: a Gramscian view in which the goal is to change individuals (e.g., values, mores, principles) and construct subjectivities, a war of position rather than a war of maneuver. It is an attempt to transform society one person, one family, and one neighborhood at a time, rather than an attempt to "capture the state" (in a Leninist sense).

In this sense the Brotherhood "won" simply by participating in elections, irrespective of whether they actually "won" seats in parliament. Even if Brotherhood candidates "lost" as a result of electoral fraud or repression, the Brotherhood gained from electoral participation because participation (and parliamentary membership) afforded the movement opportunities to engage in political *da'wa*. This was the actual goal of participation, not "winning elections."[84] Understood in this manner, the Brotherhood "won" elections even when it "lost."

In the wake of the "January 25 revolution," the establishment of the Brotherhood's Freedom and Justice Party (FJP), and the possibility of genuinely free and fair elections, the question now becomes whether the Brotherhood's electoral strategy will change. One might expect the FJP to function increasingly like an "ordinary" political party and participate in elections with the primary objective of winning seats, influencing policy, and gaining state power. Exploring such transformations, as well as their implications for the Muslim Brotherhood organization, is surely a worthy subject for future research.

Notes

1 Earlier versions of this chapter were presented at Georgetown University, U.C. Berkeley, Princeton University, and the Woodrow Wilson International Center for Scholars. I would like to thank Nick Garcia-Mason, Adam Farrar, Nancy Farley and those who attended these presentations for helpful comments and suggestions, and Mostafa Hefny for his excellent research assistance. The research and writing were funded in part through generous grants from the Woodrow Wilson Center for International Scholars and the Carnegie Corporation of New York. I sincerely thank both institutions for their support.

2 The 1990 boycott was to protest the lack of guarantees that the elections would be free and fair. A boycott of parliamentary elections was also organized in 2010 by the National Association for Change (NAC) led by Mohamed El Baradei, the Nobel Prize-winning former director of the International Atomic Energy Agency. The Muslim Brotherhood formally participated in discussions with the NAC and also assisted El Baradei with a

signature campaign demanding political reform in Egypt. Many had hoped that the Brotherhood, as the leading opposition force in the country, would join the 2010 boycott, giving it teeth, but they did not. Several other opposition parties did join the boycott, including the Ghad (Tomorrow) Party, Democratic Front Party, and Karama Party. In 2008, the Brotherhood announced a boycott of municipal council elections the day before the vote, as only 21 of the approximately 10,000 candidates they had hoped to run (for 50,000 municipal council seats) were allowed on the ballot. Over 1,000 Brotherhood members were arrested before the elections and other repressive measures were used against the group before the vote. See "Muslim Brotherhood Statement on Local Election Boycott," *Ikhwanweb*, April 8, 2008. Available at: http://www.ikhwanweb.com/article.php?id=16606&ref=search.php.

3 In doing so, this chapter also raises questions about the Brotherhood's conception of power and its future electoral participation. Although I cannot adequately address these questions here, I provide some initial reflections on these subjects in the conclusion (p. 133).

4 Electoral participation in the form of campaigns often allows organizations such as Egypt's Muslim Brotherhood to engage in political activity that is usually prohibited. This is in stark contrast to democratic contexts, where political parties can engage in these types of activities even outside of election periods.

5 Of course, not all opposition groups participate in "authoritarian elections" for the same reasons.

6 Voter registration lists are wildly inaccurate in Egypt and often include fictitious names as well as names of the dead, who sometimes mysteriously vote. The names of thousands of non-residents in each district also often appear on voter registration lists. Moreover, spelling and other typographical errors frequently prevent actual registered voters from voting. One assessment of the 2005 elections noted that "It is widely accepted that problems with the voter registry in Egypt are an intrinsic weakness that severely limits the opportunity for democratic elections to take place. A complete overhaul of the list is necessary in order to enhance the fairness of elections." International Republican Institute, *2005 Parliamentary Elections Assessment in Egypt*, November 15–21, 2005, p. 11. For the names of the dead on voter registration lists, see Independent Committee for Election Monitoring, *Preliminary Report on Election Day Voting and Counting Process*, September 8, 2005, available at http://www.eicds.org/english/activities/news/preliminaryreport05.htm; K. Abaza, *Political Islam and Regime Survival in Egypt*, Policy Focus 51, Washington, DC: Washington Institute for Near East Policy, January 2006, p. 8.

7 For example, see G. Shahine, "See for Yourself," *Al Ahram Weekly*, October 27–November 2, 2005. "Rights groups have already reported a string of violations as well as violence which marred the first day of candidate registration in the parliamentary campaign. Local monitors said executive powers showed clear bias to members of the ruling National Democratic Party (NDP), allowing them to apply before other candidates and allowing them to receive the two most prominent electoral signs, the camel and the crescent." Speaking optimistically about the 2005 elections before they took place, a prominent human rights activist declared that he believed the polls would be better than in previous years, when "rigging, violence and police interference were the norm." The 1995 elections were particularly bloody and fraudulent. Even before the run-off elections were held, because of the extent of fraud, the "administrative courts ruled that the results of the first round in more than 50 constituencies were null and void." See S. Shehab, "Challenging the Results," *Al Ahram Weekly*, December 14–20, 1995. See also G. E. El-Din, "Taking the Poll to the Courts," *Al Ahram Weekly*, November 30–December 6, 2000.

8 Othman held the post of Minister of Social Affairs for 16 years. Her 2000 election "victory" was also tainted by electoral fraud. In that election she also ran against a popular Muslim Brotherhood candidate, Ma'moun El Hodeibi. El Hodeibi had twice been elected to parliament in 1984 and 1987. He served as the Brotherhood's spokesman and was appointed Deputy General Guide of the organization in 1986; he held that post in

2000 when he ran against Othman. He later became the General Guide of the organization, in 2002. An Egyptian court invalidated Othman's 2000 election victory, finding that the "polling had been rife with grave irregularities, at the top of which was police intervention." See G. E. El-Din, "Selective Submission," *Al Ahram Weekly*, August 14–20, 2003.

9 J. Stacher, "Damanhour by Hook or by Crook," *Middle East Report* 238, 2006, 26–27. Stacher describes regime tactics on election day designed to engineer the desired outcome, including violence and fraud.

10 *Al Masry Al Youm*, November 24, 2005. As a result of the overwhelming demand for the newspaper, copies of the issue ran out almost immediately. The newspaper reprinted Noha El Zeini's testimonial on the front page the following day and she quickly became a nationally known figure.

11 "137 Judges Supervising Damanhour's Elections Support Noha El Zeini's Testimonial to Al Masry Al Youm," *Al Masry Al Youm*, November 25, 2005.

12 For example, see the front page of *Al Masry Al Youm*, December 2, 2005. The headline reads "Prevention Is the Solution: Security Forces Surround Polling Stations...and the Interior Ministry Describes It as 'Security Measures'." The headline is accompanied by a photo showing Central Security Forces preventing people from entering polling stations. The headline is a play on the Muslim Brotherhood's slogan "Islam is the solution."

13 See *Al Masry Al Youm*'s election coverage in November and December 2005, especially, November 24, December 2, and December 9, 2005. For accounts of violence during the 1995 elections, including the use of sulfuric acid against rival candidate supporters, see "Violence Mars Round Two" and S. Shehab, "Brawn in the Ballot," *Al Ahram Weekly*, December 7–13, 1995.

14 See the numerous reports of the Independent Committee on Election Monitoring (ICEM) during and after the 2005 elections, as well as the report by Democracy Reporting International and the Egyptian Organization for Human Rights entitled *Assessment of the Electoral Framework: Final Report, Arab Republic of Egypt*, April 2007. See also International Republican Institute, *2005 Parliamentary Elections Assessment in Egypt*, November 15–21, 2005. Election monitors have frequently been harassed, detained, attacked, and prevented from monitoring Egyptian elections. In addition to the ICEM reports, see also the National Democratic Institute's "Election Monitors Denied Their Right to Monitor the Voting Process," Municipal Elections Monitoring Campaign, April 2008, available at http://www.ndi.org/node/14738.

15 In addition to the references cited above, see Human Rights Watch, *Elections in Egypt: State of Permanent Emergency Incompatible with Free and Fair Vote*, December 2010; D. Williams, "Police Attack Voters During Last Day of Egypt Election," *Washington Post*, December 8, 2005.

16 Hala G. Thabet reports about "80 people dead and 1,500 wounded" during the 1995 polls, while Maye Kassem, citing the Centre for Human Rights Legal Aid, puts the figure at 51 dead and 878 wounded. See H. G. Thabet, "Egyptian Parliamentary Elections: Between Democratisation and Autocracy," *African Development* 31, 2006, pp. 11–24, p. 19, and M. Kassem, *In the Guise of Democracy: Governance in Contemporary Egypt*, Ithaca: Ithaca Press, 1999, p. 172.

17 M. Kassem, *Egyptian Politics: The Dynamics of Authoritarian Rule*, Boulder: Lynne Rienner, 2004, p. 76. Kassem writes, "The 2000 legislative elections brought state-directed violence in which the most blatant tactics were used to target and confront citizens. This fact is confirmed by one independent report that noted that 'while violence between their candidates and supporters decreased, the violence from security forces against voters increased.' Indeed, 'Approximately 80% of the killings and injuries resulted from bullets or tear gas fired by security forces and not through rival fighting.'" The quotation is from J. Ouda, N. el-Borai, and H. Abu Saada, *A Door onto the Desert: Egyptian Legislative Elections of 2000*, Cairo: United Group and Friedrich Neumann Foundation, 2001, p. 75.

18 See G. Essam El-Din, "Time for Delivery," *Al Ahram Weekly*, December 15–21, 2005.

19 The ruling party "won" over 80 percent of seats in the November/December 2010 elections and "independent" NDP candidates won another 10 percent. Many parties boycotted the vote, while the Brotherhood boycotted the second round of voting, after the extent of electoral fraud became apparent. The Brotherhood did not win a single seat in the first round of voting. The Independent Coalition for Election Observation described the elections as "a moral and a political catastrophe" and urged the government to annul the results. Mohamed Morsy, a member of the Brotherhood's Guidance Office, said the elections "scandalised the ruling regime, while giving a boost to our legitimacy and popularity." Mohamed El Baradei described the elections as "a farce." See "Egypt: Election Coalition Urges President Mubarak to Dissolve Parliament," *Los Angeles Times*, December 7, 2010; "Egypt Election: Hosni Mubarak's NDP Sweeps Second Round," BBC, December 7, 2010, available at: http://www.bbc.co.uk/news/world-middle-east-11935368. See also "Egypt's Parliamentary Election a Farce: ElBaradei," BBC, December 8, available at http://www.bbc.co.uk/news/world-middle-east-11952055.

20 Reports from the Independent Committee for Election Monitoring describe "a systematic and planned campaign of intimidation against opposition voters, in particular, Muslim Brotherhood supporters and candidates." See Press Statement, Independent Committee for Election Monitoring, '*Preliminary Report on Election Day Voting and Counting Process for the Second Round of the Parliamentary Elections*,' November 23, 2005.

21 "Egypt Police Arrest Brotherhood Ahead of Polls," Islamonline, November 30, 2005, available at: http://www.islamonline.net/English/News/2005–11/30/article07.shtml. Former Guidance Bureau member and prominent Brotherhood leader Abdel Monem Aboul Fotouh estimated that up to 2,000 Brothers had been arrested before the conclusion of the 2005 elections. Before the 1995 elections Mustafa Mashhour (before he became the group's General Guide) interpreted the arrest of Brotherhood members as "an act of interference on the part of the government, which was seeking to prevent them from running for election. It is obvious governmental interference to prevent them from exercising their constitutional right." See the interview with Mashhour in A. Howeidy, "Soldiers of the Shari'a," *Al Ahram Weekly*, November 16–22, 1995.

22 See Human Rights Watch "Egypt: Muslim Brothers Arrested Ahead of Elections," June 12, 2007.

23 The Guidance Office (or Bureau) is the organization's highest governing body, consisting of between 12 and 20 elected members entrusted with the most important decisions regarding the organization and its activities.

24 Interview with Mohamed Habib, Cairo, Egypt, March 12, 2008. Although Habib believed in the utility of electoral participation, he described the debates that took place about these issues within the Guidance Office. One prominent former Guidance Office member recently made his own views explicit. In a long interview in early 2010, Abdel Monem Aboul Fotouh stated that the Brotherhood should withdraw from electoral politics for the next 20 years. He argued that the regime uses the Brotherhood as an excuse with the West in order to rig elections. Withdrawing from electoral participation would eliminate this excuse. Aboul Fotouh also argued that between 1928, when the group was established, and 1984 the Brotherhood did not have a single representative in parliament but this did not limit the group's effectiveness or its national presence. It should be noted that this has not always been Aboul Fotouh's position. See A. M. Aboul Fotouh, "Dr. Abdel Monem Aboul Fotouh: I Call on the Brotherhood to Withdraw from Elections for Twenty Years," *Al Dustour*, February 10, 2010, available at http://www.dostor.org/politics/egypt/10/february/10/5915. Aboul Fotouh's comments generated quite a bit of attention. The journalist and blogger Abdel Monem Mahmoud wrote a long commentary about the interview on his own blog on February 14, 2010 entitled "Dr. Abdel Monem…the call for the Brotherhood to withdraw from political life is organizational pragmatism [and] not in the national interest." See http://ana-ikhwan.blogspot.com/2010/02/blog-post_479.html. It is important to note that although Aboul

Fotouh calls for the Brotherhood to withdraw from electoral politics in the interview, his understanding of the purpose and benefits of electoral participation reflects the argument I present here about *da'wa*. Aboul Fotouh says, "no one wants to believe: we compete over the interests of the nation but we do not compete to rule the nation, because we are not occupied [concerned with] with ruling the nation even though this is our right."

25 "*Al Hidha Fuwq Al Kilma fi Majlis Al Sha'b*," *Al Masry Al Youm*, January 12, 2009. Farid was responding to an article entitled "Shoes above Words in the People's Assembly" that described a heated debate that erupted in parliament when one Brotherhood MP (Ali Laban) raised his shoe while making an impassioned speech during the 2008–09 Gaza War. Several days earlier another Brotherhood parliamentarian (Ashraf Badr El Din) raised his shoe in what appears to have been an insult to a ruling party MP in a dispute about the Gaza War. Farid's statement that "we are without representatives in our district … and this is better" refers to the fact that Aga did not have representatives in the People's Assembly between 2005 and 2010. Because of administrative problems during the 2005 elections in Aga, the district was without parliamentary representation (i.e., MPs) during this period. Farid states that his district is better off without representatives because they are useless.

26 See H. R. Ezzat, "Ahlam Al 'Asafir," *Al Dustur*, June 8, 2008. Ezzat notes that "the government benefits from their presence [Brotherhood MPs] more than the people or the nation" and writes that the Brotherhood MPs "cannot tame the ruling party that is holding onto to the chairs of power by their teeth."

27 G. Essam El-Din, "People's Assembly Still Toothless," *Al Ahram Weekly*, August 10–16, 2006. Describing the first session after the election of 88 Brotherhood MPs to the Assembly, El-Din writes that many still consider the parliament to be "little more than a rubber stamp." El-Din described the previous Assembly (between 2000 and 2005) as "toothless." See his "Lacklustre Session for Toothless Assembly," *Al Ahram Weekly*, July 8–14, 2004. Democracy Reporting International and the Egyptian Organization for Human Rights came to similar conclusions: "The Parliament … in which the ruling NDP has held a two-thirds majority since the inception of multi-party politics, is a weak institution which rarely acts on its own initiative and is widely perceived as a rubber-stamp body." See their report entitled *Assessment of the Electoral Framework: Final Report, Arab Republic of Egypt*, April 2007, p. 2.

28 As quoted in B. Magaloni, *Voting for Autocracy: Hegemonic Party Survival and Its Demise in Mexico*, Cambridge: Cambridge University Press, 2006, p. 9. The original reference is J. Gandhi and A. Przeworski, "Dictatorial Institutions and the Survival of Dictators," paper presented at the Annual Meeting of the American Political Science Association, August 30–September 2, 2001. The original quotation is: "Under dictatorships, parties do not compete, elections do not elect, and legislatures do not legislate."

29 For example, Maye Kassem writes that "the legislature remains, in general, a weak and dependent institution in Mubarak's Egypt, as it was during the Nasser and Sadat eras." *Egyptian Politics: The Dynamics of Authoritarian Rule*, Boulder: Lynne Rienner, 2004, p. 36. The Egyptian parliament is described as "marginalized" and "politically impoverished" in a book that is ostensibly about the importance of Arab legislatures. See A. Baaklini, G. Denoeux, and R. Springborg, *Legislative Politics in the Arab World: The Resurgence of Democratic Institutions*, Boulder: Lynne Rienner, 1999 (see chapter 10, pp. 221–46). In *A Grand Delusion: Democracy and Economic Reform in Egypt*, London: I. B. Tauris, 2000, Eberhard Kienle refers to the parliament as an "empty shell" (p. 23) and writes that "The executive's grip on legislation has been a constant feature in contemporary Egyptian politics."

30 The number of representatives in the People's Assembly has varied from a low of 360 members in 1976 to 454 members between 1995 and 2005. Sixty-four new seats reserved for women were added in 2009. The first elections that included these seats took place in 2010, increasing the assembly's size to 518.

31 See S. Shehata, "Inside an Egyptian Parliamentary Campaign," and E. Lust-Okar, "Competitive Clientelism in Jordanian Elections," in E. Lust-Okar and S. Zerhouni (eds.) *Political Participation in the Middle East*, Boulder: Lynne Rienner, 2008.

32 This is similar to what Beatriz Magaloni calls "punishment regimes," where regime supporters receive benefits (i.e. state spending) whereas opponent supporters do not. See her *Voting for Autocracy: Hegemonic Party Survival and Its Demise in Mexico*, New York: Cambridge University Press, 2006, p. 20. It should also be noted that despite the regime's hostility Brotherhood MPs have managed to provide some government services to their constituents. In fact, Brotherhood MPs take pride in their ability to provide assistance to district residents. But access to government resources is not the primary reason the organization competes in elections.

33 K. Janda, "Comparative Political Parties: Research and Theory," in A. W. Finifter (ed.) *Political Science: The State of the Discipline II*, Washington DC: American Political Science Association, 1993, pp. 163–91.

34 For example K. Strom, "A Behavioral Theory of Competitive Political Parties," *American Journal of Political Science* 34, 1990, pp. 565–98; W. C. Muller and K. Strom, *Policy, Office, or Votes? How Political Parties in Western Europe Make Hard Decisions*, Cambridge: Cambridge University Press, 1999.

35 The more recent interest in authoritarian elections includes S. Mainwaring, "Party Objectives in Authoritarian Regimes with Elections or Fragile Democracies: A Dual Game," in S. Mainwaring and T. R. Scully (eds.) *Christian Democracy in Latin America: Electoral Competition and Regime Conflicts*, Stanford: Stanford University Press, 2003, pp. 3–29; B. Geddes, "Why Parties and Elections in Authoritarian Regimes?" paper presented at the American Political Science Association meeting, 2005; A. Schedler (ed.), *Electoral Authoritarianism: The Dynamics of Unfree Competition*, Boulder: Lynne Rienner, 2006; B. Magaloni, *Voting for Autocracy: Hegemonic Party Survival and Its demise in Mexico*, New York: Cambridge University Press, 2006; K. F. Greene, *Why Dominant Parties Lose: Mexico's Democratization in Comparative Perspective*, New York: Cambridge University Press, 2007; J. Gandhi, *Political Institutions under Dictatorship*, New York: Cambridge University Press, 2008, in addition to works cited in notes 28, 31, 36, 37, and 39 in this chapter. Some of this literature is relevant for understanding why opposition parties participate in "limited" or "controlled" elections. For example, Mainwaring is rightly critical of the assumption that parties are "exclusively interested in winning votes or seats" (p. 8). He claims that "contexts of authoritarian regimes with competitive elections... often dramatically alter parties' objectives and strategies for reaching those objectives," and concludes that parties in such contexts play "two games," an "electoral" and a "regime game" (p. 8). For the Brotherhood, as I have argued, elections are clearly more about the "regime game." Greene's intriguing analysis is also relevant. His idea of "message seekers" who aspire to transform voters' "hearts and minds" (as opposed to "office seekers") and what he calls the "expressive benefits" of participation resemble aspects of what I call political *da'wa* (pp. 120, 129). But his conception of "expressive benefits" appears more psychological and narrower than the model of political *da'wa* I present here. In Greene's account, the benefits of participation are primarily "expressive" and serve to explain why elites join opposition parties and run for office. This is quite different from the tangible, concrete benefits of political *da'wa* I describe here. Rather than there being shortcomings in analysis, however, Greene's focus and the object of his outstanding study are significantly different than my own. Of course, there is also an older literature on communist elections and elections in one-party states that is only marginally relevant for the discussion here. For example, see J. M. Gilson, "Soviet Elections as a Measure of Dissent: The Missing One Percent," *American Political Science Review* 62, 1968, pp. 814–26; and F. Dinka and M. J. Skidmore, "The Functions of Communist One-Party Elections: The Case of Czechoslovakia, 1971," *Political Science Quarterly* 88, 1973, pp. 395–422.

36 See J. Gandhi and A. Przeworski, "Authoritarian Institutions and the Survival of Autocrats," *Comparative Political Studies* 40, 2007, pp. 1279–1301; and J. Gandhi and E. Lust-Okar,

"Elections under Authoritarianism," *Annual Review of Political Science* 12, 2009, pp. 403–22.

37 J. Gandhi and E. Lust-Okar, "Elections under Authoritarianism," *Annual Review of Political Science* 12, 2009, p. 407. They write: "In most cases, the emerging picture is that elections are not uncompetitive exercises simply returning preselected candidates, but rather exercises in 'competitive clientelism,' wherein candidates vie for the privilege of acting as intermediaries in patron–client relations." Writing about why most candidates enter elections, Gandhi and Lust-Okar state: "Most candidates apparently enter elections to vie for a portion of the spoils, since their control over policy outcomes is limited" (p. 409).

38 This is also unlikely to be why most Islamist groups participate in elections.

39 A. H. Sinno and A. Khanani, "Of Opportunities and Organization: When Do Islamist Parties Choose to Compete Electorally?" in M. A. Mohamed Salih (ed.) *Interpreting Islamic Political Parties*, New York: Palgrave Macmillan, 2009, pp. 29–49.

40 They further "predict" that the ability to benefit from participation determines whether (some) Islamists choose to participate electorally or not.

41 Sinno and Khanani, op. cit., p. 39.

42 It is interesting to note the possible confusion in the article about what exactly is being explained. The article's subtitle is "When Do Islamist Parties Choose to Compete Electorally," while the authors describe their own ambitions, in part (on the article's first page), as explaining (among other things) "why some are willing to participate in electoral competition while others are not, [and] why some even participate in elections organized by autocratic regimes that manipulate results and only allow the parliament limited powers." However, there is an important difference between explaining when Islamists participate (i.e., the conditions under which they choose to participate) and why they participate (or, stated differently, the benefits of participation). The authors do a commendable job of explaining why some Islamists are more interested in electoral participation than others, as well as when these Islamists participate. Their "explanation" of why Islamists participate, however, is hollow: (some) Islamists benefit from electoral participation. How they benefit more specifically is not addressed.

43 M. El-Ghobashy, "The Metamorphosis of the Egyptian Muslim Brothers," *International Journal of Middle East Studies* 37, 2005, 373–95. For another analysis of the Brotherhood's electoral participation, see T. Masoud, "Why Do Important Social Movements Run in Rigged Elections for Seats in Rubber-Stamp Legislatures?" paper presented at the Middle East Studies Association meeting, November 18, 2008. Masoud's meticulous analysis is outstanding and there are significant similarities, as well as differences, between his account and my own. The most important difference is that Masoud's analysis is framed largely through the framework of "political party formation."

44 M. Ottaway and A. Hamzawy, *Islamists in Politics: The Dynamics of Participation*, Carnegie Papers 98, November 2008.

45 Ibid., pp. 1, 5, 9, 11–12.

46 Ottaway and Hamzawy, op. cit., p. 20.

47 Ibid., p. 20.

48 By "only part of the story" I mean only one of several motivations for participating in "authoritarian elections."

49 More empirical and cross-country research needs to be done on the periods immediately before elections in semi-authoritarian regimes in order to determine whether what is true in Egypt is also true in other semi-authoritarian regimes that hold elections (i.e., whether there is increased political space before elections, and, if so, how much and in which circumstances). This phenomenon has frequently been observed by journalists covering elections in such regimes. For example, increased political space, albeit temporary, was allowed before the 2010 Sudanese presidential elections. A Reuters journalist covering the elections noted that "The election campaign has witnessed some rare political freedoms. Direct newspaper censorship was lifted, opposition politicians were given

some air time on live television and about 30 young Sudanese protested outside the National Elections Commissions, carrying a coffin which they said symbolized the body's integrity." See O. McDoom, "Sudan Polls to Start Despite Fraud Claims, Boycotts," *Reuters*, April 8, 2010.

50 For the desire of autocrats to be seen as democrats, see K. Roth, "Despots Masquerading as Democrats," *Journal of Human Rights Practice* 1, 2009, pp. 140–55. There is also a corresponding desire for elections to look free and fair, or at least not completely fraudulent.

51 Muslim Brothers are also very aware of the phenomenon of increased space for political activity, including campaigning, during election periods. Interview with Essam El Erian, Cairo, March 10, 2008.

52 This is in stark contrast to democratic contexts, where political parties can engage in these types of activities even outside of election periods.

53 For an outstanding account of the Brotherhood's more general practice of *da'wa* as "ideological outreach," see Carrie Rosefsky Wickham, *Mobilizing Islam: Religion, Activism, and Political Change in Egypt*, New York: Columbia University Press, 2002, esp. ch. 6.

54 It makes sense for some opposition groups in semi-authoritarian regimes, in the context of "authoritarian elections" and "toothless parliaments," to use electoral participation and parliamentary membership in this manner.

55 In an excellent article about the Brotherhood's overall "goals and strategies," Sana Abed-Kotob briefly touches upon this understanding of the group's use of elections. She writes: "the contemporary Brotherhood views the election campaign as an ideal apparatus for promulgating its message of Islam as the solution....Participation in the existing electoral system is thus a major tool used by the Brethren to advance their *da'wa* by sidestepping the many legislative restrictions that otherwise prevent promulgation of their message." See S. Abded-Kotob, "The Accomodationists Speak: Goals and Strategies of the Muslim Brotherhood of Egypt," *International Journal of Middle East Studies* 27, 1995, 331.

56 Interview with Mohamed Habib, Cairo, Egypt, December 26, 2007. Later in the same interview, Habib said, "I want to stress that the question is not about competition for power. We want to find outlets for the message. We want to create environments and spaces where we can communicate with the masses."

57 With even more cameras, lights, and attention focused on MPs in parliament than candidates during a campaign, membership in parliament provides a microphone in the arena of domestic politics.

58 Eighty-eight Muslim Brothers were elected to parliament but two died in the first years of the 2005–10 session.

59 For more on this, see S. Shehata and J. Stacher, "The Brotherhood Goes to Parliament," *Middle East Report* 240, 2006.

60 *Al Masry Al Youm* also carried a picture on the front page the following day (March 20, 2007) of Muslim Brotherhood MPs wearing the sashes outside of parliament.

61 Interview with Hamdy Hassan (MP from the Mina Al Basal district in Alexandria), Alexandria, Egypt, January 3, 2007. Hassan implied that this was the first time the Muslim Brotherhood parliamentary bloc held internal elections. He said that previously their numbers were too small to have use for internal elections. "Before our numbers were small, 15, we did not need elections...88 is a number where we can have real elections. At the beginning, we did not know each other and at the beginning, the choice was made by the Guidance Office, in the second year we did it (held elections). They were real elections."

62 M. Mohamed, "Brotherhood Representatives in the People's Assembly Choose a New Head of the Bloc Tomorrow and Hussein and Al Baltagy Are the Leading Candidates," *Al Masry Al Youm*, September 22, 2006. Not surprisingly, Sorour did not show up.

63 The elections took place without nominations and as a result more than one round of balloting was required in order to fill certain posts. In other words, Brotherhood

parliamentarians could vote for anyone among themselves for these posts. See *Al Masry Al Youm*, September 22, 2006.

64 See M. Mohamed, "Al Katatny Is the Head of the Brotherhood Parliamentary Bloc and Ibrahim is Deputy without Nominations," Al *Masry Al Youm*, September 24, 2006.

65 The media activities of the Brotherhood, including those of the parliamentary bloc, are worthy of an entire research project.

66 At least one Brotherhood parliamentarian in the Mansoura area has gone even further, opening an office in a neighboring district, in order to serve those residents as well as his own.

67 See S. Shehata, "Inside an Egyptian Parliamentary Campaign," in E. Lust-Okar and S. Zerhouni (eds.) *Political Participation in the Middle East*, Boulder: Lynne Rienner, 2008.

68 The Brotherhood's web presence is worthy of an entire research project. Suffice it to say here that its online activities are extremely impressive, far more so than the regime's or the ruling National Democratic Party's, despite far fewer resources. In addition to the group's main websites in both Arabic and English and the Muslim Brotherhood parliamentary bloc's website (www.nowabikhwan.com), individual parliamentarians have their own sites, in addition to Brotherhood sites for different Egyptian governorates. The main websites and the parliamentary bloc's sites include continuous updates, news and news aggregation from other sites, original articles about the Muslim Brotherhood, and live streaming audio interviews, in addition to other features. The parliamentary website also includes transcripts from parliamentary sessions, which are otherwise difficult to obtain. The Brotherhood's sophisticated web presence is an exceptional tool for political *da'wa*. See the group's own history of its web presence, A. Hafez, "Muslim Brotherhood Websites," *Ikhwanweb*, December 13, 2008, available at http://www.ikhwanweb.com/article.php?id=18865&ref=search.php.

69 The newsletter also encourages readers to join the Alexandria MPs in a no-smoking campaign.

70 A number of the pictures are of the MPs in the district, with constituents, doing various things like visiting poor areas, listening to residents' complaints, attending community events, participating in demonstrations, etc.

71 This is especially true for Islamists as they are often portrayed as radical or revolutionary, if not irresponsible and violent, to domestic populations and foreign governments by incumbent authoritarian regimes.

72 See K. El Shatir, "No Need to Be Afraid of Us," *Guardian*, November 23, 2005. One of the recurring Muslim Brotherhood refrains during the 2005 election campaign was the motto "participation not domination." The simple fact that the organization only nominated 160 candidates is an indication that they never intended to come to power through elections.

73 Some observers even commented that the Brotherhood's boycott of the April 2008 municipal council elections only two days before the vote and after suffering 1,000 arrests and other harassment demonstrated the group's commitment to electoral participation. The Brotherhood only attempted to field 10,000 candidates for 50,000 elected positions, further signaling its limited electoral aspirations.

74 See A. Howeidy, "'Participate, Not Contest,'" *Al Ahram Weekly*, October 14–20, 2010. The Party of Justice and Development (PJD) in Morocco also intentionally ran fewer candidates than it could have in the 2002 legislative elections. It did this so as not to threaten the Moroccan government and to signal that it is only interested in participation, not in coming to power. This is similar to what I wrote earlier regarding why the Brotherhood chooses to run relatively few candidates compared with the number of seats available. See M. J. Willis, "Morocco's Islamists and the Legislative Elections of 2002: The Strange Case of Party that Did Not Want to Win," *Mediterranean Politics* 9, 2004, pp. 53–81. Nathan Brown, Amr Hamzawy, and Marina Ottaway also describe this phenomenon, stating that, "At the same time, Islamist movements started developing sophisticated strategies to increase their credibility and appease fears of their intentions. Conscious of the vicious circle of violence perpetrated by security forces and radical

Islamists precipitated by the threatened Islamists' victory in the 1991 Algerian elections, the strongest movements have deliberately curbed the scope of their political participation to limit their electoral success and avoid scaring governments into adopting repressive measures. The Moroccan PJD and the Egyptian Muslim Brotherhood decided to field candidates in fewer than 30 percent of districts in their respective countries' most recent legislative elections, thus limiting the extent of their possible success. Suspicion of these movements by the respective governments, secular parties, and international actors has not disappeared, but it is not as high as it would be had they shown less restraint. "Participation, not domination" seems to be the motto of Islamists taking part in electoral politics." See *Islamist Movements and the Democratic Process in the Arab World: Exploring Gray Zones*," Carnegie Paper 67, 2006.

75 See "Egypt's Brotherhood Eyes Big Political Role," *Al Jazeera*, April 30, 2011, available at http://english.aljazeera.net/news/middleeast/2011/04/2011430155749502855.html; A. Eleiba, "Muslim Brotherhood Announces Future Plans after Two-day Meeting," April 30, 2011, *Ahramonline*, available at http://english.ahram.org.eg/NewsContent/1/64/11102/Egypt/Politics-/Muslim-Brotherhood-announces-future-plans-after-tw.aspx.

76 Interviews with Muslim Brotherhood members in the group's headquarters in Cairo, Egypt, spring 2006.

77 Interview with Essam El Erian, Cairo, Egypt, March 10, 2008.

78 There have been a number of occasions in which high-ranking Brotherhood officials have not been allowed to leave the country for various reasons. This has included the previous General Guide Mahdi Akef, Gamal Hishmat, Essam El Erian, and others. See the U.S. State Department's "Egypt: International Religious Freedom Report 2005," available at http://www.state.gov/g/drl/rls/irf/2005/51598.htm. See also M. Salah, "Banned from Traveling," *Dar Al Hayat*, September 1, 2008, available at http://www.daralhayat.com/archivearticle/251651. In some cases, Brotherhood MPs have been allowed to travel to conferences overseas whereas other Muslim Brothers (non-parliamentarians) have been prevented from traveling to the same event. A number of Brotherhood MPs have traveled extensively to attend conferences and represent the organization since entering parliament. See "Another MB Figure Banned from Travelling to Attend Economic Conference," *Ikhwanweb*, October 28, 2006, available at http://www.ikhwanweb.com/article.php?id=3167.

79 This is the case despite other senior figures in the organization being detained, arrested (including Mohamed Morsy and Essam El Erian), and found guilty and given long prison sentences (e.g., Khairat El Shatir, among others).

80 This can be particularly important in Egypt, with its notorious bureaucracy, and in other states that suffer from poor governance. Many Egyptians have neither the connections nor the money (e.g., bribes) often needed to "finish (government) paperwork." This can include anything from the paperwork required to transfer a child from one school to another to procuring necessary documents from a ministry or other government agency (e.g., military service records). A connected official can often expedite such bureaucracy. See S. Shehata, "Inside an Egyptian Parliamentary Campaign," and E. Lust-Okar, "Elections under Authoritarianism and Democracy Promotion in the MENA," both in E. Lust-Okar and S. Zerhouni (eds.) *Political Participation in the Middle East*, Boulder: Lynne Rienner, 2008.

81 Interview with Essam El Erian, Cairo, Egypt, March 10, 2008.

82 Ibid.

83 I do not mean to imply that the Brotherhood's electoral participation is merely "tactical" and that the organization is not sincerely committed to the principle of democratic elections. The Brotherhood's previous electoral participation (despite the costs of participation and the limitations of Egyptian elections), in addition to regular internal elections within the organization, should demonstrate the group's commitment to elections.

84 One can find a number of instances in which Brotherhood leaders, at different times during the last several decades, make this explicit. For example, in the daily statements issued by the Brotherhood entitled "The World Today" for Thursday, July 30, 2009, the

first news item (reporting on an article in the newspaper *Al Youm Al Sab'*) is entitled, "Akef: The Brotherhood Does Not Compete for Office." The first line reads: "Mahdi Akef, the Muslim Brotherhood General Guide, assured that they [the Muslim Brotherhood] are not competing with anyone for office but their goal is only the service of the nation." Almost 15 years earlier, Mustafa Mashhour, who held the post of Deputy General Guide and then General Guide in the 1990s, expressed similar sentiments in an interview shortly before the 1995 elections. He denied that the Brotherhood was "infiltrating civil institutions," stating: "What they call infiltration is not done with the objective of overthrowing the government, ever. We do not seek power like the political parties. We just want someone to rule by shari'a and we are ready to be his soldiers." See A. Howeidy, "Soldiers of the Shari'a," *Al Ahram Weekly*, November 16–22, 1995.

Bibliography

"137 Judges Supervising Damanhour's Elections Support Noha El Zeini's Testimonial to Al Masry Al Youm," *Al Masry Al Youm*, November 25, 2005.

Abaza, K., *Political Islam and Regime Survival in Egypt*, Policy Focus 51, Washington, DC: Washington Institute for Near East Policy, 2006.

Abded-Kotob, S., "The Accomodationists Speak: Goals and Strategies of the Muslim Brotherhood of Egypt," *International Journal of Middle East Studies* 27, 1995, 321–39.

Aboul Fotouh, A. M., "Dr. Abdel Monem Aboul Fotouh: I Call on the Brotherhood to Withdraw from Elections for Twenty Years," *Al Dustour*, February 10, 2010, available at http://www.dostor.org/politics/egypt/10/february/10/5915.

"Akef: The Brotherhood Does Not Compete for Office," *The World Today*, July 30, 2009.

"Another MB Figure Banned from Traveling to Attend Economic Conference," *Ikhwanweb*, October 28, 2006, available at http://www.ikhwanweb.com/article.php?id=3167.

Baaklini, A., Denoeux, G., and Springborg, R., *Legislative Politics in the Arab World: The Resurgence of Democratic Institutions*, Boulder: Lynne Rienner, 1999.

Brown, N., Hamzawy, A., and Ottaway, M., *Islamist Movements and the Democratic Process in the Arab World: Exploring Gray Zones*, Carnegie Paper 67, 2006.

Democracy Reporting International and Egyptian Organization for Human Rights, *Assessment of the Electoral Framework: Final Report, Arab Republic of Egypt*, April 2007.

Dinka, F. and Skidmore, M. J., "The Functions of Communist One-Party Elections: The Case of Czechoslovakia, 1971," *Political Science Quarterly* 88, 1973, 395–422.

"Egypt: Election Coalition Urges President Mubarak to Dissolve Parliament," *Los Angeles Times*, December 7, 2010.

"Egypt Election: Hosni Mubarak's NDP Sweeps Second Round," BBC, December 7, 2010, available at: http://www.bbc.co.uk/news/world-middle-east-11935368.

"Egypt Police Arrest Brotherhood Ahead of Polls," Islamonline, November 30, 2005, available at http://www.islamonline.net/English/News/2005–11/30/article07.shtml.

"Egypt's Brotherhood Eyes Big Political Role," *Al Jazeera*, April 30, 2011, available at http://english.aljazeera.net/news/middleeast/2011/04/2011430155749502855.html.

"Egypt's Parliamentary Election a Farce: ElBaradei," BBC, December 8, available at http://www.bbc.co.uk/news/world-middle-east-11952055.

Eleiba, A., "Muslim Brotherhood Announces Future Plans after Two-day Meeting," April 30, 2011, *Ahramonline*, available at http://english.ahram.org.eg/NewsContent/1/64/11102/Egypt/Politics-/Muslim-Brotherhood-announces-future-plans-after-tw.aspx.

El-Ghobashy, M., "The Metamorphosis of the Egyptian Muslim Brothers," *International Journal of Middle East Studies* 37, 2005, 373–95.

El Shatir, K., "No Need to Be Afraid of Us," *Guardian*, November 23, 2005.

Essam El-Din, G., "People's Assembly Still Toothless," *Al Ahram Weekly*, August 10–16, 2006.

Essam El-Din, G., "Time for Delivery," *Al Ahram Weekly*, December 15–21, 2005.

Essam El-Din, G., "Lacklustre Session for Toothless Assembly," *Al Ahram Weekly*, July 8–14, 2004.

Essam El-Din, G., "Selective Submission," *Al Ahram Weekly*, August 14–20, 2003.
Essam El-Din, G., "Taking the Poll to the Courts," *Al Ahram Weekly*, November 30 December 6, 2000.
Ezzat, H. R., "Ahlam Al 'Asafir," *Al Dustur*, June 8, 2008.
Farid, A., "Al Hidha Fuwq Al Kilma fi Majlis Al Sha'b," *Al Masry Al Youm*, January 12, 2009.
Gandhi, J., *Political Institutions under Dictatorship*, New York: Cambridge University Press, 2008.
Gandhi, J. and Lust-Okar, E., "Elections under Authoritarianism," *Annual Review of Political Science* 12, 2009, 403–22.
Gandhi, J. and Przeworski, A., "Authoritarian Institutions and the Survival of Autocrats," *Comparative Political Studies* 40, 2007, 1279–1301.
Gandhi, J. and Przeworski, A., "Dictatorial Institutions and the Survival of Dictators," paper presented at the Annual Meeting of the American Political Science Association, August 30–September 2, 2001.
Geddes, B., "Why Parties and Elections in Authoritarian Regimes?" paper presented at the American Political Science Association meeting, 2005.
Gilson, J. M., "Soviet Elections as a Measure of Dissent: The Missing One Percent," *American Political Science Review* 62, 1968, 814–26.
Greene, K. F., *Why Dominant Parties Lose: Mexico's Democratization in Comparative Perspective*, New York: Cambridge University Press, 2007.
Hafez, A., "Muslim Brotherhood Websites," *IkhwanWeb*, December 13, 2008, available at http://www.ikhwanweb.com/article.php?id=18865=search.php.
Howeidy, A., "'Participate, Not Contest,'" *Al Ahram Weekly*, October 14–20, 2010.
Howeidy, A., "Soldiers of the Shari'a," *Al Ahram Weekly*, November 16–22, 1995.
Human Rights Watch, *Elections in Egypt: State of Permanent Emergency Incompatible with Free and Fair Vote*, December 2010.
Human Rights Watch, "Egypt: Muslim Brothers Arrested Ahead of Elections," June 12, 2007.
Independent Committee for Election Monitoring, *Press Statement: Preliminary Report on Election Day Voting and Counting Process for the Second Round of the Parliamentary Elections*, November 23, 2005.
Independent Committee for Election Monitoring, *Preliminary Report on Election Day Voting and Counting Process*, September 8, 2005.
International Republican Institute, *2005 Parliamentary Elections Assessment in Egypt*, November 15–21, 2005.
Janda, K., "Comparative Political Parties: Research and Theory," in A. W. Finifter (ed.) *Political Science: The State of the Discipline II*, Washington, DC: American Political Science Association, 1993, pp. 163–91.
Kassem, M., *Egyptian Politics: The Dynamics of Authoritarian Rule*, Boulder: Lynne Rienner, 2004.
Kassem, M., *In the Guise of Democracy: Governance in Contemporary Egypt*, Ithaca: Ithaca Press, 1999.
Kienle, E., *A Grand Delusion: Democracy and Economic Reform in Egypt*, London: I. B. Tauris, 2000.
Lust-Okar, E. and Zerhouni, S. (eds.), *Political Participation in the Middle East*, Boulder: Lynne Rienner, 2008.
McDoom, O., "Sudan Polls to Start Despite Fraud Claims, Boycotts," *Reuters*, April 8, 2010.
Magaloni, B., *Voting for Autocracy: Hegemonic Party Survival and Its Demise in Mexico*, New York: Cambridge University Press, 2006.
Mahmoud, A. M. "Dr. Abdel Monem...the Call for the Brotherhood to Withdraw from Political Life Is Organizational Pragmatism [and] Not in the National Interest," February 14, 2010, available at http://ana-ikhwan.blogspot.com/2010/02/blog-post_479.html.
Mainwaring, S., "Party Objectives in Authoritarian Regimes with Elections or Fragile Democracies: A Dual Game," in S. Mainwaring and T. R. Scully (eds.) *Christian*

Democracy in Latin America: Electoral Competition and Regime Conflicts, Stanford: Stanford University Press, 2003, pp. 3–29.

Masoud, T., "Why Do Important Social Movements Run in Rigged Elections for Seats in Rubber-Stamp Legislatures?" paper presented at the Middle East Studies Association Annual Meeting, November 18, 2008.

Mohamed, M., "Al Katatny Is the Head of the Brotherhood Parliamentary Bloc and Ibrahim Is Deputy without Nominations," *Al Masry Al Youm*, September 24, 2006.

Mohamed, M., "Brotherhood Representatives in the People's Assembly Choose a New Head of the Bloc Tomorrow and Hussein and Al Baltagy Are the Leading Candidates," *Al Masry Al Youm*, September 22, 2006.

Mohamed Salih, M. A. (ed.), *Interpreting Islamic Political Parties*, New York: Palgrave Macmillan, 2009.

Muller, W. C. and Strom, K., *Policy, Office, or Votes? How Political Parties in Western Europe Make Hard Decisions*, Cambridge: Cambridge University Press, 1999.

"Muslim Brotherhood Statement on Local Election Boycott," *Ikhwanweb*, April 8, 2008. http://www.ikhwanweb.com/article.php?id=16606=search.php.

National Democratic Institute, "Election Monitors Denied Their Right to Monitor the Voting Process," Municipal Elections Monitoring Campaign, April 2008, available at http://www.ndi.org/node/14738.

Ottaway, M. and Hamzawy, A., *Islamists in Politics: The Dynamics of Participation*, Carnegie Papers 98, November 2008.

Ouda, J., el-Borai, N., and Saada, H., *A Door onto the Desert: Egyptian Legislative Elections of 2000*, Cairo: United Group and Friedrich Neumann Foundation, 2001.

Roth, K., "Despots Masquerading as Democrats," *Journal of Human Rights Practice* 1, 2009, 140–55.

Salah, M., "Banned from Traveling," *Dar Al Hayat*, September 1, 2008, available at: http://www.daralhayat.com/archivearticle/251651.

Schedler, A. (ed.), *Electoral Authoritarianism: The Dynamics of Unfree Competition*, Boulder: Lynne Rienner, 2006.

Shahine, G., "See for Yourself," *Al Ahram Weekly*, October 27–November 2, 2005.

Shehab, S., "Challenging the Results," *Al Ahram Weekly*, December 14–20, 1995.

Shehab, S., "Brawn in the Ballot," *Al Ahram Weekly*, December 7–13, 1995.

Shehata, S., "Inside an Egyptian Parliamentary Campaign," in E. Lust-Okar and S. Zerhouni (eds.) *Political Participation in the Middle East*, Boulder: Lynne Rienner, 2008.

Shehata, S. and Stacher, J., "The Brotherhood Goes to Parliament," *Middle East Report* 240, 2006.

Stacher, J., "Damanhour by Hook or by Crook," *Middle East Report* 238, 2006.

Strom, K., "A Behavioral Theory of Competitive Political Parties," *American Journal of Political Science* 34, 1990, 565–98.

Thabet, H. G., "Egyptian Parliamentary Elections: Between Democratisation and Autocracy," *African Development* 31, 2006.

U.S. State Department, "Egypt: International Religious Freedom Report 2005," available at http://www.state.gov/g/drl/rls/irf/2005/51598.htm.

"Violence Mars Round Two," *Al Ahram Weekly*, December 7–13, 1995.

Wickham, C. R., *Mobilizing Islam: Religion, Activism, and Political Change in Egypt*, New York: Columbia University Press, 2002.

Williams, D., "Police Attack Voters During Last Day of Egypt Election," *Washington Post*, December 8, 2005.

Willis, M. J., "Morocco's Islamists and the Legislative Elections of 2002: The Strange Case of Party that Did Not Want to Win," *Mediterranean Politics* 9, 2004, 53–81.

8

MOBILIZATION AND IDEOLOGY IN THE IRAQI INSURGENCY

The role of Islam

Ahmed S. Hashim

Introduction

Whatever the original goals of the American invasion and occupation of Iraq, they fell out of reach long ago. Iraq witnessed a stunning display of violence by a wide variety of forces *after* the fall of Saddam Hussein's regime. From the vantage point of the present, it is clearly inaccurate to refer to this violence simply as an insurgency. After "the war," Iraq became embroiled in what I have referred to elsewhere as multi-level, complex violence where a large number of actors were pitted against one another, within shifting and tactical alliances.[1] In the words of one astute journalist who spent considerable time in Iraq, the situation after 2003 was characterized by a "dizzying mosaic of battle lines" in which Sunni insurgents confronted Al-Qaeda, U.S. troops and Iraqi security forces fought Sunni groups, Shi'i militias, and Al-Qaeda fighters, Shi'i militias fought Sunni insurgents and Al-Qaeda, and in the south Shi'i militias battled each other for control.[2] My focus in this chapter, however, is on the insurgency that emerged in Iraq after the invasion. Consisting of a variety of Sunni groups, the insurgency lasted for at least four years and witnessed major developments and changes in its motivational and ideological bases. It began as an ad hoc and not terribly well-organized or ideologically cohesive resistance, but developed considerably after the spring of 2003. It became more deadly, better organized, and capable of sophisticated and complex military operations.[3] I argue here that Islam become increasingly important in the insurgency, but that this significance was vastly complicated by the peculiarities of the Iraqi sociopolitical environment both before 2003 and after the invasion.

The purpose of this chapter is threefold. First, I briefly examine Iraqi society's political, socioeconomic, and cultural developments, particularly during the last decade of Saddam Hussein's Ba'thist regime. It is only by doing so that one can address the relevance of Islam as a political phenomenon in post-Saddam Iraq.

Second, I address the roles played by Islam (1) in motivating Iraqis to fight, (2) as a tool for mobilizing popular support, and (3) as an ideological prop for the insurgency.

Third, I explore the problems that the insurgency faced as a result of using Islam in the three ways mentioned above. The point is that Islam was not entirely a unifying factor for the insurgency. Iraq was, and remains, a bitterly divided society, and the Sunni insurgency was viewed from the beginning with suspicion by the majority Shi'i population. Moreover, divisions existed within the Sunni community between what I refer to as the national-Islamist insurgents, on the one hand, and the Sunni religious extremists – whom I will refer to as the Salafi-Jihadist group – on the other. The former group increasingly relied on promoting Islamic motifs and beliefs, and largely referred to the struggle against foreign forces in the country as a *muqawama*, or resistance. The latter group viewed the insurgency in terms of a *jihad*, or holy struggle, against both the Coalition occupation and the Shi'i majority.

Islam and the structure of power in Ba'thist Iraq

Ba'thist ideology and goals

The Ba'thist regime that came into power in July 1968 described itself as progressive, modernizing, and socialist. Indeed, after it had violently consolidated power against a number of enemies, the regime embarked on a dizzying program of economic development and social progress following the nationalization of the oil industry and the dramatic rise in oil prices in 1973. The phenomenal increase in oil revenues allowed the state to provide extensive social services and goods, promote the growth of heavy industry, and implement greater control over society.[4] The Ba'thists also managed to establish one of the most terrifying systems of government in the Middle East. Moreover, despite its "progressive" orientation, it relied heavily for its top leadership on one community within the Iraqi body politic: the Sunni Arab population.

What has been misunderstood, whether deliberately or through ignorance, is the regime's relationship to Islam. The ideology of Ba'thism to which the regime subscribed was not avowedly secular. The journalistic accounts that referred to Saddam's Iraq as the most secular regime in the Arab world were part of the political folklore picked up and repeated ad nauseam, including by one of the key architects of the U.S. quagmire in Iraq, Paul Wolfowitz. The following statement by Wolfowitz about Iraq is indicative of this:

> The Iraqi population is completely different (from the truculent Saudis). The Iraqis are among the most educated people in the Arab world. They are by and large quite secular. They are overwhelmingly Shiite, which is different from the Wahabbis of the Peninsula. They don't bring the sensitivity of having the holy cities of Islam on their territory.[5]

There are many things wrong with this analysis, including the comment about the level of Iraqi education; the sanctions regime destroyed that system and the middle class it had built. However, my focus is on the alleged secularism of Iraq. Presumably, that secularism had been constructed and institutionalized over the course of three decades under the very regime that Wolfowitz and his group were seeking to overthrow. Two quotations from Michel 'Aflaq, co-founder of the Ba'thist ideology, should dispel the notion that adherents of Ba'thism had an Arab nationalist world view that saw Islam as its antithesis:

> The pure nationalist idea in the West was consistent with itself when it separated nationalism from religion. Religion entered Europe from the outside; therefore it is alien to its character and history. It is a combination of otherworldly faith and morals. It was not revealed to them originally in their languages. It did not express the needs of their environment nor was it fused with their history. Islam, on the other hand, neither is to the Arabs, not only an otherworldly faith nor is it merely a moral code, but it is also the clearest expression of their universal feeling and their view of life. It is the strongest expressions of the unity of their personality in which word, feeling, thought, mediation, action, soul, and destiny, are all integrated and work in harmony together.[6]

Or, the following:

> The connection of Islam to Arabism is not, therefore, similar to that of any religion to any nationalism. The Arab Christians, when their nationalism is fully awakened and when they restore their genuine character, will recognize that Islam for them is nationalist education in which they have to be absorbed in order to understand and love it to the extent that they become concerned about Islam as about the most precious thing in their Arabism. If the actual reality is still far from this wish, the new generation of Arab Christians has a task which it should perform with daring and detachment, sacrificing for it their pride and benefits, for there is nothing that equals Arabism and the honor of belonging to it.[7]

The Ba'th party's strategy in Iraq was to control religion, and – particularly as the years went by – any political manifestation of religion which could be seen as a challenge to its project. That this was necessary stemmed from very profound structural factors, including some internal to the party itself. First, the Ba'th party sought to control all social spaces, of which religion was one. Second, the Ba'thists were met with opposition almost from the very onset of their rule from both Sunni and Shi'i religious organizations, whose leaders recognized the terrifying totalitarian political project of the party. Among the first political movements to suffer the wrath of the Ba'thist regime was the Iraqi branch of the Muslim Brotherhood.[8] Sunni Islamic activism has a longstanding but checkered history in Iraq. The Iraqi branch of the famed *Jama't al-Ikhwan al-Muslimun* (Society of the Muslim Brotherhood, a political movement that was started in Egypt by Hasan al-Banna in

1928) was established under the aegis of Sheikh Muhammad Mahmud al-Sawwaf, a religious scholar, in 1947. Its stronghold was the northern city of Mosul, where it immediately threw itself into the political life of the country under the discredited monarchy.

The role of Islam under conditions of crisis and warfare

The regime's efforts to suppress *al-zahira al-diniyya al-siyasiyah* – the phenomenon of political Islam – in Iraqi political life failed. Though most Shi'a and other opponents of the regime sought to avoid framing their opposition in specifically religious terms, SCIRI (the Supreme Council for Islamic Revolution in Iraq) and Da'wa (Da'wa al-Islamiyya Party), the major opposition groups, did. But the Shi'i religious parties and organizations are not the focus of our attention here; rather, we are concerned with the use of Islam as an ideological tool mobilized by the Sunnis. While religion was not as well organized among the Sunnis for this purpose as it was among the Shi'a, it would be inaccurate to argue that the Ba'th regime succeeded in eradicating Sunni Islamism as a political phenomenon. Indeed, several major events had an impact on the revival of religiosity among Sunnis.

First was the impact of the Iranian Revolution and of the Iran–Iraq War. The Iranian Revolution described itself in ecumenical terms as an Islamic revolution, not a Shi'i revolution. Its leadership believed, of course, that the revolution would have a greater effect and traction if it appealed to the wider Islamic world, particularly the Sunni Arab countries. However, the most significant impact was naturally on the Shi'i populations in Arab countries. The Ba'thist regime responded by strengthening its Arab nationalist discourse in the face of this revolutionary theocratic message. It could not very well attack Shi'ism itself, since the majority of the country's population was Shi'i. Indeed, the vast majority of the common ranks within the Iraqi military were Shi'i, and these soldiers had proved their loyalty to the Iraqi nation by fighting loyally and for eight sanguinary years against their co-confessional brethren in Iran. But when Ayatollah Khomeini fatefully decided in 1982 to put forth a counter onslaught against Iraq and "export the revolution," the Sunnis decided that the defense of Iraq required a fusion of Arab nationalism and Sunni religious sentiment.

The second important factor in understanding the religious revival among Iraqi Sunnis was the abject and humiliating defeat in Desert Storm in 1991, which was followed by the most comprehensive and devastating sanctions regime ever applied against a country. The effects of the sanctions began as early as 1992–93.[9] By the mid to late 1990s the sanctions regime had dismantled Iraqi society and left it with a bleak view of the future.[10] Iraq's social disintegration was reflected in the rising trend of impoverishment, the destruction of the education system, and the de-professionalization of the society. Moreover, as a result of the rise in poverty and increase in the number of qualified professionals leaving Iraq, the middle class, often considered a prerequisite for a stable society, vanished as a recognizable social stratum. Education had been free of charge at all levels prior to the sanctions, but it became expensive after they were instituted. Parents were forced to send their children onto the streets to beg or look for work. In 1990, 56 percent of Iraqis between the ages of six and 23 were enrolled in school; this figure dropped to 26 percent by 1994. Furthermore, 89 percent of adults were literate in 1985, while only 59 percent were in 1995. De-professionalization also occurred. This phenomenon refers to two groups: (1) youth who either did not enter college or dropped out of college because they needed to work; and (2) adults with higher degrees who were forced to make a living through non-professional or menial work. In 1995, one journalist wrote: "In the Shorje market in downtown Baghdad, it is not uncommon to find academics, accountants, and engineers selling powdered milk or soda pop."[11]

What does this have to do with Islam? In the 1990s, the environment of dismay and disintegration caused many Iraqis to turn to religion for succor and also for aid. Of course, one cannot generalize and argue that only people in dire circumstances turn to religion, as this would contradict the reality of affluent middle class people in many societies who subscribe to religious piousness. But many Iraqis I spoke with in 2003 and 2004 during my times there related that much of their turn to religion stemmed from the effects of the sanctions.[12] Indeed, an Iraqi economist was quoted in early 2003, just before the invasion, as saying, "Religion is on the rise in Iraq. The tide is strong, and there are definite signs of radicalism."[13]

Third, after the Kuwait war debacle Saddam himself initiated a "return" to religion, known as *al-hamla al-imaniyyah*, or the Return to Faith. This was the same leader who, in a speech in 1978 following mass Shi'i disturbances, stated that the party must oppose the institutionalization of religion and its introduction into political life. But given the dire circumstances in which the country found itself, it was not surprising that he would initiate this call – a necessity to ensure the regime's survival. Ba'thist ideology had been discredited in the aftermath of the disaster in Kuwait, and the party cadre proved incapable of dealing with the south's increasing discontent and uprisings. A new ideological underpinning had to be found.

Under the Return to Faith campaign, the government began spending money on promoting mandatory Qur'anic studies in schools, and it built training centers for imams, including Saddam College (for Iraqis) and the Saddam University of Islamic Studies (for foreigners). Radio stations were dedicated to airing Qur'anic lessons, and alcohol was banned in restaurants. The campaign also encouraged mosque-building, and Hussein planned to construct three gigantic mosques, as much to commemorate his regime as to honor the Prophet. As a result, Ba'th party officials and army officers rediscovered religion.[14] The rise of religiosity in Iraq was viewed approvingly by an official at the Saddam University of Islamic Studies: "Iraq is witnessing a religious renaissance. There was religious stagnation and a tendency toward materialism here. Nightclubs, bars, and pubs were spreading. Saddam has helped correct that."[15] In short, Iraq was undergoing a profound religious revival in both confessional systems as the United States and its allies prepared to invade the country and ostensibly bring it the joys of political liberalization and freedom.

Islam and the onset of the Iraqi insurgency

Political Islam was thus waiting in the wings in Iraq during the dying years of the Ba'thist regime. The regime's downfall in April 2003 allowed it to come fully into the open and take its place in the cacophony of political movements and organizations that made their appearance at that time. Moreover, the fact that Iraq was now occupied by foreign forces was crucial to the articulation of opposition in religious terms by Iraqis – both Sunnis and Shi'is – to that presence.

However, the role of Islam in the early days of the Sunni insurgency was significant but not dominant. Many of the early insurgent leaders were out-of-work former army officers who had become more pious over the course of the 1990s as described above. Yet when the insurgency broke out in the spring and summer of 2003, the narrative for many of its commanders was clustered around the theme of legitimate resistance to foreign occupation. In an interview with the Arabic newspaper *Al Riyad* in the fall of 2003, one of these former officers who led an insurgent group explained his motivations for fighting, which were largely nationalistic:

> The Iraqi land is currently under occupation. Therefore, it is our duty to sacrifice our blood for it. The occupation harms our dignity and people. Many of our kinsfolk have been killed. So, what else is there to live for? … The Americans are in a predicament, and we will continue to beat their heads until they admit the fact that they are greedy occupiers who implement Israel's policies … The struggle for the homeland has been decreed upon us. Our fathers and grandfathers fought against British colonialists and we now fight against the Americans. No occupier will remain in our homeland, no matter how long it takes.[16]

Patrick Graham, a Canadian journalist who spent a considerable period of time with the Iraqi insurgents in the movement's early years, came to know one insurgent leader. He quotes him as follows:

> When we see the U.S. soldiers in our cities with guns, it is a challenge to us. America wants to show its power, to be a cowboy … Bush wants to win the next election – that is why he is lying to the American people saying that the resistance is Al Qaeda … I don't know a lot about political relations in the world, but if you look at history – Vietnam, Iraq itself, Egypt, and Algeria – countries always rebel against occupation … The world must know that this is an honorable resistance and has nothing to do with the old regime. Even if Saddam Hussein dies we will continue to fight to throw out the American forces. We take our power from our history, not from one person."[17]

Even years later, when Islam began to play a greater role in the resistance narrative, fighting foreign occupation continued to be strongly based on the notion of the legitimate right of resistance. Among the mainstream insurgents, for example, many within the Ba'th Party continued to base their justification for resistance to occupation on what we would call, for want of a better phrase, nationalist and legal principles. Thus in late October 2006, "Dr. Abu-Muhammad," a Ba'th Command spokesman, told *Al-Jazeera*:

> What concerns us is the legitimacy of the occupation. Is the occupation legitimate, and are its actions legitimate? This is the question. According to international law, it is well known that what is established based on falsehood, is false. Since the occupation of Iraq is immoral, illegitimate, illegal, and in violation of international law, it is therefore an aggression and an invasion that is not based on logic or law ... Therefore, the legitimate Iraqi state is the resistance with all its national, pan-Arab, and Islamic groups.[18]

The spokesman then enumerated a number of goals, none of which was religious in origin. He called for: (1) complete and unconditional withdrawal of American forces from Iraq; (2) full acknowledgement of Iraq's sovereignty and its national and pan-Arab independence; (3) maintenance of the national unity of Iraq's people, territory, holy places, and wealth; and (4) rejection of all laws that are "aimed at dividing and fragmenting Iraq."[19]

However, it is undeniable that the Sunni clerical establishment began to awaken politically in the aftermath of the invasion and occupation. This political activism had already started in the 1990s when Sunni clerics began to rail against the sanctions regime and the collapse of Iraqi society. Those clerics who dared to attack the regime, whether implicitly or explicitly, were imprisoned or exiled. Hence the vast majority kept silent, but this changed with the downfall of the regime.

The hitherto dominant Sunni community found itself devoid of well-organized political parties or organizations, although some, such as the Iraqi Islamic Party (IIP), which is affiliated with the Muslim Brotherhood, reactivated itself, particularly in the Mosul area. However, the IIP faced considerable obstacles and problems from its earliest days. First, it was not well organized or well funded. Second, and as a consequence of weak organization, its network was neither extensive nor deep. Third, it was constantly harassed by Coalition forces who suspected it of collaboration with Sunni insurgents. Finally, its participation in the political process in the immediate post-invasion era ironically led it to be viewed with distaste by many within the Sunni community and with suspicion by the insurgency. This stood in contrast to the Shi'i and Kurdish communities, many of whose parties – previously in exile – were well funded, well organized, and resonated with their respective communities.

Sunni clerics thus began to take charge of the sociopolitical space of their communities due to a lack of prominent or decisive political leaders. In turn, they began to be recognized as key political players. In 2004, when interim Prime Minister Iyad Allawi wanted to negotiate with insurgents in the then war-torn town of

Fallujah, he went through the mosques. Sunni clerics began to press for an important role at the national level as well as in Baghdad, where they sought to build a political base.

Harith al-Dari, a cleric from one of the leading Sunni families in Baghdad who returned home from the United Arab Emirates after Hussein's ouster, was one of the most prominent of these leaders. He quickly installed himself in the "Mother of All Battles" Mosque, a sprawling complex Hussein built to celebrate surviving the first Gulf War, and established the Association of Muslim Scholars (AMS). The AMS held that Iraqis have a legitimate right to oppose foreign presence in their country and to combat it by force. The group, however, referred to the fight against foreign presence as *muqawama*, or resistance, rather than *jihad*, or holy struggle. The AMS began by calling for a united resistance linking Sunni and Shi'a against foreigners. Al-Dari himself sought on numerous occasions to build bridges to Shi'i leaders, but this became increasingly difficult over the course of 2005–06 as the country descended into an orgy of sectarian bloodletting and as the Shi'i-dominated governments in Baghdad began to accuse the AMS of direct support for the insurgency.

Sheikh Mahdi Ahmed al-Sumaidi, who was detained in Abu Ghraib prison after a weapons cache was found in his Ibn Taymiyyah mosque in Baghdad, was another of the earliest preachers to take an activist political role. His distaste over the American presence turned into undisguised hostility after his release: "Neither the occupation forces nor the government they installed is acceptable. The legitimate power is the resistance."[20] Moreover, he argued that the American invasion conclusively showed the necessity of turning to Islam: "God uses many tools. America's brutality has caused many to understand that Islam is the answer to our problems. The only solution is Islamic government."[21]

In sum, the political vacuum and psychological dislocation occasioned by the invasion and its chaotic aftermath helped promote a rise in religious sentiment within the Sunni community. As one Sunni in Baghdad put it: "During the U.S. invasion, I saw so much chaos and death that I turned to God. Now there is so much corruption and violence that we need an Islamic government according to Shari'a. That would stop a lot of the suffering we have now."[22] Sunni clerics and preachers began to take an activist political role to articulate Sunni grievances and goals and to present a cohesive narrative legitimizing resistance to foreign occupation from within an Islamic framework.

Islam in the struggle within the Iraqi insurgency

"Mainstream" insurgency versus Al-Qaeda in Iraq

Islam as an ideology did not function as a unifying factor within the camp of Sunni insurgents, however. The insurgency was complex: the dividing lines were often blurred, and shifting alliances occurred. This situation was made even more complex by the fact that many insurgent organizations were reluctant to admit that they coordinated or worked with groups that were ideologically different. However, for the sake of simplicity and clarity, we can divide the insurgency into two distinct entities. On one side was a group I have chosen to call the mainstream insurgents. This vast group included the following:

- *Baʿthists*: consisting mainly of former regime officials, officers (military and security), and paramilitary personnel, such as the former Fida'yin Saddam. Some remained "true believers" in the Baʿthist ideology, while others have turned more and more toward religion but still choose to function under the Baʿthist umbrella.[23]
- *National-Islamist fusion*: consisting mainly of former Baʿthist army officers, intellectuals, and middle class citizens who became disillusioned with the party and its ideology after the regime's downfall.
- *Tribally based*: consisting of sheikhs and young men who chose to fight the occupation in their tribal areas and within the framework of the support structure of their tribal networks.
- *Islamists*: consisting primarily of Salafist groups such as the Islamic Army of Iraq, the Army of the Mujahidin, and the 1920 Revolution Brigades, who were thoroughly against Al-Qaeda in Iraq (AQI) and its various evolutions, including its transformation into the so-called Islamic State of Iraq (ISI) in October 2006.

As for AQI/ISI and its adherents, it may have had a significant foreign presence before 2007 but not afterward; it went through several phases and gained more local adherents. This was one of the major reasons behind its conflict with the mainstream insurgency, which I will describe below.

Divisions within the "mainstream" insurgency

We heard a great deal, particularly toward the end of 2006 and the beginning of 2007, about the intensifying struggle between the mainstream insurgency and AQI/ISI. However, the mainstream insurgency was itself not united; indeed, despite tactical and operational coordination between various mainstream insurgents, there were profound differences over ideology, including the role of Islam. Many of the insurgent groups were thus reluctant to unite to form more potent organizational frameworks. Abu Naemi, a commander of the 1920 Revolution Brigades based in Duluiyah, a city north of Baghdad, remembers a meeting among various groups to discuss forming an umbrella organization. The idea fell through, he said, over concerns about turf: "Every commander of an organization said, 'I have my own method that I am following, and so I am going to follow it.'" Local insurgent commanders, Abu Naemi continued, are also reluctant to submerge their groups within a larger organizational framework because they fear they will be edged out: "If there is greater organization, they worry that in the future they will lose power in their areas. So they work separately." Indeed, Abu Naemi's group splintered from the Brigades in early 2007.

Notwithstanding these profound differences and rampant factionalism, the mainstream insurgents agreed on the desire to throw the foreign occupation out of Iraq, and many were willing to negotiate with the United States about the parameters of its withdrawal. Yet some insurgents were more Islamically oriented than others and wished to see the implementation of Shari'a or divine law in Iraq after the removal of the foreign presence, while others were more concerned with formulating a nationalist set of goals that sought to reverse all the occupation has done, e.g. the Iraqi constitution (which is seen as a prelude to the division of the country), the promotion of federalism, and the encouragement of ethnic and confessional differences.

Apart from implying that Islam would be important in the body politic and sociocultural affairs, these groups were all vague on the specific type of state that would emerge once the foreign occupation ended. But all the groups – even those with a pronounced Islamist agenda – were not intent on a *jihad* against the United States, nor were they motivated by the desire to create an Islamic caliphate. The General Command of the Islamic Resistance Movement or Hamas-Iraq, one of the more Islamically oriented members of the mainstream insurgency, issued a lengthy statement which included the following section directed at the U.S.

> Finally, we address the American people that continue to suffer from losses in the lives of their sons and in their resources as a result of the reckless adventures of the present administration of "lies" in the White House, and the merchants of war who are controlling the administration, and we say to them: "We do not believe in the inevitability of the conflicts of civilizations and we do not aim at spilling blood. However, this is a war that was imposed on us, and we have no option but to defend our religion, our country, and our future, even if the fight continues for many generations."[24]

The head of the Association of Muslim Scholars, Harith al-Dari, gave an extensive interview to the Lebanese paper *Al Safir* on the fourth anniversary of the invasion of Iraq in 2007. Al-Dari expressed the opinion that if the occupation forces did not leave Iraq in short order, the country would continue to disintegrate as the rifts between its various communities deepened. Al-Dari elaborated: "it is a failed process that would not lead to the liberation of Iraq and to rescuing it from the situation in which the occupation has put it."[25] Al-Dari also attacked the Iraqi constitution, asserting that it was designed to lead to a breakup of the country and the destruction of its Arab and Islamic identity. The U.S. project in Iraq, he also noted, depends on the institutionalization of an ethno-sectarian process. On the right of legitimate resistance to occupation, al-Dari said:

> We – and others like us that recognize the legitimacy of resistance and the right of nations to resist against their enemies and occupiers – believe that the resistance should be against the occupying enemies and their obvious agents that cooperate with, support, and fight with the occupiers. Those that target innocent and peaceful Iraqis from all sects, denominations, and faiths are

> condemned criminals that transgress against Shari'a and are outside the law and the national values.[26]

The resistance in Iraq, says al-Dari, is "an Islamic and national resistance," with majority support, in which most of the people who participate are Sunnis.

The 1920 Revolution Brigades, another mainstream insurgent organization, was part of the General Command of the Islamic Resistance Movement, which promised to continue its "blessed *jihad*" to force the occupation in all its forms out of Iraq. The Brigades, which has written extensively on its beliefs and goals, issued a message in January 2007 that stated:

- "Our goal at this stage is to fight the invader who occupied our land." The *jihad* in this phase is defensive and not offensive; the debate in Islam between defensive and offensive *jihads* has been extensive and divisive.
- The operational method is an "all-encompassing *jihad*," meaning that it incorporates all dimensions, including military, political, and indoctrination.
- There is a prohibition against the killing of Muslims and of non-combatants, whatever their religion, sect, or nationality.
- "The basis of our *jihad* is not to cause harm to the civilians." The organization does not believe in the notion of the end justifying the means.
- The organization demands discipline and obedience from its members.
- "The basis of our *jihad* is to investigate the evidence, and to interpret it on the basis of Islamic jurisprudence and its accepted principles." The organization supports the right to *ijtihad* – the process of making a legal decision by independent interpretation of the legal sources of the Qur'an and the Sunnah.[27]

The 1920 Revolution Brigades showed nothing but scorn for the Ba'th insurgent group led by the former vice-president of the Iraqi republic under Saddam, Ibrahim Izzat al-Duri; indeed, it declared its total disavowal of any connection with the Ba'th Party.

Another split within the ranks of the mainstream insurgency was evident in the polemics between the Ba'th party and the Army of the Mujahidin (AM) in April 2007, which began when a Ba'thist spokesman stated unequivocally that the Ba'th party was the original brains behind the insurgency and that it continued to be a key element within it. The spokesman said that the Ba'th party cooperates with the Islamic Army of Iraq (IAI), a bona fide Salafist group, and the AM, and he distinguished this cooperative group from AQI and its affiliates:

> It has a methodology, a vision, and a strategy that differs from the methodology, vision and strategy of the Ba'th and the rest of the other nationalist resistance factions, so, from our perspective as Ba'thists and resistance factions, there is absolutely no form of any relationship whatsoever with Al-Qaeda.[28]

This statement prompted quick responses by both the IAI and the AM. The former issued a statement that denied any "relationship or coordination at all between the Islamic Army and the so-called Ba'th."[29] The AM's response was more caustic. It stated that it was the Islamists who rose up against the occupation from the very beginning; as for the Ba'thists, the AM asserted, they surrendered the country to the foreigners and went into hiding, leaving behind no presence in the field except in the media. The AM also stated emphatically that there is no ideological compatibility between the Ba'th and the combatant Islamic factions, and that the latter "consider the Ba'th's doctrine an infidel doctrine that removes its adherents from the community of the faith."[30]

The AM's attack prompted a Ba'thist counter-response by Salah al-Mukhtar, a former regime official writing on one of the insurgent internet websites. He lauded the presence of the Ba'thist party in the field of battle and argued that it had the numbers, extensive military capabilities, and knowledge of the environment derived from decades of rule over Iraq to have aided in the formation and development of Islamic insurgent factions. Al-Mukhtar's screed prompted another diatribe by the now thoroughly disgruntled AM.[31] The statement reiterated the claim that the Ba'thists did not have a strong presence in the insurgency. Moreover, it said, many members of the Shi'i death squads and militias are former Ba'thists, a seemingly curious claim but not so if one understands that close to two-thirds of the Ba'th Party was Shi'i. The rise of religious sentiment among Sunni Ba'thists paralleled the rise of religious sentiment among the party's Shi'a.

The IAI's response to the Ba'th statement also included the idea that its "creed is the absolute belief in God's uniqueness in lordship and worship." In other words, the IAI adheres to the notion of *tawhid* (monotheism) and stresses literal adherence to the Qur'an and the tradition of the Prophet, such that politics and consensus must derive from Islamic laws and not from charismatic people or celebrities. The IAI sought unity and coordination with other jihadist groups, but stressed that it denounces and rejects several activities: actions committed by a Muslim that contradict Islam; the declaration of others as infidels unless by agreement of Salafi scholars; and harming the reputation of the mujahid, even if the action is permissible. In addition, the IAI believes that those who are power hungry must be prevented from climbing up the ranks within the resistance. The statement did not allude to anyone in particular, but it could very well have been implicitly referring to Abu Mus'ab al-Zarqawi (the Jordanian Al-Qaeda leader who was killed in 2006) and his successors within the ranks of AQI. The IAI clearly wanted to see the establishment of an Islamic polity in Iraq but not under the leadership of AQI.

An extensive October 2006 newspaper interview with an Iraqi insurgent commander from an unnamed Sunni group who goes by the *nom de guerre* Abu Umar provides rich detail on the more nationalist-oriented insurgent groups' approach to the role of Islam in the political process. Abu Umar argued for a separation of religion from politics: "We do not care if people perform their rites, each according to his religion and doctrine, but we are against using the true religion [Islam] politically … the radical Islamic trends, be they Sunnis or Shi'a, have failed to build the state of the new Iraq, and the Iraqi street is fed up with these ideas." He suggested the formation of a national salvation government that shies away from sectarian quotas and depends on a strong statesman like former Prime Minister Iyad Allawi, "who, although he is a Shi'a and I am a Sunni, showed that he is non-sectarian. The man is acceptable to the majority of the resistance factions, the Ba'thists, the secularists, the nationalists, and the military." Abu Umar's distaste for the politicization of religion comes through clearly in his excoriation of AQI's Islamic State of Iraq: "The Islamic state plan will not succeed in Iraq … We, the Iraqis, are one nation. I do not want to use a sectarian language. There are no Sunnis or Shi'a, but rather Iraqis, whether Muslims or non-Muslims. The sectarian confrontations in Iraq were planned by radical Sunnis and Shi'a. We strongly reject calling the Shi'a brothers infidels, and we also reject the murder of Sunnis at the hands of Shi'a militias."[32]

Divisions between the "mainstream" insurgency and AQI/ISI

The violent confrontation that emerged between Sunni insurgent groups and AQI in late 2005 added yet another layer of complexity to the violence in Iraq. Insurgent leaders offered different explanations for their split with AQI. Many said their link to the Al-Qaeda groups tainted their image as a nationalist resistance force. Others say they no longer wanted to be tools of the foreign fighters who lead Al-Qaeda. Their war, they insist, is about pressuring the U.S. forces to leave Iraq.

One can trace the origins of the divisions between the mainstream insurgents and AQI to one of the most divisive figures in the insurgency: the notorious Jordanian Abu Mus'ab al-Zarqawi (AMZ), who was killed in June 2006 by an American air strike. He first appeared in Iraq as the leader of the *Tawhid wal Jihad* (Unity and Holy War) insurgent group, merging it in late 2004 with Osama bin Laden's Al-Qaeda network. Zarqawi rose to greater international prominence after the U.S. invasion of Iraq, when Unity and Holy War claimed responsibility for some of the worst terrorist outrages, notably the brutal beheadings of the British hostage Ken Bigley, and of the U.S. hostages Nick Berg, Eugene Armstrong, and Jack Hensley. After being subsumed under the umbrella of Al-Qaeda, AMZ's group became known as *Tanzim al-Qaeda fi bilad al-rafidayn* (Al-Qaeda in the Land of the Two Rivers). On March 21, 2005, AQI issued its creed and methodology as written and sanctioned by its Legal Committee:

- "We believe that there is no god other than God Almighty in the highest. We worship Him alone."
- "We believe in defending *tawhid* and eliminating polytheism. We testify that there is no deity but God alone who has no partner. This is the most important aspect of our creed … Someone who does not adhere to the conditions of *tawhid* or who commits an act that contradicts *tawhid* is an infidel even though he claims he is a Muslim."
- "We excommunicate those who do not believe in God and His apostle. Everyone who believes in a religion other than Islam is an atheist whether or not he is aware of the truth … "
- "We view the Rafidin (Shi'a) as a sect of polytheism and apostasy."

- "We believe that atheist countries are the countries that are dominated by atheism – where atheist, not Islamic, rules are implemented. This does not mean that we excommunicate the population of these countries since the state of Islam has not been established ... We do not agree with radicals who say that people are unbelievers until proven otherwise. Rather, every person, including an unbeliever, has individual circumstances."
- "We believe that all tenets of secularism – including nationalism, communism, and Ba'thism – are a blatant violation of Islam. A person who believes in any of them is non-Muslim."
- "*Jihad* becomes an individual duty if assailant infidels attack Muslims. There is no condition to *jihad*, which should be launched by the means readily available. Next to faith, there is nothing more important than repulsing an assailant enemy who ruins the religion and the world."[33]

AQI's ideology is clearly Salafist and also advocates the *takfir* (excommunication) of Muslims who do not subscribe to its tenets. Initially, AQI under Zarqawi's helm won a measure of local support for its success in targeting U.S. troops and Shi'i militias. But in late 2005, its focus on attacking Iraqi police and army recruits and on promoting sectarian divisions between Sunnis and Shi'a became increasingly incompatible with the aims and modus operandi of the mainstream Sunni insurgent groups. AMZ's rigid and inflexible ideological stance, particularly towards the Shi'a, whom he accused of polytheism, and his use of Islam to justify the worst excesses against both the Coalition and the Shi'a, even began to create problems within the ranks of Al-Qaeda.

On January 18, 2006, six jihadist insurgent groups led by AQI announced the formation of the Mujahidin Shura Council (MSC). They claimed that they were uniting to more effectively wage their *jihad* against the enemy forces, but it is possible that this new umbrella movement was created to curtail AMZ's unsavory and independent ways. An Iraqi known as Abdullah Rashid al-Baghdadi was installed as the new group's commander. The new entity extended an invitation to all other insurgent groups to join; though there were few takers, the reaction was not overly hostile. Then, the MSC's decision to set up the Islamic State of Iraq on October 15, 2006 was welcomed by the vast majority of the online jihadist community, but was met with consternation by all the Iraqi insurgent groups that were not affiliated with AQI and by Sunni political groups in the capital. In addition, groups such as the IAI and the Al-Fatihin Army argued that the timing was not propitious for the formation of an Islamic state.

Key Sunni militant groups began cutting their links with Al-Qaeda in Iraq. In the Sunni heartland, mainstream insurgents bitterly accused Al-Qaeda of killing, kidnapping, and torturing dozens of their fighters, clerics, and followers. In Diyala province, Al-Qaeda killed or kidnapped several Sunni insurgent leaders and religious and academic figures.

On March 27, 2007, AQI allegedly killed the nephew of Harith al-Dari, the most prominent Sunni cleric in Iraq and head of the AMS. Al-Dari's nephew was a senior leader in the 1920 Revolution Brigades. The murder of al-Dari, among other things, set off a major verbal assault on Al-Qaeda by the Brigades. As far as they and other insurgent groups were concerned, AQI had developed the nasty habit of killing the members, particularly leaders, of other resistance organizations who did not see the benefits of subordinating themselves to the umbrella jihadist organization and its so-called ISI. Mahmud al-Zubaydi, a Brigades spokesman, issued a statement in which he said that the Brigades did not target innocent civilians, implying indirectly that AQI did: "As for the 1920 Revolution Brigades," al-Zubaydi stated, "it has never claimed any operation against civilians. Its vision is clear and its policy is also clear. It is fighting against the occupier, its henchmen, lackeys, and agents. It does not attack civilians and has never claimed any such operation." Al-Zubaydi admitted that all the insurgents are brothers in arms, but stressed that many of the insurgent organizations reject Al-Qaeda's modus operandi of the "killing of civilians, bombings, indiscriminate attacks, and attacks on the mujahidin groups in the country." When asked by an Arab journalist whether the Brigades agreed with Al-Qaeda on operations against the Coalition but disagreed with it on the killing of innocent civilians, al-Zubaydi answered: "Yes, exactly." The bitter opposition to AQI did not, however, imply any recognition of or desire to work with the al-Maliki government: "Concerning the political process, we have no faith in this government. Neither do we plan to participate in it now or in the future. We do not believe in it part and parcel."[34]

The IAI claimed that AQI killed more than 30 fighters from different armed groups in early 2007. The group even posted a nine-page letter urging bin Laden to stop those killing in his name: "He should rise up for his faith and assume religious and organizational responsibility for Al-Qaeda and search for the truth. It is not enough to disown those actions, but it is imperative to correct the path." The IAI attack on the ISI and AQI was unprecedented in the short history of the insurgency. It accused AQI of a whole set of illegitimate actions, including killing 30 members of its organization, tarnishing the image of the IAI, and engaging in open conflict with other major resistance groups such as the 1920 Revolution Brigades, Mujahidin Army, Ansar al-Sunnah Group, and the Islamic Front for Resistance. The IAI also accused AQI of robbing from and killing innocent Sunni civilians, including clerics, and transgressing Islamic law as a result of its methods. The IAI also refused to acknowledge the so-called Islamic State of Iraq, referring only to AQI throughout the letter rather than to the ISI.[35] The document then accused Al-Qaeda of killing innocent people with gases like chlorine, and implied that this had been an immoral method. Furthermore, the IAI castigated AQI for killing IAI leaders and clerics because they had expressed a willingness to negotiate with the Americans over the latter's exit from Iraq. They also expressed disdain for the AQI tactics of imposing Taliban-type codes of conduct on the local populace in Sunni areas.

This depth of distaste for AQI was expressed by a number of other insurgent commanders. Abu Mohammad al-Salmani, a commander in the IAI, stated that "al-Qaeda has killed more Iraqi Sunnis in Anbar province during the past month than the soldiers of the American occupation have killed within three months. People are tired of the torture. We cannot keep silent anymore."[36] Other insurgent groups were also critical of AQI's tactics of "mindless" killings of both innocent Sunnis and Shi'a: "We do not want to kill the Sunni people nor displace the innocent Shi'a, and what the al-Qaeda organization is doing is contradictory to Islam," said Abu Marwan, a religious leader of the Mujahidin Army in Baqubah, northeast of Baghdad. He concluded that "we will strike whoever violates the boundaries of God, whether al-Qaeda or the Americans."[37] Khalid Awad, a commander of the Jamiat Brigades, an insurgent group in Anbar, said: "We must confess that if it was not for al-Qaeda, neither Iraq nor Afghanistan would have been occupied. For al-Qaeda has awakened the American ogre against the Islamic nation after the September 11th events, and it is still causing disasters."[38]

In short, for many insurgent groups, AQI's ideology, its presence in Iraq, and its modus operandi had become a major problem. What is surprising, however, is that many of these groups were reluctant to engage in extended running battles with AQI/ISI as the Al-Anbar tribal militias did with U.S. encouragement and help. However, the tribes' battles with AQI/ISI caused considerable strain within the tribal coalition, due to increasing dissatisfaction with its cooperation with the U.S. and the perceived megalomania of its leader, Sheikh Abdul Sattar Abu Risha.[39] Thus, the tribes were beginning to splinter in mid-June 2007.

The divisions within the insurgency between the mainstream groups began to worry some key figures within the anti-occupation forces, including those operating openly in Baghdad, such as the Association of Muslim Scholars. At the end of March 2007, a spokesman for the AMS Muhammad Bashar al-Faydi warned the resistance against "preoccupying themselves with fighting al-Qaeda and thus forgetting about the Americans."[40]

The growing criticism of AQI prompted warnings by the so-called Islamic State of Iraq. It warned that it would kill any Sunni who sought to negotiate with or worked for the Americans and the Iraqi government. An ISI spokesman, Abu Hasna al-Dulaimi, stated in mid-April 2007 that "[the Sunni insurgents] have no choice. They have to either join us in forming the Islamic state project in the Sunni areas or hand over their weapons to us before we are forced to act against them forcefully. It will not save them that they have fought the Americans or resisted them in the last few years."[41] It is not clear that the issues that separated the mainstream insurgents from AQI/ISI in terms of both ideology and modus operandi could have been resolved. Although the situation in Iraq has changed considerably since 2007, differences over the role of Islam in Iraq and the use of religion to justify certain actions or operations will persist.

Conclusion

Islam clearly played an important role during the course of the insurgency in Iraq, as it had in post-Saddam Iraqi political life in general. I began by making the claim that we cannot fully understand the role of religion in Iraqi political life and in the insurgency without reference to the politics of the Ba'th regime and the socioeconomic situation in which Iraq found itself between 1991 and 2003. In short, Islam grew in importance in Iraqi society during that period, a dynamic that the regime tried to shape and control to its liking.

The role of religion within the insurgency grew in intensity from 2004 onwards. The reasons are not difficult to discern. Political Islam, as I demonstrated above, was making a comeback in Iraq during the last decade of Saddam's rule. Moreover, secular ideologies were increasingly discredited. However, some of the mainstream insurgent groups proved quite ideologically flexible in that they were able to concoct a fusion of nationalism and Islamism as an ideological construct to oppose the occupation of Iraq by foreign forces.

Islam proved to be a potent motivator for many disgruntled Sunnis. The rise of Sunni clerics to prominence – in the absence of respected politicians – contributed to the dissemination of Islam as an ideology of national resistance within the insurgency. This was achieved through Friday prayers, the media, and the internet. Yet it is also clear that no consensus developed among the entire insurgency on the proper role of Islam within the movement. Neither the Sunni Arab community nor the Sunni insurgency was united on the issue of an Islamic government or about how Islam should be used in justifying operations. Although the use of religion was a potent motivator for the insurgents and for the purposes of indoctrination, it did not entail consensus about what Islam meant for the resistance or how it was to be interpreted.

Notes

1 A. S. Hashim, *Insurgency and Counter-Insurgency in Iraq*, Ithaca: Cornell University Press, 2006.
2 S. Raghavan, "Sunni Factions Split with Al-Qaeda Group," *Washington Post*, April 14, 2007.
3 For extensive analyses of the increased lethality of the insurgency by well-informed journalists, see R. Oppel, "Attacks Surge as Iraq Militants Overshadow City," *New York Times*, April 16, 2007, p. 1; J. Partlow, "Troops in Diyala Face a Skilled, Flexible Foe," *Washington Post*, April 22, 2007.
4 C. Siemsen, "Oil, War and Semiperipheral Mobility: The Case of Iraq," *Studies in Comparative International Development* 30, 1995, available at http://www.uwsp.edu/geo/faculty/saed/myweb/corsi/g100/siemsen.htm.
5 S. MacLeod, "Mideast Diary: Iraq's Shiite Awakening," *Time*, April 24, 2003, available at http://www.time.com/time/columnist/macleod/article/0,9565,446545,00.html.
6 http://albaath.online.fr/English/Aflaq-04-on%20heritage.htm.
7 Ibid.
8 See B. al-Azami, "The Muslim Brotherhood: Genesis and Development," in F. Jabbar (ed.) *Ayatollahs, Sufis and Ideologues: State, Religion and Social Movements in Iraq*, London: Saqi Books, 2002, pp. 162–76.
9 See H. al-Husayni, "Plight of Iraqis under Saddam's Rule Explained," *Al-Sharq al-Awsat*, August 5, 1993, p. 8, in *Joint Publications Research Service – Near East and Africa – 93–109*, November 5, 1993, pp. 34–35; see also E. Bronner, "Hussein Standing as State Totters," *Boston Globe*, July 23, 1995; A. Borowiec, "As Iraq's Poor Starve, Its Rich Officials Grow Fat," *Washington Times*, October 24, 1995.
10 For more details on the impact of the sanctions regime on Iraqi society, see the excellent series of articles by Larry Johnson, especially "A Nation Sagging under the Weight of Sanctions," *Seattle Post-Intelligencer*, May 11, 1999, available at http://seattlepi.nwsource.

com/iraq/life2.shtml; L. Johnson, "A Nation Sagging under the Weight of Sanctions: Iraq's Youth Faces a Bleak Future," *Seattle Post-Intelligencer*, May 11, 1999, available at http://seattlepi.nwsource.com/iraq/life3.shtml; see also A. Gresh, "Iraq's Silent Agony," *Le Monde Diplomatique*, July 1999.

11 J. Battersby, "Saddam, Sanctions Plunge Iraq into 'Irreversible' Ruin," *Christian Science Monitor*, October 30, 1995.

12 A. S. Hashim interviews in Iraq, November 2003–March 2004.

13 M. Basu, "Secular No More, Saddam Adopts Radicalized Islam," *Christian Science Monitor*, January 3, 2003, available at http://ebird.dtic.mil/Jan2003/s20030106144356.html.

14 Ibid; and interviews in Iraq, fall and winter 2003–04.

15 Ibid.

16 Abd al-Wahhab al-Qaysi, "An Officer in the Resistance Tells Al-Riyad that Iraqi Resistance to the Americans Will Escalate during the Month of Ramadan," *Al Riyad*, October 14, 2003, GMP20031014000027, *Foreign Broadcasting Information Service*, October 14, 2003.

17 P. Graham, "Beyond Fallujah: A Year with the Iraqi Resistance," *Harper's Magazine*, June 2004.

18 G. Bin Jiddu, "Open Dialogue: Interview with Dr. Abu-Muhammad," *Al-Jazeera*, Doha 19:05 GMT, October 21, 2006, GMM20061022618001, *Open Source Center*.

19 Ibid.

20 Ibid.

21 Ibid.

22 Quoted in D. Murphy, "Radical Islam Grows Iraq's Sunnis," *Christian Science Monitor*, July 28, 2004, available at http://www.csmonitor.com/2004/0728/p01s04-woiq.html.

23 There are, of course, some caveats brought about by multiple ideological identities, e.g. many officers have found religion, but also remain nationalist or believers in Saddam and the Ba'th; others, like members of the Fida'yin Saddam, are largely young and poorly educated Sunni youth from the Sunni heartland who have succumbed to religion. Senior Ba'thist officials such as Ibrahim Izzat al-Duri, a Sufi, seem to have allowed the Ba'thist insurgency to become influenced by religion.

24 GMP20070330302001, *Open Source Center*, Jihadist Websites, March 30, 2007.

25 K. Harb, "Interview with Shaykh Harith al-Dari," Al Safir, March 24, 2007, GMP20070326636001, *Open Source Center*.

26 Ibid.

27 GMP20070124302003, *Open Source Report*, Jihadist Websites, January 18, 2007.

28 "Growing Rifts within Insurgency in Iraq, Part II: Baathists vs. the Army of Mujahideen," *Global Issues Report*, Center for International Issues Research, OSD-Policy, April 11, 2007.

29 Ibid.

30 Ibid.

31 *Rad min jaysh al-mujahidin ala akhadib al-ba'thi Salah al-Muktar* (A Response from the Army of the Mujahidin to the Lies of the Ba'thist Salah al-Mukhtar), *Alhanein.com*, April 5, 2007, available at http://www.alhanein.com/vb/showthread.php?t=10162.

32 M. Fayad, "Iraqi Insurgent Leader: Premier's Initiative Rejected, Dialogue with U.S. Halted," *Al-Sharq al-Awsat*, October 23, 2006.

33 "Al-Zarqawi's Group Creed and Methodology Reiterates Mandate of Jihad, Battling Infidels, Apostates, Shia," GMP20050324000125, *FBIS Report*, Jihadist Website, March 24, 2005.

34 In apparent contradiction of what al-Zubaydi said, there is some evidence that the Brigades is one of the various mainstream insurgent organizations that has had contact with the United States.

35 "Prominent Iraqi Jihadist Group Denounces Al-Qaeda in Iraq," British Broadcasting Corporation, Caversham, 13:30 GMT, April 6, 2007, GMP20070406950023, *Open Source Center*, 6, 2007.

36 S. Raghavan, "Sunni Factions Split with Al-Qaeda Group," *Washington Post*, April 14, 2007.

37 Ibid.
38 Ibid.
39 J. Partlow and J. W. Anderson, "Tribal Coalition in Anbar Said to Be Crumbling," *Washington Post*, June 11, 2007.
40 "Secret War Against Weapons Hideout, Reinforcements and Finance Lines; Al-Qaeda Inflames Struggle Inside Sunni Cities; HAMAS-Iraq Secedes from 1920 Revolution Brigades," *Al-Hayah*, March 31, 2007, GMP20070331825001, *Open Source Center*, March 31, 2007.
41 Ibid.

Bibliography

al-Azami, B., "The Muslim Brotherhood: Genesis and Development," in F. Jabbar (ed.) *Ayatollahs, Sufis and Ideologues: State, Religion and Social Movements in Iraq*, London: Saqi Books, 2002.al-Husayni, H., "Plight of Iraqis under Saddam's Rule Explained," *Al-Sharq al-Awsat*, August 5, 1993, in *Joint Publications Research Service – Near East and Africa – 93–109*, November 5, 1993

al-Qaysi, A., "An Officer in the Resistance Tells Al-Riyad that Iraqi Resistance to the Americans Will Escalate during the Month of Ramadan," *Al Riyad*, October 14, 2003, GMP20031014000027, *Foreign Broadcasting Information Service*, October 14, 2003, available at http://albaath.online.fr/English/Aflaq-04-on%20heritage.htm.

"Al-Zarqawi's Group Creed and Methodology Reiterates Mandate of Jihad, Battling Infidels, Apostates, Shia," GMP20050324000125, *FBIS Report*, Jihadist Website, March 24, 2005.

Basu, M., "Secular No More, Saddam Adopts Radicalized Islam," *Christian Science Monitor*, January 3, 2003.

Battersby, J., "Saddam, Sanctions Plunge Iraq into 'Irreversible' Ruin," *Christian Science Monitor*, October 30, 1995.

Bin Jiddu, G., "Open Dialogue: Interview with Dr. Abu-Muhammad," *Al-Jazeera*, Doha 19:05 GMT, October 21, 2006, GMM20061022618001, *Open Source Center*.

Borowiec, A., "As Iraq's Poor Starve, Its Rich Officials Grow Fat," *Washington Times*, October 24, 1995.

Bronner, E., "Hussein Standing as State Totters," *Boston Globe*, July 23, 1995.

Fayad, M., "Iraqi Insurgent Leader: Premier's Initiative Rejected, Dialogue with U.S. Halted," *Al-Sharq al-Awsat*, October 23, 2006.

GMP20070124302003, *Open Source Report*, Jihadist Websites, January 18, 2007.

GMP20070330302001, *Open Source Center*, Jihadist Websites, March 30, 2007.

Graham, P., "Beyond Fallujah: A Year with the Iraqi Resistance," *Harper's Magazine*, June 2004.

Gresh, A., "Iraq's Silent Agony," *Le Monde Diplomatique*, July 1999.

"Growing Rifts within Insurgency in Iraq, Part II: Baathists vs. the Army of Mujahideen," *Global Issues Report*, Center for International Issues Research, OSD-Policy, April 11, 2007.

Harb, K., "Interview with Shaykh Harith al-Dari," Al Safir, March 24, 2007, GMP20070326636001, *Open Source Center*.

Hashim, A. S., *Insurgency and Counter-Insurgency in Iraq*, Ithaca: Cornell University Press, 2006.

Johnson L., "A Nation Sagging under the Weight of Sanctions: Caught in a Spiral of Poverty and Death," *Seattle Post-Intelligencer*, May 11, 1999.

Johnson, L., "Iraq's Youth Faces a Bleak Future," *Seattle Post-Intelligencer*, May 11, 1999.

MacLeod, S., "Mideast Diary: Iraq's Shiite Awakening," *Time*, April 24, 2003.

Murphy, D., "Radical Islam Grows Iraq's Sunnis," *Christian Science Monitor*, July 28, 2004.

Oppel, R., "Attacks Surge as Iraq Militants Overshadow City," *New York Times*, April 16, 2007.

Partlow, J., "Troops in Diyala Face a Skilled, Flexible Foe," *Washington Post*, April 22, 2007.

Partlow, J. and Anderson J. W., "Tribal Coalition in Anbar Said to Be Crumbling," *Washington Post*, June 11, 2007.

"Prominent Iraqi Jihadist Group Denounces Al-Qaeda in Iraq," British Broadcasting Corporation, Caversham, 13:30 GMT, April 6, 2007, GMP20070406950023, *Open Source Center*, April 6, 2007.

Rad min jaysh al-mujahidin ala akhadib al-ba'thi Salah al-Muktar (A Response from the Army of the Mujahidin to the Lies of the Ba'thist Salah al-Mukhtar), *Alhanein.com*, April 5, 2007, available at http://www.alhanein.com/vb/showthread.php?t=10162.

Raghavan, S., "Sunni Factions Split with Al-Qaeda Group," *Washington Post*, April 14, 2007.

"Secret War Against Weapons Hideout, Reinforcements and Finance Lines; Al-Qaeda Inflames Struggle Inside Sunni Cities; HAMAS-Iraq Secedes from 1920 Revolution Brigades," *Al-Hayah*, March 31, 2007, GMP20070331825001, *Open Source Center*, March 31, 2007.

Siemsen, C., "Oil, War and Semiperipheral Mobility: The Case of Iraq," *Studies in Comparative International Development* 30, 1995.

9

HIZBULLAH AND REGIONAL NON-STATE ACTORS

Rola el-Husseini[1]

The Lebanese group Hizbullah is an object of fascination. It is often reviled in the West and Israel as a terrorist group, and it is lionized by some people in the Arab and Muslim world as a successful resistance organization. Other regional groups have been either accused of, or have declared themselves to be, following the Hizbullah model in their relations with the United States and Israel. The members of Hizbullah and those who are sympathetic to its causes see the U.S. and Israel as colonizers, and they view the U.S. in particular as an empire attempting to impose its hegemony on the region. Resistance to this hegemony is the key to Hizbullah's identity.

I explore the relationship between Hizbullah and other regional resistance movements to articulate my claim that Hizbullah is first and foremost an anti-imperialist organization.[2] It is a temptation too often indulged to focus on Hizbullah's overt religious character and to try to explain the organization's activities as a feature of religious identity and religious difference. To really understand Hizbullah's trajectory, it is more important to focus on and take seriously the group's defining ideology of resistance against perceived economic and political oppression. It is Hizbullah's specific interpretation of political problems and solutions that gives the organization its defining character within the landscape of the Middle East. To make this argument, I begin by sketching a brief history of Hizbullah, and I describe its ideology as manifested in the group's 1985 "Open Letter" and its 2009 manifesto. I show how the intellectual genealogy of the party can be traced to the concepts of resistance against oppression and colonization developed by Ali Shari'ati and Frantz Fanon. I then turn to the nature of Hizbullah's relationship with Hamas in the Palestinian territories and the Mahdi Army in Iraq. I argue that Hizbullah's support for these diverse groups is consistent with its perceived ethos of resistance, and with its role as a mentor for other organizations in the region that form what has been known as the "axis of resistance."[3]

Hizbullah's emergence

In 1974, Musa al-Sadr, an Iranian cleric residing in Lebanon, established *Harakat al-Mahrumin* (the Movement of the Deprived) as a means of organizing and aiding the country's politically and economically disadvantaged Shi'i community. Feeling that the Shi'a needed to defend themselves in an increasingly violent and factionalized society, al-Sadr soon created a military wing for his organization, which he called *Afwaj al-Muqawama al-Lubnaniyya* (Brigades of the Lebanese Resistance). This group became known by its acronym: AMAL. In 1982, following the Israeli invasion of Lebanon, a group of particularly militant clerics seceded from AMAL to establish a new and more forceful locus of opposition. The existence of the new organization was officially announced in February of 1985 with the publication of Hizbullah's "Open Letter." This document provides insight into the group's worldview – it starkly declares that the world is divided between oppressed and oppressors, and it indicates that the U.S. is considered to be the main oppressor. The United States is presented as condoning Israel's regional behavior, if not ruthlessly urging its ally to inflict suffering on Lebanese Muslims. With the 1985 Open Letter, Hizbullah presented itself as a militant counter to the actions of Israel and Western superpowers, and as an advocate for the creation of an Islamic state to oppose what it considered to be Western puppet regimes in the Middle East.[4]

In the early 1990s, after the end of the Lebanese civil war, the death of Iran's Ayatollah Khomeini, and a significant change in internal leadership, Hizbullah came to adopt a more nuanced attitude toward Lebanese politics – a policy of opening that came to be known as "Lebanonization." The significance of this "Lebanonization" was in Hizbullah's newfound tolerance for participating in the diverse and multi-sectarian Lebanese state, leading to the organization's gradual and incomplete integration into the rules of the political game in Lebanon. Since 1992, Hizbullah has participated in all of the country's representative elections, whether legislative (1992, 1996, 2000, 2005, and 2009) or municipal (1998, 2004, and 2010). The party's candidates have achieved a number of significant electoral victories, and after the 2005 legislative elections Hizbullah representatives were for the first time able to secure appointments in the nation's ministerial cabinet.

The most recent party manifesto, issued in November of 2009,[5] does not include the emphatic calls for Islamic statehood that were an important part of the group's 1985 charter. However, it continues to emphasize resistance against American *istikbar* (arrogance). It is clear that Hizbullah has not changed its reductive views regarding the actions of the United States and Israel. In the section entitled "Domination and Hegemony," the new manifesto describes the dangers of U.S. influence, stating that Americans "believe that they own the world." The manifesto adds that after the September 11 attacks in the United States "terrorism has become an American pretext for hegemony." It declares that the Palestinians have the right to resist this hegemony through any means necessary, and it calls for a "direct Lebanese–Palestinian dialogue" to orchestrate resistance. The 2000 Israeli withdrawal from southern Lebanon and 2005 withdrawal from Gaza, and the survival and consolidation of Hizbullah during the 2006 July War, are portrayed as victories against Israel that should encourage the Palestinians to follow the Hizbullah model.

The 2009 manifesto shows a greater degree of political sophistication than the Open Letter. Benedetta Berti has argued that the shift in terminology between 1985 and 2009, especially the transformation in Hizbullah's depiction of the U.S. (from an evil and almost supernaturally oppressive force to a greedy nation seeking global hegemony), indicates Hizbullah's growing familiarity and concordance with the terminology of international leftist and anti-globalization movements.[6] However, while significant rhetorical shifts have taken place, the language of the 2009 manifesto also indicates that the vehemence of the party's rhetoric and policy vis-à-vis Israel and the U.S. has not changed. After Israeli withdrawal, there was a significant debate within Hizbullah about whether "to focus on Lebanese politics and themes or to maintain the resistance posture in Lebanon and the Middle East."[7] Following internal party discussions, official Hizbullah policy remained on a resistance footing, and the "Lebanonization" of the group was left as a work in progress. It is important to note that Hizbullah did not *need* to maintain its broad posture of regional resistance in order to consolidate its power or to justify its raison d'être. As the central party of the Lebanese Shiʿa, the organization could have been satisfied by a role that was entirely focused on internal Lebanese politics. Continuing to focus on resistance against the occupier even after the Israeli withdrawal was a *choice* made by the Hizbullah leadership, one that was motivated by Hizbullah's ideological affiliations.

According to Larbi Sadiki, the concept of resistance carries various meanings. "The ideas of defiance, protest, challenge, struggle, rebellion, and revolution represent varying degrees of intensity in resistance. The Arabic term *muqawamah* literally means the act of 'standing up to' injustice, domination, or hegemony (*haymanah*)."[8] Since Hizbullah subscribes to a vision of the U.S. and Israel as domineering powers in the Middle East, it is not surprising that the organization continues to be motivated by a righteous desire to counter their influence – whether through mere defiance or through outright rebellion. Seen from this perspective, Hizbullah's relations with groups such as Hamas or the Mahdi Army are not surprising. Though they have their differences, these organizations are all heirs to a long-standing anti-hegemonic dimension within political Islam. It is important to take into account the reasons why these adherents of political Islam tend to adopt intractable, anti-hegemonic stances. Islamist movements and their ideologies first arose during a period of intense Western colonization. While some of the most tragic abuses of the past are all but forgotten in the West, they have not been forgotten by those who suffered them, and their consequences in the region have not evaporated. Meanwhile, the authoritarian regimes that governed many Muslim countries until the Arab Spring continued to maintain their power through ties of dependency to Western governments and economic institutions, and U.S. policy towards Muslim countries, especially Middle Eastern nations, does in fact largely serve to maintain these dependencies.[9]

Resistance as choice

Throughout the "Lebanonization" period from 1992 to the present, Hizbullah has retained its military apparatus. It is the only faction that was not officially demobilized after the end of the civil war in Lebanon.[10] The ostensible reason for this was to allow Hizbullah to continue its resistance operations against the Israeli occupation until UN Security Council Resolution 425, calling for an Israeli withdrawal from Lebanon and "strict respect" for Lebanon's territorial boundaries, was fully implemented. The partial transformation of Hizbullah into a Lebanese political party, combined with an ongoing commitment to independently confront Israel in southern Lebanon, led to what Richard Norton calls "a Janus-faced organization,"[11] with seemingly contradictory missions and behaviors. Through a war of attrition in southern Lebanon that intensified throughout the 1990s, and that relied on tactics such as suicide bombings, Hizbullah was in fact able to drive Israel out of Lebanon by making the cost of war too high, on both the human and financial level, for the Jewish state. This success made Hizbullah into a hero and a role model for many in the Arab world.

After the Israeli withdrawal, a territorial dispute took place over a 15-square-mile border region called the Shebaa Farms. Lebanon and Syria asserted that the area is Lebanese land, while Israel (backed by the UN) declared it part of the Golan Heights and, therefore, Syrian territory – though occupied by Israel.[12] The continuing conflict was aggravated by Israel's refusal to produce maps of landmines it had left in Lebanon, and by its rejection of demands for the release of Lebanese prisoners taken during the war. Hizbullah seized upon these issues to argue the continuing need for resistance – a stance that became increasingly unconvincing to others in the Lebanese polity as the immediate threat of occupation declined.

Hizbullah's primary, self-defined role has always been to resist occupation and liberate Lebanese territory from Western/Israeli control. This role is seen by members of the group as an obligation and the highest of all priorities.[13] In the words of Larbi Sadiki, Hizbullah "worked to perfect muqawamah [resistance], constructing it into an ethos, a way of thinking, being, and acting, and an ever-widening site of holistic struggle in which the AK-47 is not, in the scheme of resistance, more important than piety, charity, schooling, propaganda, or music."[14] This uncompromising and all-inclusive ethos – combined with the historical and ongoing reality of foreign interference in the Middle East – allowed Hizbullah to create a society of resistance (*mujtama' muqawim*) among its constituents, and to become a role model for other regional groups that have coalesced around an opposition to Western hegemony.

Intellectual underpinnings

The strict division of the world into oppressed and oppressors that is seen in Hizbullah's 1985 Open Letter draws on the language of Iran's Ayatollah Khomeini and of his dyad *mustazaf/mustakbir* (the impoverished and weak vs. the powerful and arrogant). This understanding of Islam as dictating a militant response against brutality on behalf of the impoverished is indebted to the Iranian sociologist Ali Shari'ati, who is often described as the "ideologue" of Iran's Islamic Revolution.[15] While many have argued that a practical relationship exists between Hizbullah and the Islamic Republic in Iran, few have been concerned with the formative role that this relationship had on the ideology of resistance that is omnipresent in Hizbullah's thought and practice. This intellectual genealogy can be traced through AMAL founder Imam Musa al-Sadr,[16] not only to Ali Shari'ati and Iran's Ayatollah Khomeini, but also from Shari'ati to the anti-colonial thinkers Frantz Fanon and Jean Paul Sartre.

Ali Shari'ati, an Iranian studying sociology in Paris in the 1960s, was captivated by the ideas of Jean Paul Sartre and Frantz Fanon, so much so that he translated Fanon's *The Wretched of the Earth* into Persian. Fanon and Shari'ati corresponded directly and exchanged ideas about the "role of Islam in the broad anti-colonial war."[17] While Fanon condemned Christianity as intrinsically tainted by its association with oppression,[18] his attitude toward Islam was more ambiguous. He actively encouraged Shari'ati to make use of the institution of Islam in the cause of emancipation and egalitarianism.[19] Fanon saw the colonial world as "a world cut into two compartmental zones: the zone of the native or colonized, and the zone of the settler or colonizer … The Manichean nature of the colonial world divides it into binaries of colonizer/colonized, light/dark, white/black and dominator/dominated."[20] This binary outlook helped to shape Shari'ati's understanding of the world and, later on, Ayatollah Khomeini's understanding of social relations within Iran. Eventually, it would also influence Hizbullah's perception of the West, especially of the United States and of its local ally Israel. In this outlook, Israel is regarded as a new colonial project inflicted on the Middle East by Western powers, an extension of foreign control that brings with it an intrinsic master/slave conflict.

While Sartre's influence on Fanon is well known,[21] his impact on Shari'ati is less concrete. Shari'ati often praised Sartre's existentialism,[22] but he explicitly rejected Sartre's concept of "*bon sens*" (common sense) as a viable guide for moral action. Instead, Shari'ati argued that a more objective moral compass was needed and that Islam could provide such a compass. As Fanon "slightly stretched" Marxism for his analysis of a global class struggle that takes into account racial injustices,[23] Shari'ati likewise made adjustments to the views of his mentors to take into account his experiences as a Muslim. Under the influence of these anti-colonial thinkers, he came to believe that Islam should be transformed into a political ideology. Shari'ati proposed a new distinction between "Alid Shi'ism" – an authentic and politically active religion identified with the authoritative figure of the first Shi'i Imam – and the more common, degenerate, and passive "Safavid Shi'ism" that had been practiced under the patronage of oppressors such as the Shahs of Iran.[24] Indeed, prior to the influence of Shari'ati's writings, Shi'ism had remained largely apolitical.[25]

Shari'ati was also struck by Fanon's understanding of violence as a fundamental means of liberation from colonialism.[26] This acceptance of violence had a great impact in the Middle East – indeed, while similar justifications of violence against occupiers can be found in the writings of contemporary Shi'i clerics such as Ayatollahs Fadlallah and Shams al-Din, it is likely that these clerics are strongly influenced by the writings of Shari'ati, and that they therefore draw from the dialogue of international anti-colonialism as much as from traditional understandings of Islam.[27] Khomeini's Islamic Revolution in Iran was highly indebted to Shari'ati's attempts to transform Islam into a political force. Khomeini's own language and worldview drew heavily from Shari'ati's amalgamation of Marxist and Islamic thought, a point that has been made by Iranian-American historian Ervand Abrahamian: "in his post-1970 writings ... Khomeini depicted society as sharply divided into two warring classes *(tabaqat):* the *mostazafin* (oppressed) against the *mostakberin* (oppressors); the *foqara* (poor) against the *sarvatmandan* (rich); the *mellat-e mostazaf* (oppressed nation) against the *hokumat-e shaytan* (Satan's government)."[28]

This view of irresolvable conflict between the oppressed and the oppressors served as a catalyst for the Iranian Revolution, with which Hizbullah politically and religiously identifies. As I have argued elsewhere,[29] the leaders of Hizbullah simply expanded Ayatollah Khomeini's concept of local revolution back into the global anti-imperial context from which it emerged. Instead of focusing on a single local tyrant (i.e., the Westernized and repressive Shah Pahlavi of Iran), the focus was shifted back to the *international* conflict between the haves and the have-nots. It is therefore not surprising to see ideas evocative of third-worldism and anti-colonialism appearing in Hizbullah's 2009 manifesto; these basic ideological premises were in fact there from the beginning.

The Second Lebanon War

In accordance with the promise made by Hizbullah's leader Hassan Nasrallah to seek the release of all Lebanese prisoners in Israel, on July 12, 2006, Hizbullah kidnapped two Israeli soldiers to barter in a prisoner exchange. This action triggered an extensive Israeli bombardment of Lebanon during the following month. Hizbullah's action was arguably within the "rules of the game" that until that point had governed the low-intensity conflict between the militia and the Jewish state – similar actions and exchanges had been agreed to by both sides during previous years.[30] This time, however, Hizbullah's hopes for an exchange were dashed when Israel retaliated by launching another full-scale war.

Israel's retaliation, known as the July War or the "Thirty-three-day War," led to more than 1,000 deaths in Lebanon – mostly civilians – and another several thousand injured. About one million people were displaced, and the economic losses for Lebanon were estimated at $12 billion U.S.[31] The attacks only ceased after UN Security Council Resolution 1701 was adopted to mandate an end of hostilities. While the conflict was a tragedy for Lebanon, it turned out to be a triumph for Hizbullah, which remained remarkably functional as an opposition force throughout the Israeli onslaught. This glorious survival in the face of Israeli firepower, and a renewed sense of outrage throughout Lebanon, led to a resurgence of support for Hizbullah's doctrine of resistance. While expressing remorse for the country's losses and the wholesale destruction of the Lebanese infrastructure, Hizbullah declared the eventual Israeli retreat to be a "divine victory,"[32] and quickly contextualized the violence in the terms of global imperialism. In a televised speech given shortly after the start of the conflict, Hizbullah's Nasrallah declared his movement to be a "spearhead of the *[Islamic] umma*" (nation) and characterized the conflict as "surpassing Lebanon ... it is the conflict of the umma." The organization's leaders took advantage of the violence to declare that the fate of the Middle East as a whole was tied to the success or failure of Hizbullah's resistance, and that Hizbullah was the central exemplar of bold action against local regimes allied with Western powers.[33]

The symbolic capital gained by Hizbullah during this violence was not limited to the organization's Shiʿi base. In Egypt and other Sunni-majority countries, Hizbullah's resistance during the invasion was highly admired, especially by other Islamist groups. Nasrallah's photo began to appear in Sunni communities, as well as in secular leftist contexts (often next to pictures of Nasser and Che Guevarra).[34] In Syria, Nasrallah was featured on posters with Syrian President Bashar Assad. Hizbullah's performance galvanized the Palestinians, and pro-Hizbullah sentiment exploded in the West Bank and Gaza. Nasrallah's appeal for pan-Arabic resistance seemed to be gaining ground, as entrenched religious divides proved to be less fundamental than the outrage against perceived Western oppression.[35] The perception of Hizbullah's victory against oppression was further reinforced by the preliminary report of Israel's own Winograd Commission in April of 2007, which harshly criticized the Israeli military's conduct during the war.

While Hizbullah enjoyed a state of celebrity in the wake of the July 2006 conflict, this prestige and Sunni-Shiʿa rapprochement would only last until the events of May 2008, when Hizbullah forces entered the predominantly Sunni area of West Beirut in an attempt to force the Lebanese government to retract decisions it had taken that affected the party's independent communication network. The extent of the popular support for Hizbullah's doctrine of resistance seems to hang in a tenuous balance between perceptions of Western interference vs. perceptions of Hizbullah's own resistance to transparency and popular rule, especially by non-Shiʿis. The regional sympathy for Hizbullah's position would take another nosedive in 2011, when Nasrallah vocally supported the Syrian regime against widespread popular protests. Hizbullah's rejection of the Syrian uprising led to protesters burning posters of Nasrallah, a phenomenon that was widely aired in the Middle East via television and YouTube.[36]

Hizbullah's regional role

The alleged involvement of Hizbullah in the Palestinian–Israeli conflict and the Iraq War may be understood as part of the organization's strategy to maintain a broad posture of regional resistance. I maintain that Hizbullah remains faithful to its ideology of anti-imperialism, and that bids to help the Palestinians or to support the Iraqi resistance would be seen as logical efforts to help fellow "resisters" against Zionist colonizers and perceived U.S. hegemony. Indeed, Nasrallah's discourse makes it clear that he views the Lebanese political situation as part of a continuing regional struggle that extends beyond national boundaries:

> From the very beginning central issues around which the Imam's revolution against the Shah revolved brought into focus the nation's position regarding the struggle against the great Satan, Israel, and against the oppression and tyranny, which this regime represented … Imam Khomeini's revolution and movement suffered in the past the same way resistance factions in Lebanon are now suffering and have suffered in the past. It is also similar to the suffering the intifada and resistance in Palestine are going through at the moment.[37]

The easy linking of the political situations in Iran, Lebanon, and Palestine in this quotation is representative of a view grounded in anti-colonial binaries, where the exploitative interference of Western powers is seen as the central, overwhelming concern for regional politics.

Hizbullah and the al-Aqsa intifada

After the Israeli withdrawal from Lebanon in 2000, Hizbullah's hostility toward Israel remained limited to occasional border skirmishes. However, the liberation of Jerusalem has always been part of the organization's discourse. Hizbullah's 1985 Open Letter includes unambiguous statements such as: "Israel's final departure from Lebanon is a prelude to its final obliteration from existence and the liberation of venerable Jerusalem from the talons of occupation." In this regard, Hizbullah's official platform is in line with that of influential Shi'i clerics such as Ayatollahs Fadlallah and Shams al-Din, who emphasize the importance of Jerusalem to the Islamic faith.[38] Despite the occasional conflicts between Palestinian and Shi'i groups – such as the ferocious "War of the Camps" that took place in 1984 – these factions are on the same page when it comes to their outrage over Israel's claims of sovereignty in Jerusalem. As Lara Deeb has argued, "Hizballah offers a nationalism that views Lebanon as an Arab state that cannot distance itself from causes like the Palestine question."[39] Since Hizbullah views itself as a "spearhead" of the Arab community as a whole and as a bulwark against Western oppression, it is not surprising that when the Al-Aqsa intifada began in Palestine in September of 2000, a few months after the Israeli withdrawal from southern Lebanon, Hizbullah was outspoken in its support for the Palestinians.

Journalist Nicholas Blanford, a longtime observer of the Lebanese political scene, perceptively notes that "the support for the Palestinian intifada was rooted in Hezbollah's anti-Israel credo, as well as a desire to offer its successful resistance to Israeli occupation in Lebanon as a model for other oppressed people to emulate and adapt to their own circumstances."[40] Hizbullah's desire to be emulated by Hamas and other resistance groups has been a long-standing feature of the organization. In an interview with the Kuwaiti newspaper *Al-Rai al-Aam* on October 5, 2000, a few weeks after the outbreak of the al-Aqsa intifada, Nasrallah stated:

> We are committed, *in principle* [emphasis added], to supporting this intifada and standing side by side with the Palestinian people; but we would rather not talk

> about the quality or quantity of our assistance to them … We have a moral, humanitarian, religious, patriotic, and national duty towards this people, and believe it is our collective duty to stand by its side.[41]

The following year, in a speech on September 29, 2001, Hassan Nasrallah elaborated that his party was willing to provide "direct interference" for the Palestinian cause.[42] Sheikh Nabil Qaouk, who acts as Hizbullah's top field commander in southern Lebanon, likewise opined in an interview that "it is contingent upon all the Arab leaders to look to see what resources they can contribute to the Palestinian struggle since they will take the brunt of it if a forced exodus … takes place." Qaouk went on to argue (repeating a metaphor used by Nasrallah) that Hizbullah is "a major Arab resource and the actual spearhead of the resistance against Israeli occupation."[43] These statements make it clear that Hizbullah does not regard its sphere of interest as ending at the Lebanese borders.

Part of the "direct interference" of Hizbullah in the Palestinian–Israeli conflict mentioned in Nasrallah's speech might have been the involvement of the party in the *Karine A* affair. The *Karine A* was a ship seized by the Israelis with more than 50 tons of weapons on board, allegedly originating in Iran and destined for the Palestinian Authority. The U.S. and Israel accused Iran and Hizbullah of involvement in this weapons shipment, though both denied any knowledge of the incident. There are also more explicit indications that Hizbullah has engaged in "direct interference." In a press conference on March 6, 2002, Nasrallah admitted that Hizbullah had been involved in training members of Hamas.[44] The extent of this training and involvement is not known, but a number of commentators have provided specific accusations of clandestine military assistance that have not been refuted by the party leadership.[45]

It seems clear that Hizbullah has provided some degree of moral and practical support for the Palestinian intifada in the West Bank and Gaza. I believe that this support was provided as a logical extension of Hizbullah's self-perception as an agent of resistance against imperialism/colonialism. This conclusion contradicts the one put forward by scholars such as Jacob Hoigilt and Reinoud Leenders, who have each maintained that Hizbullah's interest in the Palestinians was a short-lived consequence of an "identity crisis" within the group after the 2000 Israeli withdrawal from Lebanon. For example, Hoigilt argued that

> victory created a serious dilemma for the party, since it geared its party apparatus and rhetoric to focus on the conflict with Israel ever since the 1980s. With the end of the occupation, the party faced the possibility of becoming marginalized, as a major cause had disappeared … Hizbullah has tried to resolve this dilemma by placing more emphasis on the Palestine question and less on the internal Lebanese politics.[46]

I disagree with this statement because I do not believe that Hizbullah's stance of resistance was ever fundamentally limited to the Lebanese context. While the Israeli withdrawal did lead to a decrease in Lebanese support for Hizbullah, it would not have been a fundamental threat to the group's identity since the oppressors, and the struggle against them, had not ceased to exist. Furthermore, the party certainly did not shy away from internal Lebanese politics in the years after the Israeli withdrawal – Hizbullah has instead continued to fully engage with both Lebanese issues and region-wide concerns. Finally, it is important to note that there is a widespread antipathy within Lebanon vis-à-vis the Palestinians. Many in the Lebanese polity regard the Palestinian conflict as the root cause of the Lebanese civil war.[47] Therefore, if Hizbullah felt a need to maintain Lebanese unity around the idea of resistance to Israel, linking itself to the Palestinian cause would not have been a politically deft maneuver. It seems most reasonable to conclude that Hizbullah's support of the Palestinians was not the hasty action of an organization in crisis, but rather a basic and consistent feature of its self-identity as an anti-imperial movement.

Hizbullah and the Iraqi Shiʿa

There are myriad connections between Hizbullah and the Shiʿa of Iraq. Iraq is home to Najaf and Karbala, the holy cities of Shiʿism, and most of the senior clerics of Hizbullah were trained at the *hawza* in Najaf before being exiled by Saddam's Hussein's regime. Given Hizbullah's opinion of the United States, however, it is not surprising that the organization would fail to see the U.S.'s displacement of Saddam as an improvement in that country's leadership. Nasrallah expressed his opposition to the U.S.-led invasion of Iraq even before the first shot was fired. In a speech on March 13, 2003, he prophetically stated:

> We declare our opposition to the American war on Iraq, and to all the deceptive, lying, and hypocritical American objectives and slogans about saving nations, instilling democracy, and granting people their freedom … [W]e declare our condemnation of this diabolical, arrogant, and Zionist administration, and say: Do not expect the people of this region to meet you with flowers, rice, and perfume; peoples of this part of the world will receive you, rather, with guns, blood, weapons, and martyrdom operations. This is the reception the people are preparing for the American invaders.[48]

In another speech following the American invasion, Nasrallah asked rhetorically: "Can we count on the Iraqi people to liberate their soil?" Drawing from his experiences in Iraq as a student, he immediately answered "We can say – not based on emotional reasons or out of friendship, but based on our knowledge and experience – yes, this is a people we can count on."[49]

Since 2003, the U.S. press has been filled with allegations of Hizbullah members actively training Iraqi "insurgents." According to the journalist Olivier Guitta, Hizbullah began building up organizational and military apparatuses in Iraq immediately after the U.S. invasion, and opened two offices in the Iraqi cities of Basra and Safwan. During the same period, Imad Mughnieh – the Hizbullah agent held responsible by the U.S. for the bombing of the U.S. embassy and the Marine barracks in 1983 – was reportedly sighted in Iraq. Guitta also alleges that in 2005, 18 members of Hezbollah were captured by Iraqi authorities.[50]

The fact that Iraqi Shi'i resistance leader Muqtada al-Sadr has described himself as "the striking arm for Hizbullah" did little to detract from the widespread assumption that Hizbullah was active in the Iraqi resistance.[51] Hizbullah is a natural ally of al-Sadr's movement. Both groups are steeped in anti-colonial Shi'i social thought and adhere to a similar type of Islamic Nationalism.[52] Journalists were quick to point to relations between the Lebanese party and al-Sadr's movement, especially after al-Sadr's visit to Beirut in 2006.[53] There were suggestions in the U.S. and international press that the two organizations were closely connected. One journalist wrote:

> The rise of radical Shiite cleric Moqtada al-Sadr and his Mahdi army in Iraq has caused many in the West to speculate about a possible Hezbollah link to Sadr's fighting force. Hezbollah secretary-general, Sayyed Hassan Nasrallah, is thought to have personal ties to the Sadr family, having studied under Mohammed Baqir al-Sadr – cousin to Sadr's father, Mohammed Sadiq al-Sadr – in the holy Iraqi city of Najaf in 1976.[54]

Hizbullah has acknowledged the existence of "political relations" with Muqtada al-Sadr's movement, but has denied any direct involvement or military support.[55] And despite the proliferation of accusations, little has emerged in the way of specific evidence for such support. In March of 2007, U.S. forces arrested Ali Mussa Daqduq, an alleged Hizbullah operative, in Iraq. However, Hizbullah quickly denied accusations made by U.S. National Intelligence Director Mike McConnell, who said (without expounding on his sources) that the resistance group was training Iraqi fighters in Lebanon and sending them back to Iraq to attack American troops. In a statement issued by its press office, Hizbullah described McConnell's allegations as "yet another American fabrication." The statement added that such accusations "only highlight the United States' abhorrence of any resistance movement fighting against its hegemony in the region."[56]

Regardless of whether or not claims about Hizbullah's material support of the Iraqi insurgents are true, it is clear that Hizbullah regards itself as ideologically affiliated with Muqtada al-Sadr's resistance movement. The latter is undertaking a fight against what it sees as an unjust occupation and an attempt by the U.S. to take advantage of Iraq's national resources. Again this clearly falls into line with Hizbullah's ideology of anti-imperialism and of defending the poor and the weak against external oppressors. Indeed, it is probably the outspoken ideological support that Hizbullah lends to the Iraqi resistance that is the most troublesome thorn in the Americans' side. In 2007, Nasrallah again confirmed Hizbullah's affinity with the insurgents, stating that the U.S. had no intention of promoting democracy in Iraq. He continued on to say:

> We support the option of the Iraqi resistance, in all its dimensions, and the military resistance first and foremost. We believe that the salvation of Iraq

> begins with the adoption of the armed resistance and struggle against the forces of the occupation.[57]

As was the case in their support of the Palestinians, Hizbullah continued to focus on building solidarity around anti-colonial arguments, while in this case also relying on the bond of sectarian religious identity.

Hizbullah has presented itself to the Iraqis, as to the Palestinians, as a successful model of anti-imperialism. As late as 2003, Muqtada al-Sadr had rejected any comparison of his movement with the Lebanese organization (especially in terms of Hizbullah's relations with Iran).[58] His later embrace of Hizbullah should be seen as an acceptance of Hizbullah's strategy and tactics. David Enders noted in the years following the U.S. invasion of Iraq that "Al-Sadr has a two-pronged strategy: vehemently resisting the U.S. occupation, while providing social services for the poor and assisting the thousands of Shiite families displaced by sectarian attacks. It is a tactic that reminds many of that employed by Hezbollah."[59] After the 2004 clashes in Iraq, Sadr encouraged his followers to develop a social services network that could provide the average Shiʿi with protection, healthcare, and sometimes jobs. This greatly expanded the influence of the movement, which was able to win 32 out of 275 parliamentary seats in Iraq's December 2005 national elections. The integration of the Sadrist resistance into the national political process was very similar to the "Lebanonization" embraced by Hizbullah starting in the 1990s.[60] Muqtada al-Sadr also made sure that his group was allocated social ministries in the new Iraqi government (e.g., health, education, transportation) instead of the so-called sovereign ministries (defense, interior, or oil). Following the Hizbullah model, access to these ministries and their allocations helped al-Sadr to further develop his base of popular support.

According to the Syrian analyst Sami Moubayed, al-Sadr worked hard "to transform the Mahdi Army into another Hezbollah, personally inspired by Hassan Nasrallah … [He decided to] take a long hard look at membership and filter out the undisciplined, the reckless, and the corrupt … against all odds, he has insisted on refraining from any sectarian rhetoric, copying the Nasrallah model in Lebanon, who always speaks of Lebanon, not of Shiʿites."[61] After briefly being forced into exile during 2009–10, Muqtada al-Sadr was able to return to Iraq in early 2011, when his organization (in alliance with Nouri al-Maliki's party) gained control of the prime minister's office and 24 out of 42 ministerial positions. In this government, following the Hizbullah model, the Sadrists once again focused on controlling the service ministries and thus increasing their influence among the popular demographic.

Conclusion

Hizbullah is not suffering a legitimacy crisis tied to its identity or to its role as a resistance movement. The organization's identity is grounded in an ideology of resistance against foreign colonization and the protection of the impoverished against external oppressors, specifically identified as Israel and the United States. This resistance is not limited to Lebanon; it can extend to any Arab or Islamic country that is perceived to be threatened by the West and its allies. As Amal Saad-Ghorayeb argues, Hizbullah's "politico-strategic program is essentially a defensive one: to protect the Resistance, maintain Lebanon's 'Arabism' and … keep Lebanon out of the US–Israeli orbit."[62]

While Hizbullah may no longer have an immediate enemy to confront within Lebanon, the resistance against imperialistic oppressors remains its core value. It continues to express this value by maintaining a capability for independent resistance and by acting as a role model for like-minded groups throughout the region. The primary change in Hizbullah after the Israeli withdrawal was not a shift in ideology or values, but a tentative willingness to seek expression of those values through the political process. This meant that the party was increasingly perceived as primarily a Shi'i party within Lebanon. Currently, Hizbullah has embraced the "rules of the game" in Lebanon, while maintaining its vigilance and arms in case it has to return to a more forceful form of resistance against direct threats to Lebanese soil. Hizbullah is vocally supportive of the more active resistance movements in Palestine and Iraq, but its material support of these factions remains, at most, limited and furtive.

Notes

1 The author would like to express her gratitude to Wesley Dean for his helpful comments and copyediting efforts. The usual caveats apply.
2 For an analysis of the group's relations with Iran and Syria, see R. el-Husseini, "Hezbollah and the Axis of Refusal," *Third World Quarterly* 31, 2010.
3 See the "Drums of War: Israel and the 'Axis of Resistance,'" International Crisis Group Report, August 2010, available at http://www.crisisgroup.org/en/regions/middle-east-north-africa/iraq-syria-lebanon/lebanon/097-drums-of-war-israel-and-the-axis-of-resistance.aspx (accessed October 6, 2011).
4 See A. R. Norton, *Hezbollah: A Short History*, Princeton: Princeton University Press, 2007, p. 38.
5 The full text of the manifesto (in Arabic) can be found on Hizbullah's official website, http://www.moqawama.org/essaydetailsf.php?eid=16245&fid=47 (accessed June 24, 2011).
6 B. Berti, "The Rebirth of Hizbollah," *Strategic Assessment* 12, 2010, 93-94.
7 Norton, op. cit., p. 90.
8 L. Sadiki, "Reframing Resistance and Democracy: Narratives from Hamas and Hizbullah," *Democratization* 17, 2010, p. 357.
9 For specific examples and further analysis, see M. Ayoob, "The United States and Political Islam: The Dialectic of Hegemony and Resistance," *Middle East Insight* 3, 2009, available at http://www.mei.nus.edu.sg/wp-content/uploads/2011/04/MEI-Insights-003.pdf (accessed May 11, 2011).
10 The Ta'if agreement that ended the civil war mandated the demobilization of Lebanese militias, and as of March, 1991, all other Lebanese militias were declared dissolved and their weapons confiscated. A large number of militiamen were incorporated into the security apparatus of the Lebanese state (the Lebanese Army and Internal Security Forces). Hizbullah alone refused to disband and disarm, arguing that its military integrity was needed to combat the Israeli occupation. For more on the demobilization of militias in post-war Lebanon, see E. Picard, *The Demobilization of the Lebanese Militias: Prospects for Lebanon*, Oxford: Centre for Lebanese Studies, 1999.
11 Norton, op. cit., p. 45.

12 According to Asher Kaufman, the Shebaa Farms situation came about due to the sloppy way that France delineated the Syrian-Lebanese borders during the original "carving up" of the Ottoman empire by Western powers at the end of World War I. After obtaining their independence from France, neither country made an effort to rectify the anomalies in different interpretations of their borders. Since 1920, most official maps have located the area within Syria. However, in all practical matters, the area functioned as part of Lebanon. For more on this issue, see A. Kaufman, "Who Owns the Shebaa Farms? Chronicle of a Territorial Dispute," *Middle East Journal* 56, 2002.
13 A. Saad-Ghorayeb, *Hizbullah: Politics and Religion*, London: Pluto Press, 2002, p. 112.
14 Sadiki, op. cit., p. 358.
15 H. Dabashi, *Theology of Discontent*, Piscataway, NJ: Transaction Publishers, 2006, p. 102.
16 Al-Sadr did not leave a body of writings, but he was a central influence in shaping the intellectual environment in which Hizbullah emerged. Sadr's indebtedness to the writings of Shari'ati has been traced in detail by Nasrin Rahimieh in her book *Oriental Responses to the West*, Leiden: Brill, 1990.
17 A. Rahnema, *An Islamic Utopian: A Political Biography of Ali Shari'ati*, London: I. B. Tauris, 2000, p. 127.
18 "I am talking of Christianity and this should come as no surprise to anybody. The church in the colonies is a white man's Church, a foreigners' Church. It does not call the colonized to the way of God, but to the ways of the white man, to the ways of the master, the ways of the oppressor." F. Fanon, *The Wretched of the Earth*, New York: Grove Press, 2004, p. 7.
19 F. Slisli, "Islam: The Elephant in Fanon's *The Wretched of the Earth*," *Critique: Critical Middle Eastern Studies* 17, 2008, p. 103.
20 N. Roberts, "Fanon, Sartre, Violence and Freedom," *Sartre Studies International* 10, 2004, p. 140.
21 Sartre, in fact, wrote the original introduction to Fanon's *Wretched of the Earth*.
22 See Rahnema, op. cit., p. 127.
23 Fanon, op. cit., p. 30.
24 Dabashi, op. cit., p. 111.
25 Dabashi, op. cit., pp. 110-13.
26 Fanon, op. cit., p. 44.
27 See R. el-Husseini, "Resistance, Jihad, and Martyrdom in Contemporary Lebanese Shi'a Discourse," *Middle East Journal* 62, 2008.
28 E. Abrahamian, *Khomeinism*, Berkeley: University of California Press, 1993, pp. 26-27.
29 El-Husseini 2008, op. cit.
30 In 2004, for example, Nasrallah presided over an exchange of prisoners when, through German mediation, over 400 Arab prisoners were released by Israel in exchange for the remains of three Israeli soldiers and for an alleged Israeli spy held by Hizbullah. For more on the "rules of the game" in this conflict, see D. Sobelman, *New Rules of the Game: Israel and Hizbollah after the Withdrawal from Lebanon*, Tel Aviv: Jaffee Center for Strategic Studies, Tel Aviv University, 2004, p. 67.
31 "Israel/Hizbollah/Lebanon: Avoiding Renewed Conflict," *ICG Middle East Report* 59, November 2006, available at http://www.crisisgroup.org/en/regions/middle-east-north-africa/israel-palestine/059-israel-hizbollah-lebanon-avoiding-renewed-conflict.aspx (accessed October 6, 2011).
32 The term "Divine Victory" is a pun on Nasrallah's name: "Nasr" is Arabic for "victory."
33 A. S. Ghorayeb, "Hezbollah's Apocalypse Now," *Washington Post*, July 23, 2006, available at http://www.washingtonpost.com/wpdyn/content/article/2006/07/21/AR2006072101363. html (accessed March 18, 2007).
34 L. Fielder, "Nasrallah Has Come," *Salon*, August 24, 2011, available at http://www.salon.com/news/feature/2006/08/24/nasrallah (accessed June 23, 2011).
35 See Norton, op. cit., p. 148.
36 "Syrian Protesters Turn on Iran and Hezbollah," *France 24*, March 6, 2011, available at http://observers.france24.com/content/20110603-angry-syrian-protesters-turn-iran-

hezbollah (accessed June 24, 2011). For an example of these protest videos, see "City of Douma: Saturday Demonstrations and Burning of Nasrallah's Pictures," http://www.youtube.com/watch?v=X90KWdSquW0 (accessed June 24, 2011).

37 N. Noe (ed.), *Voice of Hezbollah: Statements of Sayyed Hassan Nasrallah*, London: Verso, 2007, p. 270.

38 See S. al-Din, *Al-Muqawama fi al-Khitab al-Fiqhi al-Siyasi li Samahat al-Imam Muhammad Mahdi Shams al-Din*, Beirut: Al-Mu'assassa al-Dawliah, 1998, p. 195.

39 L. Deeb, "Hizballah: A Primer," *Middle East Research and Information Project*, July 31, 2006, available at http://www.merip.org/mero/mero073106.html (accessed March 10, 2007).

40 N. Blanford, "Introduction," in N. Noe (ed.) *Voice of Hezbollah: Statements of Sayyed Hassan Nasrallah*, London: Verso, 2007, p. 10. Blanford is the Lebanon correspondent of the *Times* and the *Christian Science Monitor.* He is also the author of a book on politics in postwar Lebanon and the circumstances that led to the assassination of former Lebanese Prime Minister Rafiq Hariri. See N. Blanford, *Killing Mr. Lebanon*, London: I. B. Tauris, 2006.

41 Noe, op. cit., p. 250.

42 Quoted in J. Harik, *Hezbollah: The Changing Face of Terrorism,* London: I. B. Tauris, 2004, p. 161.

43 Ibid., p. 162.

44 Ibid., p. 188.

45 See Blanford 2007, op. cit., p. 9; also B. Slavin, "Mullah, Money, and Militias," Washington, DC: United States Institute of Peace, Special Report 206, 2008, available at http://www.usip.org/files/resources/sr206.pdf (accessed June 24, 2011).

46 J. Hoigilt, "Islamism, Pluralism and the Palestine Question: The Case of Hizbullah," *British Journal of Middle Eastern Studies* 34, 2007, p. 125.

47 For example, Farid el-Khazen has argued that the presence of the Palestine Liberation Organization in Lebanon was central to the breakdown of the Lebanese state. See F. el-Khazen, *The Breakdown of the State in Lebanon 1967-1976*, Cambridge, MA: Harvard University Press, 2000.

48 Noe, op. cit., p. 285.

49 Ibid., p. 298.

50 O. Guitta, "Nasrallah's Other Fight," *Asia Times*, July 29, 2006, available at http://www.atimes.com/atimes/Middle_East/HG29Ak02.html (accessed June 24, 2011).

51 O. Guitta, "Iraq: A New Lebanon?," *American Thinker*, April 30, 2004, available at http://www.americanthinker.com/2004/04/iraq_a_new_lebanon.html (accessed October 6, 2011).

52 M. Etherington, *Revolt on the Tigris*, Ithaca: Cornell University Press, 2005, p. 165.

53 For example, see D. Enders, "Hezbollah on the Tigris," *Salon*, May 8, 2006, available at http://www.salon.com/news/feature/2006/05/08/sadr/ (accessed May 8, 2006); N. A. Youssef, "Shiite Cleric Seen Trying to Broaden his Base of Support," *Knight Ridder*, May 1, 2006, available at http://www.realcities.com/mld/krwashington/14475068.htm (accessed June 19, 2006); A. Taheri, "The Road to Iraq's Riots," *New York Post*, April 6, 2004, available at http://www.benadorassociates.com/article/3198 (accessed April 14, 2006); and P. Cockburn, *Muqtada*, New York: Scribner, 2008, p. 169.

54 A. Soussi, "The Enigma that Is Lebanese Hezbollah," *worldpress.org*, June 14, 2004, available at http://www.worldpress.org/Mideast/1873.cfm (accessed April 21, 2006).

55 Ibid.

56 *Daily Star*, Beirut, March 2, 2007.

57 Interview on January 19, 2007 with Hasan Nasrallah on *al-Manar* TV. Quoted in Nir Rosen and Amer Mohsen *http://www.iraqslogger.com/index.php/post/912/Hizbullahs_Leader_on_Iraq*, accessed February 19, 2007.

58 M. N. Musawi, *Sadr al-Iraq al-Thaleth*, Damascus: Markaz waliallah lil Dirasat wal Tawjih wal Irshad, 2004, p. 63.

59 D. Enders, op. cit.

60 See G. Bruno, "Muqtada al-Sadr," *Council on Foreign Relations*, May 16, 2008, available at http://www.cfr.org/iraq/muqtada-al-sadr/p7637 (accessed June 23, 2011).
61 S. Moubayed, "Muqtada Unleashes New Improved Army," *Asia Times*, April 30, 2010, available at http://www.atimes.com/atimes/Middle_East/LD30Ak02.html (accessed June 25, 2011).
62 A. Saad-Ghorayeb, "In Their Own Words: Hizbollah's Strategy in the Current Confrontation," Carnegie Endowment for International Peace, *Policy Outlook*, January 2007, available at http://www.carnegieendowment.org/files/saadghorayeb_hizbollah_final.pdf (accessed February 3, 2007).

Bibliography

Abrahamian, E., *Khomeinism*, Berkeley: University of California Press, 1993.

al-Din, S., *Al-Muqawama fi al-Khitab al-Fiqhi al-Siyasi li Samahat al-Imam Muhammad Mahdi Shams al-Din*, Beirut: Al-Mu'assassa al-Dawliah, 1998.

Ayoob, M., "The United States and Political Islam: The Dialectic of Hegemony and Resistance," *Middle East Insight* 3, 2009, available at http://www.mei.nus.edu.sg/wp-content/uploads/2011/04/MEI-Insights-003.pdf.

Berti, B., "The Rebirth of Hizbollah," *Strategic Assessment* 12, 2010 91–100.

Blanford, N., "Introduction," in N. Noe (ed.) *Voice of Hezbollah: Statements of Sayyed Hassan Nasrallah*, London: Verso, 2007.

Blanford, N., *Killing Mr. Lebanon*, London: I. B. Tauris, 2006.

Bruno, G., "Muqtada al-Sadr," *Council on Foreign Relations*, May 16, 2008, available at http://www.cfr.org/iraq/muqtada-al-sadr/p7637.

Cockburn, P., *Muqtada*, New York: Scribner, 2008.

Dabashi, H., *Theology of Discontent*, Piscataway, NJ: Transaction Publishers, 2006.

Deeb, L., "Hizballah: A Primer," *Middle East Research and Information Project*, July 31, 2006, available at http://www.merip.org/mero/mero073106.html.

"Drums of War: Israel and the 'Axis of Resistance,'" International Crisis Group Report, August 2010, available at http://www.crisisgroup.org/en/regions/middle-east-north-africa/iraq-syria-lebanon/lebanon/097-drums-of-war-israel-and-the-axis-of-resistance.aspx.

el-Husseini, R., "Hezbollah and the Axis of Refusal," *Third World Quarterly* 31, 2010, 803–15.

el-Husseini, R., "Resistance, Jihad, and Martyrdom in Contemporary Lebanese Shi'a Discourse," *Middle East Journal* 62, 2008, 399–414.

el-Khazen, F., *The Breakdown of the State in Lebanon 1967–1976*, Cambridge, MA: Harvard University Press, 2000.

Enders, D., "Hezbollah on the Tigris," *Salon*, May 8, 2006, available at http://www.salon.com/news/feature/2006/05/08/sadr/.

Etherington, M., *Revolt on the Tigris*, Ithaca: Cornell University Press, 2005.

Fanon, F., *The Wretched of the Earth*, New York: Grove Press, 2004.

Fielder, L., "Nasrallah Has Come," *Salon*, August 24, 2011, available at http://www.salon.com/news/feature/2006/08/24/nasrallah.

Guitta, O., "Nasrallah's Other Fight," *Asia Times*, July 29, 2006, available at http://www.atimes.com/atimes/Middle_East/HG29Ak02.html.

Guitta, O., "Iraq: A New Lebanon?" *American Thinker*, April 30, 2004, available at http://www.americanthinker.com/2004/04/iraq_a_new_lebanon.html

Harik, J., *Hezbollah: The Changing Face of Terrorism*, London: I. B. Tauris, 2004.

Hizbullah's official website, http://www.moqawama.org/essaydetailsf.php?eid=16245=47.

Hoigilt, J., "Islamism, Pluralism and the Palestine Question: The Case of Hizbullah," *British Journal of Middle Eastern Studies* 34, 2007.

"Israel/Hizbollah/Lebanon: Avoiding Renewed Conflict," *ICG Middle East Report* 59, November 2006, available at http://www.crisisgroup.org/en/regions/middle-east-north-africa/israel-palestine/059-israel-hizbollah-lebanon-avoiding-renewed-conflict.aspx.

Kaufman, A., "Who Owns the Shebaa Farms? Chronicle of a Territorial Dispute," *Middle East Journal* 56, 2002, 576–95.
Moubayed, S., "Muqtada Unleashes New Improved Army," *Asia Times*, April 30, 2010, available at http://www.atimes.com/atimes/Middle_East/LD30Ak02.html.
Musawi, M. N., *Sadr al-Iraq al-Thaleth*, Damascus: Markaz waliallah lil Dirasat wal Tawjih wal Irshad, 2004.
Noe, N. (ed.), *Voice of Hezbollah: Statements of Sayyed Hassan Nasrallah*, London: Verso, 2007.
Norton, A. R., *Hezbollah: A Short History,* Princeton: Princeton University Press, 2007.
Picard, E., *The Demobilization of the Lebanese Militias: Prospects for Lebanon*, Oxford: Centre for Lebanese Studies, 1999.
Rahimieh, N., *Oriental Responses to the West: Comparative Essays in Select Writers from the Muslim World*, Leiden: Brill, 1990.
Rahnema, A., *An Islamic Utopian: A Political Biography of Ali Shari'ati,* London: I. B. Tauris, 2000.
Roberts, N., "Fanon, Sartre, Violence and Freedom," *Sartre Studies International* 10, 2004, 139–60.
Saad-Ghorayeb, A., "In Their Own Words: Hizbollah's Strategy in the Current Confrontation," Carnegie Endowment for International Peace, *Policy Outlook*, January 2007, available at http://www.carnegieendowment.org/files/saadghorayeb_hizbollah_final.pdf.
Saad-Ghorayeb, A., "Hezbollah's Apocalypse Now," *Washington Post*, July 23, 2006, available at http://www.washingtonpost.com/wpdyn/content/article/2006/07/21/AR2006072101363.html.
Saad-Ghorayeb, A., *Hizbullah: Politics and Religion*, London: Pluto Press, 2002.
Sadiki, L., "Reframing Resistance and Democracy: Narratives from Hamas and Hizbullah," *Democratization* 17, 2010, 350–76.
Shatz, A., "In Search of Hezbollah," *New York Review of Books* 51, 2004.
Slavin, B., "Mullah, Money, and Militias," Washington, DC: United States Institute of Peace, Special Report 206, 2008, available at http://www.usip.org/files/resources/sr206.pdf.
Slisli, F., "Islam: The Elephant in Fanon's *The Wretched of the Earth*," *Critique: Critical Middle Eastern Studies* 17, 2008, 97–108.
Sobelman, D., *New Rules of the Game: Israel and Hizbollah after the Withdrawal from Lebanon*, Tel Aviv: Jaffee Center for Strategic Studies, Tel Aviv University, 2004.
Soussi, A., "The Enigma that Is Lebanese Hezbollah," *worldpress.org*, June 14, 2004, available at http://www.worldpress.org/Mideast/1873.cfm.
"Syrian Protesters Turn on Iran and Hezbollah," *France 24*, March 6, 2011, available at http://observers.france24.com/content/20110603-angry-syrian-protesters-turn-iran-hezbollah.
Taheri, A., "The Road to Iraq's Riots," *New York Post*, April 6, 2004, available at http://www.benadorassociates.com/article/3198.
Youssef, N. A., "Shiite Cleric Seen Trying to Broaden His Base of Support," *Knight Ridder*, May 1, 2006, available at http://www.realcities.com/mld/krwashington/14475068.htm.

10

HAMAS AS A RULING PARTY

Jean-François Legrain

In the early 2000s, the theme of democratizing the Arab world gained increasing prominence in the media as well as in international diplomatic circles. During this time, the parliamentary elections in Iraq (December 2005) and the presidential elections in Palestine (January 2005, which saw the victory of Mahmoud Abbas), as well as the Syrian departure from Lebanon (June 2005), among other events, were interpreted by some as proof of the rightness of an interventionist approach, at a time when stalemates in Syria, Tunisia, Egypt, and elsewhere were thought to call for stronger external pressures. Others, on the other hand, warning of the dangers of intervention, preferred to bet on the internal dynamics that in certain countries had led to undeniable progress in gaining certain freedoms.

In 2005–06, as parliamentary elections were about to take place in Palestine, the prevalent approach on the international scene to understanding the main Palestinian Islamist movement – the Islamic Resistance Movement, or Hamas – sprang out of this context. Interpretation focused on a transformation within the framework of democratization, revealing a highly ideological and politicized approach to the Palestinian question.

The transparency of the 1996 elections that had confirmed the power of Yasser Arafat at the head of the Palestinian Authority (PA) had been discarded. Democratization was supposed to have begun with the marginalization of Arafat, beginning in 2002–03 and reaching its consecration with the election of Mahmoud Abbas as head of the PA in 2005. At the end of the road, the virtuous dynamics of democratization imagined by the international community were supposed to integrate all the Palestinian forces into a political scene where they would finally submit to the order dreamed of by successive U.S. governments. In this way, Hamas was supposed to have completed its transformation into an entirely civil party by abandoning its military ambitions and rejecting its previous political positions. At no moment did it appear that the international community considered the possibility, in such contradiction with its notion of democratization, of an electoral victory for Hamas achieved before the completion of the imagined process.

But on January 25, 2006, Hamas carried the absolute majority of seats in the Palestinian Legislative Council (PLC) of the Interim Self Government. On March 28, the PLC granted investiture to a cabinet headed by Ismail Haniyya, head of the Reform and Change ticket that had won the elections. As Arafat's Fatah movement was unable to reach agreement on a program of national union, the cabinet was comprised exclusively of Hamas members and the movement's allies.

As soon as this victory was announced, the international community – led by the United States and the European Union – exerted political, economic, and military pressure on the victors. Some thought this policy was aimed at accelerating Hamas' transformation as imagined by the international community. Others saw in it simply the desire to hasten the failure – before any contagion could spread – of the experiment of an Islamist government that had gained power through the ballot box. The international community's goal, then, was to turn public opinion around and, with new elections, once again find its "good" interlocutors.

With Hamas' military seizure of the Gaza Strip on June 14, 2007, the discourse on democratization abandoned the theme of transforming the movement and returned to a call for fighting against "terrorism" and "obscurantism." Approaching the conflict between Hamas and Fatah (and, beyond, the Palestine Liberation Organization (PLO)) in Islamist versus secular terms was reactivated, and an order of compliance with an international policy that *de facto* submitted to Israeli interests since the 1990s was put forward.

Thus, with Hamas commemorating its twentieth anniversary on December 14, 2007, it appears more than ever opportune to review the reality embodied by this Islamic resistance movement and inquire as to its identity. To answer this question, I first base my discussion on facts acquired during extensive research I conducted about the mobilization strategies used in the legislative elections of 1996 and 2006. The 1996 elections followed a "traditional" mode of mobilizing based on familial and local allegiances within a neo-patrimonial context. The 2006 elections, however, revealed the emergence of a completely new reality for Palestine that some would qualify as "modern": the promotion by the electorate itself of a national political party called upon to govern – Hamas.

I then turn to Hamas' history, from its origins as a Muslim Brotherhood movement in Palestine to its entry into politics and its electoral victory, while considering its military ambitions. Was its evolution in becoming a ruling party inscribed from the beginning in the very identity of the movement? What stages did its internal debate on political participation go through before the votes of the electorate were sought?

I then endeavor to detail the various measures adopted by President Abbas, Fatah, Israel, and the international community aimed at preventing Hamas from exercising the mandate it received in the January 2006 legislative elections. It will then be possible to decipher the dynamics of the violent events of 2006–07 that – far from being some ideological move concerning the need for Islam and the application of international injunctions – seem clearly to be a struggle for power in a context of contradictory democratic elections and foreign intervention.

Political mobilization, from "traditional" to "modern"

After an interval of ten years the population of the Palestinian territories was summoned to elect its representatives to the PLC. While it boycotted the 1996 election, Hamas participated in the 2006 vote. What tells us how fundamentally new this situation was is not so much the victory of the Islamist movement itself – it was anticipated, even if the extent of the vote may have been surprising – but rather the vastly different patterns of electoral mobilization in both elections. Indeed, while voters still registered some support for nationalist forces and independents in accordance with the traditional clan and localist logics, they gave Hamas a victory that was decisive and unattached to familial and local allegiances. The Islamist electorate of 2006 thus made of Hamas a true national party called upon to govern.

The logic of ethno-localism (1996)

The 1996 elections, for the first time in recent history, allowed the entire population of the West Bank and the Gaza Strip to express itself at the ballot box. The examination of the results obtained by each of the candidates at each of the polling stations via factorial correspondence analysis (FCA)[1] has allowed me to bring to light the mobilization strategies and the geography of operative allegiances as expressed through the vote.[2]

Contrary to expectations, the political factor (in the sense of belonging to a party or even by reputation of belonging to, or by closeness to, a party) was never a major feature in the consistency of how people voted. In almost all cases, the choices expressed can be explained by the geographical link between the polling station, on the one hand, and the origin of the candidate on the other. Voters, in defense of their own interests, placed their confidence almost solely in candidates who were from their own circle of local allegiances, regardless of their own, or their candidates', political affiliation. Belonging to those areas that are geographically delimited and restricted to a neighborhood, city, village, group of villages, or a refugee camp seemed to be the key to allegiances for which voting was the channel of expression.[3]

FCA allowed me to map the physical geography of allegiances with great accuracy due to the precision of geographical linkages shown in polling stations.[4] Surprisingly, this map reflected, for the villages, the outlines of the *nâhiyyas* (the smallest Ottoman administrative units) of the eighteenth and nineteenth centuries.[5] Thus, far from having imposed an administrative division upon a restive group of people, the Ottomans considered the configuration of human allegiances that had taken shape from the Mameluke period onward. Also, and particularly in spite of such profound political, demographic, and economic upheavals since the beginning of the twentieth century, the January 1996 vote expressed the permanence of these allegiances.[6] Far from establishing a definitive break with the traditional order of cities and villages before 1948, the refugee camps themselves seemed in some respects the restoration of that order. Every camp thus set itself up as a new closed space of allegiances, substituting its own internal network for the old *nâhiyya* allegiances it had lost.

The dynamics of the Palestinian political order were thus still embedded in the traditional play between the population and a power perceived as being external – the Ottoman Porte (Istanbul), the Hashemite Kingdom (Amman), and the PLO (Amman, Beirut, then Tunis and, since 1994, Gaza and Ramallah). As a result, even after they were repatriated, the leaders of the PLO remained external: adulated as liberators and then denounced as predators, while at the same time both liked and scorned, the "returnees" were soon referred to in the street as "Tunisians."[7]

A system based on such a dichotomy, however, can only function because of constant interconnections. The concept of the "politics of the notables," once used to characterize Ottoman order in the region,[8] seems capable of accounting for the situation. It refers to a society in which one observes a chasm between population and power. Mediation between the two is ensured by the "notables" who ensure the representation of the authority among the population and that of the population among the authority. Sending the "neo-notables" to the PLC thus constituted for the population of the West Bank and Gaza Strip a means of appropriating the new institutions controlled by the external repatriated leadership. The presidential election's results did not reflect a choice: in giving Arafat more than 87 percent of the vote, the Palestinians simply indicated the site of real power within the political sphere. But as a reward for the allegiance they offered, they sought resources from the central power via its neo-notables (e.g., local infrastructures, positions in the administration, assistance, not to mention security and protection against the occupant).

The party logic (2006)

Ten years later, the January 2006 legislative elections reveal a completely different mobilization process.[9] The FCA indicates that in contrast to the practices of 1996, the Islamist voter in 2006, much more than the nationalist one, gave primacy to political affiliation over ethno-localism;[10] affirming a "party ticket vote" independent of clannish and local allegiances, he further voiced an identical opinion on both the national and district ballots.[11] The nationalist parties' electorate and candidates, on the contrary, the leftist ones more than Fatah, remained prisoners of a logic based on local allegiances. As in 1996, votes cast for each candidate in many cases depended on the person's origins and geographic location rather than political affiliation. Thus, in district balloting, Fatah candidates never managed to equal the votes achieved by their movement in national balloting.

Ethno-localist solidarities have not gone away even though they no longer constitute the basis for the choice in the election. The cities, like the camps and the groups of villages, appear each one as a group with its own personality, as they are often coherent in their political choice. Nevertheless, no general sociology is able to explain these differences: the categories of "urban dwellers," "villagers," or "refugees of the camps" are not able to account for the diversity of political allegiances.[12]

Thus, for the first time perhaps in contemporary Palestine, a movement – namely Hamas – was viewed by the electorate as a real party at the national level: in 2006, to vote for Hamas constituted the result of primarily individual decisions.[13]

Hamas and political participation

A few months before the 2006 elections, Hamas oscillated between its identity as an associative movement of re-Islamization – attached to its Muslim Brotherhood origins – and its identity as a political, military, and social organization aspiring to eventually become a ruling party. Haniyya's faction that had until then been in the minority convinced the entire movement to participate in previously boycotted national elections. At no time, apparently, had the possibility of a victory endowed with an absolute majority that would lead it into executive power been considered. But the electorate placed Hamas at the heart of the political scene and granted it the status not only of a party but also, and above all, of a governing party.

The quietism of the Muslim Brotherhood in Palestine

Hamas has its ideological and organizational roots in the Muslim Brotherhood, founded by Hassan al-Banna in Egypt in 1928. It emerged out of the Palestinian branch, created in Jerusalem in 1946, and it participates in contemporary Sunni Islamism.[14] In Palestine, however, unlike other regional cases, Islamization of its political language has been late in coming. In the absence of its own state, to criticize the PLO – which was struggling for liberation in the name of Arab and/or Palestinian nationalism – was at the time perceived as tantamount to working for the occupiers.

At the end of the 1970s, however, the Islamic movement developed by giving center stage to the active, and more or less authoritarian, preaching (*da'wa*) of Islam. Limiting their incursions onto the political scene to denouncing the atheistic Communist Party, the Muslim Brothers then maneuvered among Israel, Jordan, and Fatah, according to the current situation. Despite an undeniable lack of political legitimacy due to their withdrawal from the anti-Israeli resistance, the Muslim Brothers managed to weave together an important charitable network, especially in the Gaza Strip, where Sheikh Ahmad Yasin (b. 1936, assassinated by the Israeli army in March 2004) stood out as a charismatic national figure.[15] In the West Bank, however, despite the proliferation of pious associations and the takeover of various student councils, the Brothers failed to set up a structured network with a true leader.

It was only with the appearance of a second current, rivaling the Muslim Brothers in the field of active Islamization but with a fundamentally different political behavior, that Islamism became integrated into the political scene – which radically transformed it as much as the Muslim Brothers themselves. This current, identified under the generic name of "Islamic Jihad," appeared in the middle of the 1980s and made Palestine the central cause of Islam today.[16]

The ideologues of this movement saw Zionism and Israeli occupation as an inescapable barrier to re-Islamization, and thus their destruction by Jihad (in all its forms, including armed struggle) became a religious duty incumbent on every believer (*fard 'ayn*). Islamic Jihad, through its military activities, subsequently allowed the whole Islamic movement access to political legitimacy – until then monopolized by nationalism (*qawmiyya*) and patriotism (*wataniyya*). But with its leadership decapitated by Israeli repression at the beginning of the first Intifada (1987–94) and hampered by its small size, Islamic Jihad failed at this moment to become the organizational catalyst for the reconciliation between patriotism and religion. Hamas was poised to take over this role.

Hamas, or the entry of the Muslim Brotherhood into politics

Breaking with their former quietism, the Muslim Brotherhood entered the active struggle against the occupation around the time that Islamic Jihad's influence was weakening. It believed that participation in patriotic mobilization was necessary for its survival as an association of religious mobilization. Members of the younger generation of the Brothers, such as Dr. 'Abd Al-Aziz Al-Rantîsî (b. 1947, assassinated by the Israeli army in April 2004 just as he was succeeding Sheikh Yasin as the head of the movement), Salâh Shahâda (b. 1954, assassinated by the Israeli army in July 2002), and Yahyâ Al-Sinuwwar (b. 1962, currently in prison), created "the active arm of the Muslim Brotherhood in the uprising," the Islamic Resistance Movement (*Harakat Al-Muqâwama Al-Islâmiyya*, or *Hamâs*, an acronym meaning "zeal"). This revolution had been fairly quickly endorsed by Sheikh Ahmad Yasin himself.

Through increasingly greater involvement in military action (but still distanced from international Jihadism)[17] and social effectiveness through its network of associations inherited from the Brotherhood (mosques, benevolent societies, kindergartens, clinics, sports clubs, etc.), Hamas has managed to seal the reconciliation between patriotism and religion, assuring for itself a future that is equally at home in *da'wa* and in politics.

The movement thus very quickly found its place on the political chessboard. During the entire first Intifada, the newly born Hamas never participated in the National Unified Command (i.e., the uprising's leadership).[18] However, at the beginning of the al-Aqsa Intifada in 2000, now robust from the work it had accomplished in the preceding years, Hamas imposed itself as a pivotal element in the National and Islamic Forces, a flexible structure whose goal was to shape political and activist mobilization in the context of the new uprising. Hamas further participated in all student, union, and professional elections, competing with Fatah to the point of imposing a quasi-dual-party system.[19]

Hamas has likewise developed diplomatic skills. Opposed to the Madrid Conference (1991) and the diplomatic initiatives taken up by the PLO, the movement immediately set up representation offices in Amman, Damascus, Beirut, Khartoum, and Tehran; it then maintained regular contact with the host governments and more irregular contact with certain Western governments.[20]

The debate over political participation

Even though Hamas virtually swallowed up the Muslim Brotherhood as soon as it was created, in the spirit of Sheikh Yasin its only *raison d'être* was its *da'wa* mission, to which politics and military operations were strictly subordinated. Time after time, its apprehension over the use of force with Israel and the PA led Hamas to distance itself from the realms of both armed conflict (through the truces of 1995, 1996, and those over the last several years) and the political (for example following Sheikh Yasin's triumphal tour of the Muslim world after his release from prison in 1998). The movement had then refocused on its traditional associative activities, and only a few cells showed disapproval by undertaking localized military operations.

Like other Palestinian movements of national liberation, Hamas has always refused to transform itself into a political party.[21] But unlike the Islamic Liberation Party (ILP),[22] for example, it has always upheld the principle of holding political or professional elections.[23] Generally speaking, the movement believes that the diversity of its positions regarding elections simply responds to the general interest – that is, the fulfillment of the rights and claims of the Palestinian people[24] – in accordance with their changing circumstances.

And so, as early as the 1990s, Hamas believed that at the local level it could, and should, exercise the principle of participation. It therefore allowed some of its members to accept PA nominations in cities and other village councils. The movement became more deeply involved in electoral politics when local elections were held in 2005, and it won major victories.

The internal debate in Hamas over its participation in national elections has never been closed, with decisions remaining tied to the particular circumstances of each election. Thus, at the end of 1995 the movement decided to follow the example of the Jordanian Muslim Brotherhood. When the first multiparty legislative elections took place in Jordan in 1989, the latter decided to enter into politics while preserving its autonomy. It founded the Islamic Action Front (*Jabhat al-'Amal al-Islâmî*), responsible for political participation, while it reserved for itself the role (*marjâ'iyya*) of managing its traditional fields of activities tied to *da'wa*. For its part, Hamas created the Islamic National Salvation Party in Palestine (*Hizb Al-Khalâs Al-Watanî Al-Islâmî fî Filastîn*), whose directorship was entrusted to one of its leaders, Ismail Abu Shanab (b. 1955; the artisan of the truce between Hamas and Israel, he was assassinated by the Israeli army in August 2003).[25] Unlike the Jordanian Brothers, however, Hamas has never assigned any real responsibilities to this party, even depriving it of participation in the January 1996 legislative elections by officially establishing it only two months later.

The January 1996 elections, in any case, revealed the movement's internal differences. Certainly, none of Hamas' officers ever proposed a formal interdiction concerning holding elections. Hamas thus summoned its partisans on November 9, 1995, to register to vote – a call that was heard, judging by the high levels of registration observed in voting districts. The circumstances in these elections, on the other hand, also led the movement to call upon "the resolute Palestinian people to boycott these [presidential and legislative] elections that want to confer legitimacy on the [1993 Oslo] Accords[26] and the bargain sales."[27]

Taking advantage of this latitude, four Hamas leaders, including Ismail Haniyya, announced their decision to register in Gaza as independent candidates after managing to collect the 500 signatures of support necessary to stand in elections. The leaders outside the Territories, for their part, unanimously distanced themselves from this move without condemning it. Within the Territories, the debate took shape through the publication of contradictory communiqués. Three out of the four leaders thereupon withdrew their candidacy. On the eve of the election, however, a communiqué circulated in Gaza under the signature of Hamas presenting seven candidates, five of them independent Islamists and two from Fatah, as recipients of the favors of the movement in Gaza City.[28]

Ten years later, the same Ismail Haniyya, joined by leaders from Gaza – a good number of whom had held high-level responsibilities in the Khalas party[29] – and leaders from the West Bank,[30] received the go-ahead from the movement to venture into direct political participation in the legislative elections.

In January 2005, however, Hamas decided to boycott the presidential election by refusing to offer a candidate and calling for non-participation. By only organizing the presidential election (without legislative elections), in Hamas' view, the PA was implementing a political program based on "patching up" its institutions that people rejected. It therefore called for holding general elections all at one time – presidential, legislative, and local.[31]

Two months later, Hamas decided to participate in the legislative elections announced for the summer of 2005, declaring that

> on the basis of adherence to the legitimate rights of our people and the preservation of the program of resistance as a strategic choice until the end of the occupation, [we want] to participate in building the institutions of Palestinian society on healthy foundations, to cure corruption and vice in all its forms, and to carry out the national global and authentic reform so that our people are able to resist occupation and aggression.[32]

Furthermore, it explained the abandonment of its 1996 position via "the changes imposed by the resistance and the Intifada and the sacrifices made by the people these last few years."[33]

The refusal to let Hamas carry out its mandate

At the end of 2006 and the beginning of 2007, the major international media continuously made a connection between the proliferating inter-Palestinian clashes and the Hamas victory a year earlier. Corruption (*fasâd*), anarchy (*fawda*), and chaotic security (*falatân*) had been feeding a dynamic already in place for several years, the culmination of which – a civil war (*fitna*) – the population feared and condemned.[34]

The 2006 election clearly demonstrated the frustration of the Palestinian people in regard to the lack of a political solution to the occupation – at least in the short term. Fatah, the icon of Palestinian national claims for the last 40 years, was removed from a situation of power it had controlled since its founding. For voters, Yasser Arafat's movement would at best have failed in the struggle against various evils; at worst, it would have been their cause. On the other hand, owing to its reputation for probity and efficiency, the people invested confidence in Hamas to carry out the mission of overcoming a civil war. But in preventing Hamas from exercising its mandate, President Mahmoud Abbas, Fatah, Israel, and the international community each contributed to transforming the security debacle into a conflict whose beginnings appeared in the summer of 2006, when Hamas decided to take by force the power it had legally acquired at the ballot box.

The Hamas Cabinet (March 2006–February 2007)

With Fatah refusing to participate in a government of national unity, the cabinet formed by the PLC at the end of March 2006 was made up exclusively of members or allies of Hamas. Declining to participate in any meeting of the council of ministers, President Abbas was particularly adamant in denying Hamas any competence in matters of internal security.[35] He did not believe that the Hamas Cabinet would last, and his initiatives in the name of "the sovereignty of the people" were planned repeatedly as a way of marginalizing, if not pushing aside, the victor of the legislative elections. Thus, in contradiction with the letter of the Basic Law, in June 2006 Abbas called for a national referendum (never to be held), summoning the population to pronounce itself on the "National Conciliation Document."[36] In December 2006, threatening to call for anticipated presidential and legislative elections, once again in contradiction with the Basic Law, he again fomented an increase in violence on the ground.

Fatah, for its part, constantly overplayed its refusal to let Hamas govern. Informal groups and members of security forces attached *de jure* or *de facto* to the Presidency assailed the very symbols of the Authority from which they felt dispossessed; ministries as well as PLC and Prime Minister's offices were vandalized.

The Israeli government, aside from its routine occupation and blockade of the Gaza Strip, froze the transfer of taxes it levied on all merchandise imported to Palestinian territories in the name of the PA, in conformity with the Paris Accords of 1994. The total sum in 2005, according to the World Bank, came to some 60 percent of the PA's revenue.

As of January 30, 2006, the Quartet (the United Nations, the United States, the European Union, and Russia) made all cooperation conditional on a "commitment to the principles of nonviolence, recognition of Israel, and acceptance of previous agreements and obligations, including the Roadmap."[37] Judging the response of the cabinet inadequate, the Quartet froze all its direct aid and rescinded the mechanisms set up in 2002 to centralize the management of funds within a transparent Ministry of Finance. In the framework of a "Transitory International Mechanism" (TIM), the Presidency and the "good" non-governmental organizations (NGOs) thus became the new beneficiaries of increased aid but deprived of its part devoted to economic development. The United States further forced the international banking system to discontinue transactions with the cabinet. These measures brought about an immediate social crisis. In the Gaza Strip, unemployment reached 36 percent, and it was estimated that 87 percent of its population was living below the poverty line.[38]

The National Unity Cabinet (March–June 2007)

Given the context of an impending civil war, Saudi Arabia convoked a summit meeting in Mecca in February 2007 and brought together the President, Prime Minister, and responsible parties in Fatah and Hamas. The parties reached an agreement for the framing of a Unity Cabinet, based on the Document of National Accord, to which was added respect for agreements signed by the PLO and an explicit reference to Arab resolutions.

The PLC approved a National Unity Cabinet on March 17, 2007. Ismail Haniyya, confirmed in his duties as Prime Minister, headed it, accompanied by a Fatah Vice-Prime Minister. With the Popular Front for the Liberation of Palestine (PFLP) and Islamic Jihad refusing to become associated with the executive, the cabinet consisted of 12 Hamas ministers, 6 Fatah ministers, 4 ministers from "small" parties, and 3 independents.

Officially, the Quartet timidly welcomed the installation of this cabinet. Announcing the resumption of its aid, it nonetheless maintained the TIM and abstained from renewing direct financing. Furthermore, the Israeli government refused to resume the transfer of the taxes it collects for the PA and to hand over the roughly $600 million it had placed in escrow.

Tensions soon reappeared over the Minister of the Interior's (an independent) control of security forces. Despairing of the ability to impose himself on forces faithful to Fatah, he resigned in May. Partisan violence began again, with clashes between familial clans that had increased in early 2007 now picking up again. They escalated in intensity beginning on May 11, 2007, when regular security forces and Al-Aqsa Martyr Brigades of Fatah (most of whom had recently been integrated into the regular forces) began a unilateral and massive deployment operation in the Gaza Strip on the initiative of the Presidency and with total scorn for the security plan adopted in April by the Unity Cabinet.

On June 14, the Ministry of the Interior's regular forces and Hamas' irregular forces (Izz al-Din al-Qassam Brigades) went on the offensive. Within a few hours, they took control of the military command of all the security forces tied to the Presidency and Fatah. Pillaging, acts of vengeance, and summary executions then set the Gaza Strip ablaze. In the West Bank, Fatah's regular and irregular forces joined together and attacked institutions, people, and property associated with Hamas.

Hamas states that its forceful strike anticipated an attempted putsch planned by Muhammad Dahlan with the support of the United States.[39] As a former head of Preventive Security on the front lines in clashes with Hamas, Muhammad Dahlan received the Presidency of the National Security Council from Mahmoud Abbas when it was reestablished on April 8, 2007, to better "keep an eye on" the Ministry of the Interior. The putsch was alleged to have been worked out with the active participation of General Keith Dayton, who was responsible for coordinating security questions with Israel and the PA at the U.S. State Department.[40]

Territorial and institutional division (June 2007)

Thereafter refusing any dialogue with Hamas and its dismissed Prime Minister, President Abbas adopted a politics of confrontation encouraged by his Israeli and international interlocutors. The territorial division between the West Bank and the Gaza Strip, established by Israel in 1993 and aimed at stopping exchanges of persons, was redoubled by this institutional and political division. Two cabinets henceforth opposed one another. The former National Unity Cabinet headed by Ismail Haniyya, reduced to Hamas ministers only, controlled the Gaza Strip, while an Emergency Cabinet, headed by Salam Fayyad, administered the West Bank. In defiance of the Basic Law, the Fayyad Emergency Cabinet – extended without a deadline in the absence of any vote of confidence from the PLC – received international support, while the Haniyya Cabinet experienced a political and economic boycott. The entire international community thus adopted the American plan, which granted support to the President and aimed to marginalize those who were faithful to Hamas through ever-hardening economic conditions.

Declared "hostile territory" by Israel in September 2007, the Gaza Strip was subjected to a blockade on persons and merchandise that sunk it into a state of misery, while Hamas managed to stabilize its rule in spite of an Israeli invasion at the end of 2008.[41]

A struggle for power

Thus, far from any ideological issue, the dynamics of violence in 2006–07 looked very much like a struggle for power in a context where successive democratic elections should have led to "cohabitation" between a Fatah President and a Hamas or a unity cabinet. During the entire period, Hamas denounced the coup d'état against the cabinet and upheld its legitimacy in defending – including by arms – its right to exercise the mandate conferred upon it at the ballot box.

The refusal of President Abbas and Fatah to alternate power reflects the inability of Arafat's movement to respond to its defeat in an organizational and programmatic way. Sapped by its divisions (returnees vs. natives, young vs. old, partisans of armed struggle vs. its opponents, etc.) and by the rival appetites for power of certain leaders (at the heart of which are those of Muhammad Dahlan), Fatah has shown itself incapable of remedying the failure of its political program regarding the Israeli–Palestinian issue through internal reform. The violence of 2006–07 can thus be understood as Fatah's desperate attempt to survive and cement its dispersed ranks, whether in a planned or unplanned manner, into a common opposition to the only national party that Hamas has become.[42]

Need for Islam and national liberation

The question of the place of Islam in society did not contribute to the dynamics of violence. As surprising as this assertion may seem to some, the transfer of power desired by the electorate from the nationalists to the Islamists cannot justify an interpretation that regards the opposition between Hamas and Fatah (and, beyond that, the PLO) in Islamist versus secular terms. If, in fact, the project for a state promoted by the PLO over the last 40 years can be characterized by a refusal of religious sectarianism, it can never be said that it has been characterized by secularism.

The "democratic state," appearing in Palestinian institutional discourse in 1968 and maintained as a strategic objective for the national struggle until 1976, was conceived as "non-sectarian" (*lâ-tâ'ifiyya*), with Lebanon as an antithesis. Different groups gave the idea varying definitions; Fatah endorsed the coexistence of Muslims, Jews, and Christians, while Marxist-leaning organizations envisaged the community in terms of Arabs and Jews. None of the normative texts of any of the major nationalist organizational members of the PLO ever characterized the expected state as "secular" (*'ilmâniyya*), an unpopular notion often associated with a supposedly Godless and immoral West.

The political development of Islam common to the Muslim world since the end of the 1970s could not leave Palestinian nationalist organizations and institutions untouched. Islam was thus inserted into the heart of their institutional mechanisms beginning in 1996, as much so in the Basic Law developed by the PLC as in the projects for a constitution prepared by the PLO. All these mechanisms make Islam "the official religion of the State" and emphasize that it "grants its respect to heavenly revelations" (an Islamic terminology that includes Jews, Christians, and Muslims as heirs to a divine revelation) without, however, involving the need for the President of the Authority to be Muslim. All likewise stipulate that "the principles of Islamic *sharî'a* constitute a principal source of legislation." The Basic Law of the PA further maintains the citizen as a member of a religious community, a statute inherited from the previous Ottoman, Jordanian, and Egyptian regimes; as such, questions of personal rights are subject to religious courts.

Thus, the dynamics of violence over the last few years have never been fueled by Hamas' desire to modify the place of Islam in the institutional structure of the PA. Furthermore, in spite of denouncing the corruption of officials in charge of affairs since the PA was established – a denunciation shared well beyond Islamist voters – and a few marginal initiatives, Hamas as a whole has never sought to impose a mode of life that some might qualify as a forced "Talibanization" of society.

Hamas also cannot simply be understood as a national liberation movement based on religion, even if the beginnings of such an identity occasionally appear. Such movements make the recuperation of territory the grounds for their actions and the basis for national unity beyond geographical dispersion. The territorial disappointment engendered by the Oslo Accords logically caused Fatah's hold over Palestinian society to waver. By the same process, that disappointment designated Hamas as its only legitimate heir – all the more easily because Hamas learned how to integrate patriotism by Islamisizing its referents while associating it with the armed struggle. It then played a preeminent role within that struggle.

Hamas does not eliminate the territory issue but, in contrast to the PLO liberation movements, situates it at a different level. The early twentieth century land of Palestine that no longer exists or a Palestine rationally divided into territories is not placed at the forefront of its discourse, even if both make up a part of it. Rather, an eschatological Palestine blessed by God for all eternity is at the heart of Hamas' discourse. The demand for its liberation, therefore, is not an immediate one; the destruction of Israel constitutes a "Koranic ineluctability."[43] On the other hand, in the name of respect for Islam and its conception of Jihad, and for the necessary defense of the general interest of the Muslim community, political pragmatism is required. Hence Hamas' highest rank leaders were serious when they put forward, on many occasions, proposals for a truce.[44]

Faced with the impossibility of retaking the territory as well as social ties that were under threat from anarchy and chaotic security, the religious referent could then function as an effective strategy. Making Palestine not the source of identity but the space of its blossoming, the Islamist movement, with the strength of its vast network of associations, both benevolent and religious, could appear to be the natural place to respond to social disintegration and the absence of national liberation. More than the armed struggle, the return to religion clearly appears in Hamas literature as the privileged expression of Jihad and Hamas has never made its military operations a strategy of national liberation. Islam here becomes the foundation of the individual and of society. Immediately available, it allows for reconstructing the unity of a group no longer dependent on a return to the territory. Moreover, in a context of permanent external interventions (e.g., military occupation), Islam appears as the ultimate rampart but also the last space for sovereignty.

The demands of the Quartet

Whether or not the demands of the Quartet are adopted is likewise outside the realm of the dynamics of violence.[45] One year later, the summer 2006 National Conciliation Document still summarizes Palestinian political consensus, and the Quartet has deemed that the Document does not meet its requirements.

Refusing to realize its stated priority – the peaceful coexistence between two states on the territory which was Palestine under the British Mandate – the international community bears a large share of responsibility for the failure to establish a solution. With the Madrid Conference in 1991 the international community adopted the myth of a "peace process" that masked the reality of its renunciation of applying its own laws by its *de facto* alignment with the Israeli *fait accompli*.[46] In the early 1990s, the

United States, coming out of the Gulf War and on the eve of the collapse of the Soviet Union, imposed Israeli demands on the world. Declining to convene an international conference under the aegis of the United Nations (a body endowed with mechanisms for constraint) and based on "all their relevant resolutions," the international community pledged its support for simple bilateral forums sponsored by the U.S. and (nominally) by the Soviet Union. Multilateral negotiations were reserved for questions that did not involve sovereignty, borders, and the end of warfare.

In strict continuity with these developments, President George W. Bush convoked the international conference on the Middle East in Annapolis, Maryland, on November 27, 2007. Its discussion continued to inscribe itself in the Israeli perspective by making international law (about return of territories occupied by force, refugees' rights, etc.) the subject of negotiations rather than their reference – and negotiations once again took place in the absence of any mechanism for enforcement.[47]

The international community's refusal to apply its own laws led it likewise to disregard the 2006 election results, though it has recognized their democratic nature. As for the demands of the Quartet, their lack of precision as well as their contradiction with international law were simply an instrument of this refusal.

The Palestinians obviously did not elect Hamas to provide them with a better position in negotiations with Israel or on the international scene. The divergence on the definitive solution to the occupation of Palestine that indeed exists between Hamas and Fatah therefore does not constitute the real stakes in their armed polarization. Their differences lie in the status of negotiations – essential for Fatah and the PLO and marginal for Hamas. Therefore, Hamas, expecting nothing from negotiations in the short or the long term, has accepted, without hesitation, to let the Presidency and the PLO manage the negotiations issue.

Conclusion

In 1987 the Palestinian population mobilized against the occupation, transforming its resistance, which had until then been passive (*sumûd*), into one of action (*muqâwama*). The Muslim Brotherhood saw that its salvation as an associative preaching movement lay only in its entrance into national mobilization, from which it had thus far kept its distance. The Islamic Resistance Movement (Hamas), which it created to that end, allowed it to unite religion and patriotism, until then monopolized by the nationalists.

As a result of that combination, Hamas assured itself of massive support. Eighteen years later, with the legislative elections of 2006, the people, in their turn, latched on to Hamas and carried it to power. They entrusted the movement with fighting corruption, anarchy, and chaotic security through the building of healthy institutions – thus saving them from a civil war. They likewise expected the reaffirmation of claims for national liberation, the return of refugees, and the liberation of prisoners after Fatah's concessions over the last few years had produced no positive result. Voters thus made Hamas a ruling party even when the movement, like Fatah and other Palestinian movements of national liberation, refused to transform itself as such.

Palestinian voters did not ask Hamas to deliver national liberation during the 2006 elections. Taking pragmatically into account the current impossibility of that goal, voters turned from those invested with that task and charged Hamas with building institutions meant to manage the expectation of liberation while saving Palestine from the evils of corruption and internal violence.

Neither a party properly speaking, nor a liberation movement, Hamas considers its resistance discourse – based on a certain conception of Islam – a central element in its mission. Its transformation from an association for religious mobilization into a quasi-party is part of the type of democracy possible in the Palestinian territories, with its variability, errors, and limits due to the occupation and the weight of history.

Hamas' evolution follows an internal coherence, and it would be illusory to imagine that external intervention by the U.S. or Israel can force it to bend its doctrines. Hamas' reading of the Qur'an and Muslim tradition forbids it from formally (*de jure*) granting legitimacy to a Jewish State resulting from the loss of Islamic land inhabited by Muslim people. A truce, however, and *de facto* coexistence without time limits can be envisaged since they do not entail recognition of the legitimacy of the illegitimate. Moreover, they must be envisaged if they represent the community's general interest, as jurisprudence demands.

In deciding to defend the right to exercise the mandate entrusted to it by the Palestinian people at any cost, including by arms, Hamas is thus invoking the necessity of defending the community's interest, in conformity with Islam, as much as the necessity of protecting the democratic outcome that has been denied by the Palestinian Presidency, Fatah, the Israeli government, and the international community.

Notes

1 J.-P. Benzecri, *Correspondence Analysis Handbook*, New York: Marcel Dekker, 1992. By using an objective scale to spacialize similarities and dissimilarities in the way people vote, the mathematical method of FCA has the advantage of avoiding subjectivity.

2 J.-F. Legrain, *Les Palestines du quotidien: Les Elections de l'autonomie (janvier 1996)*, Beirut: Centre d'Etudes et de Recherches sur le Moyen-Orient Contemporain (CERMOC), 1999, p. 452 (http://www.gremmo.mom.fr/legrain/palestine00.htm).

3 Such electoral behavior signified the permanence of blood ties and their centrality in the functioning of Palestinian society. But they likewise implied the need to extend the notion of "clan polarization" as the basis for areas sketched out by the *'asabiyya* (the "*esprit de corps*" defined by Ibn Khaldûn in the fourteenth century) to that of "ethno-localism," at the heart of which blood ties, while still highly significant, can nonetheless be transcended and articulated by a common reference to a local whole. Cf. Olivier Roy, *Groupes de solidarité au Moyen-Orient et en Asie centrale: États, territoires et réseaux*, Paris: Centre d'Etudes des Relations Internationales, 1996. (http://www.ceri.sciences-po.org/publica/cahiers/cahier16.pdf).

4 Urban dwellers thus voted for inhabitants of their own city (for example, Bethlehem, Bayt Jâlâ, and Bayt Sahûr each have specific votes), as did refugees (near Dayr al-Balah, for example, the vote of Nusayrât camp differed from that of Burayj, like that of Maghâzî). Meanwhile, the Fatah voter from the city of Nablus abstained from voting for a Fatah candidate originating from the camps and even preferred to vote for non-Fatah candidates "but" from the city itself in addition to the Fatah urban candidates. Being a

member of Fatah, the "ruling party," was only a "plus" which would facilitate a deputy's access to the authority and would thus improve his capacity to obtain the awaited benefits.

5 In the area of Bethlehem, for example, the *nâhiyya* of al-Wâdiyya was still distinguished from those of al-'Arqûb and Banî Hassan; in Jenin, Machârîq Al-Jarrâr still marked its difference with Bilâd Al-Hâritha and Cha'râwiyya.

6 This hypertrophy of localist attachment in Palestine, when compared to the situation in neighboring countries, can be read as a "natural" protection adopted by the population to defend itself from the policies of the occupant aiming at destroying the social link.

7 Nadine Picaudou and Isabelle Rivoal (eds.), *Retours en Palestine: Trajectoires, rôles et expériences des returnées dans la société palestinienne après Oslo*, Paris: Karthala-IISMM, 2006.

8 Albert Hourani, "Ottoman Reform and the Politics of Notables," in William R. Polk and Richard L. Chambers (eds.) *Beginnings of Modernization in the Middle East: The Nineteenth Century*, Chicago: University of Chicago Press, 1968, pp. 41–68.

9 In conformity with the new election law adopted in June 2005, the number of PLC members went from 88 to 132. Unlike the January 1996 elections, which were organized in the framework of a simple plurinominal system in 16 electoral districts, those of 2006 followed two different systems. Only half the representatives were elected according to the 1996 system, while the other half were elected by national balloting through proportional party lists. In setting up proportional balloting by party, the PA sought to block a Hamas victory it feared would occur in the framework of majority balloting. This initiative turned out to be effective without, however, blocking Islamists from gaining an absolute majority. In the balloting by list, in fact, Hamas won 29 representatives, with 42.2 percent of the vote, followed by Fatah, which had 28 of its own elected, with 39.4 percent of the vote (only 30,000 votes separated the two factions, out of a little over one million voters and a participation rate of 78 percent). In addition, the party vote underscored the slump suffered by the other political forces: their nine lists were reduced to sharing the 18 percent of the remaining votes. The scope of the Fatah defeat came from the majority balloting by election districts. Hamas's 56 candidates – that is, only 13.5 percent of 414 candidates – won 40.8 percent of the vote and took 45 seats, in addition to 4 seats won by independents supported by the movement. Fatah's 66 candidates – that is, 15.9 percent of all Fatah candidates – won 35.6 percent of the vote and took only 17 seats. The bipolarization of the political scene, already manifest in the proportional voting, became consolidated as none of the candidates belonging to or supported by parties other than Hamas and Fatah won seats in district balloting.

10 Jean-François Legrain, *"La Ville dans la tête": Bethléem 1996–2006*, Lyon: Maison de l'Orient et de la Méditerranée, 2006, p. 264 (http.//www.gremmo.mom.fr/legrain/bethleem.htm).

11 Another difference from the 1996 elections is that the 2006 elections constituted a real choice. Power and society thus would not be experienced as radically distinct any more. The dichotomy between "inside" and "outside" that still existed in 1996 thus would have now disappeared and its end would have involved a chasm between the ruler and the ruled today. In the same movement, the electorate would have appropriated the Palestinian Authority when it dismissed the movement which held power since its foundation.

12 For example, the town and the camp of Khân Yûnis expressed a common support for Hamas. The town of Dayr Balah, in contrast, preferred Fatah. The camp of Dayr Al-Balah, like that of Maghâzî, also supported Fatah, while the Nusayrât and Burayj camps preferred Hamas.

13 In 1976 the PLO, whose leadership at the time had taken refuge in Beirut, gained control of municipal elections in the West Bank by means of the new allegiance shown it by the main notables, who at the same time were turning away from Hashemite Jordan. Their action allowed the PLO – and more particularly Fatah, its driving force since the end of the 1960s – to take control of the political scene in the Occupied Territories, whereas the movement had until then found itself confined to marginal and often clandestine circles. Thirty years later, the Hamas victory stems from a

fundamentally different process. The new saliency of the movement does not stem from a rallying of notables making a break with Fatah; rather, the electorate itself imposed the victory, as much on the whole country, whose notables were still tied to the old nationalist leadership, as on the movement.

14 In recent years, works on Hamas have proliferated, but Khaled Hroub, *Hamas: Political Thought and Practice*, Washington, DC: Institute for Palestine Studies, 2000, remains a reference point. See also Zaki Chehab, *Inside Hamas: The Untold Story of the Militant Islamic Movement*, London and New York: Nation Books, 2007; Azzam Tamimi, *Hamas: Unwritten Chapters*, London: Hurst & Co., 2007; and, more recently, Beverly Milton-Edwards and Stephen Farrell, *Hamas*, Malden, MA: Polity Press, 2010. Concerning current events, see the various reports of the International Crisis Group (ICG) (http: www.crisisgroup.org/home/index.cfm?id=2745&l=1). The best recent overall work by the movement itself is *Fi Dhikrâ Intilâqatihâ al-Tâsi Ashara, Hamâs Haraka San'at al-Târikh* (On Its Nineteenth Anniversary, Hamas, a Movement that Has Made History), Governorate of Ramallah and al-Bira: Hamas, 2006 (http://alquds.ws/pdf/19net.zip).

15 The Muslim Brothers conducted no anti-Israeli operations during this period, even if Sheikh Yasin and several of his associates were arrested in 1984 and sentenced for having "founded an armed cell aimed at the destruction of Israel." The weapons seized had never been used.

16 Palestinian Islamic Jihad has never appeared as the subject of an academic monograph in a Western language (in 2011, a book written by Wissam Alhaj, Nicolas Dot-Pouillard, and Eugénie Rébillard was published by La Fabrique in Paris). The thesis of one of the members of the Anwar 'Abd al-Hâdî Abû Taha movement has a rich store of information: *Harakat al-Jihâd al-Islâmî fi Filastîn. Al-Usûl, al-Idiyûlûjyâ, al-Tahawwulât* (The Islamic Jihad Movement in Palestine: Principles, Ideologies, Transformations), 1998 (http://www.qudsway.com/Links/Jehad/4/Html Jehad4/4hje1.htm).

17 All of Hamas' military forces inherited from various cells, some of which were created before the birth of the movement, were grouped together in 1992 under a single label, *Katâ'ib 'Izz al-Dîn al-Qassâm* (the Izz al-Din al-Qassam Brigades). After limiting its operations to armed targets (soldiers and settlers), the movement changed its position following the 1994 suicide operation led by an Israeli settler in the Abraham Mosque at Hebron. Its operations against civilians, including inside Israel itself, then, are presented as the only response they can bring against acts of aggression on Palestinians. See the website of the Information Office of the Ezzedeen Al-Qassam Brigades – Palestine (http://www.alqassam.ps/english/?action=aboutus).

18 The National Unified Command consisted of Fatah, the Popular Front (PFLP), the Democratic Front for the Liberation of Palestine (DFLP), and the ex-communist People's Party.

19 Outside the Territories, at the beginning of the 1990s, the movement joined with the Alliance of Ten Palestinian Forces based in Damascus, opposed to the politics led by Arafat. In the same period, the Palestinian National Council (PNC), the Parliament in exile of the PLO, offered it membership. After Hamas gave its agreement in principle, however, it nullified it by demanding 40 percent of its representation. More recently, Hamas has signed on to various national initiatives – the Cairo Declaration (March 2005), the Prisoners' National Conciliation Document (June 2006), and the Mecca Agreement on a government of national unity (February 2007), all of which stipulate that in the framework of reforming Palestinian institutions, the entirety of Palestinian forces, including Hamas, are called upon to join the ranks of the PLO to reestablish its status as the sole and legitimate representative of the Palestinian people.

20 *Filastîn al-Muslima*, August 2005, unofficial mouthpiece of Hamas, lists the contacts made from 1993 to 2005 (http://www.fm-m.com/2005/Aug2005/story18.htm).

21 This refusal is not new in Palestine and remains tied to the absence of a state. Also refusing to transform itself into a party, Fatah has nonetheless "governed" since autonomy was established in 1994. Only Fida, the ex-communist Palestinian People's Party and new groupings, most tied to reforms, are parties.

22 Founded in 1953, the ILP (*Hizb al-Tahrîr*) has always been headed by a Palestinian even after it became international. Fundamentally, the ILP believes that the sovereignty of the people is simply the negation of the sovereignty of God. The implantation of democracy in the Muslim world is thus only the instrument of the Crusading West aimed at destroying Islam, and the ILP, refusing all collaboration with current regimes that it considers to be impious, demands the reestablishment of the Caliphate. Regarding the boycott of Palestinian legislative elections, see its official communiqué of January 22, 2006, "*Intikhâbât Majlis al-Darâr al-Tashrî'î al-Filastînî. Khita min Khitat al-Kuffâr Taharram al-Mushâraka fihâ*" (Elections of the Evil Palestinian Legislative Council: One of the Measures of the Infidels with which It Is Forbidden to Participate) (http://www.hizb-ut-tahrir.org/index.php/AR/wshow/26/).

23 On this subject Hamas has taken very political positions and *de facto* marginalizes the approach in terms of *fiqh* (Islamic jurisprudence). Thus, Palestine-Info, its unofficial website, ignores any study of *fiqh* on the question of participation on its portal devoted to legislative elections (http://www.palestine-info.com/arabic/spfiles/2006/enthkabat tshre31 06/entkhabat tshre31 06.html). Its portal "Fatwas and Rootedness in the *Sharî'a*" (http://www.palestine-info.info/arabic/fatawa/index.htm) confines itself to reproducing a declaration of the League of Ulemas of Palestine reaffirming the duty to register for elections (http://www.palestine-info.info/arabic/fatawa/alfatawa/2005/tasjeel.htm). A single study, *Hukm al-Mushâraka fî al-Majlis al-Tashrî'î al-Filastînî (Dirâsa Fiqhiyya)* (The Decision to Participate in the Palestinian Legislative Council, a Study of *Fiqh*), anonymous and distributed by the Islamic Movement of Hebron, was reproduced in May 2005 in the section on books (http://www.palestine-info.info/arabic/books/2005/derasah/derasah1.htm). The few rare studies on jurisprudence distributed in the Hamas movement (including this latter text) were reproduced in a portal entitled "Being Rooted in the Sharî'a" (http://www.pal-election.com/pages/deen/deen.htm) on the pal.election.com site (which later became http://www.pal.election.org). Created at the end of April 2005 between the first two rounds of local elections, this site emanates from a Higher Election Committee acting through a Palestinian Center in charge of elections and making use of the name "Islamic Movement," even though only Hamas is involved. In the field, the Committee prints and distributes a weekly, *Minbâr al-Islâh* (likewise online at the site). All activities stopped in October 2006 with the destruction of the committee office in Ramallah by Fatah sympathizers.

24 This move was made clearly explicit by Muhammad Ghazzâl, who was in charge of announcing Hamas' decision in March 2005 to participate in legislative elections (http://www.palestine-info.info/palestoday/reports/report2005/grar.htm). See also the FAQ published by Hamas on January 6, 2006, on its concept of political participation, especially concerning legislative elections (with a reassessment of its position of 1996) (http://www.palestine-info.info/palestoday/reports/report2006 1entkhabat06/enthabat tashsre3i 06/6 1 06.htm).

25 The Khalas party puts its political program, bylaws, and communiqués online; http://alkhalas.tripd.com as of 2007 is the way the site was in 1998, while http://alresalah.info/alresalah/alkhalas%20movment/index.htm brings it up to date with a few changes dating from 2005.

26 In 1993, in exchange for its recognition of Israel and its renunciation of terrorism (though not its right to resist the occupation), the PLO entered into a direct negotiation with Israel. It expected that via the Oslo Accords international law would end the military occupation, create a state on the territories occupied in 1967, and implement the right of refugees to return or to receive compensation. Nearly 20 years later, the creation of a real sovereign state appears more utopian than ever.

27 Hamas Communiqué, no. 130, December 6, 1995.

28 About 50 of the 672 candidates were reputed to maintain more or less close ties with the Islamic religion, defined, however, in the most diverse manners. Six were elected, to whom should be added the four Fatah winners connected to the inner religious current of the movement.

29 'Atif Adwân, Minister of Refugee Affairs, and 'Atallâh Abû al-Subh, Minister of Culture, assumed responsibilities in Khalas, as well as Ghazi Hamad, spokesman of the cabinet and former editor of *al-Risâla*, the movement's weekly, Ahmad Bahr, interim President of the PLC, and Salâh al-Bardawil, President of the Hamas block at the PLC (these two were members of the Political Bureau of the party).

30 While the Gaza Strip, with the exception of the Khalas party, would have been reticent to see Hamas participate in elections, the West Bank, undoubtedly because of the Jordanian tradition of political participation by the Muslim Brotherhood, would have seen it favorably, especially under the aegis of Sheikh Hasan Yûsuf of Bayt Hanîna and leaders from Nablus, such as Muhammad Ghazzâl and Nâsir al-Dîn al-Shâ'ir.

31 Communiqué of December 1, 2004 (http://www.palestine-info.com/arabic/hamas/statements/2004/1 12 04.htm).

32 Communiqué of March 12, 2005 (http://www.palestine-info.com/arabic/hamas/statements/2005 12 3 05.htm).

33 The Intifada is considered to have definitively buried the Oslo Accords. Khaled Hroub, "A 'New Hamas' through Its New Documents," *Journal of Palestine Studies* 35, 4, Summer 2006, pp. 6–27 (http://www.palestine-studies.org/final/en/journals/printer.php?aid=7087) analyzes the election program of Hamas, the draft for a program of a National Unity Cabinet, and the program for the Hamas Cabinet.

34 Massively used by participants and observers of all sorts, these four terms were finally joined together into a whole: the "4 fs." Danny Rubinstein, "Longings for Arafat," *Haaretz*, June 27, 2005 (http://www.haaretz.com/hasen/pages/ShArt.jhtml?itemNo=592483), appears to be the first to have popularized this expression, whose origin remains unknown.

35 Thus, in the absence of any constitutionally required agreement by the cabinet, at the beginning of April 2006, he appointed a director general (from Fatah) for the Internal Security Forces (ISF) (Police, Preventive Security and Civil Defense), whose members, further, refused to obey the Minister of the Interior, their authority according to the Basic Law. The creation of an "executive force" by the Minister of the Interior (Hamas) in April falls into this context. Conceived of as an adjunct unit of the police, its missions were aimed at fighting against various expressions of security disorders – armed men but also gangs of car thieves, financial trafficking, drug trafficking, etc. The order by the minister to create this force was immediately abrogated by a presidential decree which, refusing to consider the force as a simple police unit, declared it contrary to the Law. Beverley Milton-Edwards, "Order Without Law? An Anatomy of Hamas Security: The Executive Force (Tanfithya)," *International Peacekeeping* 15, 5, November 2008, pp. 663–76.

36 Composed in an Israeli prison and made public on May 10, this document was signed by the upper echelons of five of the principal Palestinian organizations (Hamas, Fatah, PFLP, DFLP, and Jihad). Its goal in this national movement crisis was to provide consensual political solutions that would culminate in the constitution of a Unity Cabinet. Taking advantage of Hamas' internal debates regarding certain points in the document, the President transformed a document developed by the forces themselves with a prospect for unity into a tool aimed at strengthening the Presidency and Fatah to the detriment of Hamas. Consensual despite last-minute discussions, the document could only be approved by Hamas voters, thus contributing to a victory of the "Ayes" that the President was seeking against the cabinet.

37 Reproduced on the U.S. Department of State website on January 30, 2006 (http://www.state.gov/r/pa/prs/ps/2006/60068.htm). The terms of the requirements differ from those issued in the declaration of January 26, 2006 (http://www.state.gov/r/pa/prs/ps/2006/59978.htm), according to which "A two-state solution to the conflict requires all participants in the democratic process to renounce violence and terror, accept Israel's *right to exist* [my italics], and disarm, as outlined in the Roadmap." While the January 30 version requires a non-state movement to recognize a state, an act which is usually a state prerogative, the January 26 version (whose terms can be found in many

other declarations) introduces a moral notion totally unknown in international law. See, for example, John V. Whitbeck, "What 'Israel's Right to Exist' Means to Palestinians," *Christian Science Monitor*, February 2, 2007 (http://www.csmonitor.com/2007/0202/p09s02-coop.html).

38 The U.S. also granted direct military aid to President Abbas in his arm-wrestling with the Ministry of the Interior. Beginning in mid-May 2006, it considerably increased cooperation with the presidential guard in terms of arms, training, and financing.

39 Hamâs, *Limâdhâ Hadatha mâ Hadatha fî Qitâ Ghazza* (Why What Happened in the Gaza Strip Happened), July 2007 (http://www.alquds.ws/pdf/report 17 8 2007.zip).

40 This fear of a putsch was based on the publication of two documents that gave a sense to realities observed in the field for the previous several months. The first was published in Jordan; "Khitta 'Amaliyya li-l-Ri'âsa al-Filastîniyya li-ʿAm 2007" (Plan of Action for the Palestinian Presidency 2007), *al-Majd* (Amman), April 30, 2007 (http://www.almajd.net/article/details/details.asp?id=2018). It was supposed to be a Jordanian government translation of a document from sources close to the White House with which Fatah and perhaps Egypt may have been associated. Its ideas reflected those of Eliot Abrams, the Deputy Counselor for National Security at the White House, who, in the 1980s, had been in charge of the Nicaraguan Contras file. The second text, known by the name of "Benchmark Document," was made public by the Israeli daily *Haaretz*: "Acceleration Benchmarks for Agreement on Movement and Access as Well as on the Gaza Security Situation," *Haaretz*, May 4, 2007 (http://www.haaretz.com). It was written by General Keith Dayton, coordinator of security questions with the PA, Dick Jones, Ambassador in Tel Aviv, and Jacob Wales, Consul General in Jerusalem, and was to be officially presented by Secretary of State Condoleezza Rice to her interlocutors during her tour of the region in mid-May 2007. The document had repercussions in the American press a year later with David Rose's, "The Gaza Bombshell," *Vanity Fair*, April 2008 (http://www.vanityfair.com/politics/features/2008/04/gaza200804). Also see Khaled Amayreh, "The War within Fatah," *Al-Ahram Weekly*, July 5–11, 2007 (http://www.ahram.org.eq/2007/852/re5.htm); Mark Perry and Paul Woodward, "Document Details 'U.S.' Plan to Sink Hamas," *Asia Times*, May 16, 2007 (http://www.atimes/Middle East/IE16Ak04.html); Jonathan Steele, "Hamas Acted on a Very Real Fear of a US-sponsored Coup," *Guardian*, June 22, 2007 (http://www.guardian.co.uk/commentisfree/2007/jun/22/israel.comment).

41 Palestinian Centre for Human Rights (PCHR), "Illegal Closure of the Gaza Strip: Collective Punishment of the Civilian Population," Gaza, December 2010 (http://www.pchrgaza.org/files/2010/Illegal%20Closur.pdf); Yezid Sayigh, "Hamas Rule in Gaza: Three Years On," Brandeis University, *Middle East Brief* 41, March 2010 (http://www.brandeis.edu/crown/publications/meb/meb41.html).

42 The international community, meanwhile, had clearly announced its definition of "democratization:" the unconditional surrender to its policy submitted *de facto* to Israeli interests over the last years.

43 According to the expression used by Sheikh As'ad Al-Tamîmî, *Zawâl Isrâ'îl, Hatmiyya Qur'âniyya* (The Destruction of Israel, a Koranic Ineluctability), Beirut, n.d. A former member of the Islamic Liberation Party (ILP), Sheikh Tamimi was the leader of one of the currents in Islamic Jihad during the 1980s. His notion of Koranic ineluctability is shared by many Islamists beyond the ranks of Jihad alone.

44 In 2008, Hamas renewed its proposals for a ten-year truce (*hudna*) with Israel on several occasions (excluding any formal recognition of Israel) in exchange for the creation of a Palestinian state on the territories occupied in 1967, with East Jerusalem as its capital, the dismantling of the colonies, and the recognition of the right of return for the refugees. The movement likewise proposed a lull (*tahdiyya*), a reciprocal and simultaneous ceasefire, to be accompanied by an end to the Gaza blockade. In spite of Egypt's involvement in negotiations, Israel refused the two proposals, qualifying them as a tactic used by Hamas to gain more time to arm itself.

45 Fatah invoked the requirements of the Quartet in justifying its refusal to let Hamas exercise power. But even if it still possessed representative bodies, Fatah would have been incapable of signing on to those requirements because the absence of an Israeli and international response to concessions made in the 1980s and 1990s went so much against what had been expected. The firing of rockets and the various suicide attacks of the last few years were certainly the work of Hamas and Islamic Jihad, but also, and especially, of groups of Fatah followers who do not refer in their by-laws either to the Oslo Accords or to the PNC decisions, but to the 1965 Basic Charter of Fatah calling for the destruction of Israel (Official Bureau of Information of the Al-Aqsâ Martyrs Brigades (http://www.kataebaqsa.org/arabic/auhtml.php?op=modload&name=about us.htmlfile=index).

46 The "peace process business" then cultivated that myth. Since the beginning of the 1990s, the "peace process" has constituted a diplomatic venture but also an economic venture for many, both actors and observers (researchers and "think tanks" not being the least of them), for whom the survival, even artificial, of the so-called "process" is an imperative. See Markus E. Bouillon, *The Peace Business: Money and Power in the Palestine–Israel Conflict*, London and New York: I. B. Tauris, 2004.

47 Further, no tangible response ever came out to the proposals made by Saudi Arabia at a meeting of the Arab League States in Riyadh in March 2007. The meeting resulted in the reaffirmation of the plan adopted at the Beirut summit of 2002, where the Arab states affirmed their readiness to normalize relations with Israel in exchange for the "creation of an independent and sovereign Palestinian State over all the territories occupied in 1967, with East Jerusalem as its capital, and for an equitable and suitable solution to the refugee problem."

Bibliography

Al-Tamîmî, S. A., *Zawâl Isrâ'îl, Hatmiyya Qur'âniyya* (The Destruction of Israel, a Koranic Ineluctability), Beirut, n.d.

alkhalas.tripd.com.

Amayreh, K., "The War within Fatah," *Al-Ahram Weekly*, July 5–11, 2007.

"Being Rooted in the Sharî'a," available at http://www.pal-election.com/pages/deen/deen.htm.

Benzecri, J., *Correspondence Analysis Handbook*, New York: Marcel Dekker, 1992.

Bouillon, M. E., *The Peace Business: Money and Power in the Palestine–Israel Conflict*, London and New York: I. B. Tauris, 2004.

Chehab, Z., *Inside Hamas: The Untold Story of the Militant Islamic Movement*, London and New York: Nation Books, 2007.

Communiqué of March 12, 2005, available at http://www.palestine-info.com/arabic/hamas/statements/2005 12 3 05.htm.

Communiqué of December 1, 2004, available at http://www.palestine-info.com/arabic/hamas/statements/2004/1 12 04.htm.

Dayton, G. K., "Benchmark Document," *Haaretz*, May 4, 2007, available at http://www.haaretz.com.

"Fatwas and Rootedness in the *Sharî'a*," available at http://www.palestine-info.info/arabic/fatawa/index.htm.

Hamâs, *Limâdhâ Hadatha mâ Hadatha fî Qitâ Ghazza* (Why What Happened in the Gaza Strip Happened), July 2007, available at http://www.alquds.ws/pdf/report 17 8 2007.zip.

Hamas, Governorate of Ramallah and al-Bira, *Fi Dhikrâ Intilâqatihâ al-Tâsi Ashara, Hamâs Haraka San'at al-Târikh* (On Its Nineteenth Anniversary, Hamas, a Movement that Has Made History), 2006, available at http://alquds.ws/pdf/19net.zip.

Harakat al-Jihâd al-Islâmî fi Filastîn. Al-Usûl, al-Idiyûlûjyâ, al-Tahawwulât (The Islamic Jihad Movement in Palestine: Principles, Ideologies, Transformations), 1998, available at http://www.qudsway.com/Links/Jehad/4/Html Jehad4/4hje1.htm.

Hizb ut-Tahrir, "*Intikhâbât Majlis al-Darâr al-Tashrî'î al-Filastînî. Khita min Khitat al-Kuffâr Taharram al-Mushâraka fihâ*" (Elections of the Evil Palestinian Legislative Council: One of

the Measures of the Infidels with which It Is Forbidden to Participate), January 22, 2006, available at http://www.hizb-ut-tahrir.org/index.php/AR/wshow/26/.
Hourani, A., "Ottoman Reform and the Politics of Notables," in W. R. Polk and R. L. Chambers (eds.) *Beginnings of Modernization in the Middle East: The Nineteenth Century*, Chicago: University of Chicago Press, 1968.
Hroub, K., "A 'New Hamas' through Its New Documents," *Journal of Palestine Studies* 35, 4, 2006, 6–27.
Hroub, K., *Hamas: Political Thought and Practice*, Washington, DC: Institute for Palestine Studies, 2000.
Hukm al-Mushâraka fî al-Majlis al-Tashrî'î al-Filastînî (Dirâsa Fiqhiyya) (The Decision to Participate in the Palestinian Legislative Council, a Study of *Fiqh*), available at http://www.palestine-info.info/arabic/books/2005/derasah/derasah1.htm.
"Illegal Closure of the Gaza Strip: Collective Punishment of the Civilian Population," Gaza: Palestinian Centre for Human Rights (PCHR), December 2010.
"Khitta 'Amaliyya li-l-Ri'âsa al-Filastîniyya li-'Am 2007" (Plan of Action for the Palestinian Presidency 2007), Amman, Jordan: Al Majd, April 30, 2007, available at http://www.almajd.net/article/details/details.asp?id=2018.
Legrain, J., *"La Ville dans la tête": Bethléem 1996–2006*, Lyon: Maison de l'Orient et de la Méditerranée, 2006, available at http.//www.gremmo.mom.fr/legrain/bethleem.htm.
Legrain, J., *Les Palestines du quotidien: Les Elections de l'autonomie (janvier 1996)*, Beirut: Centre d'Etudes et de Recherches sur le Moyen-Orient Contemporain (CERMOC), 1999, available at http://www.gremmo.mom.fr/legrain/palestine00.htm.
Milton-Edwards, B., "Order without Law? An Anatomy of Hamas Security: The Executive Force (Tanfithya)," *International Peacekeeping* 15, 2008, 663–76.
Milton-Edwards, B. and Farrell, S., *Hamas*, Malden, MA: Polity Press, 2010.
Official Bureau of Information of the Al-Aqsâ Martyrs Brigades, available at http://www.kataebaqsa.org/arabic/auhtml.php?op=modload&name=about us.html=index.
Perry, M. and Woodward, P., "Document Details 'U.S.' Plan to Sink Hamas," *Asia Times*, May 16, 2007.
Picaudou, N. and Rivoal, I. (eds.) *Retours en Palestine: Trajectoires, rôles et expériences des returnées dans la société palestinienne après Oslo*, Paris: Karthala-IISMM, 2006.
Rose, D., "The Gaza Bombshell," *Vanity Fair*, April 2008.
Roy, O., '*Groupes de solidarité au Moyen-Orient et en Asie centrale: États, territoires et réseaux*,' Paris: Centre d'Etudes des Relations Internationales, 1996, available at http://www.ceri.sciences-po.org/publica/cahiers/cahier16.pdf.
Rubinstein, D., "Longings for Arafat," *Haaretz*, June 27, 2005, available at http://www.haaretz.com/hasen/pages/ShArt.jhtml?itemNo=592483.
Sayigh, Y., "Hamas Rule in Gaza: Three Years On," Brandeis University, *Middle East Brief* 41, March 2010.
Steele, J., "Hamas Acted on a Very Real Fear of a U.S.-sponsored Coup," *Guardian*, 22 June, 2007.
Tamimi, A., *Hamas: Unwritten Chapters*, London: Hurst & Co., 2007.
U.S. Department of State, January 30, 2006, available at http://www.state.gov/r/pa/prs/ps/2006/60068.htm.
U.S. Department of State, January 26, 2006, available at http://www.state.gov/r/pa/prs/ps/2006/59978.htm.
Whitbeck, J. V., "What 'Israel's Right to Exist' Means to Palestinians," *Christian Science Monitor*, February 2, 2007.
www.palestine-info.com/arabic/spfiles/2006/enthkabattshre3106/entkhabattshre3106.html.
www.palestine-info.info/arabic/fatawa/alfatawa/2005/tasjeel.htm.
www.palestine-info.info/palestoday/reports/report2005/grar.htm.
www.palestine-info.info/palestoday/reports/report20061entkhabat06/enthabattashsre3i06/6106.htm.

11

A DECADE OF REFORMISTS AND ISLAMISTS IN POWER IN THE ISLAMIC REPUBLIC OF IRAN

1997–2007

Saïd Amir Arjomand

In July 2006, President Mohammad Khātami offered the following justification of his administration's policy of "development of non-governmental formations." Political organizations set up by governments were "like artificial flowers put in a vase without roots; whereas political organizations should come out of the context of society, resulting in political parties and more extensive political organizations with roots among the people of the country."[1] His claim to strengthen civil society and "non-governmental formations" is born out by the sevenfold increase in the number of women's non-governmental organizations (NGOs) from 67 to over 480 during his two terms in office (1997–2005).[2] As Tolstoy showed long ago, taking refuge in historical and sociological determinism is an easy way of avoiding taking responsibility for one's action.[3] The truth is that the undeniable importance of the social roots of political organizations is no substitute for decisive political action. The moment for decisive political change to democratize the regime of the Islamic Republic of Iran in a definitive way came between March and August of 2000. The first date marks the attempted assassination of the main architect of the stunning electoral victory of the reformists who had gained control of the Majles; the second the stark failure of the same reformists and of President Khātami to stand up to the Supreme Leader when he ordered them to stop discussing a bill to liberalize the press law. With this submission, the possibility of irreversible democratization was foreclosed, and the Ahmadinejad administration has had no difficulty rolling back the gains of the civil society NGOs, and certainly their political participation and agency.

Analytical introduction

In my recent papers on the rise and fall of Khātami and the reform movement, I have offered a dual conceptual frame that links "constitutional politics" and the sociology of revolution, and can easily be extended to explain the coming to power of Ahmadinejad and his followers, whom I shall call "populist hardliners."[4]

From the perspective of constitutional politics,[5] I have argued that the contradictions among the heterogeneous principles of the Constitution of 1979 – namely, theocratic government, the rule of law, and participatory representative government – can exhaustively account for the confrontation between the Supreme Leader, Ayatollah or clerical monarch, Sayyed 'Ali Khāmane'i and the former President, Mohammad Khātami. The Leader stood for the first principle; aligned behind him were the conservative clerics who came to power as a result of the Islamic Revolution and are in control of the revolution-generated system of collective rule by clerical councils, foundations (*bonyāds*), and foundation-supported unofficial groups, including the thuggish Helpers of the Party of God (*ansār hizb allāh*), the judiciary, and the commanders of the Revolutionary Guards and its Mobilization Corps. The President stood for the last two principles (e.g., the rule of law and participatory representative government), which were fused together in his new political discourse of the rule of law, democratic participation, and civil society; behind him were the technocrats for reconstruction, the reformist and excluded clerics, women and students, and the disenfranchised middle classes.

As for the sociology of revolution, my account highlights two features of the Iranian political situation which may not be immediately evident. First, what I called clerical conciliar rule would appear as the typical form of collective government that emerges during the period of succession to the charismatic leader of a revolution and is gradually consolidated. But the clash of clerical conciliarism with the democratization espoused by the reform movement has also set in motion a non-institutional process of accumulation of power by the Supreme Leader. The result was the consolidation of a system of personal rule that is increasingly, and perhaps misleadingly, referred to as clerical monarchy. The Islamic Revolution thus established a hybrid political regime, with an elected Parliament and President subordinated to clerical authority – a theocratic republic. As time went by, contrary to what one might expect, clerical authority enhanced its control over the state. After the death of Khomeini, the charismatic leader, the government of the Islamic Republic can be characterized as a system of collective rule by clerical assemblies or councils.[6] The country is divided into a small clerical elite of religious jurists (*mojtaheds*), which maintains its power through the system of conciliar rule and is supported by a "second stratum" of lay civil servants in control of the administration, and a huge lay population which has no share of political power but votes once a year for the President, the Majles, or the local and municipal councils that are often effectively neutralized by the structures of clerical domination. It should also be pointed out that a sizeable proportion of the second stratum come from clerical families.[7] Having an uncle who is or was a cleric helps enormously with becoming Deputy Minister of Foreign Affairs or Industry.

Second, the rift between the "establishment clerics" and the "reformists" in the 1997–2005 period, and between the latter and the hardliners from a military-mobilizational background led by Mahmud Ahmadinejad after 2005 (calling them "conservatives," as do the U.S. media, is a complete misnomer), can be seen as two rounds of a delayed but typical pattern of revolutionary power struggle. This struggle is greatly complicated by the fact that the quarter-century delay first caused a great (180-degree) ideological shift in the position of the radicals, and then a turn-around to revive the neglected, albeit secondary, populist element of Khomeini's revolutionary heritage. Each round was carried out by those children of the Islamic Revolution who had been pushed aside and excluded from real power. Some observers wondered why Saturn did not devour his children in the case of the Iranian Revolution, apart from the Mojahedin-e Khalq. The power struggle may well be the result of Saturn's unsatisfied appetite. What stands out in this analysis is that the reformists are very much the children of the revolution, as are the populist hardliners currently in power and, before them, were the so-called "religious-nationalist" (*melli-madhhabi*) followers of Bāzargān, Khomeini's revolutionary partner and the first prime minister of the Islamic Republic.[8] I think what we see here is the transformation of the quick and violent revolutionary power struggle captured by the Saturn image and a slower, much less violent pattern of intra-elite circulation similar to Pareto's long-term and historical circulation of elites.

The reformists in power, 1997–2005

> We the protesting Representatives have had a share and role in the Revolution and have struggled for its victory and consolidation in various arenas, have learned the lessons of honor, truth-telling, piety, and freedom in the school of Imam Khomeini (God's mercy be upon him), and consider his way and Tradition (*sonnat*) the path to the salvation and high standing of the Islamic Republic of Iran.

So begins the last letter of protest of February 17, 2004, from the 131 Representatives of the Sixth Majles, who had gone on strike in January after the Council of Guardians had disqualified 80 of them from running again in the impending elections for the Seventh Majles. The reformists presented themselves as spokespersons for "the forces loyal to the Revolution and democracy (*mardom-sālāri*)," and complained that "the forces faithful (*mo'men*) to the Revolution and the regime" had no option but to retreat from political involvement. The reformists ended their letter with an admonition in the manner of the councilors to old kings: "We are very worried about the future when our regime, with the nostalgia of its immense lost popular support, would be forced to submit to the open and hidden onslaught of foreigners." This belated but pure Islamic revolutionary discourse fell absolutely flat among the students, the women and the urban poor – the presumed social base of the reform movement. It revealed its deeper discourse beneath the novel neologism-filled discourse of democracy and civil society introduced by the reformist press and Khātami in the late 1990s which had taken root in important segments of Iranian society. This letter was really the epitaph of the reform movement that began in 1997 and caused a tremendous burst of enthusiasm in Iran and throughout the world.

The reformist strike had begun in January 2004, and Interior Minister Musavi-Lāri announced that he was not willing to hold the elections on schedule when the

Council of Guardians promptly rejected a bill passed by the Majles "to solve the election crisis."[9] But on the 25th anniversary of the Islamic Revolution on February 11, President Khātami let down his Interior Ministry and cabinet and capitulated to the Leader, confirming that the elections would take place on schedule. This was yet another instance of the President's caving in rather than standing firm and provoking a constitutional crisis. Khātami did nothing to protect his followers in the Majles, just as he had failed to support his followers among the students earlier, and completed his second term after another year of ineffectual grumbling in 2005.

During the crisis, Mohsen Kadivar, the reformist cleric who had been jailed for over a year for writing an erudite refutation of Khomeini's theory of the Mandate of the Jurist (*velāyat-e faqih*), called upon him to resign rather than accept an unfair election. More poignantly, in a letter urging the striking parliamentarians to push for a new constitution, the jailed reformist Hāshem Āghājari had aptly referred to the "Tragedy of Khātami."[10] The stuff of the tragedy is of course the destruction of the "smiling Sayyed" (*sayyed-e khandān*), who had been elected President in 1997 and 2001, by the ruthless Ayatollah who was selected by his clerical colleagues as Khomeini's successor as the Supreme Leader (*rahbar*). This destruction was already complete in 2000, before Khātami's second victory in June 2001.[11] I would place it in the spring and summer of 2000 and at the time of the astonishing defeat of the pro-clerical candidates in the national elections of the Sixth Majles. It came in the Supreme Leader's several deadly embraces after the almost successful assassination of the President's most important reformist aide, the clampdown on the pro-President reformist press, and the slap on the face of the newly elected reformist Majles. With each embrace came Khāmane'i's affirmation that "Khātami is one of us"; the latter did not have the courage to push him away and say he was *not* one of them. From then on, Khāmane'i knew he could do anything he wanted with the smiling Sayyed. Khātami was a defeated man. His maudlin speech for Nawruz (New Year) 1380/March 2001, read by many as expressing his intention to quit, surely reflected his sense that he did not have the strength to stand up to the Supreme Leader and the price of clinging to presidential power would be capitulation and further humiliation. On August 6, 2000, the Leader told the Majles to stop its deliberations on the new press law. The reformist Majles lost the best and probably the only chance it had as the Legislative Power for confronting the Leader, who had clearly stepped beyond his ample constitutional jurisdiction by telling Parliament to shut up. It was far too timid to challenge the authority of the Leader and took the slap in the face without any vigorous reaction.

I will not examine the more exciting first term of the Khātami presidency, except for emphasizing that this firm, indeed ruthless, response by Khāmane'i to the stunning electoral victory of the reformists in 2000 was a decisive turning point in the reformists' struggle with the Supreme Leader, and also adding that this struggle had an important institutional dimension as struggles between the Majles and the Council of Guardians, on the one hand, and between the judiciary and the press and the Majles, on the other. Instead I will briefly focus on a less decisive turning point in the same direction (of defeat) in 2002, during Khātami's second term. While the President's resignation and a national referendum were being discussed by the reformists as ways to overcome the predictable recalcitrance of the Council of Guardians and the Maslahat (Expediency) Council, Rahim Safavi, Commander of the Revolutionary Guards, announced his readiness to unleash revolutionary violence against the reform movement.[12] Meanwhile, the political abuse of clerically controlled judiciary power had become more blatant. A number of reformists outside the Majles were arrested in the fall of 2002, and on November 6, one university lecturer, Hāshem Āghājari, was sentenced to death for his anticlerical remarks, which the judge considered as insults to the Prophet. The students joined the constitutional struggle with protests against judicial abuse.[13] Unrest continued into December, resulting in numerous arrests, and even a hardline judicial spokesman resigned in protest against the gross miscarriage of justice in the Āghājari case.[14]

At this point, Āghājari introduced a radically novel oppositional tactic into the constitutional politics of the Islamic Republic. Sensing the futility of the President as the leader of the uncoordinated opposition within and outside Parliament, Āghājari refused to ask for the pardon hinted by the Supreme Leader and demanded instead that the unjust death sentence be carried out. His example was followed by the "religious-nationalist" dissident leader, the late 'Ezzatollāh Sahābi, who wrote an open letter to the heads of the three powers asking that he be executed rather than subjected to continued harassment after his release from jail.[15] I am inclined to attribute the admittedly very small victory of these two dissident individuals (to which we can add Akbar Gangi's hunger strike in prison two years later) as tactically brilliant innovations in the Islamic revolutionary discourse that turned it to the advantage of dissidents and against the Leader and the IRI establishment. By comparison, the stale deeper discourse of the big losers, the reformist Majles deputies, couched in terms of loyalty to Khomeini and the Islamic Revolution, tilted the discursive terrain hopelessly against them and in favor of the Leader. A further theoretical and analytical point, the reformists' being trapped in their own rhetoric reveals the more subtle political-discursive dimension of constitutional politics as distinct from its more evident legal-constitutional dimension. Political-ideological discourse, too, set the parameters of constitutional politics, as does the letter of the law and the Constitution.

At the more evident level of constitutional politics, Khātami had appointed a Commission for the Implementation of the Constitution and constitutional supervision, citing Article 113 of the Constitution in 1998. Article 113 was one of the few unchanged articles from the original draft modeled on the 1958 constitution of the French Fifth Republic, which makes the protection of the Constitution one of his main duties. The Commission did not display much energy. It avoided confronting the Council of Guardians and the judiciary, which under a more assertive head, Ayatollah Hāshemi-Shāhrudi, was putting forward its own claim to constitutional interpretation.[16] In September 2002, Khātami finally introduced the bill to increase the powers of the President as the guardian of the Constitution, announced in his second inaugural speech a year earlier. The bill was passed by the Majles but, needless to say, promptly rejected by the Council of Guardians. It was in any case ill-conceived and too timid to make a significant difference. It missed the opportunity to make the first step toward introducing a form of judicial review under the aegis of the

President, which was technically possible,[17] by couching the bill in administrative rather than judicial terms. The proposed presidential commission was given the power of "inspection" to determine violations of the Constitution, and it was not explicitly given jurisdiction to hear cases of human rights violations. Obliquely and at the end, the President was given the power to provide a budget for compensating victims of human rights violations!

The loss of the only serious constitutional struggle Khātami and the reformists had mounted against the Supreme Leader evidently led to widespread disaffection that manifested itself in the elections of the local and municipal councils in February 2003. The turnout outside of the major cities was not low (about 50 percent for all of Iran), partly because the Ministry of the Interior had stood its ground and the candidates were not vetted by the Council of Guardians, and quite a few reformists seem to have been elected in smaller towns. But the drop in participation in the big cities was sharp, and with less than one-third of voters turning out (the official breakdown of the Tehran vote has apparently never been made public) the municipal council of Tehran went entirely to the pro-Khāmane'i hardliners, with Mahmud Ahmadinejad being elected Mayor. As several people told a researcher, "what can we expect from local councilors, when even the President of the country is stymied from pursuing his agenda?"[18] It cannot be said that the reformists have looked after the Councils. In fact, in their typical inattention and disarray, the reformist Majles has passed the 2003 Tax Amalgamation Law, which removed what little financial autonomy the Councils have had. The same general disaffection with Khātami was evident in the widespread and continuous student protests and youth unrest in a large number of cities through the summer of 2003. The Majles reformists, to their great discredit, disowned the students.

This brief survey should suffice to show that the major problem of the political wing of the reform movement as the true children of the Islamic Revolution of 1979 and its undoing was a double disconnect: a disconnect between the President and the reformist members of the Majles at the organizational level, and a disconnect of both Khātami and the reform movement from the people in general, and from the new generation, and the university students in particular. Nor was the reform movement able to build any bridges connecting to the urban poor. This double disconnect was the other side of the entrapment of the reformist children of the revolution as insiders (*khodi*) in the revolutionary discourse reflected in their final letter. The empty slogans they clung to for salvation in their last moment of desperation were in fact the millstones that drowned them.

Dilemma of the Supreme Leader: expansion of personal power or clericalist institution-building

Toward the end of Hāshemi-Rafsanjāni's second term, the idea was aired that the Constitution be amended to allow him to run for another term. The idea was vetoed by the Supreme Leader, who was slowly being called Imam and was less and less inclined to share power. He was under some pressure from the clerical Assembly of

Leadership Experts, with a commission to monitor the conditions of the Leader as specified by the Constitution to consolidate the system of collective clerical rule,[19] and decided to revitalize the Maslahat Council in the spring of 1997, which would also provide a suitable job to ease Rafsanjāni out of the presidency. This and other instances of institution-building toward the end of Rafsanjāni's presidency and throughout Khātami's were accompanied by a non-institutional, personal bid for power by the Leader, Ayatollah Khāmane'i. While firmly retaining his control over the Revolutionary Guards and its Mobilizational Corps (Basij), Khāmane'i eliminated Rafsanjāni's men one by one, replacing some of them with his own men, such as the Lārijani brothers, but also putting his men, notably the cleric Ezheh'i, in key positions in the judiciary.

The economic basis of the Supreme Leader's power should not be neglected. All the banks and large industrial companies were expropriated after the revolution. Khomeini did not allow the state to take them over, however, but treated them as booty in Islamic law and set them up as independent foundations, appointing mullahs – Islamic clerics – as their heads.[20] These economic foundations, known as Bonyāds, control an estimated 40 percent of the Iranian economy; their heads are not responsible to the state but only to Ayatollah Khāmene'i, whose official title is the Leader of the Islamic Revolution.[21] Nepotism is rife in the economy, as it is in the appointment to governmental positions. Indeed, the term *āqāzādehgān* (sons of masters) was coined to refer to the new politico-economic elite consisting of the families of the clerical upper stratum. Closely connected to the *āqāzādehgān* in government and foundation business are a more numerous group of *bazaaris* (bazaar merchants and businessmen) and former revolutionaries turned businessmen through the foundations and as the mediators in the 1979 bazaar–Khomeini alliance that overthrew the Shah. The best representative of this group is the ruffian monopolist Habibollāh Asgar-awlādi head of the "Coalition Groups" (*hey'atha-ye mo'talefa*).

With the expansion of the reach of the clerical conciliar system and the growth of the personal, extra-legal power of the Supreme Leader, both of which are typical modes of post-revolutionary concentration of power, the trend toward democratization initiated by Khātami has been reversed. The pro-clerical hardliners, who include the newly elected President and had the Seventh Majles elections won for them by the clericalist Council of Guardians in 2004, do have a plan of their own for *perestroika*. The plan, as unveiled by their leader Haddād-ădel, proposes to make Iran into a new China or Japan by performing the economic miracle of combining political and religio-cultural conservatism with economic liberalization. I consider this policy impossible because it requires the destruction of the economic base of the Islamic Republic as I have just described it. But in the extremely unlikely event that they do succeed, they would dig their own graves, as did the Soviet Union after 1989.

Islamism and populism: Ahmadinejad's presidency

The victory in the 2004 Majles elections of the hardliners, many of whom were the Supreme Leader's men in the security apparatus and mobilization, extended Ayatollah

Khāmane'i's agglomeration of personal power to the Majles. The final popular defeat of the reformist movement came in the presidential elections of June 2005. The reformist candidate, Khātami's lackluster Education Minister, Mostafā Mo`in, rejected by an unduly apprehensive Council of Guardians but shrewdly reinstated by the Leader, who is much better at taking the popular pulse of the nation, came fifth in the first round and was eliminated.[22] The hardliner Mahmud Ahmadinejad, who had become mayor of Tehran in the municipal elections of 2003, the first massive expression of disillusionment against the reformists with the lowest ever turnout, but whose career as a child of the Islamic Revolution was otherwise the same as Mo`in's, won the final round against Hāshemi-Rafsanjāni by a wide margin. It is interesting to note that quite a few students, presumably disillusioned with the reformists, joined his campaign. The ineffectiveness of the student and anti-regime boycott of the presidential elections was demonstrated by the larger than expected turnout, even though the official 60 percent figure should be discounted. Finally, the Ahmadinejad vote also demonstrated that the reformists had not only alienated the students by letting them down, but also failed to attract masses of the urban poor. Trapped in their insider rhetoric and narrow vision and refusing to use the huge reservoir of secular professionals in his administration, Khātami and his reform movement also came to naught because of their failure to build bridges to the significant and growing social forces that were their easy potential constituencies.

The election of Ahmadinejad with the backing of the Leader-controlled security and mobilization apparatus in June 2005 can also be seen as the culmination of the trend in accumulation of extra-constitutional power. If so, it also signaled the beginning of the end of the trend toward concentration of the personal power of the Leader. The control of a personal system of power is difficult, and the hardliners, formerly Khāmane'i's men, are not as easy to control, with the Majles and presidency as their additional power bases. Although the military-mobilizational hardliners turned politicians have not remained united, and some of them in the Majles and local government have distanced themselves from him.[23] Nevertheless, the realization of the difficulty to control Ahmadinejad seems to have motivated the Leader gradually to begin tilting the balance of power a little back to the clerical elite and the Hāshemi-Rafsanjāni's faction.[24] Furthermore, he has even made a gesture toward the reformists for the same reason. This is my interpretation of the ending of the suspension of publication of three reformist papers, most notably *Sharq*, by the judiciary, which is under the thumb of the Leader.

Ahmadinejad is reliably reported to have predicted his highly improbable election in the summer of 2009 as a favor from the Hidden Imam, whom he also believes to have supernaturally intervened to make the eyes and ears of the delegates open to his message during the speech he delivered at the General Assembly of the UN in September 2005. In an early cabinet decision, Ahmadinejad's administration allocated the equivalent of $17 million to the Jamkarān pilgrimage site near Qom and about a hundred kilometers south of Tehran, where the Hidden Imam is believed to have disappeared down a well and have ordered the building of a mosque in a dream revealed to a virtuous believer. Furthermore, there are rumors that he threw the names of the cabinet ministers before their presentation to the Majles down the Jamkarān well, and had had plans as mayor of Tehran for building a modern road connecting Jamkarān to the center of Tehran in expectation of the imminent appearance of the Mahdi.[25] It is, however, not at all clear that Ahmadinejad is encouraging millennial yearnings in order to exploit them for mobilizational purposes. In fact, the more common and plausible explanation is that he is using them to strengthen his own purely secular authority vis-à-vis the Leader, Ayatollah Khāmane'i, whose office of the supreme jurist (*faqih*) would be made quite redundant by the return of the Hidden Imam.

What he does use for mobilizational purposes is populism, seeking to revive the long-neglected populist heritage of Khomeini and the Islamic Revolution. His nuclear policy, too, was astute purely as a tactic in domestic politics, and made him popular with the middle class.[26] He has traveled extensively in the provinces, diverting a large proportion of government expenditure and investment away from Tehran, and has promised to divide up the stocks of all nationalized industry as "shares of justice" on a per capita basis among the entire population of Iran. This program follows Mongolia's model of privatization, and boosted the President's popularity. Its implementation, however, has been delayed, and the lowest decile of the population with which it was to begin is yet to receive its shares. Perhaps for this reason, as well as his failure to deliver on the anti-corruption campaign, the crowds Ahmadinejad has been drawing in his provincial rallies are dwindling. Furthermore, Ahmadinejad's 'Well Serving Faction" did poorly in the December 2006 elections for municipal councils, while his rival hardliner in the 2005 presidential elections, Qālibāf, now the Mayor of Tehran, did very well and has secured the support of the economically conservative Coalition Groups alienated by the anti-corruption campaign, as well as that of Hāshemi-Rafsanjāni.

To conclude, let me return to the mellowing forces in the revolutionary process that produce moderation. In Iran, this began with the Hāshemi-Rafsanjāni Thermidor 1989–97 and continued through Khātami, 1997–2005. The military-mobilizational hardliners are the last and the rudest faction of the Islamic revolutionary elite to undergo moderation and corruption in power. In the last few years, the Revolutionary Guards have strengthened their economic enterprises and have become the government's biggest contractor by far. Petrodollars are finally sapping their hardline revolutionary zeal.

Postscript

Since this chapter was written, the growing power of the Revolutionary Guards and the assertiveness of Ahmadinejad gave them confidence to carry out the electoral putsch of June 2009, and declare Ahmadinejad President for a second term. Ayatollah Khāmane'i not only went along but fully endorsed the suppression of the massive protests against electoral fraud during the summer and fall of 2009, creating a rift between himself and a considerable section of the clerical elite headed by Hāshemi-Rafsanjāni.[27] This appears a costly mistake, making the Ayatollah's balancing act between the hardliners and the clerical elite and his checking of Ahmadinejad's assertiveness increasingly difficult.

Notes

1 As cited in F. Sadeghi, "Siyāsat-zodā'i az jāmi'a-ye madani: Tajroba-ye sāzmānhā-ye ghayr-e dawlati dar dawra-ye eslāhāt", *Goftogu* 47, January 2007/Dey 1386, 45.
2 Ibid., 46.
3 I. Berlin, "The Hedgehog and the Fox," in H. Hardy and A. Kelly (eds.) *Russian Thinkers*, Harmondsworth: Penguin Books, 1979, pp. 22-81.
4 The description of this groups as "conservatives" by the press is completely misleading. They came to power as hardliners faithful to the Islamic Revolution.
5 Constitutional politics consists of political contention, and struggle for the definition and constitution of order takes place among groups and organizations aligned behind different principles of order by their material and ideal interests. These principles of order are heterogeneous and potentially contradictory. In the process of constitutional politics, the contending groups and organizations are forced to reconcile the respective logics of these principles through compromise, concession, and reinterpretation. Some principles of order are clustered into ideologies, and may be incorporated into written constitutions. The principles of order amalgamated in fundamental laws set the parameters of constitutional politics. See S. A. Arjomand, "Constitutions and the Struggle for Political Order: A Study in the Modernization of Political Traditions," *European Journal of Sociology* 33, 1992, 39-82.
6 S. A. Arjomand, "Democratization and the Constitutional Politics of Iran since 1997," *Polish Sociological Review* 136, 2001, 349-63.
7 W. Buchta, *Who Rules Iran? The Structure of Power in the Islamic Republic*, Washington, DC: Washington Institute for Near East Policy, 2000.
8 It is not an accident that, apart from the "reformist" children of the revolution, one of the most important dissident leaders, 'Ezzatollāh Sahābi, and most of the 42 persons arrested in April 2001 were members of Bāzargān's Islamic liberal nationalist movement and junior partners in the initial Islamic revolutionary coalition in 1979.
9 This was to be done by making being a Muslim in good standing to run attestable by neighbors and acquaintances according to custom (*'orf*) rather than requiring the determination of the Council of Guardians.
10 BBC Persian website, February 15, 2004.
11 Khātami won 77 percent of the popular vote, running against nine other candidates. The turnout, however, was not as heavy as in 1997. It was 67 percent of eligible voters (aged over 16), as compared to 88 percent in May 23, 1997, when Khātami received 69 percent of the popular vote. It should, however, be pointed out that according to official figures the turnout and the percentage of popular vote cast for Khāmane'i in 1981 and the percentage of popular vote cast for Hāshemi-Rafsanjāni in 1989 were much higher (95 percent) than those for Khātami's 1997 'landslide' victory. See W. Buchta, op. cit. p. 36.
12 *Financial Times*, November 2, 2002.
13 *The Economist*, November 16, 2002.
14 *The New York Times*, December 11, 2002.
15 Emrooz website, February 12, 2003.
16 In January 2002, the judiciary even denied Mehrpur's request to visit dissident political prisoners. See *New York Times*, January 9, 2002.
17 I had urged the Office of the President, through Vice-President Abtahi and a number of reformist members of the Majles, to do so.
18 K. Tajbakhsh, "Fate of Local Democracy under Khātami," Woodrow Wilson Center website, Events, December 16, 2003, 2.
19 Personal interview.

20 S. A. Arjomand, *The Turban for the Crown: The Islamic Revolution in Iran*, New York: Oxford University Press, 1988.
21 J. Amuzegar, *Iran's Economy under the Islamic Republic*, London: I. B. Tauris, 1997.
22 Former Majles Speaker Mehdi Karrubi, who belonged to the clerical wing of the reformist movement, came third in the first round partly by magnifying a leaf out of George W. Bush's book and promising every Iranian a substantial, monthly negative tax paycheck, and justifiably complained of electoral fraud. But the fact remains that the total hardline vote in the first round was larger than the total reformist vote.
23 As has the former Revolutionary Guard General Zarghāmi as the Head of the National Radio and Television.
24 A similar shift in foreign policy would be an encouraging sign for the resolution of the nuclear crisis. Khāmene'i remains firmly in control of Iran's foreign policy and has appointed as Iran's chief nuclear negotiator 'Ali Lārijāni, his relative by marriage and a pragmatic strategist. If he decides that the balance of power has tilted too much in favor of the President's security-military faction and against the clerical establishment, he can act on the nuclear issue and reach an agreement with the UN and International Atomic Energy Agency. As an indication of a possible shift under suitable circumstances, he stated on January 18, 2006: "The West knows very well that we are not seeking to build nuclear weapons," which are "against our political and economic interests and Islamic beliefs." See N. Fathi, "Iran's Ayatollah Affirms Peaceful Nuclear Plans," *New York Times*, January 19, 2006.
25 S. Peterson, "Waiting for the Rapture in Iran," *Christian Science Monitor*, December 21, 2005.
26 Ahmadinejad's insistence on Iran's nuclear "rights" is popular with the Iranian masses and has a powerful civil constituency. This is the one factor that unfortunately makes the nuclear issue especially intractable. The President's policy of championing Iran's national right to nuclear energy (for peaceful purposes), carefully promoted by government-controlled television and other media, comes close to a stroke of evil genius to cover the regime's violations of human rights and civil liberties by appealing to long frustrated nationalist sentiment - at a time of widespread disillusionment with Islam, revolution, and reform. The portrayal of Iran being bullied by an America armed to the teeth with nuclear weapons and threatening to invade it while preventing her development of nuclear energy has been quite effective in arousing popular indignation and demands for the assertion of Iran's national rights and dignity. (Iranians were very scared by George W. Bush's "axis of evil" State of the Union speech in 2002 and haven't forgotten that either.) This significantly broadens the social basis of the President's support beyond revolutionary veterans and the urban poor.
27 S. A. Arjomand, *After Khomeini: Iran under His Successors*, New York: Oxford University Press, 2009, pp. 165-71.

Bibliography

Amuzegar, J., *Iran's Economy under the Islamic Republic*, London: I. B. Tauris, 1997.

Arjomand, S. A., *After Khomeini: Iran under His Successors*, New York: Oxford University Press, 2009.

Arjomand, S. A., "Democratization and the Constitutional Politics of Iran since 1997," *Polish Sociological Review* 136, 2001.

Arjomand, S. A., "Constitutions and the Struggle for Political Order: A Study in the Modernization of Political Traditions," *European Journal of Sociology* 33, 1992, 39-82.

Arjomand, S. A., *The Turban for the Crown: The Islamic Revolution in Iran*, New York: Oxford University Press, 1988.

Berlin, I., "The Hedgehog and the Fox," in H. Hardy and A. Kelly (eds.) *Russian Thinkers*, Harmondsworth: Penguin Books, 1979.

Buchta, W., *Who Rules Iran? The Structure of Power in the Islamic Republic*, Washington, DC: Washington Institute for Near East Policy, 2000.

Fathi, N., "Iran's Ayatollah Affirms Peaceful Nuclear Plans," *New York Times*, January 19, 2006
Peterson, S., "Waiting for the Rapture in Iran," *Christian Science Monitor*, December 21, 2005.
Sadeghi, F., "Siyāsat-zodā'i az jāmi'a-ye madani: Tajroba-ye sāzmānhā-ye ghayr-e dawlati dar dawra-ye eslāhāt," *Goftogu*, 47, 2007.
Tajbakhsh, K., "Fate of Local Democracy under Khātami," Woodrow Wilson Center website, Events, December 16, 2003.

INDEX